D1383139

This original and ground-breaking study deals with a specific set of institutions in nineteenth-century Athens. Relying on matrimonial contracts, travellers' accounts, memoirs and popular literature, the authors show how distinctive forms of marriage, kinship and property transmission evolved in Athens in the nineteenth century. These forms then became a feature of wider Greek society which continued into the twentieth century.

Greece was the first post-colonial modern nation state in Europe whose national identity was created largely by peasants who had migrated to the city. As Athenian society became less agrarian, a new mercantile group superseded and incorporated previous elites and went on to dominate and control the new resources of the nation state. Such groups developed their own, more mobile, systems of property transmission, mostly in response to external pressures of a political and economic character. These same pressures resulted in a distinctive ethic of family life that in turn influenced models of kinship, marriage and property transmission in the rural areas. Of particular significance was the impact of the growth of the dowry and massive cash transactions upon the position of women.

This is a persuasive piece of detective work, full of brilliant insights, which advances our knowledge of modern Greece. It is a model for future scholarship on the development of family and other 'intimate' ideologies where nation states encroach upon local consciousness.

Cambridge Studies in Social and Cultural Anthropology

Editors: *Jack Goody, Stephen Gudeman, Michael Herzfeld Jonathan Parry*

77

The Making of the Modern Greek Family

A list of books in the series will be found at the end of the volume

THE MAKING OF THE MODERN GREEK FAMILY

Marriage and Exchange in Nineteenth-Century Athens

PAUL SANT CASSIA
University of Cambridge

with

CONSTANTINA BADA
University of Ioannina

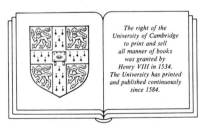

The right of the
University of Cambridge
to print and sell
all manner of books
was granted by
Henry VIII in 1534.
The University has printed
and published continuously
since 1584.

CAMBRIDGE UNIVERSITY PRESS
Cambridge
New York   Port Chester
Victoria   Sydney

Published by the Press Syndicate of the University of Cambridge
The Pitt Building, Trumpington Street, Cambridge CB2 1RP
40 West 20th Street, New York, NY 10011-4211 USA
10 Stamford Road, Oakleigh, Victoria 3166, Australia

© Cambridge University Press 1992

First published 1992

Printed in Great Britain by the University Press, Cambridge

British Library Cataloguing in Publication Data
Sant Cassia, Paul
  The making of the modern Greek family: marriage and
  exchange in nineteenth-century Athens – (Cambridge studies
  in social and cultural anthropology.)
  1. Families. Social aspects, history
  I. Title II. Bada, Constantina
  306.8509

Library of Congress cataloguing in publication data
Sant Cassia, Paul.
  The making of the modern Greek family: marriage and exchange in
  nineteenth-century Athens / Paul Sant Cassia with Constantina Bada.
    p. cm. – (Cambridge studies in social and cultural anthropology; 77)
  Includes bibliographical references and index.
  ISBN 0-521-40081-3
  1. Family – Greece – Athens – History – 19th century. 2. Marriage –
  Greece – Athens – History – 19th century. 3. Athens (Greece) –
  Economic conditions. I. Bada, Constantina. II. Title.
  III. Series.
  HQ662.5.Z9A847   1991
  306.8'09495'12—dc20   90-43072 CIP

ISBN 0 521 40081 3 hardback

This book is dedicated to my grandmother, Lady Genoveffa Boffa, who, in a different Mediterranean land than that dealt with in this book, originally stimulated my interest in the anthropology of the recent past.

Paul Sant Cassia

Contents

List of illustrations   *page* x
List of tables   xii
Acknowledgements   xiv

1 Introduction: history, family and the 'other' in Greece   1
2 Men and houses, women and households   33
3 Marriage, women and land in nineteenth-century Athens   48
4 Gifts and commodities, cash and trousseaux   80
5 'For one's soul': adoption, fosterage and the growth of
   koumbaria   145
6 The family and emotional life   164
7 Conclusion: exchange, marriage and the person   228

Notes   256
References   262
Index   275

Illustrations

PLATES   *page*

1   An Athenian bride. Photograph by O.M.B. de Stackelberg,
    1825 (1825;30). Courtesy of the Benaki Museum, Athens   136

2   Costume of a migrant villager settled in the Athenian
    suburbs. Photograph by O.M.B. de Stackelberg, 1825
    (1825;4). Courtesy of the Benaki Museum, Athens   137

3   Family grave of the *arkhon* Kantzillieri family. First
    Cemetery, Athens (Section A). Photograph by K. Manolis   138

4   Grave of Maria Kassimati, a member of the *nikokirei*. First
    Cemetery, Athens (Section A, 115). Photograph by K.
    Manolis   139

5   Nationalist poster, 1913, depicting Mother Greece flanked
    by her sister/daughter regions and linked by the banners of
    eleftheria (Freedom) and *enosis* (Union). Photograph by G.
    Chouliaras. Courtesy of the Folklore Museum, University
    of Ioannina   140

6   Nationalist poster, Cyprus, 1960, depicting Mother Greece
    and her enslaved daughter, Cyprus. Photography by G.
    Owen   140

7   Annunciation Icon by the artist Loverdos Stelakatos, 1851.
    Courtesy of the Folk Museum, Stemnitsa   141

8   *Liberaci Maria da ogni male*. Italian oleograph of a type
    which circulated in Athens in the 1930s and 40s. Photograph
    by K. Manolis. Courtesy of J. Skourdoubi   142

9   Popular religious poster depicting Christ blessing the daily
    family meal. Photography by G. Owen   143

10 An Athenian couple (J. Kairophylas, 1982;37). Photograph by G. Chouliaras 144

FIGURES
1 Dower flows from titled/untitled grooms to titled/untitled
brides above 500 groshia 91
2 Marriages and the transmission of goods in the family
Fragoyiannis 129
3 Marriages and the transmission of goods in the family
Karoris 130

Tables

1	Population growth in Athens (1834–1976)	15
2	Land and population in Greece, 1828	25
3	Dowry houses supplied by brides	36
4	Correlation between house transfer and conditional terms	38
5	Endowment of brides with dowry houses according to family situation	39
6	Transmission of dowry houses according to unusual donors	41
7	Transmission of dowry houses to daughters according to presence of siblings	45
8	Marriage patterns of brides' parents	59
9	Frequency of endogamy/exogamy within titled groups	60
10	Endowment of fields to titled and untitled brides at marriage	64
11	Parental transmission of livestock to titled and untitled brides at marriage	64
12	Endowment of vineyards to titled and untitled brides at marriage	66
13	Endowment of olive trees at marriage to titled and untitled brides	67
14	Comparison of dowries between all untitled brides, migrant countrywomen and adopted daughters	68
15	Transmission of olive trees as dowries before and after 1830	70
16	Cash endowments as dowries before and after 1830	71
17	Cash dowries to titled and untitled brides at marriage	86
18	Cash endowments to daughters at marriage according to status of grooms	86

19 Cash dowers according to status of grooms   89
20 Dowries and dowers compared   93
21 Features of cash and trousseaux in matrimonial exchanges   104
22 Incidence of items of clothing and jewellery transferred
    with different types of costumes (1688–1834)   112
23 Transmission of resources to brides according to costume
    type   116
24 Cash dowers according to costume types worn by titled/
    untitled brides   118
25 Relationship between costume type (A–D) and other com-
    ponents of the dowry   126
26 Correlation between adoption and titled families   149
27 Distribution of maids in the total working female popula-
    tion, Athens, 1853–79   192
28 Differences between Athenian social groups in terms of
    family and social organisation   193

Acknowledgements

It is always a great pleasure to acknowledge and thank the various individuals who have generously given of their time and friendship in the writing of a book which makes it in some senses a collective enterprise. My greatest thanks and appreciation are due to my co-author Constantina Bada Tsomokou, who collected the raw statistical data upon which this book is based, and carefully inputted it. The lengthy discussions which we had over three years in Cambridge, Athens and Ioannina formed the basis of this book.

In Cambridge various people kindly assisted us in our endeavours. Roger Schofield of the Cambridge Group for the History of Population and Social Structure generously gave us of his time to devise a programme for the inputting of data on the Statistical Package for the Social Sciences (SPSS) package. Janet Hall expertly retrieved this data for us in the form we requested. Colleagues in the Department of Social Anthropology, Cambridge, read various chapters and made very useful comments and provided encouragement for ideas about which I was at times uncertain. I should especially like to thank Keith Hart, Chris Hann, Carrie Humphrey and Ernest Gellner. I should also like to thank Peter Loizos and Michael Herzfeld who patiently read through an earlier draft of this manuscript and who provided, as ever, many stimulating insights and detailed comments. An anonymous reviewer for Cambridge University Press also made some incisive, useful and corrective observations which I have tried to take into account. David Holton also kindly helped guide me through various aspects of nineteenth-century Greek literature.

In Greece (Ioannina) I should like to thank Magda Stroungari, Yiannis Persinakis and Vasilis Nitsiakos for their warm friendship and hospitality. In Athens Jenny Skourdoubi kindly provided accommodation as well as many valuable insights into domestic life among Athenian middle class families in an earlier period. I have benefited from all too brief discussions with my friend Akis Papataxiarhis. Jack Goody, my former supervisor, was also kind enough to discuss various aspects of this work during our visit to the Lot. The first draft of this book was written during a sabbatical; Hilda Lateo provided companionship and encouragement during this period. To all these people I should like to express my deepest thanks and appreciation. Finally, Pam Dearlove, Caroline Hunter and especially Franca Vincent expertly typed various chapters. Franca Vincent, to whom special and warm thanks are due, generously and patiently guided this book through its various typing changes to its final version.

Paul Sant Cassia

1

Introduction: history, family and the 'other' in Greece

Anthropological research on the Greek world, as elsewhere in the Mediterranean, has long concentrated on the family, the household, the transmission of property (especially the dowry) within the family, and more recently on the construction of gender identities and power relations in rural areas. From various accounts we are now aware of significant variations in all these practices. Yet we know very little about the historical evolution of the Greek family and the processes which have contributed on a wide variety of fronts to its formation, its ethics and its patterns of property transmission in the forms we recognise today.

These important gaps in our knowledge are due to a number of factors. The Ottoman period has left us a relative poverty of historical documentation and archival material such as household censuses, matrimonial contracts and documents of all sorts, which would enable us to construct a picture of the family in past times in Greece, as scholars of other southern European societies (Spain, Italy, Portugal, France, all notarial cultures) have been able to do. Few Ottoman archives survive in Greece and the prospective scholar is faced with the daunting prospect of working on Ottoman archives in Turkey, many of which deal with fiscal matters rather than the family. Church records in Greece, the source of many reconstructions of family life elsewhere in southern Europe, are uneven and disjointed. A second factor is the particularly tumultuous history of Greece since the Turkocratia, the period of Turkish rule in the eighteenth century where war and radical and extensive population movements have been a constant feature. Such disturbances and the incorporation of new populations and refugees as Greece progressively extended its national frontiers hardly contributed to the ordered accumulation of data so necessary for historical research on the family.

Yet the study of the evolution of the Greek family does merit attention by anthropologists and historians for both general and particular concerns. On a general level it is now almost a received orthodoxy among anthropologists that the Mediterranean is in some sense a 'cultural unit'. This notion has a long and complicated history which is intertwined with the development of anthropology itself and the territorial redirection of its interests in the period of decolonisation. The unity of the Mediterranean also received a powerful stimulus from the work of historians, notably Fernand Braudel (1975), and demographers and historians of the family (Hajnal, 1965; Laslett and Wall, 1972; Laslett, 1983; Wall, 1983). Whilst Braudel was interested in the interaction of men within a commonly defined mental and geographical framework that formed and stamped their experiences, Hajnal and Laslett were more concerned with the differences between north and south, west and east, in Europe. Yet the precise nature of southern Europe in these schemata was less specified, and indeed the criteria often selected as the differentiating features between the various areas of Europe (age at marriage, family forms, patterns of property transmission, residence patterns, and the like) were perhaps developed more to highlight the specificity of northwest Europe. The thrust of most of the argument was to explain why this part of Europe was different from the rest of Europe and hence provide a fuller context for the emergence of industrial capitalism, 'individualism', and so on.

Such comparisons, while useful, nevertheless tend to construct arguments along certain lines. To begin with, the type of data required is not always available. Even more seriously, perhaps such approaches risk bypassing the question of whether it is suitable to apply such universalistic criteria to other societies. Furthermore, they do not address the critical questions of why and how we construct such models, as well as where and at what level this 'unity' of the Mediterranean lies, if at all?

Jack Goody (1983) has recently offered a historical explanation. In a wide ranging survey of the development of the family and kinship in Europe, especially in its western regions, he shows how historically both northern and southern shores of the Mediterranean had many common features. Continuous intervention by the Church, however, on the 'rules' of marriage had the result of transforming the family and kinship along lines we recognise as distinctly 'European'. This point has been taken even further by Alan Macfarlane (1978, 1986) who sees English society as having long differed from the rest of Europe. Should we follow this lead and view all Mediterranean societies as different from each other? Or should we move sideways away from the lines of enquiry proposed by historians of the family and try to specify other areas for comparison? Recently a noted historian of the Tuscan Renaissance family signalled her dissatisfaction with the conventional models proposed to typologize the European family patterns by asking:

Does [the Tuscan model] provide evidence – happily preserved through Florentine documentation – of a medieval phase in the evolution of family and marriage of which we only know later forms in northern Europe? Or should we see it as a typically Mediterranean model, closer, in the last analysis, to central and eastern European structures than to those of north-western Europe? From what some studies – all too few of them – have told us about marriage and domestic structures in the modern period, the second hypothesis seems preferable.

(Klapisch-Zuber, 1985; 20)

This study on the evolution of the Greek family indicates strong similarities and parallels to the Tuscan material, both in 'form' (settlement patterns at marriage, the 'dowry', men and 'houses', etc.) and on a deeper and more subtle level less open to statistical analysis, in 'cultural content' (women 'as' gifts and women 'with' gifts at marriage, the symbolic role of clothing and its relation to the construction of the person, etc.). This lends some credibility to the notion of a 'Mediterranean model', but it also raises the problem again in sharper focus. How can one compare two (or even more) societies distinct in space and time without for example reviving the old schemata of cultural unity (such as 'honour and shame', private and public spheres) explored by the first generation of Mediterraneanists and with which there is now uncomfortable dissatisfaction?

Such themes may now have to be analysed as part of the northern European construction of 'the other', yet intimately linked and incorporated into northern European perceptions of itself. For 'the Mediterranean' is an insidious category and it has been held up in anthropological and historical discourse not to indicate what we are not (as in more 'exotic' societies), but what we 'were'. Even Braudel's masterful survey of the Mediterranean concentrates on its 'Golden Age' – which is where its interest is presumed to lie; after that what is 'interesting' and 'significant' and has to be 'explained' occurs in the North, where industrial capitalism and Protestantism emerged. Yet, while northern Europe 'overtook' the Mediterranean, these societies are preserved in a historical discourse which posits them as representing an earlier stage in the evolution of European culture. As Herzfeld (1987) has aptly remarked, Mediterranean peoples are now held up as the 'aborigines' of Europe. Put differently, the 'other' is the past, the 'self' is the future.

What we mean by this is that in many Mediterranean societies the issue of 'time and the other' (Fabian, 1983) becomes particularly problematic. To begin with, the 'other' in the Mediterranean context does not merely inhabit the epistemological frame in Western anthropo-logical discourse of allochronicity ('other time'), i.e. 'the science of other men in another time' (Fabian, *ibid.*; 143). Rather, to coin another neologism, Mediterranean societies occupy an ambiguous position in time and space. On one level they are allochronic, but they also occupy an idiotopic (same space) frame within Europe. From the Encyclopaed-ists, Shelley, Byron and Chateaubriand, to Walter Pater, Winkelmann and Bernard Berenson, Mediterranean societies were held to represent 'our ancestors'. Indeed so pervasive initially was this view that in the early nineteenth century Greeks were believed to be the direct descendants of the ancient Hellenes, prompting Shelley to rhetorically invert the distinction between time and the other by proclaiming 'We are all Greeks . . .'

Increasingly the West's disenchantment with its inability to fit the products of its imagination with the irreducibility of 'the other' resulted not in a rejection of the West's perception of itself as the 'heir' to Graeco-Roman-Christian civilization and culture, but a denial of the identity of 'the other' in the Mediterranean. Scholars such as Fall-merayer attempted to disprove that modern Greeks were descended from the ancient Greeks. The effects of this disjuncture were far reach-ing. The Greek state, which had largely emerged through the West's support based partly upon such beliefs, became increasingly concerned with reappropriating the past in order to gain legitimacy. Indeed Greece experienced particular problems in secularising the state and its ideology (nationalism) as well as in naturalising time. The Church, which had been cast in the role as the carrier of the ethnos (national and ethnic sentiment) subscribed to a very distinct Judeo-Christian pre-enlightenment notion of time which did not lend itself to a secular nationalism. Instead the state adopted an ideology of religious national-ism which had been mainly formed by the Church. The War of Independence, embedded as it was in Western European desires to liberate the Christian descendants of the ancient Hellenes from Muslim oppression, implied not only the appropriation of the (Greek) past by the West as its own history, but also assumed the nuances of a war of religious and ethnic liberation for the Greeks themselves. Religion and ethnicity became inextricably linked. And because the new Greek state started off only with the Peloponnese, and many Greek-speaking areas were still under Ottoman control, irredentism became a powerful force in Greek politics and culture until the catastrophe in Asia Minor of 1922. The state's expansion to incorporate all Greeks within its boundaries, their liberation from 400 years of 'slavery' and 'darkness' became a sacred and political imperative. In effect the whole process of liberation of Greeks outside the confines of the kingdom represented an attempt to transcend the poverty of the present and recover the lost glory of Greece. The 'future' could only be achieved by recovering the lost glory of the past, and a past, moreover, which the West was increasingly appropriating for itself as the heir to classical civilisation and denying modern Greeks their identity as descendants of the ancient Hellenes.

In this way Greek culture and society became progressively locked in a world view where time and space were not naturalised or secularised. Time was not naturalised because the evolution of the Greek state was perceived in terms of a recovery of the glory of ancient Greece. Space was not secularised because the world was divided into those areas liberated from Ottoman rule, those areas where Greek 'brothers' were waiting to be liberated (especially 'the City', Constantinople, the centre of national and religious aspirations which had to be recovered as the embodiment of Hellenism's 'golden age' before 'the Fall' to the Ottomans), and finally those areas beyond the pale which included both the West (Europe) and the East (Asia). In many respects Greek nationalism was as much anti-Western as anti-Oriental. Expansion in space, bringing the light of Hellenic Christian culture to areas under Ottoman rule, implied salvation through a transcendence of time, and a recovery of lost grace. It was a view of time and space, and ultimately of identity, which had to recapture the past in order to achieve the future. If, as Fabian has suggested communication is about creating shared time, Greece communicated in a very distinctive way with both the West and the East. With the West its communication was via the past; with the East the shared time was denied by being characterised as 'slavery' and 'darkness' under Ottoman rule.

Thus for many Mediterranean peoples, history and identity hold very distinct values. Because Mediterranean peoples were incorporated into a northern European discourse about itself in a manner different from 'exotic' societies, and because they often shared the 'same history' with the West, the 'self' often lies in the past to be reappropriated, or even held up as an ideal as to why they are now different (and sometimes 'better'), although certainly part of the discourse on knowledge and identity dominated by northern Europeans. One form this has taken lies in the construction of national cultures. Nineteenth-century Greeks tried to discover links and continuities with the classical past in order to establish a national identity; twentieth-century Italian Fascism evoked the glories of Ancient Rome and its domination of the *mare nostrum* to place Italy on an equal footing with the Great Powers, while in less belligerent contemporary times the Renaissance is held up as a model of

Italian inventiveness and 'style'; the Arabs recall the ideal theocracy of the first community of believers and develop a vocabulary of justification to explain their fall from grace (Gellner, 1985). 'Grace' in the modern world is of course linked to power through commodity production and display, in product innovation and so on.[1] As we shall try to show, this concern with the past as a means to discover identity had particular implications for the family and its emotional life.

The semi-incorporation of Mediterranean societies within European discourse as representing the past within the present may even extend to the categories we employ. Terms such as 'dowry', 'dower', 'marriage' and the like, embedded as they are in western legal concepts and classifications, may appear unequivocal to us. Yet while they were often incorporated in official state legal systems in countries such as Greece and may therefore appear unproblematic to us, they may also hold different additional significances and meanings at the grassroots level (Herzfeld, 1980). This is not to deny that such institutions may be suitable for comparative purposes, but their uses and significances at the grassroots may well be different and deserving of analysis. At the very least examination of their semantic significances for the actors themselves may help shed light on and inform us how we should construct our comparisons and affect our conclusions.

This problem is even more acute when we examine notions which are both anthropological abstractions and appear in everyday discourse, such as 'honour', 'shame', 'private', 'public', and so on. As ethnographers who had previously lived and worked in different parts of the Mediterranean, we were struck as much by the differences as by the similarities between the 'customs' and *mentalités* of 'our' respective societies, not only at similar points in time, but also across time. How can we explain such deceptive similarities and differences without making any evolutionary assumptions? Clearly we need to move to other levels of analysis and perception which are not limited to statistical data. These would include a consideration of other aspects of culture, a hidden logic of constructing the world, the person, and exchange. Mediterranean societies may well share a 'common aesthetic' in a manner similar to that claimed by Marilyn Strathern for Melanesia (1988; 341). Such an approach would take cognizance of both similarities and differences between different societies.

On a more particular level, the study of the development of the Greek family also merits attention. Of all the southern European societies Greece is especially distinctive in its social evolution. To begin with, until the early nineteenth century it formed part of the Ottoman world. It was perhaps less subject to the changes experienced in southern

European societies, including the Napoleonic wars, the sweeping away of *anciens régimes*, the imposition of new legal codes, and internal revolts. Yet Greece was certainly exposed to the brisk new winds of change blowing from the West, although the extent to which the new climate of liberalism was actually genuinely felt in Greece has been hotly debated by historians and by the Greeks themselves. The country was the first Ottoman province to wrest its independence from its Muslim masters, and a 'modern' nation-state was established forty years before the Italian Risorgimento, for which it was an inspiration. De Pouqueville's *Story of the Greek revolution of the events 1740–1824* was translated into Italian in 1829 and not surprisingly published in Piedmont, where it exercised considerable influence on Italian nationalists.

In other respects the evolution of Greek society, its polity, economy and institutions, has been singularly distinctive. In contrast to that other 'geographical expression', Italy, the establishment of the nation-state was not due to the incorporation of the society under the hegemony of a regional Kingdom (Piedmont) which established its control over the rest of society. Nor was it achieved through the shedding of an empire and the working out of internal political processes as in Spain. Rather, the state was created through a somewhat sporadic nationwide revolt, politically not well co-ordinated, and reliant upon external European assistance. This reliance and a healthy suspicion of European motives indelibly influenced the construction of national identity. As Legg has pointed out, 'in Greece, the power to unite the State came from outside, there was barely sufficient common identification, much less solidarity, to create the nation-state' (1969; 89). Nor were its territories fixed, a fact which contributed to regular and massive influxes of refugees and the destitute at regular intervals for a hundred years since the state's establishment in 1830 to the catastrophe in Asia Minor in 1922, when Greece's ill-fated attempt to capture Asia Minor from Turkey (areas of Greek settlement for millennia) resulted in defeat and the forcible settlement of over a million refugees in Greece (Pentzopoulos, 1962). In one very crucial way the new Greek nation-state was the first post-colonial state in Europe, foreshadowing in its experiences the irredentism of European countries in the 1930s and the often obligatory repatriations of millions of Europeans and Russians in the twentieth century.

Other, related factors were perhaps of more significance for the evolution of the family in Greece. In contrast to many other Mediterranean societies, there was no continuity in elites and ruling groups across time. The old elite of primates, *arkhontes*, formed under the Ottomans, were for various reasons bypassed and discredited in the nation-state and they merged with a new rising urban bourgeoisie formed primarily by the growth of the state and its bureaucracy. This was a peaceful replacement but in the last decades of the eighteenth century and early nineteenth century it involved a wide variety of factors, including the Church and its attempts to regulate the manner of property transmission within the family. Nor were there competing elites in the modern Greek state, as with Spain, where one regionally based elite (in Catalonia) was 'politically overrun' by Castile. Indeed for a considerable part of the nineteenth century the Greek elite, which was mercantile-based, was concentrated not in the Greek kingdom but in Greek cities under Ottoman control (Smyrna and Constantinople). Within Greece, the growth of the State's bureaucracy, which had to be established *ex nihilo* after the Ottoman departure, attracted rural notables to the cities, the new centres of power, and increasingly the dispersed mercantile elite. The lack of a common national culture, because of different regional ones whose only common element was the Greek language, and a despisal of the departed Ottoman overlords, meant that a new culture was to emerge in a rapidly expanding urban setting which indelibly influenced the ethics of the family and the significance of kinship in relations between family groups.

This is not to say that the old elite of *arkhontes* lost all its previous power in one fell swoop in 1833, as did the Russian nobility in 1917. Rather, the *arkhon* class ceased to operate as an administratively defined class concerned with defining and defending its privileges and wealth according to certain Ottoman-imposed criteria. Many families, especially in certain Peloponnesian regions (such as the Barbitsiotei and the Mavromichaelei in the Mani) retained their wealth, extensive landholdings and power in spite of the attempts by the first Prime Minister Capodistrias to the contrary; in certain cases many even managed to extend their holdings and influence in the new Greek kingdom due to extensive networks of rural patronage pledged to urban politicians. But increasingly the old *arkhon* class in Athens and later elsewhere merged with a new and emerging urban middle class defined predominantly by participation in the state administration whose ethics and family organisation were formed mainly out of a dialectical and selective rejection of the past (i.e. the Turkocratia system of privileges, defined erroneously as *feudarhismo*, or 'feudalism', thus incorporating Greece within Western historical categories) and attempts to 'Europeanise' themselves and the wider society. In contrast to Tsoukalas (1981) and Burgel (1976) we do not believe that the *arkhontes* retained its pristine identity as a class in the nineteenth century by means of heavily patrolled borders, control over the means of production and a specific distinct rationality. As McNeill has observed: 'during and immediately after the war of Independence a central issue was whether or not leaders of the revolution would be able to convert their social position into land ownership on the model of the Turkish pashas whom they had massacred. In the end, the "Christian Turks" as their enemies called them, failed' (1978; 57). As the magnet of Athens increased its pull over the countryside and its slowly expanding incorporated territories, social and geographical mobility became progressively common, albeit with distinct regional biases.[2] Even in the twentieth century, with some distinct regional exceptions (such as Thessaly), class sentiments have been remarkably absent in most parts of Greece, rendering class analyses particularly problematic. Education and wealth, the two being largely synonymous in modern Greece, and a transformed custom largely transcended social differences. In fact the term *morfomenos anthropos* means both a formally educated man and a 'Europeanised' man. It also includes the notions of being 'shaped' and 'cultivated', and having the knowledge and facility necessary to deal with the outside world. 'Culture' which 'forms' individuals is thus presented as coming from the 'outside world', not the village, and is available to and recognizable in anyone regardless of his social origins.

The absence of a landed aristocracy had far-reaching implications for patterns and styles of leadership, and moulding of aspirations, as well as the perceptions of individual and family mobility. No social group or class, with the possible exception of the Ionian aristocracy (of whom Capodistrias was a member) had a 'mission to lead', and the latter lost their homogeneity after 1864 when Britain handed over the Ionian islands to Greece.[3] Instead, a peasant-type 'Weberian' competitive culture was carried over to the city, a source of many aspirations to political leadership. Within the city, education increasingly became one of the main means of social mobility as the aged but prescient tamed mountain warrior Kolokotronis had predicted in the early nineteenth century. Indeed education became identified with the city, with *politismos* (a distinctive Greek notion of 'civilisation' and the 'civilised' life), and it evolved into one of the safest means to stabilise the seesaw changes in family fortunes which inevitably characterised the tumultuous city-based political life of the new Greek nation state. In contrast to their counterparts in France, Italy and Spain in the nineteenth and twentieth centuries, Greek peasants as peasants never entered the political stage; rather they did so as urbanites, actual or potential.

Urbanisation and the political and economic significance of the city are perhaps the main keys for an understanding of the evolution of the Greek family, its ethics and its concerns from the nineteenth century, even in rural areas. This marked a radical redirection from what had previously been the trend for the two hundred years of Ottoman rule where there were generally progressive movements away from the city to safer highland areas. Thus in one basic sense Greek society, its politics, economy and culture, are 'new' products of the growth of the nation state, paradoxically much 'newer' than the younger states of Italy and Spain where there has been a far greater continuity in ruling groups, regional cultures and identities with a long history of political autonomy and representation.

The society was young in its economy, bureaucracy, law, and national and cultural identity. After the departure of the Ottomans, the rural economy had to be created anew, in the wake of centuries of neglect, and the physical environment required reclamation by man from nature. Slaughter and Kasimis note of Boeotia: 'The dry language of social-economic analysis, to the effect that post-Revolution Greek agriculture suffered above all from lack of capital, cannot convey the enormity of the task facing these communities. Without implements, with very few draft animals, even with many of the best young and active men lost in the fighting, and with no money, they set about making a living with their bare hands' (1986; 112). Small peasant holdings predominated partly because the state subscribed to this ideal and partly because it was unable or unwilling to resolve the land question until well into the end of the nineteenth century. Yet because land was distributed on an auction basis and credit was not readily available, peasants were dependent upon money lenders and merchants. They also lacked secure property titles. Because the state required revenue which could only be obtained through taxation, the actual state of affairs for a considerable part of the nineteenth century was in effect no different from the Ottoman system it had supplanted, and Greece entered the twentieth century as an under-developed country (Mouzelis, 1978; McNeill, 1978). In the north, Arta and Thessaly, the areas of large landholdings ex-*chifliks*, a by-product of Ottoman rule, entered the Greek kingdom in 1881. Yet while the big landowners of Thessaly were prominent in Greek politics, investment in their estates remained low, and liberalisation of land distribution had to wait until 1917–28. Large landowners moved to Athens and increasingly sold off their land in order to finance the education of their offspring and to enter into lucrative state employment or politics. Small peasant hold-ings and the legal insecurity of tenure in the countryside, as well as regular influxes of refugees and the lack of resources supplied by the state for agricultural improvement, contrasted sharply with the politi-cally and economically expanding towns. Steady urbanisation in the nineteenth century, which shot up in the twentieth century, populated the cities with former peasants, refugees and other migrants attracted by new opportunities, sometimes more imaginary than real. The state and its bureaucracy absorbed a good number: the rest entered small-scale urban enterprises employing less than five people. In such a prevailing climate of insecurity of private-sector employment, which contrasted sharply with the security of government employment, the newly formed urban populations had to rely extensively on kinship links and mutual support. This had profound implications for the interaction between town and country across time. For example, while Friedl (1964) talks about 'lagging emulation' of urban life in the contemporary countryside, it is equally valid to speak of the lagging retention of country values in the town across time.

Although the effects of urbanisation and aspirations to an urban lifestyle have now permeated most corners of the Greek countryside, historically since the nineteenth century it has been the country that has largely populated the cities, sometimes creating new and distinct sub-cultures, as with the popular shadow theatre of Karaghiozis, an offshoot of the Turkish *hamam* plays, which retained a distinctly 'Turkish' flavour opposed by military and civil servants as well as the Church for its 'Oriental' and 'non-Greek' (a legitimated code for 'plebeian') qualities in much the same way as the *rebetiko* culture of songs developed in Athens by Asia Minor refugees was hounded by the authorities a century later in the 1930s.[4] The contrast between Greece and its nearest Mediterranean neighbour, Italy, is striking. If central Italy is imbued with the urban and urbane values of *civiltà* (an ideology derived from the traditional elites which intertwines local identity and urban values, suggesting that the present possesses the civility and culture of the past) down to the smallest Tuscan or Umbrian hamlet, as Silverman (1975) has suggested, it is country values (for example of *poniria*, or cunning-ness) that have imbued the main Greek cities, including Athens, creating in the process a distinctive culture. Thus whereas central Italian villagers pride themselves on the *civiltà* of even their smallest hamlets, which are defined by reference to the past (including local autonomy), Greek villagers define *politismos* (the nearest equivalent in Greek to *civiltà*, but with other nuances) differently. It is the past which has less *politismos/civiltà* than the present. The past is the remembered past rather than the mythic past learned through schoolbooks and national rhetoric which ascribes all European culture to the Ancient Greeks: 'before, life here was primitive, it was a wasteland; now everybody has his television, video, washing machine and so on'. *Civiltà/politismos*, in the experience of villagers, is not a simple matter of the continuity of local tradition, however much national rhetoric may have attempted to suggest it (Herzfeld, 1982). For there is little obvious continuity with the past, certainly not in the built environment. While on one level the idealised past has penetrated the consciousness of villagers in the sense that they are the 'descendants of the ancient Greeks', it is more that they are the heirs to that tradition rather than able to identify a tangible continuity with that past. Indeed it is mainly in those towns with long histories of urbanisation, such as Nafplion (the first capital of the Greek state), and which resemble Italian towns most closely, that there is nostalgia for the 'aristocratic' values of the past (Zinovieff, 1989). By contrast, for most village dwellers *politismos* is associated with the related concept of *politelia* (comfort, smartness, luxury). In such cases *politismos* is predicated upon the contrast of time, either between the experienced past and the present, or between the here and now, and the future, as when villagers rhetorically ask '*horio dhen ine?*' ('Isn't this only a village?' i.e., 'don't expect much from life here in the village'), the implication being that of an inverted Confucianism: the adoration of one's more urbanised and more economically independent, or salaried descendants and their way of life, rather than of one's rural ancestors whose life was full of toil and certainly lacking in charm.

The society was young in its legal structures and in its national cultural identity. We are not competent to discuss the complex development of law in Greece and its relationship to social factors, for which there is a voluminous literature. But the promulgation of a civil code was long in coming in Greece and was intimately intertwined with two factors: the desire to 'discover' ancient custom which would palpably demonstrate the continuity of Greek culture across, and in spite of, centuries of foreign oppression, and to indicate that Greek 'custom' and hence 'law' were essentially 'European' rather than 'Asiatic' (Herzfeld, 1985b; Argyriades, n.d.). A few words should be said here about the legal system, especially as regards property ownership and devolution. Although land under the Ottomans technically belonged to the Porte, *de facto* property rights were recognised and increasingly so with the development of large estates or *chifliks*. As the Ottomans lacked a salaried scribal class and relied on local power holders to collect taxes and administer the peace, the functions of adjudication especially as regards property disputes and transmissions within the various Greek communities were largely in the hands of the Patriarchs and the Orthodox Church. While the latter relied heavily upon the complications of Byzantine law, especially the Exavivlos of Armenopoulos, a Thessalonikan jurist, in practice this was tempered by two other factors. First, reference was also made to customary law (*synethio, ethimo tou topou mas*), and second, appeals could always be lodged with the local

Ottoman *qadi* (judge). It is perhaps difficult to establish at this stage with precision how the system worked in practice, and its variations from place to place, and much research still needs to be done. Yet it is clear from the numerous encyclicals on various topics (for example, the custom of unigeniture in the Aegean, the practice of cohabitation among the poor and the inflation of dowries), that the Church, decentralised as it was and staffed at the lower levels by priests who were villagers, was unable to impose its laws strictly, especially in the countryside. In this respect, Ottoman Greece was dominated by customs which brought communities in line with the general rules of the Church.[5]

This study examines matrimonial patterns and property transmissions in the Athenian family at a crucial turning point in the evolution of Greek society, namely the end of the Turkocratia and the establishment of the Greek state (late eighteenth and early nineteenth centuries). It has two aims. The first is to highlight the nature of property trans-missions within the various classes that made up Athenian society. At issue here are a host of questions, which bear ultimately upon the subsequent development of the contemporary Greek family, in spite of its regional variations. To begin with we are interested in the matrimonial and property-transmission patterns of a traditional agrarian-based hierarchical society in a context of limited urbanism. How did family forms and property transmission patterns differ between various social groups and classes? Were social groups largely endo-gamous or was social mobility through marriage possible? If so, were there any particular conflicts, and what institutions did this involve? We hope to show how a traditional agrarian-based society with its 'indi-genous' elites (to the Ottoman system) became increasingly urbanised and more complex. As Athenian society progressively lost its agrarian character, a new mercantile-oriented group, the *nikokirei*, largely superseded and incorporated previous elites and went on to dominate and control the new resources created by the nation state. Such groups evolved their own particular systems of property transmission, which were more mobile than the previous dominant ones, and they devel-oped, too, a particular ethic of family life, an ethic of family, work and kinship which was to crucially influence the models of kinship, property transmissions, and the family in rural areas.

The term 'embourgeoisement' does not cover the processes involved here, at least not in the sense of the penetration of sentimentalised values into family life, of the equality between children, and of the primacy of 'love' over 'economic interests', in short of 'emotion' over 'interest' (Medick and Sabean, 1984). Indeed Greek social development departs significantly from parallel processes in state and class formation occurring elsewhere in southern Europe, and even more so from Northern Europe. The reluctant and precarious urbanisation of country folk is perhaps a more suitable description for the processes involved. This placed a particular emphasis on the mobility of dowry goods; neolocality; the massive endowment of daughters as a means of achieving social mobility; the primacy of the matrimonial contract, of a legal agreement, to establish trust and security in an uncertain and threatening urban environment; the use of godparenthood as a means to lure strangers into potential allies; the distinction between the 'public' and the 'private', the concern to distinguish oneself from one's social origins, and the cult of motherhood and seclusion within the home. Certainly some features are common to other Mediterranean societies, but we are concerned here with an amalgam of features which fieldworkers and anthropologists would recognise as specifically 'Greek', rather than Italian, Spanish or other.

Of critical importance to the constitution of this ethic is the significance of a particular form of urbanisation, specifically that undergone by Athens. The role of Athens as the national centre, the capital of the new Greek state, the centre of national Greek culture, of the 'rediscovery' of new values, as the site of government employment in a highly centralised state administration, and as the ultimate destination of peasants in search of a 'better life', is unparalleled in other Mediterranean cities. Indeed if there is one critical feature in modern Greek history and society, it must surely be the phenomenal growth of Athens, as is testified in table 1.

In such a context it is hardly surprising that the 'models' of *politismos*, of 'civilised life', of family life, of the transmission of property, of the new uses to which kinship and fictional kinship could be put, and of the respective roles of men and women, were primarily formed within this rapidly growing city. These 'models' increasingly came to dominate rural life partly because of the ideological, political and economic primacy of the capital which superimposed itself over regional differences where regional elites were largely absent or at best heavily dependent upon the centre. Indeed while some areas at best utilise the language of rhetoric supplied by the national centres, as Herzfeld's (1985a) Cretan villagers do, there was never a series of autonomous regional identities consciously and consistently developed in opposed rejection of the state (as with Sicily, Catalonia, Corsica or the Basque country).[6] Another reason for the primacy of the urban-Athenian model of family, kinship and property transmission patterns is its strong pull on migrants who also retained, where possible, strong links with their natal

Table 1. *Population growth in Athens (1834–1976)*

Year	Population
1834	10,000
1848	31,500
1896	179,700
1928 (greater Athens)	802,600
1951 (greater Athens)	1,378,500
1971 (greater Athens)	2,540,200
1976 (greater Athens)	3,000,000

McNeill, 1978.

villages and thus acted as conduits for the dissemination of Athenian values and social change in their home regions.

The second aim of this study is to insert, as it were, the features of family life in Athens in the late eighteenth and early nineteenth centuries, in a framework which takes cognisance of contemporary regional variation in Greece across time. By identifying those features of family life, embryonic in Athens during this period, we hope to show how these features subsequently interacted with, and influenced, regional patterns of family organisation and property transmissions which, initially, were largely responses to local ecological, political, economic and cultural factors. By studying a critical period in the development of the Athenian family we should be better able to understand a specifically urban type of phenomenon and thus be more able to comprehend regional variations.

Observers have long noted that patterns of property transmission, settlement at marriage, household composition, marriage ages and family forms have been extremely variable in Greece and the Balkans. Apart from the problems that this variability raises for comparative purposes, especially within a broader 'Mediterranean' or 'European' framework, what is at issue here is whether they possess any common features or characteristics. Such features would almost by definition not be the ones normally pursued by historians of the family, for which ones could be taken as 'typical' of Greece. While typologising these systems in terms of geographical area, productive system, ecology and the like may provide some insights, what needs to be explained is whether they possess anything in common. The alternative would be a type of cultural nominalism. Furthermore, to reduce these different systems to the bare bones of the workings of a 'property transmission complex' (for example, that of 'diverging devolution') may explain some matters but not others, especially the cultural values held by the actors themselves, how they perceive their situation and how they respond to their structural predicaments. Even certain institutions such as the dowry, the 'house', etc., may be classified in one way by a legal system and perceived in a completely different manner by the actors themselves. For let us not forget that the family and kinship are as much questions of morality and values (as Fortes has suggested) as property relations, as Leach has asserted for another part of the world. This morality in Greece and other Mediterranean societies is a complex one; in contrast to other areas perhaps it does not simply underlie the religious and jural systems but is heavily influenced by them and interacts in many complex ways, and changes across time. Even the irreducible 'amity' of kinship may change its form and be expressed in different ways in different contexts and across time, as the historians of sentiments and indeed Mauss in a different context have suggested. We therefore need to explore not just the 'bones' (the structural workings of a property transmission system), nor just the 'flesh' (the cultural responses to this system), but also the 'clothing' or 'fashion' (the changing perceptions of the actors them-selves) of the family across time. Thus while we need to discover a type of hidden logic of a culture, its 'aesthetic', if one prefers that word, we still need to retain a comparative perspective and thus be able to see how cultures separated in time and space (such as Renaissance Tuscany and early nineteenth-century Greece) responded differently to a similar set of problems, for example dowry inflation.

One way of doing this is to take a key set of institutions and values recognised as particularly significant in contemporary Greece (the dowry, migration, massive endowments of daughters often with town houses, neolocality, the emphasis on education and state employment, and the distinction between the 'private' and 'public' domains) and examine how they were constructed and operated, if at all, at an earlier critical period. That some values and trends in the organisation of family life on both material (in property transmission patterns) and symbolic levels, the organisation of domesticity and gender construction, have become dominant in Greece over the past decades is indubitable, but what about earlier periods? How new or old are these patterns of organising the family and its material and symbolic universes? Regional variation, to use a convenient shorthand, was certainly strong in Greece and still is, but increasingly less so, especially where the family and its culture are concerned. As regards traditional patterns, Couroucli (1987; 329) has identified four different systems of domestic organisation with corresponding distinctions in property transmission: pastoralists with extended families and a trousseau given to daughters at marriage; the continental farmers with nuclear families, patri-virilocality and land and trousseaux given to daughters as dowries; neolocal island farmers who give mainly trousseaux as dowries, and fishermen with uxorilocality and a bias towards the heavy endowment of daughters, especially of houses. These latter often practise unigeniture with the eldest daughter (*protokori*) receiving the bulk of the family estate. The custom is an old one, found in nineteenth-century Lesbos (Papataxiarhis, 1985), seventeenth-century Naxos (Kasdagli, 1988) and in Nisyros as early as the second half of the eighteenth century (Skouteri-Didaskalou, 1976; 72). There was considerable variation in details (*ibid.*, 73), but it appears that in the larger islands this unigeniture was somewhat more liberal. In Naxos daughters were endowed from the patrimony and sons from the matrimony; in Karpathos bilinearity was practised. The eldest daughter inherited from the mother and the eldest son from the father (Vernier, 1984). By contrast mainlanders in Epirus, the Peloponnese, Mani, as well as inhabitants of large islands such as Crete (Herzfeld, 1985a), Cyprus (Loizos, 1975; Sant Cassia, 1982) and Corfu in the nineteenth century (Couroucli, 1985a) can best be described as 'agnatically oriented'; sons often received the bulk of family property (though women certainly received goods at marriage), residence is patrivirilocal, and so on. A plethora of different patterns co-existed geographically and also changed across time. Such differences had major implications for relations between men and women, the constitution of the family, and the nature of politics within the community. But what were they due to, and what about patterns in the towns? On one level the desire to retain resources intact within the family, or at least to prevent their undue pulverisation, underlies most of these systems though with different emphases. It has been suggested that such practices have been strongly influenced by a recent pastoral past, an argument applicable to the mainland and large islands, but not to the myriad small islands of Greece where scarcity of land and a difficult terrain probably encouraged such conservative practices. But what happened when villagers moved to the city, and even more importantly, what occurred among permanently settled urbanites? What patterns evolved especially among those whose wealth was generated within an urban context? Did a specific 'urban pattern' evolve which was to subsequently influence the varied rural patterns, certainly not necessarily toward identical uniformity, but nevertheless toward a common matrix of cultural principles?

Recent studies on patterns of property transmission and settlement seem to suggest that major changes were occurring in different societies at different times but in a broadly convergent direction. For example, Loizos (1975) shows a movement from virilocality to uxorilocality in the Morfou region, Cyprus, in the early twentieth century with the emergence of a greater emphasis on the dowry. He explores this change by reference to changes in demographic patterns with nubile girls becoming scarcer. In contemporary Cyprus uxorilocality and large dowries prevail (Sant Cassia, 1982). In the region of Laconia, dowries are large in Sparta with daughters receiving a dowry house, but in the surrounding countryside (for example at Mistras) residence is patrivirilocal and the dowry is relatively small (De Waal, personal communication to author). Michael Herzfeld (personal communication to author) reports that while Cretan towns are marked by uxorilocality, overall the surrounding countryside is characterised by patrivirilocality (with the exception of Sitia prefecture).

Contemporary studies of city suburbs, such as Piraeus, seem to reinforce the views that something distinctive appears to be happening to the family and kinship in urban settings. Hirschon's studies (1983; 1989) of Asia Minor refugees (many, but not all of whom were from urban areas) indicate that in the city a certain uniformity in matrimonial practices emerged. In Piraeus, residence is often uxorilocal and that the focus for extended family co-operation tends to centre on a man's relations with his affines (Hirschon, 1983), rather than his agnates. Admittedly this study concentrates on Asia Minor refugees who experienced sudden and traumatic uprooting, were transposed to an alien environment and suddenly swelled the ranks of propertyless labourers. Where men had to move in search of shifting and insecure employment it is hardly surprising that the mother-daughter link should have been given particular enduring emphasis, and a man's strongest links were with his affines through his spouse, rather than with his widely dispersed agnates. Nevertheless it indicates that both among propertyless refugees and ex-peasants, both migrants to the cities, similar patterns emerged. Our data demonstrate that such tendencies were already emerging in the early nineteenth century in Athens, a fact which induces us to conclude that such practices are largely an effect of growing urbanisation and commoditisation, in short that we are in the presence of specifically urban patterns of family organisation and property transmission.

It is in this respect that family forms and patterns of property transmission in Greece, especially in urban areas, are 'new', rather than continuations of traditional rural patterns or their 'rediscovery'. The contemporary pattern of investing daughters with large dowries, especially of urban real estate to attract a suitable groom; the tendency towards uxorilocality; the emphasis on the nuclear family rather on lineage ties, on affinity rather than agnation, on *koumbaria* (godparenthood) rather than adoption or fosterage, on equal partible inheritance and the like; are features which first emerged in early nineteenth-century Athens, especially among its emerging middle class, and which were legitimated by the Church. Because Athens came to dominate Greek society in the new small nation state politically, economically and culturally, to an inordinate extent (certainly greater than Rome and other European Mediterranean capitals), and because this was a society composed mainly of small-holding peasants with no strongly based regional hegemonic elites, the family features that permeated through the rest of society were heavily influenced by Athenian urban patterns. This study aims to show how these came about.

The nature of matrimonial contracts

This study initially grew out of an analysis of 523 marriage contracts drawn up in Athens between 1788–1834, a particularly eventful period for Athens as well as for Greece. It is also supplemented by travellers' accounts, memoirs, and other literature where relevant. The period covers the end of the Turkocratia and the establishment of the Greek kingdom with Athens as its capital, a period marked by prosperity, political unrest, insurrection, war, famine and massive population changes as well as by the more anthropologically familiar notion of 'social change in peaceful conditions'. Nevertheless, in spite of the restless and politically tumultuous times we are dealing with (and perhaps also because of it), we hope to show how changes in political organisation, the movement towards a monetary economy, relations between social classes and changes in clothing fashion, among other developments, were reflected in the matrimonial contracts entered into during this period. We are equally interested in the way property transmissions within and between families, and how they changed across time, influenced relations between social classes, the position of men and women in society, and the shaping of civil society in a nationalist age.

Such an aim may appear particularly ambitious for the material and data at our disposal. Yet as we hope to show, our point of departure which is the contracts themselves, contain a veritable mine of information which enables us to relate to other literature on this period as well as to other material on Mediterranean societies. We therefore begin by discussing the nature of our data. This includes all the published matrimonial contracts of Athens as well as archival research and all the available records on unpublished contracts for this period. Our matrimonial contracts come from three sources in the form of three codices belonging to five notaries: Manuscript 11 Codex, consisting of 125 sheets containing the acts of Notary Antoniou Karori, between

1788–1823 (unpublished, General State Archives, Athens); Manuscript 12 Codex, consisting of 60 sheets containing the acts of Notaries Lambrou Neri, Andreas Neri and Nicolaou Neri who worked in Athens between 1815–23 (unpublished, General State Archives, Athens); Manuscript 1 Codex of Athens Notary Panayi Poulou, who worked in Athens between 1822–34 (G.A. Petropoulos, 1957). As far as we have been able to ascertain our data thus comprises all the hitherto accessible and available known matrimonial contracts for Athens during this period. We believe that our data is based on a sufficiently large sample to enable us to make some general statements about Athenian society in the late eighteenth and early nineteenth centuries.[7]

Of equal significance is the nature of the contracts themselves. Athens and some islands were distinct in Greece in that they possessed a notarial culture, due to Venetian influence (Visvizis, 1965; 64–5). Few consistent, sustained and easily accessible matrimonial contracts survive for other parts of Greece, and the researcher must plough through much material in order to select his primary data upon which to base his analysis. The nature of the transcribers themselves is also important. In Athens it appears that most contracts (*prikosymfona*) were registered in front of a small number of notaries who were highly literate, followed certain formulas, and centralised their records. In other parts of Greece there were a greater number of transcribers (usually the village *papas*) with the consequent uneven details, inconsistency and lack of continuity which inevitably reduces their comparative and statistical potential. On the other hand, by restricting themselves to standardised formulas Athenian notaries excluded references to details on the quality of life for which we have had to turn to other sources, such as memoirs and travellers' accounts.

The tendency to record and register *prikosymfona* in Greece was insisted on by the Orthodox Church and encouraged by self-interest, particularly in the towns. In accordance with its long expressed aim to control marriage practices (Goody, 1983) the Church insisted that agreements be recorded in special registers and drawn up either by the *papas* or by notaries, where they existed. This was a condition to obtain a marriage permit, as the Circular letter of 1796 by Theofilos, Bishop of Kozanis, indicates:

Without drawing up the marriage contract in front of the appointed cleric, they will not be able to obtain a marriage permit . . . After this has been obtained the [same] marriage contract must be signed by the [same] appointed cleric who must register and copy it in a special book kept for such purposes and to avoid any future disagreements.

(M. Kalinderis, 1951; 95)

It is doubtful whether such directives were closely followed, especially in the countryside and among the urban poor. As is well known in Greece, as in other parts of the Mediterranean, grassroots matrimonial practices differed radically from Church dogma. Village priests (*papas*, plural *papades*) in many cases were also unlikely to follow such rigid and complex rules. Many country people were content with an agreement which involved just the two parties to the match, rather than a costly and potentially troublesome third party. This was known as the *ksofili*, an agreement drawn up at the matchmaking in front of the parents but not by a notary and given to the groom and bride (I. Visvizis, 1965; 56–60).

In the highly stratified urban environments of the late eighteenth and early nineteenth centuries, such as Athens, there was a greater tendency to register *prikosymfona* with neutral third parties. There were a number of reasons for this: the Church's power was more secure, a notarial culture was more diffused and widespread, there were greater population movements and people were less likely to know each other 'in the round' as in the villages, although Athens was certainly far from an anonymous place. Of equal importance was greater commercialisation, and the desire to register such transfers with the authorities to prevent Ottoman usurpation of property or inflated tax demands. Athenians also utilised notaries out of self-interest; some contracts explicitly state that the *prikosymfono* was drawn up and registered with the notary 'for the bride's insurance' (Manuscript 11; 109). Registration also gave legal force to the parental transmission of property and prevented the emergence of disagreements at a later stage. Dowry cultures are often associated with scribal cultures.[8]

The contracts were drawn up in front of a large number of witnesses, mainly the bride's and groom's kin, and appear to have constituted an integral part of the whole marriage complex. This was done either some time before the ceremony took place, especially at the time of delivery of some goods (usually the bridal costume supplied by the groom among the main productive population), or a few days after the ceremony. Three copies were produced for the groom, the bride and the notary's archives.

It is unlikely that all Athenian marriages were recorded in this way, especially among the mass of the Athenian population. Nevertheless, we believe, from an examination of the nature of resources transferred, that many ordinary Athenian marriages were so recorded. The large number of our contracts also encourages us in this view. It is also possible that other notaries operated in Athens, apart from our five, whose codices have been lost. However, references in our codices to the 'general notary' or the 'town's notary' would suggest that not many notaries operated in Athens during this period. For these reasons we believe that our data constitute a sufficiently representative sample (if not the majority) of all *prikosymfona* drawn up in Athens during this period.

Athens under Ottoman rule

Athens became incorporated into the Ottoman Empire in 1456. During the first 200 years of Ottoman rule it held a somewhat privileged status as it was the *has* (prebend of substantial size) of high Ottoman officials and we know that after 1640 it became the *has* of Kislar Agas, chief-eunuch of the Sultan's harem. Population figures are somewhat uncertain for all periods of Ottoman rule, being based on taxation records, travellers' accounts and the like, and they must therefore be treated with caution. By the beginning of the sixteenth century the town's population is estimated to have stood at 13,000 (in 2,297 house-holds); this grew annually at a rate of 10.2 per cent between 1529–70 to reach 17,000 inhabitants in 3,207 households, making it the fourth largest town in the Balkans after Constantinople, Thessaloniki and Adrianople. For 1667 a report exists of 8–10,000 inhabitants, three-quarters Greek, one-quarter Ottoman, and divided into 8 parishes or quarters (George Wheeler, in Andrews, 1979). Other reports refer to smaller numbers of Muslims (2 per cent),[9] and it is likely that the population fluctuated. Between 1772–96 Panayis Skouzes estimated the population at 1,500 Christian families, 350 Ottoman families, 25 Muslim gypsy families of blacksmiths and 30 'Ethiopians' (black families). Andrews (*ibid.*; 118) suggests a total population figure of 12,500, includ-ing the Turkish garrison, on the basis of 6 individuals per family (although there are suggestions that this number may be too large). Numbers of Albanians had also settled in the hinterland around Athens by 1674 (Giraud, in Andrews; 94). Richard Chandler who visited the area in 1765 observed 'the lordly Turk and lively Greek neglecting pasturage and agriculture, that province has been obtained by the Albanians' (*ibid.*; 113). Skouzes refers to 1,500 families in the surround-ing villages (*ibid.*; 118).

By 1810 John Hobhouse observed that the number of houses in Athens stood between 12–13,000, of which 400 were occupied by Turks, 500–600 by Greeks, and 300 houses by Albanians. The town at the end of the eighteenth century was not rigidly segregated according to ethni-city, for 'half of the Turkish houses were in one part of the town, and the other half dispersed here and there among the houses of Christians' (Skouzes, in Andrews, 1979; 119).

Under Ottoman rule the population in Athens, as elsewhere, was divided into a number of distinct taxation groups. Such distinctions covered other aspects of public life such as clothing and costume, the painted facades of houses and rights to ride on horseback, and it appears that the Church also based itself on these distinctions when drawing up sumptuary laws covering dowry-size endowments at marriage. Some historians have identified these distinctions with social groups, to which they did correspond to a certain extent. D. Kampouroglous divided Athenian society into four groups: *arkhontes* (ruling group), *nikokirei* (household gentlemen), *bazarides* (bazaar sellers) and *ksotarides* (migrants to the city). K. Christomanos identified their manner of address as the following: 'Sior' (from the Italian 'Signore') for the first group; 'Kyr', 'Kyrie' (Mr) for the second; 'Mastro' (lit., boss or master craftsman) for the third; and 'Koumbaros' and 'Koligas' (from 'Kolligos', sharecropper, farmer) for the final group (Kampouroglous, vol. 3, 1982; 139). Such forms of address were apparently in wide use. The revolutionary hero Kolokotronis consistently addressed members of the *nikokirei* group by the title Kyrie and it is clear from his memoirs that he afforded them considerable deference and respect. Similar distinctions obtained in other parts of Greece. Leake, who visited Ioannina in the early nineteenth century, noted that the population there was divided into four taxation classes and that each group was restricted to a particular value bracket for dowry endowments (Clogg, 1976; 9–11).

Ottoman administration was under the control of a governor (*voivode*), but as occurred elsewhere in the Ottoman Empire a salaried scribal class of functionaries was lacking and the Porte was obliged to rely on pre-existing local elites to provide the personnel and the necessary continuity in the practical daily administration of the community. In contrast to other Ottoman regions such as Cyprus where the Church fulfilled the role of tax-estimator and collector (Sant Cassia, 1986), this function was assumed by the resident Athenian aristocracy of *arkhontes*. The *arkhon* class had been formed during the Venetian occupation with whom they continued to trade during the Turkocratia. They were major landowners, living off rents for their land which was worked by others. Their basic obligations were the drawing up of taxation lists to be paid by the community, their collection and the settlement of civil cases within the Christian community (I. Benizelos, 1902; 275). They thus possessed an immense source of power, ranging from land-ownership, administration, taxation and justice; they also supplied personnel for the higher clergy, straddling the polity, the economy, and the Church. I. Benizelos, a chronicler of this period and himself a member of the *arkhontes*, gives the names of the oldest and wealthiest members of the *arkhon* class in Athens, identifying them as houses (*'ai evgenesterai kai plousioterai kai palaioterai oikai isan'*). A close examination of these names indicates that some were of Byzantine origin, but others betray a strong Latin or Frankish element (*ibid.*; 265).

The Greek community elected its elders (*kotzabashides*) from among the *arkhon* class. In 1676 Wheeler noted that 'having divided the town in eight Quarters . . . out of every one of these, one of the most substantial and reverend ancient men is chosen who they can call Epitropi [committee members]' (Andrews, 1979; 101). Their periods of appointment varied from a yearly turnover, as in the Peloponnese, to lifetime appointments, as in mainland Greece and including Athens (Kaldis, 1963; 23). Inevitably within a prebendal system the *arkhontes* developed strong links with highly placed Ottoman officials to their mutual benefit. Hadji Ali Haseki, the governor of Athens between 1772–96, 'aimed to amass within a short while and to turn all Athens into his own private property, or a chiftlik as happened elsewhere' (Benizelou, 1902; 306) in which he was assisted by the *arkhontes*: 'he discovered the Athenian aristocracy to be sycophants and in a short while he turned them into his friends and followers' (P. Skouzes, 1975; 65–66).

High taxes, the mortgaging of properties to obtain cash to pay taxes and usurious rates of interest in an imperfectly monetised economy resulted in the alienation of land away from the peasant-cultivators and its concentration in private hands, either Ottoman or Greek. This process occurred in many parts of the Ottoman world and its general features have been outlined by McGowan (1981). Yet McGrew has suggested that land was perhaps less significant for direct production and for income: 'the *arkhon* class under Turkish rule had drawn its relative wealth only to a limited extent from actual ownership of land, which it normally leased out for grazing or cultivation. More significant was income derived from tax-farming, usury, administrative prerogatives and emphyteutic rights to a portion of the surplus produced by peasant farms and transhumant flocks' (1985; 220–21). A contemporary account by the reliable Consul Jean Giraud noted that whereas Albanian peasants had owned most of the land in the villages surrounding Athens in 1650, by 1674 nearly two-thirds of all land had passed into Ottoman hands, the peasant cultivators becoming mere labourers on the land to which they had previously held greater rights (Collignon, 1913; 38). Ottoman land-holding was sufficiently complex to caution us against drawing too radical conclusions from this observation, but it seems clear nevertheless that part of Athens' population growth probably was seasonal, being swelled by displaced peasants who returned to the villages as seasonal labourers. What seems generally clear is that by

Table 2. *Land and population in Greece, 1828*

Land area in hectares	Greeks	Percentage	Ottomans	Percentage
Peloponnese	1,500,000	33.3	3,000,000	66.7
Continental Greece	3,444,100	57.0	2,528,720	43.0

McGrew (1985) has questioned the validity of the data upon which this report is based.
S. Asdrachas, 1986.

the eve of Independence a considerable amount of land was Ottoman-owned. Asdrachas (1986; 74) quotes an 1828 estimate giving the proportions listed in table 2.

Concurrently, while the Ottomans concentrated on amassing land which was given over to cereal cultivation, in which a healthy illegal export trade developed,[10] other properties were obtained by the Christian population, mainly in the Church and among Greek landed-families. The transfer of properties to the Church may well have been a strategy by peasants to prevent Ottoman usurpation of their land, as occurred in Cyprus (Sant Cassia, 1986a). Christian landholding concentrated on olive cultivation, and under the Ottoman Code trees could be owned separately from the land on which they were situated. Olives not only formed part of the staple diet of the population but were also sold on the market far afield either in their raw state or as soap, produced by urban craft guilds (Beaujour, 1974; 113). Olives were generally more lucrative than cereals: in 1797 one stremma (one-third of an acre) devoted to good quality cereals yielded 200 francs income, whereas a similar area under olives yielded 300 francs. In certain cases costs could be recouped relatively quickly. In 1807 an Athenian purchased 80 olive trees for 2,000 groshia; next year when demand was high he sold his entire harvest for 2,500 groshia, thus recouping his initial outlay. Cereals, however, required less involvement in the organisation of production from the landowner and the fields could be rented out to pastoralists after harvesting; they were thus more suitable for absentee Ottoman landowners.

Other productive activities included apiaries and honey collection, mainly by monasteries (D. Karidis, 1981; 184–85) and pastoralism. Dairy products were consumed within the town while tanneries processed leather mainly for export to Constantinople. Yet the degree to which pastoralism represented a genuine alternative to agriculture is debatable. McGrew views the largely pastoral nature of much of the Greek countryside as an attempt to escape from oppressive taxation and general deterioration in the lowlands. On the other hand, while this is undoubtedly true, pastoralism was not exclusively subsistence-oriented and some surpluses were certainly extracted through cultivation dues, exchange in the market place, taxes, and so on. The large numbers of livestock in Attica for 1794 quoted by Sibthorp (1820; 141) – 100,000 goats, 60,000 sheep, 6,000 oxen and cows – suggest that an appreciable number of pastoral activities occurred in areas under central control.

By 1760, somewhat later than in other Ottoman territories, Athens became fully incorporated in the prebendal regime (*mulikame*, or *malikâne*, a holding leased for life). As happened elsewhere conditions for the local population worsened as the city and its environs were leased to the highest bidders who undertook to pay the Porte a fixed income. Inevitably such men were more interested in recouping their initial expenses and making their bid pay, rather than in long-term security, both commercial and political (D. Karidis, 1981; 127–31, 159–64). The years 1772–96 were particularly difficult for Athenians under the grasping and tyrannous rule of Hadji Ali Haseki. Under an oppressive tax regime and various natural and man-made disasters the population plummeted to roughly 10,000 inhabitants (Stuart, in Kampouroglous, 1892). It is recorded that many Athenian families secretly left for the countryside and for the mountainous areas where conditions were less politically oppressive but certainly more impoverished; according to J. Sibthorp (1820; 144) the total number of households which left Athens in 1784 was 250. Skouzes records that 'the tyrant set guards at the entrance to the alleyways to keep the people from escaping. For they would go out by the town gates, saying they were off to gather olives for the tyrant's own oil, and they got out easily that way, both the men and the women' (Andrews, 1979; 125). Between 1780–90 we have reports that the city's population comprised 1,500 Christian households, 350 Muslim households, 25 'Turkogypsy' households and 30 'Ethiopian' households (P. Skouzes, 1975; 110).

Other factors undeniably contributed to population decline, probably to a greater extent than did harsh taxation. Plague hit Athens in 1788 and was followed by famine. Panayis Skouzes, our major chronicler for the period, wrote: '. . . the plague wrought great havoc. Three, five, six people died each day. The population scattered. Only the Turks remained behind; because of their religion they were not afraid: wherever they went, they said, death would find them if so it were written' (Andrews, 1979; 123). That year I. Benizelos reported that 'approximately 1700 people died: 1200 Christians [i.e. Greeks] and 500 Muslims [i.e. Turks]' (Kodrikas, 1963; 12). In 1792 the plague struck again and claimed 1,100 lives; 800 Christians and 300 Muslims. The price of land plummeted while credit was squeezed: 'But who in those days had anything to lend? The few Turks who survived the plague would not lend but bought up land at a fraction of its value' (Skouzes, *ibid.*). The plague hastened the movement of the population to the countryside with the result that many countrymen left: '. . . people were coming from other towns to buy, because they had learned that in Athens things were going cheap. The villagers loaded caiques with every moveable object, even their herds, their cattle and other animals, and they fled secretly to Anatolia with their families. If someone escaped from this or that quarter the other parishioners would have to pay his tax. So what did they do? They would break into the fugitive's house, but they would find nothing within. As if there was anything left before he fled!' (Skouzes, in Andrews, 1979; 123–25). By the end of the eighteenth century the population recovered somewhat due to the return of about 1,000 inhabitants following Ali Haseki's death (J. Sibthorp, 1820; 145). At the same time the surrounding 60 Attica villages had a population of approximately 12,000 inhabitants. Reports exist of 12,000 inhabitants in 1813 (Holland and Forbin, in Kampouroglous, 1896; 135).

For most of the eighteenth century Athens, while an administrative centre, was in effect much like a large village. It lacked the necessary military and commercial might to completely dominate the countryside to which townsmen regularly fled in search of less oppressive conditions. Our data confirms Yannoulopoulos' observation that the

agrarian features [of towns] were quite pronounced since most of their inhabitants were incompletely separated [economically and socially] from the surrounding countryside. Their roles as centres of craft production was secondary to that of being centres of consumption. The town did not predominate over the countryside by subjecting its agriculture to a pattern of new economic relations; on the contrary it lived off the latter's surplus which was directed toward the provincial capitals in the same fashion as the surplus from the provinces was capital city-oriented.   (1981; 32)

In the early nineteenth century there were regular and apparently more frequent movements between Athens and its surrounding villages, and vice versa. This can be attributed to the general uncertainty of the times. For example De Pouqueville (1820; 92) refers to about 3,000 Ottoman inhabitants in Athens, a substantial increase; Albanian peasants also settled in the environs of Athens, leaving their villages due to uncertainty, as happened elsewhere (Antoniadou-Bibikou, 1979; 219, and Todorov, 1979; 277).

The War of Independence devastated both city and countryside and Athens was not spared. An American visitor described it during this period as

A large village of originally mean houses, pulled down to the very cellars, and lying choked in its rubbish. A large square in ruins, after a fire in one of our cities, looks like it. It has been destroyed so often by Turks and Greeks alternately, that scarce one stone is left upon another. The inhabitants thatch one corner of these wretched and dusty holes with maize-stocks and straw, and live there like beasts.

(quoted in McGrew, 1985; 3)

The war also rendered the demographic pattern complex and anomalous. The Consul Don Origone noted that a new flight from Athens occurred (Zoras, 1972; 10), a picture confirmed by an official report based upon records from the city's parishes which listed the number of Christian households in 1822 as 1,265, a substantial decrease. Such a chaotic situation must have decisively influenced fertility patterns and the like; unfortunately insufficient data is available at this stage to explore these implications. In 1830 Athens was described as a 'miserable village' (Matton, 1963; 215; Ross, 1976; 48–49). That same year however the London protocol was signed which recognised Greece's right to independence, and a fresh influx of people settled in Athens. These were not only Athenians, many of whom had moved to Salamina, Aegina and Zakynthos in 1827, but also others attracted by the possibility of purchasing Ottoman owned land. By 1834 when Athens became the new capital of the Greek kingdom the population had returned to its pre-war level of 10,000; in 1862 it had risen to 43,000.[11]

By far the majority of the Athenian population in the period under discussion consisted of ordinary townsmen. A certain percentage were involved in craft production and some were identified by the professional title of *maestros*. A more considerable proportion were migrants from surrounding villages and they appear to have retained close links with their natal villages, returning there at critical periods during the year. The majority of the population lived by a combination of domestic industrial activity (water-carriers, servants, stevedores, builders and so on) and income from a small holding, supplemented at the lower end of the scale by animal husbandry. Skouzes writes that there were also about 1,000 paupers (*ptohon*) in 1775; these were 'homeless and landless' persons who lived in the cells of the 36 parishes of the city and worked as seasonal agricultural workers (in Andrews, 1979; 118). As McGrew has so painstakingly demonstrated we are dealing with a tumultuous period after long centuries of agricultural pauperisation. Yet we must be cautious in permitting such a fact to over-influence our awareness of the complexity of the period and society. Agricultural neglect and pauperisation did not necessarily imply that wealth and resources of all kinds were unavailable in Athens. Whilst the mass of Athenians were not better off than those in the countryside, certain groups which were more historically significant had access to cash, land, political power and resources of various kinds. Nor was Athens an autarchic self-subsisting community similar to a mountain village; this was a monetary economy, surpluses were extracted from the surrounding hinterland by various means, and agricultural products were processed there for local consumption and export. Even in the countryside the economy appears to have become more complex and cash was present, despite the impression that might be gained from a cursory reading of certain historical accounts (e.g. McGrew) which may suggest that the new kingdom started from a base line of zero. In the late eighteenth and early nineteenth centuries throughout Greece the phenomenon of dowry inflation appeared and affected townsmen and countrymen alike, though to a varying extent. Our analysis of marriage contracts as well as our reading of other accounts for other areas of Greece suggest that cash and resources of all kinds were available in spite of the destruction of houses and the movement of people and loss of life which accompanied the War of Independence.

The late eighteenth, early nineteenth centuries were also a period of radical political conflict in Athens, as elsewhere in Greece. The *arkhon* class was beginning to lose its economic power, and was increasingly threatened economically and politically by a rising *nikokirei* class. In 1765 Richard Chandler observed that 'the *arkhons* are now mere names, except a tall fur cap, and fuller and better dress than is worn by the inferior classes. Some have shops in the bazaar, some are merchants or farmers of the public revenue. The families, styled *arkhontic*, are eight or ten in number, mostly on the decline' (Andrews, 1979; 113).

Arkhon decline was due to various external and internal factors. By the mid eighteenth century, the Venetians, the *arkhons'* major trading partners, had been largely supplanted by the French as the main eastern Mediterranean traders (Chateaubriand, in Andrews, 1979; 138). The latter increasingly worked through the more mobile Aegean Greeks who possessed their own ships and the *arkhontes* were obliged to work through Ottoman intermediaries. By 1810 English manufactured goods had also begun to make their appearance (Hobhouse, in Andrews, 1979; 15). In Athens the *nikokirei* class, more diverse in its geographical origins, began entering trade (internal, but also external), threatening the monopoly of the *arkhon* class. But because successful trade and capital accumulation was largely a function of, and dependent upon, control over political and administrative posts, dissatisfaction was soon expressed in the political arena. R. Clogg (1976) has published a number of political tracts circulated during this period including the *Rossanglogallos*, a bitter satire against local elites, which speaks of the *kotzabashides* 'who in all else imitated the Turk, in clothing, in external manners and in his house. His case was similar to that of the Turk, and only in name did he differ. Instead, for example, of calling him Hasan, they called him Giannis, and instead of going to the mosque he went to church. Only in this was there a distinction' (Khrysanthopoulos, quoted in Clogg, 1976; 21).

This last quotation dates to the post-Greek War of Independence and is somewhat inexact in detail (for example on clothing), having been written by an opponent of the *arkhontes*, but it is generally correct in identifying the close cooperation between Ottoman overlords and the *arkhontes*, as well as the latter's close emulation of the former, a phenomenon found in most parts of Greece. We are however fortunate in having an eyewitness account of Athens during this period from a member of the *nikokirei* group. Throughout his memoirs P. Skouzes, a merchant, refers to the *archons* as the tyrant Hadji Ali's 'henchmen' (Andrews, 1979; 120), as 'villainous' (*ibid.*; 121) and as his 'stool-pigeons' (*ibid.*; 122); it is clear that he reserved his strongest vituperations for the Athenian elite. Skouzes recorded his social origins in this way: 'My father Dimitrios of Nikolao Skouze, my mother Samaltana, daughter of Thanasi Limperiou Panayiotatzi. Both were from families which belonged to the second class, that is except the twelve families of the Athenian aristocratic Kotzabashides' (Skouzes, 1975). He also gives details of his family's occupations: 'My father was a child of a soap merchant. However, my mother's father was also a soap merchant. My grandfather was also a merchant dealing in local products' (*ibid.*; 64). Elsewhere he states that his 'grandfather' had a shop which dealt in all the cheese of Attica with 'the brother of Ilias Skouze and Georgion Skouze' (*ibid.*; 102). Skouzes also notes down the property of his paternal grandfather in 1760: 'over 1,200 olive trees, 80 flocks of sheep with 30 head per flock, two large vegetable gardens, 40 stremmata vineyards, a team of oxen, 500 stremmata arable land, two olive presses, a soap factory, two shoe factories, a place for the storage of cut grass (*grasidotopos*), three houses, and capital ["*kapitale*", here he uses the Italian word rather than the Greek *kefaleon*] all those who owed him money for oil, cheese, butter, wheat, honey, etc., ["from his shop"]' (*ibid.*; 102).

In eighteenth-century Athens such wealth was considerable and spanned most of the resources available in this period. Yet the *nikokirei* were not only becoming increasingly economically powerful in Athens; they were also a more dynamic group. Skouzes notes that the twelve leading families of Kodjabashis respected the twenty-four families of *nikokirei* 'as having money and some education' (Andrews, 1979; 117). Their kinship networks made extensive use of kinsmen networks for trade. The Athenian *nikokirei* paralleled other *nikokirei* groups elsewhere in Greece. Henry Holland who travelled to Epirus in 1812–13 noted that

> the greater part of the exterior trade of Turkey, in the exchange of commodities, is carried on by Greek houses, which have residents at home, and branches in various cities of Europe, mutually aiding each other. An instance at this time occurs to me of a Greek family, with which I was intimate where, of four brothers, one was settled in Ioannina, another at Moscow, a third at Constantinople, and the fourth in some part of Germany; all connected together in their concerns.
>
> (Clogg, 1976; 28)

In Hydra common geographical origins and a strong sense of place enabled the establishment of trust in loans which were usually oral (*ibid.*; 31), a situation paralled in Athens where most of the rich landowners sold their produce to the Christian merchants 'without bills of trade or other complications' (Skouzes, in Andrews, 1979; 119). The famous man of letters Adamantios Korais first went to Amsterdam on the request of his father because 'he wished to have there a relative and not to trade through Dutchmen, as my grandfather did' (*ibid.*; 124).

The tension between the *arkhon* and *nikokirei* classes was not restricted to trade and economic activities and the concomitant issues of political representation and control of administrative posts. In this pre-industrial society it was expressed and pursued in other areas of social life revealed in our contracts. Although some *nikokirei* families had managed to intermarry with the *arkhontes* by the end of the eighteenth century, the latter resisted these incursions mainly because their power base rested ultimately upon control of administrative and political posts (taxation, justice and so on) which were transmitted within the family. The Orthodox Church was deployed to attempt to control the amount of goods offered at marriage, and the contracts reveal a close, almost phobic, concern with the types and quality of bridal costumes, cash endowments and dowers, all issues which bear on boundary-maintaining mechanisms. Both groups entered the early nineteenth century with different types of households and historical experiences, and deployed and valued different resources according to different rationales to preserve or pursue economic and political dominance.

In 1785 matters reached a head when 'a general meeting of Athenians expelled the Kotzabashides who had been the followers of Hadji Ali . . . and the Athenians changed the system such that every year free elections would be held for the posts of *kotzabashides*, and not as before where such positions were inherited' (Skouzes, *ibid.*; 70).

The liberating effect of such a meeting was perhaps less extensive than Skouzes suggests, for it merely widened the electoral college to include the 24 *nikokirei* 'families', according to the chronicler 'the heart of the Athens' ('*I Kardia ton Athinon*'). The use of the word *kardia*, or heart, is designed to suggest that the *nikokirei* were more in touch with the feelings of the population and were their natural representatives.

As we intend to show, wider historical events beyond the control of the *arkhon* class, their loss of legitimacy during and after the Turkocratia, and the creation of new resources in the nation state, combined to weaken the dominance of the *arkhon* class and it eventually became incorporated into the *nikokirei*. Within the new Greek kingdom, especially in Athens but also in other towns, it was the *nikokirei* 'model' of kinship and marriage which became dominant. These family forms which emphasised the nuclear family, the massive endowment of daughters at marriage as a means to secure and pursue prestige, the strategic uses of *koumbaria*, which had been partly developed in the last competitive decades of the Turkocratia, were more suitable for the realities of the Greek state. The *nikokirei* model of household, kinship and marriage was legitimated by the Church and by popular literature, and eventually became the cultural norm not merely for townspeople but for those in the countryside as well. Such features in turn helped to shape the particular development of the Greek state and the mobilisation of the countryside.

2

Men and houses, women and households

Introduction

We begin our analysis by addressing a central question: where did the mass of Athenians settle at marriage? Answering this question can shed light on a host of related issues. To begin with it can indicate the nature of power relations within the household, the position of women as sisters, wives and widows, and the nature of co-operation within the family. But other issues are involved, especially when material from nineteenth century Athens is compared with that of other Mediterranean societies, and when the situation in contemporary Greece is taken into account. In general terms it appears that on both shores of the Mediterranean, until recently, residence after marriage was patrivirilocal. In the Balkans, in Renaissance Tuscany (Klapisch-Zuber, 1985) and in North Africa (Cuisenier, 1976) most women appear to have moved to their husband's household at marriage. In contemporary Greece and Cyprus, although the ideal, especially in the towns, is towards neolocality (Loizos, 1975), the pattern did not become established until recently in many parts of the countryside. Boeotian villagers (du Boulay, 1974), Peloponnesians, and Epirot Sarakatsani (Campbell, 1964) practised patrivirilocality with important consequences for gender identity, the nature of the household and for co-operation between affines. Some islands, by contrast, seem to have long practised uxorilocality, possibly because the men were often away. As early as 1749 Lord Charlemont, who visited Greece and Turkey, commented not only on the differences between the Aegean islands (such as Mykonos, which were uxorilocal) and the mainland in terms of settlement patterns, but also in terms of the comparatively freer status enjoyed by women in the islands (Stanford and Finopoulos, 1984; 126).

An analysis of residence patterns together with other factors can shed light on wider kinship links. Some Greek observers of the Sarakatsani have noted features of residual agnation, in contrast to Campbell (1964). Such observations find echoes in other literature on the Mediterranean. Historians of Renaissance Tuscany have suggested that lineage ties (similar to the French *lignages*) were particularly strong (Kent, 1977; Klapisch-Zuber, 1985; 21), a view echoed by Couroucli (1985a) for eighteenth-century Corfu under Venetian control. Often this was expressed in a tendency towards the non-division of property held by the agnatic group across a number of generations, the election of a common spokesman, the *de facto* exclusion of women either as sisters or as wives from any significant immovable property ownership, and the retaining of strong sentiments of agnatic solidarity after marriage. Yet in contemporary Greece and Cyprus the ideal is towards the establishment of an independent nuclear family at marriage (Loizos, 1975). To what extent is this a relatively recent phenomenon? An analysis of settlement patterns in Athens in the late eighteenth and early nineteenth centuries can go some way towards answering this question. As we shall try to show, Athenian patterns were not uniform and there was considerable variation between social strata.

Settlement at marriage

Contrary to contemporary Greek society, the house does not appear to have been important in late eighteenth- and early nineteenth-century Athens. By this we mean a number of things: that the house as bricks and mortar was not an important public reference point; that it was not a significant economic resource; that for the mass of the population a separate house was not a necessary precondition to marriage, and that most people did not expect, nor necessarily aspire, to live in their own house as a distinct separate building at marriage. Indeed the house was important not to establish a marriage, but to link different generations together. The low economic profile of the house is also shown in the wills and divisions of property of this period, further indicating that once the parents were dead the house found its place as a relatively insignificant economic resource.

Our data categorically indicate that the dowry house did not figure prominently in most marriage contracts; indeed 63 per cent (330) of all brides did not receive a dowry house at marriage, while 19 per cent (99) received an entire house and 18 per cent (94) received part of a house. The latter includes 16 cases of widow remarriage where 11 widows brought a house with them to their second marriage.

The figures therefore suggest that some daughters (37 per cent) resided at marriage either with their parents, or shared a house with some other married siblings, or in the case of widows shared a house with siblings. Was this the result of cultural expectations or a response to a specific set of circumstances?

In Athens and often elsewhere on the mainland (especially the Peloponnese), most couples at marriage lived not in an independent household, nor with the bride's parents or her kin, but with the groom's kin in his parental household. Similar practices have been recorded for the Peloponnese village of Dimitsana, where only 15 per cent of brides between 1890–1900 received a dowry house (Kalpourtzi, 1987; 94). In contrast to nineteenth-century working-class Lancashire, such practices were due more to choice than necessity. This applied to the majority of Athenian-born couples, although non-native Athenian grooms tended to marry Athenian brides with dowry houses. As early as 1676 the visitor George Wheler noted that

> when a Virgin is to be married, she is brought to the Church as richly attired as the Fortune of her Relations will bear, but her Face is so bedaubed with gross Paint, that it is not easie to determine whether she be Flesh and Blood, or a Statue made of Plaister. She returns with a great Crown of gilded Metal on her Head, accompanied by all the Guests, and her near Relations, with Pipes, and Hand-Drums, and the best Musick they can make: whil'st she, in the mean time, is conducted at so slow a pace, that it is scarcely perceivable that she moveth. And so soon *as she is entered into the house of her spouse*, they throw Sugar-plumbs out of the Windows, upon the People, who are crowded and throng'd at the Door:
>
> (Andrews, 1979; 103: our italics)

We have quoted this passage at length because it highlights some themes which we wish to explore at a later stage: the procession of the bride, her attire as a symbol of wealth, features found in other patrivirilocal contexts such as contemporary North Africa. In all these contexts, and especially in rural ones, such symbolism emphasises alliances (Segalen, 1986; 127). Yet the passage is unequivocal on the settlement pattern, especially of the wealthy social groups whom Wheler had in most likelihood observed. In order to bring out more clearly the differences between social groups in our data, rather than to separate the different variables on which to peg the transmission of dowry houses, we have listed them for a synoptic appreciation of the complexity of settlement patterns in table 3.

The table breaks down the transmission of dowry houses according to a variety of criteria which are listed in the 'Variables' column. Although these variables are consistent we are interested in the differences between the social groups concerned. It appears that titled families tended to endow their daughters with houses to a lesser extent than untitled families did (A1, 2). The tendency was even more pronounced when there was no ambiguity in the bride's status, that is when she

Table 3. *Dowry houses supplied by brides*

			House supplied by bride		
		Variables	Entire house	No house	Part of a house
				(in per cent)	
A	1	No title in bride's family	19.5	59.9	20.5
	2	At least 1 title in bride's family	15.4	79.7	4.7
	3	Titled brides (*'Kiria'*)	13.9	80.6	5.6
	4	Untitled brides	19.6	61.6	18.8
B	1	Brides wearing costumes of untitled Athenians	19.8	61.3	16.9
	2	Brides wearing costumes of country women	21.2	63.6	15.2
	3	Brides wearing costumes of titled groups	11.5	66.6	21.7
	4	Brides wearing new costume (post 1833)	23.0	50.0	27.0
	5	Total brides wearing non-rural costumes	11.9	83.6	4.5
C	1	Grooms: native of Athens	18.4	64.6	17.0
	2	Grooms: non-native	33.3	22.2	44.4
D	1	Groom's titles: 'Sior'	–	75.0	25.0
	2	Groom's titles: 'Kir'	5.6	88.9	5.6
	3	Titled grooms (Kir) marrying into titled brides	–	96.3	3.7
	4	Maestros	–	40.9	20.0
	5	Untitled grooms	20.0	61.1	18.9
Total			18.9	63.1	18.0

It should be noted that grooms in categories C2, D1 and D4 comprise but a small number within the overall sample.

herself was registered as titled on the contracts (A3). This is because a bride may have had just one titled parent, but if she married into a lower social group she may not have been registered as titled. Women who were endowed with a countrywoman's costume (B2) were (slightly) more likely to receive a whole house than were untitled brides (A4, 21.2 per cent versus 19.6 per cent), and women who wore the costume of titled families (B3) were even more unlikely to receive a whole house than were titled brides (A3, 11.5 per cent versus 13.9 per cent), but more likely to receive part of a house. We discuss the significance of costume in chapter 4, but at this point we wish to indicate that there was some flexibility in the correlation between those brides who wore costumes of titled women and those women who were actually titled. Finally of note is the greater tendency in the post-1833 period for daughters to be endowed with houses (B4) due to the migration of men to Athens, and the emerging pattern of neolocality.

From the perspective of the grooms we can examine where dowry houses tended to concentrate. Over 33 per cent of non-native grooms

(C2) tended to receive houses, especially parts of houses (44 per cent), in contrast to the total average (18.9 per cent), whereas titled grooms from Athens most certainly did not marry brides with houses (D1, 2, 3). We thus believe that while overall averages are significant, there were, nevertheless, important differences between social groups and categories. Clearly some of these categories overlapped, although they were not identical.

The endowment of daughters with houses, a practice which deviated from the cultural norm, was a specific response by certain Athenian families at the lower end of the social scale to the problem of old-age insurance. Non-native grooms were perceived to possess a lower social standing than native-born Athenians. Although they received a house at marriage, this was not a major economic resource, and they generally tended to receive smaller dowries in terms of the more significant resources such as cash, olives, vineyards and fields. An insignificant number of these migrant grooms married into titled families either of the *arkhon* or *nikokirei* class, but the majority took wives from the poorer strata of Athenian society; indeed many of them were of rural origin. Uxorilocality was partly a concomitant of male migration from the villages and elsewhere to Athens.

The transfer of a house to a daughter was not merely the transfer of one resource among the many available to Athenians. It represented the entrusting of care in old age to the succeeding generation, and moreover to a child who would not otherwise be expected to provide care. It is, therefore, hardly surprising that of the 100 *prikosymfona* which had conditions attached, 57 specifically referred to the house, a clear indication of an attempt to forestall tension in a situation which deviated from the dominant viri-patrilocal settlement pattern.

Table 4 indicates the correlation between house transfer and the specification of conditions imposed by the older generation. The correlation between houses and conditions is significant at the 0.001 level, which is particularly high. Predictably the main condition was that the new couple, upon receipt of the house or part of the house, was expected to care for the elderly parents until their death. When the new couple received part of the house, the elderly parents retired to the *hamomayero* (literally, ground floor cooking area) or *hamospito* (ground-floor house) and made over the top floor, which contained the bedroom, for the new couple. Cooking was therefore likely to have been collective and did not mark the division of the house into two separate households. Significantly the elderly parents retained control over the physical area where cooking took place. In such situations the

Table 4. *Correlation between house transfer and conditional terms*

	House given			Row total
	Whole	None	Part	
Total sample size				
Number	99	330	94	523
Percentage	18.9	63.1	18.0	100.0
Conditions present				
Number	33	43	24	100
Percentage	33.0	43.0	24.0	19.1

Chi-square: 23.34525. D.F.: 2.

new couple was under the control of the preceding generation; various proverbs emphasised the low status of the *esogambros*, who was a stranger and not the master in his house.[1]

Demographic and economic factors determined this tendency towards uxorilocality. It appears that many daughters were endowed with a house when there were no sons. In other cases the elderly couple was childless and had adopted a daughter. As we demonstrate later, 45.3 per cent of all adopted girls received a house (including part of a house), compared with an overall inclusive average of 38 per cent. This tendency was even more pronounced when the parental house was divided and part of the house transferred. It is, therefore, understandable that the elderly parents attached conditions when they were transferring part of their house to an adopted daughter and her non-Athenian spouse, and particularly so in those cases where the bride's father was dead and survived by his widow. Table 5 provides a breakdown of the familial situation of brides who received a dowry house.

The table requires some explanation. Parents are registered as dead or absent because in certain cases some appear not to have been present when the *prikosymfono* was drawn up. They may have been absent or they may very well have been dead. In certain cases the contracts refer specifically to deceased parents. It proved impossible to distinguish between the two; for the purposes of table 4 they are grouped together. Furthermore some contracts were likely to have been registered after the marriage, hastened by a change in the bride's family situation (e.g. the father died and the heirs were eager to regularise a pre-existing distribution of property). In other cases, because we are dealing with a lengthy period of time, some parents may both have been registered as

Table 5. *Endowment of brides with dowry houses according to family situation*

Bride's family situation	Total number of cases	Percentage of total	Number of cases in which bride received a dowry house and source	Percentage of brides who received dowry houses
Both parents alive	158	30.2	47	24.3
Father dead/absent; mother alive	160	30.5	63	32.6
Mother dead/absent; father alive	52	9.9	2	1.0
Both parents dead/ absent	153	29.2	From other dowry donors: 81	41.8
Total	523	99.8	193	99.7

Table includes the transfer of whole houses and parts of a house, as well as adopted daughters.

Where both parents were dead or absent other donors intervened, including siblings, grandparents, adoptive/foster parents, or the bride herself. Thus for example, siblings provided 57 brides with a dowry and 2 of these received a house.

In those cases where the brides received dowries from other donors (41.8 per cent) the dowry sources were, as follows: siblings, 57 or 11.91 per cent (of these 23 gave their sisters a house); unusual donors, 22 or 5.6 per cent (of these 11 gave a house); and brides who supplied their own dowry houses, 47 or 24.3 per cent.

alive at one daughter's wedding while the family situation may have changed at the time of a younger daughter's contract (for example, the father may have died in the interval). The total number of cases, 523, thus refers to contracts (i.e. marriages) rather than to parents, the number of which is likely to have been smaller. We are on firmer, less ambiguous ground when the parents were either both alive or dead, since in such cases contracts are more specific.

Given these caveats we nevertheless believe that the picture that emerges of the Athenian family is not totally improbable. Roughly 30 per cent of all daughters of marriageable age possessed both parents alive; another 30.5 per cent had a widowed mother,[2] and 9.9 per cent a widowed father, making a total of 70.6 per cent of two-generation family units. What appears unusually high is the number of brides with both parents dead (29.2 per cent). Yet this figure also includes adopted girls whose biological parents were alive in some cases. Other factors which can partly help to explain these high figures are differences in marriage ages between men and women (which complements the 30.5 per cent of widowed mothers), the plague which claimed many lives (including probably many children, although the splitting of families may have helped mitigate the effects), and severe dislocation due to war, famine and oppression. Our figures cannot therefore be utilized to draw conclusions regarding mortality, illegitimacy patterns and the like, but rather as a rough guide to the familial situation in which brides found themselves at the time of their marriage.

At this stage we are interested in the family context of those brides endowed with houses at marriage. Of particular significance is that brides whose parents were both alive generally made up a small percentage (24.3 per cent) of total house endowments. Indeed these brides generally tended not to receive houses (overall 30.2 per cent of all brides had both parents alive, while only 24.3 per cent of brides who received a dowry house had both parents alive). Daughters in an anomalous situation (for example with either one parent alive or both parents dead or absent), by contrast, present a different profile. Brides with widowed fathers were even more unlikely to receive a house (only 1 per cent of all house-endowed brides versus the overall average of 9.9 per cent of brides with widowed fathers). Such men who could, and did, often remarry would have found it difficult to maintain and preside over an extended household consisting of second wife, daughter and groom.

With widowed-mother family contexts the situation changes, reflecting the ambiguous status and precarious position of widows in many Mediterranean societies. Such women tended to endow daughters with houses to a proportionally greater extent than did widowers or surviving conjugal couples; 32.6 per cent of all brides who received a house had widowed mothers, compared with the overall average of 30.5 per cent of brides having widowed mothers. The tendency increases among brides with both parents dead or absent. In such cases brides were 'over-endowed', while 29.2 per cent of all 523 brides had no parents, 41.8 per cent of brides who did receive a house had no parents. Various sources contributed to a dowry, and in certain cases a house; these may have been siblings, unusual donors such as grandparents, adopted parents, many of whom supplied a house, or the girl herself. Brides with both parents dead also included widows entering their second marriages (16, of whom 11 supplied a house); it is clear that widow remarriage was quite rare in Athens. By far the majority of unusual donors were grandparents and foster/adoptive parents who exhibited a greater tendency to transmit part of a house (41 per cent versus the overall average of 18 per

Table 6. *Transmission of dowry houses according to unusual donors*

Donor	House given			Row total
	Whole	None	Part	
Unusual donors				
Number	2	11	9	22
Percentage	9	59	41	4.2
All other donors				
Number	97	319	85	501
Percentage	19	64	17	95.8
Column total				
Number	99	330	94	523
Percentage	18.9	63.1	18	100

cent, table 6), suggesting that the girls in question were already living with them and that adoption and the transmission of houses was linked to old-age care and insurance.

The data thus indicate that most parents did not share a house with their married daughters. Only 29.7 per cent of all living parents endowed a daughter with a house or part of a house (47 out of 158, table 5), and only 39.3 per cent of all widows and 3.8 per cent of all widowers resided with a daughter, making a total average of 24.2 per cent for all parental combinations. Thus nearly 75.8 per cent of all parents, jointly or singly, lived elsewhere, that is with their married sons; to put it more precisely, their sons remained in the parental home at marriage.

Of less significance in explaining the endowment of daughters with houses were economic factors. For particularly poor Athenians possessing little land and cash, the house may have represented the most costly resource they could muster. For a poor girl a house was her dowry; indeed many such girls received few other resources at marriage. But for the majority of our sample the cost of a house was certainly within their means, even although its ownership was not usually transferred at marriage. Some comparative figures are useful here. In 1796 a town house cost 50 groshia; this doubled in 1803 and again by 1811. By 1820 an average house cost 230 groshia, roughly the same price which 12 olive trees fetched that year. Only 19.4 per cent of our sample did not provide their daughters with olive trees and well over 37 per cent endowed daughters with over 40 olive trees (see table 15). It is clear therefore that a considerable portion of Athenians had the economic might to provide daughters with a dowry house had they wished to. Titled parents were even more unlikely to supply their daughters with a house, a clear indication that cultural rather than strictly economic factors were at work here.

If the majority of brides did not receive a house at marriage, this was because the expected settlement pattern was viri-patrilocality, at least for the first few years after marriage. The matrimonial contracts do not, however, provide hard evidence partly because we believe that the establishment of a separate household at marriage was not a cultural aspiration for the majority of Athenians. Another reason is that the matrimonial contracts were more specific on the goods brought by the bride. In this respect the dowry represented a type of pre-mortem settlement on daughters at marriage, whereas most sons expected to receive their share of the family estate at death. A letter written during this period refers to parental property held by men as *intrigada* (full of intrigues and complications), which suggests that many years often elapsed after the death of parents before the property was eventually divided between heirs, especially between sons. Within our sample only 79 (15.1 per cent) of grooms formally received parental property at marriage, although this did not exclude the gradual transfer of control over resources to sons at marriage and increasingly as the parents grew older. Significantly, many of the grooms legally received parental property at their marriages due to the death of one of the parents. A considerable portion of these grooms (65 per cent) received a house (including 19 or 24 per cent who received part of a house), which may well have been due to the requirement to assume overall responsibility for the household.

At this stage we wish to further demonstrate that the dominant settlement pattern was viri-patrilocal although our contracts do not precisely specify this. There are a number of arguments we can bring to bear. First, most grooms had access to sufficient resources at marriage to purchase a house had they wished to, or considered it in their interest to do so. A second and related reason is the long-term potential risks in establishing a separate household at marriage. Establishment of a separate household away from the parents ran the risk of diminishing the son's rights to parental property (especially land) or, amounting to the same thing, placed a son at a grave disadvantage in obtaining *de facto* control of parental property during the latter's lifetime. This situation parallels similar practices in modern Tunisia, where a son's movement out of the parental house is not to be taken lightly as it removes him from effective leverage and control over parental resources (Sant

Cassia, 1986b). As Cuisenier has pointed out, the heirs often ask not 'who has rights over the property', but 'with whom do we have to divide?' (Cuisenier, 1976). Cumulatively such practices led to the complex (*intrigada*) status of parental property. The third reason is that we are dealing with a culture which specified property transfers in minute detail. Moreover it took great pains to link the transfer of a house to daughters with old-age care, an indication that such a practice was extraordinary enough to merit particular caution. It would have been particularly uncharacteristic of this culture to have excluded such an important detail as the endowment of sons with a house at marriage unless it was an established and culturally legitimated pattern which did not require notarial attention.

Fourth, many brides were endowed at marriage with household furnishings which were transferred to their new house. Such goods indicate that the bride was expected to provide the necessary 'markers' to claim and personalise a small area of private domestic space within an alien environment. A final reason is that most grooms did not expect to actually cohabit with both parents at marriage. In the majority of cases the groom's father was, likely, dead by the time his sons married. Although we lack reliable data specifically pertaining to the groom's familial situation, we do know that 59.7 per cent of all brides married with their fathers already dead. Thus if we assume that sons married at a later age than daughters, it was even more likely that they married as adult orphans (i.e. with their fathers dead). Possibly less than 30 per cent of all grooms married with their fathers alive, a situation paralleled in Corfu during the same period where Couroucli reports a figure of 27 per cent (1985a; 53 n. 2). The controlling hand of patriarchal power was therefore weak and of short duration.

Our final piece of evidence comes from the account of Richard Chandler, a visitor to Athens in 1765. Although they deal not only with Greek but also with Turkish and Albanian marriages, we quote his observations at length because we believe that there were few distinctive differences between the various groups in this pre-nationalist age at least in so far as viri-patrilocality was concerned. The rituals which he describes, so evocative of contemporary rural North Africa (such as Tunisia; Sant Cassia, 1986b), indicate a close concern with the incorporation of the bride into the groom's household, the use of women as matchmakers, the transfer of goods to the house and a display similar to the *kiswah* procession in Tunisia:

Marriages are commonly announced by loud music at the house of the bridegroom. A Turk or Greek neither sees nor speaks to the maiden beforehand but for an account of her person and disposition relies on his female relations. The Turk, when terms are adjusted with her family, ratifies the contract before the cadi or judge, and sends her presents. If he be rich, a band of musicians precedes a train of peasants, who carry each a sheep, lamb, or kid, with thorns gilded on their shoulders; and these are followed by servants with covered baskets on their heads, containing female ornaments, money and the like for her use; and by slaves to attend her. Years often intervene before he requires her to be brought to his home. A papas or priest reads the service at the Greek weddings, the two persons standing and holding each a wax taper lighted. A ring and gilded wreath or crown is used. At the end of the ceremony the bride is as it were enthroned in a chair, and the husband remains at a respectful distance, with his hands crossed silent and looking at her; until the women enter and take her away, when the men carouse in a separate apartment. The Albanians convey the bride to the house of her husband in procession, on horseback, with a child astride behind her, a loose veil or canopy concealing her head and face, her fingers laden with silver rings and her hands painted red and blue in streaks. I was present at one of their entertainments, which consisted of a great variety of dishes, chiefly pastry, ranged under a long low arbour made with boughs; the company sitting on the ground.

(Andrews, 1979; 114–15)

We now wish to examine those cases where the groom was legally invested with a house, or part of a house, at marriage. Of a total of 52 cases, in 19 the groom received part of a house. There were almost invariably situations when the groom's father was dead and survived by his widow. In these cases the widow transferred part of the house to her son but, reflecting a sense of unease in her weakened political strength in the two-generation family, insisted on making the transfer conditional upon her being cared for by the new couple. The implication is that when a groom married during his father's lifetime, transfer of a house was rarely legally effected. The final property division between the sons would occur at the death of both parents.

There were thus various types of households in late eighteenth and early nineteenth-century Athens, depending upon the social origins of bride and groom, and the stage in the development cycle. Overall our data indicate the following proportions of house transmission: approximately 37 per cent of brides received houses or parts of a house, 3.6 per cent of all grooms were formally endowed with a house, and the remaining 58 per cent of all couples do not appear to have been formally endowed with a house at marriage. We have outlined above the reasons why we believe that the majority of these remaining couples were likely to reside with the groom and his kin. The nuclear family and a tendency towards neolocality were far from the cultural norm at least at marriage; indeed the majority of house transmissions to both sons and daughters was explicitly linked to old-age care of an elder parent.

Table 7. *Transmission of dowry houses to daughters according to presence of siblings*

Siblings present	House given			
	Whole	None	Part	Row total
No other siblings present				
Number	69	203	63	335
Percentage	20.6	60.6	18.8	64.1
Brother(s) only				
Number	23	113	18	154
Percentage	14.9	73.4	11.7	29.4
Sister(s) only				
Number	3	2	9	14
Percentage	21.4	14.3	64.3	2.7
Both present				
Number	4	12	4	20
Percentage	20.0	60.0	20.0	3.8
Column total				
Number	99	330	94	523
Percentage	18.9	63.1	18.0	100.0

'Siblings present' refers to whether siblings were present at the time of drawing of the contract; it should not be taken as a firm indication as to whether brides actually possessed siblings. *Ceteris paribus*, however, the data are significant.

In any population sons and daughters are not distributed evenly among couples. In Athens, childless couples especially among the poorer families, tended to adopt or foster girls for old-age insurance. Table 7 indicates that when no other siblings were present at the drawing up of the *prikosymfono*, daughters tended to receive houses to a proportionally greater extent (20.6 per cent received whole houses versus the overall average of 18.9 per cent). Couples having only daughters certainly tended to transfer part of a house to a daughter (64.3 per cent versus the overall average of 18 per cent); this tendency increased when a deceased father was survived by his widow.

Yet in the majority of cases where there were both sons and daughters, the general rule of the developmental cycle was that daughters moved at marriage while sons remained. Most couples thus started their conjugal careers in complex households, which were either extended (containing the widowed mother) or to a lesser extent, in a multiple household, made up of two couples linked by ties of consanguinity (Laslett and Wall, 1972). Children were thus often brought up in extended households, a situation vividly brought out by Stratis

Mirivilis in his iridescent novel *I Panayia I Gorgona* (The Mermaid Madonna) which deals with early twentieth-century Lesbos. At a later stage, especially by the time the elderly father had died, some of these married sons were likely to have moved out to a new house. Yet because death dissolved unions early it is unlikely that patriarchal power was long-lasting and unmarried sons were likely to be endowed with part of a house by the widowed mother. Finally, as children reached a marriageable age the development cycle would be repeated.

The social origins of the groom and bride tended to influence this pattern. The general rule seems to be that the higher up the social scale, the greater the resources the family was able to muster, the greater the tendency towards viri-patrilocality, and the emphasis on agnatic links, similar to the old French *lignages*. At the lower end of the social scale, among migrants and poor families, the greater the tendency towards uxorilocality.

These were not minor differences, for they encompassed major distinctions in rationality, family organisation and household composition which an arid discussion on pure settlement patterns can easily conceal. Indeed they warrant labelling as two 'models' of kinship, household and marriage when taken in conjunction with other factors. At the top a small elite of *arkhontes*, tightly knit and closely intermarried, are identified throughout the society as houses (*ikii*) or 'hearts' (*tzakia*) in a manner similar to Tuscan families which were known as *case* (Klapisch-Zuber, 1985). Heavily interdependent, they maintained a strong sense of agnatic solidarity manifested in a tendency to retain parental property (especially from the father's side) intact and hence a source of potential disquiet to an outsider such as Melos, who refers to it as *intrigada*. This solidarity was also expressed in an ideological commitment to the parental house, a symbol of continuity and identity. Their households were often not nuclear for they included, apart from the married brothers, family retainers and foster children. They exhibited a strong sense of place and identified themselves with the city within which they acted as patrons in the traditional mode. This sense of common identity and interconnected interests was facilitated by their small number, intermarriage, and reinforced by administrative privileges devolved upon them by the Ottomans. At the bottom end of the scale was the 'model' practised by a large group of migrants and seasonal workers. These probably possessed a more dispersed kin network divided between Athens and its surrounding hamlets. Uxorilocality was much more common among this group and the central dyad was often the link between the elderly widow and her resident married daughter, with other daughters often moving out. Men's links with their agnates were much weaker due to geographical dispersion and the lack of resources.

Such patterns were consonant with a traditional horizontally stratified society in a pre-industrial, pre-nationalist agrarian age, and were paralleled in other parts of the Mediterranean. Writing on Renaissance Tuscany, Klapisch-Zuber notes that

among the poor, each new couple founded its own household, but many households were not based on a new union. Among the rich, the independent 'establishment' of the children does not follow their marriage either, since the sons continued to live under the parental roof. Unlike families in northern Europe, marriage and the establishment of a household did not go hand in hand in Tuscany. Furthermore, the double model of marriage in Italy does not conform to the western model, as modern historians and demographers have defined it.

(1985; 19)

Parallels such as these should at least alert us to the possibility of exploring and identifying distinctive Mediterranean patterns in kinship and marriage for the pre-modern period. The differences, however, are equally significant. For while in Tuscany sons inherited equally and excluded their 'appropriately dowered' sisters from inheritance, especially of landed property, in Athens daughters inherited property including landed property, although this was often, but not exclusively, through dowries. There was, in short, a greater residual notion of some form of equal partible inheritance which was further encouraged by the phenomenon of dowry inflation expressed in and through cash endowments. These subverted traditional status distinctions which were based primarily not on wealth, but on administratively (politically) defined privileges, and resulted in a more egalitarian *de facto* system of property transmission. As we hope to show, the evolution of the Greek family and kinship in the modern period was singularly distinctive. Emerging out of the matrix of these models, and at points developed in conscious opposition and contradistinction to them, was the new *nikokirei* model, which was to exert a considerable influence on the future evolution of the Greek family.

3

Marriage, women and land in nineteenth-century Athens

Introduction

Athens in the eighteenth and early nineteenth century was a society with a pronounced agricultural base. Yet although many had settled there, it was not a large village inhabited by peasants. Athenians distinguished themselves from the surrounding villages as *polites*, town dwellers, possessing a distinctive culture – despite the fact that the basis of their wealth did not differ substantially from the surrounding villages. Lord Charlemont, who visited Athens in 1749, observed that the Athenians 'are infinitely more polished than their neighbours and look down upon the rest of Greece with a sort of contempt. Wheeler informs us that the Athenians were in his time the most polished people among the Greeks. They still remain so' (Stanford and Finopoulos, 1984; 114).

This sense of differentiation was due to two factors. First, administrative power over the district was based in the town, and second, Athens possessed a social structure which was more complex than that of the villages. Although Athenians successively discovered to their cost that political oppression and harsh taxation were most exacting in the town, the quality of life there was immeasurably more complex, diversified and politically vibrant than in the largely subsistence-oriented villages. In the eyes of its inhabitants Athens possessed *politismos*, meaning civilisation or the civilised life. *Politismos* is of course cognate with *polites*, city dwellers, and with the *polis*, the city, and while these terms had variable meanings in Greek history (*the* city was of course Constantinople), the ideological importance of Athens was given a strong reinforcement by the neo-Classical ideology of the new state. The sense of *politismos*, of partaking in city life, also differed substantially between the various social groups. The *arkhon* class, which initially dominated Athenian political and economic life, appears to have considered Athens as its fiefdom, at least according to the accounts of contemporary (bourgeois) observers, for whom to a certain extent it was. The *nikokirei* group, some of whom developed extensive commercial links with North European trading interests (especially the French) and who eventually supplanted the *arkhon* group as the most commercially dynamic stratum was perhaps less initially tied to Athens having kinsmen and commercial contacts scattered in various European and Ottoman trading centres. The ex-peasants, a small group consisting mainly of Albanians settled in Athens, appear to have maintained their discrete lifestyle, partaking of both urban and seasonal rural employment. Even horizontal strata were differentiated internally. The Albanians lived in their separate neighbourhoods and the *vox populi* was certainly not homogeneous in language or political attachments. Between 1809–11 it was noted that 'the Greeks sometimes marry Albanian women, but an Albanian man is rarely thought noble enough to marry with a Grecian family' (Galt, in Andrews, 1979; 144). Yet some Albanians certainly moved to Athens. Vaporiis quotes an 1820 report which states that one third of Athens and much of Attica spoke Albanian (1985; 155). Finally there were the urban poor, the *ptohon* who according to Skouzes, 'had no home'. Yet by most accounts work was readily available mainly through systems of redistribution and the role of the church:

The people of the parish hired them, men and women both, for work in their houses and fields, and so they had a livelihood. The parishioners would send them bread, a little oil, olives, plates of food, firewood, etc. They would take on the women as servants by the day and get them to run errands and to spin cotton and yarn and silk and sailcloth, and in the harvest season to gather the grapes and olives. So the poor who had no fields of their own and the old who had no home were able to live without having to beg.

(Skouzes, in Andrews, 1979; 118)

This passage enables us to bring out an important point. On the one hand this was a classical pre-industrial, pre-national society, hierarchically stratified with external relations between the various strata regulated by Ottoman-imposed law, custom and dress; in other words by formality. On the other hand certain informal social relations transcended these distinctions within the Christian, i.e. Greek, community, giving rise to that distinctive sense of solidarity and equality which many foreign observers regularly noted. Such solidarity was manifested in redistribution of the sort described above, the breaking of bread together by wealthy and poor alike, and so on, all practices which conflicted with the much more rigidly stratified and interiorised sense of social differentiation covering wider areas of social life in Western Europe, the background of such observers. This was in effect a status-based society which aspired to a class-based one but which never quite managed to make that transition in Ottoman Greece. And because status was imposed within an agrarian system, rather than as an expression of long-established differences in the ownership of the means of production, social mobility became increasingly possible in spite of the formal impediments to the contrary. This was the case especially when certain up and coming social groups could dispose of resources which symbolically and materially threatened the traditional hegemony of the ruling groups.

Paradoxically the subsequent evolution of the new Greek state further reinforced the tendency towards status distinctions rather than class ones. Apart from the evolution of the Greek economy, other factors played an important part. Nationalist rhetoric in the new Greek state progressively tended to identify Ottoman rule with the oppression of all Greeks. Those who had escaped oppression by means of co-operation with the Ottomans were characterised as non-Greeks, as having betrayed their ethnicity and religion, and as having become 'Christian Turks'. The implication was that the only true and genuine Greeks were those who were poor and oppressed, and it was this group that nationalist rhetoric turned to and progressively invested with the source of Greek identity (though not without contradictions). The syllogism which underlay the ideological orientation of the new Greek state can be expressed in the following proposition: all true Greeks were equally oppressed under the Ottomans, therefore in a non-Ottoman Greek state all true Greeks should at least begin as equals and achieve their true potential. Hence any social system that replicated or resembled the Ottoman system of inherited social differences had to be proscribed. The irony was of course that the Ottoman *millet* system was not based upon class distinctions but on religious ones.

Yet Greek nationalist rhetoric which was influenced by a heady and ultimately tension-laden mixture of three ideologies: French bourgeois revolutionary thought (via Adamantios Korais), European phil-Hellenism (which had strong anti-'Oriental' elements), and a historically besieged orthodoxy which had fallen from grace and pre-eminence in 1453 (and which aspired to recapture that lost grace through irredentism), tended to interpret the Ottoman millet system in a distinctive way. The religious basis of stratification under the Ottomans was viewed as a concealment of a class-based system which upheld the dominance of a corrupt and inefficient ethnic group which had little right to rule. Hence the particular character of the clever Greek folk hero Karayeorghis – a Greek servant much more capable than his Turkish master who always comes out on top, yet remains oppressed through no fault of his own. Class-based distinctions thus appear to modern Greeks as not only alien but as inimical to ethnic sentiments. Hence while it is widely held that all

Greeks, regardless of social origins, have the moral right to achieve great heights of power and wealth in society expressed in the notion of *aksiocratia* (the rule of the worthy), a vocabulary of counter-justification is invoked to explain why most have not been able to do so. This is that society is flawed – those who have achieved such positions have done so through corruption or betrayal, much like the 'Christian Turks' of the past allied themselves with outsiders. Values such as *filotimo* and *eghoismos* are thus not merely the (Greek) values born out of interpersonal relations in a small scale Mediterranean society, but are also the by-product of the development of a specific (Greek) state ideology. They are 'ethnic' values in a very substantial sense enmeshed in historical experiences.

In this chapter we deal with marriage in a traditional agro-literate hierarchical society about to enter a nationalist age. We examine the resources associated with the various strata of Athenian society, and matrimonial patterns. We ask to what extent social distinctions were watertight. Did individuals marry across social boundaries? If so which groups were mainly involved and how did men, women, and children circulate? How were daughters endowed and were there any significant differences between groups in their manner of endowment?

At issue here is how a traditional elite lost its pre-eminence due to a combination of political, economic and historical factors, and how Athenian society was subsequently shaped in the first decades of the nineteenth century. One key to this decline is that in the late eighteenth century dowry inflation emerged in Athens and other parts of Greece. This was not just a matter of the increase of goods transmitted at marriage to daughters, with all the attendant difficulties it caused for parents to find a suitable groom. The political implications are more complex than are apparent. The Church, allied with the higher classes, made strenuous but largely ineffectual efforts to restrict such practices. For what was critical here was that the growth of endowments at marriage, itself an expression of a new rising social group, threatened social distinctions which were largely created and imposed by the Ottoman system of government. The elite's power base was largely a function of its role within the Ottoman delegation of power, which was politically and administratively defined, and it did not possess a sufficiently autonomous power base to be able to resist incursions from a new, more commercially dynamic, emerging social group. Nor did they develop and exploit new resources, either political or economic, in the latter years of the Turkocratia or the first decades of the new Greek state. The *arkhon* class was not able or willing to assume a monopolist leadership role within the new Greek kingdom, partly but not exclusively because of their politically embarrassing association with the departed and hated Ottoman overlords. They gradually lost their distinctive cohesiveness, in marked contrast to traditional elites elsewhere in the Mediterranean (for example in Catalonia, see McDonogh, 1986) and merged with the new *nikokirei* group, some of whom Makriyiannis, the famous revolutionary, singled out for their cynical self-interest.

Another, more anthropological, reason for the decline of the old elite is the system of property transmissions within the family. Here a digression to compare Greek patterns of property transmission with those obtaining in other Mediterranean societies is useful. It must be kept in mind that contemporary patterns in Greece are no necessary guide to past practices, a condition which doubtless obtains for other Mediterranean societies. Among the *arkhon* class a system of unequal partible inheritance prevailed. This was paralleled in other parts of Greek territory where a *de facto* form of unigeniture was practised (e.g. in Lesbos, Papataxiarchis, 1985; in Karpathos, Vernier, 1984). But this was certainly not a uniform practice; in many smaller Aegean islands some form of relatively equal partible inheritance prevailed (Kenna, 1976) with daughters receiving a dowry house and other immoveables. This is reinforced by earlier accounts in the eighteenth century (Charlemont). This same visitor also noted considerable variation:

In their mode of inheritance the Sciotes follow the Turkish law. Whatever a man dies possessed of is divided into a certain number of equal parts, two of which each son inherits, and each daughter one, the married daughters refunding their portions into the common stock, and getting their respective shares. One custom they have peculiar to themselves. If a wife should die without children, her father has a right to demand from the widower one sixth of her portion for her virginity and the mother one sixth in consideration of the *suck which she has given her*.

(Stanford and Finopoulos, 1984; 32, original italics)[1]

The foregoing observation indicates two facts. First, daughters received a dowry portion at marriage which was considered to constitute a share of their pre-mortem inheritance. The account is unclear as to exactly what resources they received (land, other immoveables, or moveables), but the subsequent discussion suggests that it was probably less than their share due to them by inheritance.[2]

Second, while some degree of unequal partible inheritance prevailed among the *arkhon* group, this was not strict unigeniture in the Western European sense which was often codified and hence enforceable through a civil code. Rather it was a custom which evolved out of the conditions of their political interstitial position as mediators between the Ottomans and their *rayah*. *Arkhontic* power depended not so much on their wealth, or on their control over the means of production (which was in any case limited although important), but upon their political privileges, which were certainly a source of wealth and income. Removal of their privileges would send them into the political wilderness. Hence their property transmission strategies were oriented primarily towards maintaining their political discreteness as a distinct group. Thus the house and the name were particularly important as symbols of continuity, power and legitimacy. Younger sons either entered the clergy (Kampouroglous, 1896; 176) or remained as cadet members of the household. Daughters, by contrast, inherited goods at their marriages, both moveables and immoveables, circulated endogamously within the *arkhon* group or married into the *nikokirei* below. As we shall show, the particular tension that emerged in the matrimonial and property transmission system was the increasing tendency of the new rising *nikokirei* to invest their daughters with massive dowries which not only strained agnatic bonds among the *arkhontes*, but also seduced younger males who had previously maintained a subdued profile into more individualistic heavily endowed marriages with the *nikokirei*. This in turn obliged *arkhon* parents to increase their own daughters' dowry endowments to keep them in the 'matrimonial market'. Dowry inflation which we explore below subverted agnatic solidarity among the *arkhon* families, and by the massive influx of goods and daughters blurred the political and economic boundaries of the ruling group.

Consider by contrast other areas of the Mediterranean. In Renaissance Tuscany, which probably most closely resembled late eighteenth-century Athens, all sons inherited an equal share of the paternal estate, and although daughters received a dowry they were excluded from inheritance. Klapisch-Zuber notes that 'the eldest [son] had no greater advantage, nor was primogeniture practiced: authority over the group was all that passed to the eldest brother' (1985; 19). The system differed from the Athenian one in that women were excluded from sharing in immoveable property and they received moveables as their dowry (*ibid.*; 214). Klapisch-Zuber sees this as an essentially metropolitan phenomenon. Similar practices appear to have obtained in Pisticci, southern Italy, in the early nineteenth century (Davis, 1976).

In rural Catalonia a much stricter form of unigeniture prevailed. There the *hereu-pubilla* system of a single designated heir (Hansen, 1977) guaranteed that property remained relatively concentrated (even though in such cases we can expect to find more flexible arrangements on the ground, where younger brothers often remained as 'family retainers' as in the Alpine villages studied by Cole and Wolf, 1974).

Iszaevich notes that in rural Catalonia marriage was independent of succession and while the main heir (either male or female) resided with the elderly couple and was subordinated to their control during their lifetime, other minor heirs were given a dowry 'upon resigning rights in their natal household' (1981; 283). But by far the greatest implication of this type of system was on the marriages of daughters. Until the 1940s, in both rural and urban Catalonia, 'daughters were "bought off" with dowries that cut their ties to family production; property was favoured over stock as the appropriate coin of the *llegitima*' (McDonogh, 1986; 51). Similar institutions operated in other parts of the western Mediterranean, such as in southern Italy and Malta where the *legitima* was often the *corredo* (trousseau).

A system of property devolution such as this, codified and enforceable (and hence more difficult to overturn unless through 'revolutionary' legislation, as occurred in Sicily in 1812), has grave implications for the nature of co-operation between affines and the way daughters are married. As regards cooperation between affines, as a Catalan informant observed to McDonogh: 'you don't want to have to work with your in-laws' (1986; 51). Marriage to daughters of powerful families was also less economically significant, mainly because the bulk of the parental estate had devolved to the single designated heir (usually male). In Barcelona 'marriages have been less a vehicle for social mobility than a confirmation of status claims. For early entrepreneurs a wedding often preceded the capture of economic power . . . It was by no means an alliance with the social class with whom the founders would interact by the end of a successful life. Such claims might occur in his own lifetime through the marriages of his children' (McDonogh, 1986; 148).

In Athens a different system prevailed. Although daughters could be 'sold off' with dowries, and in the Turkocratia received probably less than their brothers, their dowries nevertheless consisted of the same types of goods as male inheritance (land and cash – we exclude here the transmission of houses). Certainly, as we shall demonstrate, certain goods tended eventually to become identified more with one sex than the other. Nevertheless there was no strict law or practice which consistently deprived women or men of certain important long-term resources (such as company stock in Barcelona). Second-born sons of the *arkhon* class could always marry into the *nikokirei* group, political rights being the only major resources transmitted to first-born sons, while daughters tended to be retained within the group. The Athenian *arkhontes* were a less unified group than the Catalan and other Mediterranean elites, mainly because their wealth depended not so much upon actual 'tangibles' (such as land) which distinguished them from other groups, but rather upon administrative prerogatives and the right to allocate taxes, which were politically determined. Furthermore, patterns of property transmission were largely variable and customary during the Turkocratia; they were not codified 'into' national law until the mid-nineteenth century. When a new codified system was established, all children were given rights to parental property. During the Turkocratia a complex interplay existed between customary practices and Church-imposed guidelines which varied from region to region, and which redefined each other across time.[3]

Such a system had a number of implications. First, in most of Greece, especially where agriculture rather than pastoralism was practised, daughters held *de facto* property rights at marriage. Equally significant, the process of urbanisation, especially in Athens, and the development of civil society, contributed in its own way to a greater endowment of daughters at marriage, especially with certain mobile resources. Second, codification of practices into national law (civil code) in the mid-nineteenth century reflected the interests and cultural perspectives of the law-makers (mainly of a specific urban and political class), and the influence of the Church.

Thus marriage in Athens and, increasingly, throughout the Greek kingdom was economically significant in a manner largely absent in wealthier, more economically diversified, unigeniture-oriented parts of the western Mediterranean. Weddings did not precede the capture of economic power; on the contrary the successful endowment of a daughter was the most visible demonstration of having 'arrived' economically and of having achieved a definite and morally safe urban lifestyle. This was in effect a petit-bourgeois culture and morality of marriage, manifested by a love of the 'new' rather than the 'old'.[4]

Another reason for the dominance of a petit-bourgeois morality of marriage is specific to the development of the new Greek state. The new Greek kingdom started off with very few resources, a practically non-existent infrastructure, and a devastated economy and countryside. Land, the main resource in a mountainous country, often needed to be reclaimed after centuries of neglect (due perhaps as much to labour shortages in a labour-intensive agricultural system, as to actual Ottoman oppression), and the handling of the national land question left little possibility for large-scale capitalist development of agriculture. Instead the small-holding predominated. With some notable exceptions, such as in Thessaly, resources were not concentrated in large-scale estates, nor in industry or banking. Instead small-scale family-dominated enterprises dominated and state employment became a major attraction for social mobility.

Proxenia: matchmaking

We begin our analysis of the relationship between marriage and social stratification by taking an example of a proposed matrimonial alliance that failed. *Proxenia*, or matchmaking, was always a delicate affair in Athenian society especially where it concerned, as it does in this case, the Athenian aristocracy with whom the prospective suitor, a merchant, was attempting to establish a matrimonial alliance. Although the example dates from the early eighteenth century, we believe it is relevant to a number of themes. In this case, *proxenia* appears to have involved only men, in three different cities, a clear indication of the dispersed merchant group, and it was conducted through correspondence. The suitor was Mihalis Melos, a merchant who had settled in Nafplion in 1715, after one of the periodic flights of Athenians from their city. His brother, Sior Georgakis (called 'Sior' here because he had settled in Venice, not because he belonged to the Athenian elite), to whom these letters were addressed, had attempted to solve Mihalis' financial problems through a good marriage into the Athenian elite. The *proxenitis* (matchmaker) written to by Sior Angelakis was Sior Leonardo, a member of the Athenian *arkhon* group. We give first the texts of the letters and then follow with a brief analysis.

On 17 February 1716 Mihalis Melos in Nafplion wrote to his brother, Sior Georgakis, in Venice:

I therefore inform you that I do not know this place [Athens] and therefore I cannot know what properties are better and which are worse and it is good that you enter an agreement as to what they [i.e. the Bride's parents] shall give me. But ensure that what my father-in-law gives me was his own wife's dowry or what he had purchased, and not from his own paternal property because such properties are often full of complications [*intrigada*] and thus they have to be divided (among the heirs) with the result that none will know what property will belong to him and what belongs to his brother. It is therefore better that I go to select that which I want.

I ask for 200 olive trees, 10 *stremmata* vineyards, 2 workships [*ergastiria*] (because my father-in-law has 9 workshops), an orchard, an oil press, and as for cash I leave it up to you to obtain that which should be given . . . because I know that he is wealthy according to what I have heard.

One year later he wrote to his brother in Venice from Smyrna:

In my other letter I wrote that you have to speak to Sior Leonardo Kapetanaki regarding the case you had spoken about as I have been written to by him [the *proxenitis*], wherein he asked me that I should put down my demands.

I therefore write to you to list all that I wish, because the woman I am due to take, if God wills, should live in the same station as she has done up till now, and as she has been accustomed to in her parents' house.

I know that you do not agree with this but I have preferred to write these details down for you so that you do not say later that I did not ask for them and we appear foolish. This is also because these affairs take place only once and Athens is not the same as you knew it where women wore only one Sunday fur, for they are now accustomed to the same things as the Nafpliots. And you should also know that the lands of Athens are like a chimera and until you cultivate them you can easily consume them, and they are not like the lands of the Morea which yield a good income. For you to understand this I say that the best workshop yields a rent of 6 *reals per annum*, and it is important that you should think about these things. I bring to your notice therefore, one by one all the things that a woman needs in order not to be unfortunate [there follows a list of various items and properties]:

Total: 1211 *reals*

Expenses for my clothing: 126 *reals*

I also ask to purchase a house, cost 300 *reals*, because his [i.e. prospective father-in-law] house, requires 300 *reals* repairs. Apart from this, the house is isolated [*erimia*] because in this neighbourhood Albanians live. I also ask for household goods; (there follows a list), value: 200 *reals* and the sum of 100 *reals* for wedding expenses: Total: 1947 *reals* and a mule to transport wood. And as long as you have noted this letter you know that I am naked of all things [i.e. do not have much property] and if this attempt [*ipothese*] is successful all will be well. And be on your guard that your affection for Sior Leonardo [the *proxenitis*, matchmaker] will not weaken your resolve to our disadvantage, for a friend who causes problems [doesn't help], can be considered an enemy [*philos epizimeos, ekthros ine*].

The woman I want to take in marriage should be able to live as others do. And also for the first year we will need living expenses of 250 *reals*, as well as other expenses to cover the period until I arrive in Athens and give a gift to the Judge and Cadi. I tell you also not to talk about the dower [*progamiea dorea*] and when I shall arrive in Athens I shall promise this myself.

(Liata, 1986; 47–53)

This example brings out a number of significant features which we wish to explore even though it dates from an earlier period than our principal data. To begin with it indicates how keen members of the dispersed merchant class were to establish matrimonial alliances with the resident Athenian aristocracy. The negotiations are lengthy and complicated, involving four distinct parties (the prospective groom; his brother in Venice; the *proxenitis*, a friend of the groom; and the father himself), and take place partly by means of correspondence. The suitor at first appears to know very little about Athens but soon proves to be informed on the incomes generated by various types of properties. He also appears not to have been particularly aware of the delicacy required when demanding a dowry and presses his more cautious brother, attempting to drive a hard bargain very different to the rationality of the *arkhon* group. He is also propertyless and reluctant to discuss the dower, the most visible marker of a groom's wealth. Indeed he phrases his demands in terms of the prospective bride's 'interests'. Paternal property rights are considered to be full of intrigues (*intrigada*) because of the system of post-mortem inheritance and the tendency to maintain the property undivided between sons for a number of years after the owner's death. An eventual division of property is considered only a remote possibility and is liable to exclude a man from the enjoyment of what is 'his'. Women's property as dowry is less encumbered because girls receive the bulk of their inheritance at marriage. This raises the interesting possibility of a double-lineal transmission of property: men's to sons, women's to daughters. Olive trees are clearly a good investment, whereas the house is not a costly component of the dowry. Finally there is a strong awareness of social differences: the suitor legitimates his demands by reference to his desire to maintain his bride in a station to which she is accustomed, and he is keen to separate himself residentially from countrymen who had recently settled in the town, as well as from the bride's parents, more a trait of the *nikokirei* than of the *arkhontes*.

Marriage and social stratification

Perhaps the best way to characterise Athenian society during this period is to state that this was a hierarchical society which aspired to the maintenance of social privileges, but which could only do so through the manipulation of the same types of resources, rather than different ones. The basis of wealth and of social stratification lies in immovable property and in cash crops. The wealthy and powerful generally possess more, rather than different, resources than the poor. 'Politics', or administrative prerogatives, distinguished the *arkhontes* from the *nikokirei*. Significantly, reflecting the agricultural base of the society, the two exceptions lie in cash and in bridal costumes, and the two are intimately related. Although cash figures in 60 per cent of all contracts, its flow is different among the various groups, and the wealthy titled groups have access to much larger amounts. Cash was a restricted resource in late eighteenth- and early nineteenth-century Athens partly because the town and central power could not totally dominate the countryside and its productive forces. Furthermore, even in the town main access to cash was through ownership of cash crops in the surrounding countryside, such as olives, rather than through more urban sectors of the economy such as petty commodity production, services or administrative employment, although workshops were important.

Bridal costumes were also significant marks of distinction. They had a double function, indicating the social origins of the bride and embodying stored wealth and labour. We discuss this in a later chapter but at this stage it is worthwhile to point out that both cash and bridal costumes were critical resources which could be manipulated strategically.

Table 8. *Marriage patterns of brides' parents*

Bride's father	Bride's mother		Row total
	'Kir' titled	Untitled	
'Kir'			
Number	13	10	23
Percentage	56.5	43.4	7.3
'Mastros'			
Number	0	13	13
Percentage	0	100.0	4.1
Untitled			
Number	9	270	279
Percentage	3.3	96.7	88.0
'Sior'			
Number	0	2	2
Percentage	0	100.0	0.6
Column total			
Number	22	295	317
Percentage	6.9	93.1	100.0

Only 317 persons are included in this table, as we possess firm data for not more than this number.

Through such manipulation of these two resources, both of which possessed strong economic and symbolic significance, families and individuals could advance their matrimonial strategies or block undesired overtones.

To what extent was status or group endogamy practised? We possess data for two generations; the parents of the brides, and the brides themselves. Generally titled families tended to marry among themselves but this was not a watertight pattern and there were significant differences between men and women. Table 8 indicates that in the preceding generation of our sample the majority of marriages were 'endogamous'; 56.5 per cent of titled grooms (of the *nikokirei* class) took titled brides, and 59.1 per cent titled brides (13 of 22) took titled grooms. The same general pattern is demonstrated for our sample of titled grooms and brides in table 9.

A few words should be said about table 9. In the Titled Grooms column we include grooms who belonged to both the *arkhon* ('Sior') and *nikokirei* ('Kir') groups. By contrast, because we are interested in the way daughters of titled families circulated at marriage, we have adopted slightly different criteria for the Titled Brides column. Titled Brides here refers to daughters of titled parents (either father, mother

Table 9. *Frequency of endogamy/exogamy within titled groups*

	Titled grooms		Titled brides	
	Number	Percentage	Number	Percentage
Endogamous	19	47.5	19	65.5
Exogamous	21	52.5	10	34.4
Total	40	100.0	29	100.0

or both). The total number of daughters of titled parents in our sample of contracts is 39, but these included 10 adopted or fostered girls. We have excluded these from the table because adoption/fosterage in these specific cases does not appear to have been a 'strategy of heirship', that is, to provide a childless couple with heirs.

Due to the relatively small number of titled families in our sample we do not feel that we can make any meaningful statistical statements about intermarriage between the *arkhon* and *nikokirei* groups. Our data indicates that by the end of the eighteenth century such intermarriages were common, and that their frequency increased in the early nineteenth century. Second-born sons of the *arkhon* class who did not join the higher clergy tended to marry into the *nikokirei* group, though *arkhon* daughters tended to be retained within their group to a greater extent. Such a pattern of seepage is common to many social systems but in this particular case the 'balance' depended upon a number of factors including the availability of women (demographic criteria) and the relative dowries of *arkhon* and *nikokirei* daughters. An increase in the dowries of the latter turns them into more attractive prospects, with the result that *arkhon* men increasingly abandon status group endogamy and *arkhon* women are obliged to marry hypogamously. Furthermore we are not dealing with a static situation; with the passage of time non-titled families could amass enough wealth to be able to claim the status of a *nikokiris* and assume the title of 'Kir'. Conversely the changing fate of families could be reflected in a downward swing of titles: 'Siori' could be referred to as 'Kirii' when changing fortunes and political expediencies so dictated. By the end of the eighteenth century some decline had set in among the *arkhon*, although it is difficult to evaluate whether this was a 'natural' byproduct of their patterns of property transmission or due to their shrinking control over the wider economy. Skouzes notes that among the poor parishioners who lived in Church-run alms houses were 'certain well-born people who had fallen on bad times and who had only a house left or a little farm, and suffered hardship because they were unused to working' (in Andrews, 1979; 119).

Table 9 nevertheless illustrates some critical features. Whereas titled women tended to marry within their own status group (65.5 per cent), titled men were more likely to take brides from lower social groups. From our data we also know that brides who were not the daughters of titled parents could also assume the titles of their husbands (for example assume a 'Kiria' title) if the husband possessed a particularly high status. Four, or 20 per cent of our sample of 20 titled brides, did not possess any titled parents. The contracts nevertheless refer to them as 'Kiria' because their husbands possessed these titles. We have included these brides in our table. Hence the number of women, daughters of titled parents, who married endogamously is even higher than this table suggests. Thus the dominant pattern is isogamy for high status women and hypergamy for lower status women, to a statistically less significant extent.

Here it is important to stress that we are referring to titles and social status rather than purely economic criteria, although the two were closely related. Eighteenth- and nineteenth-century Athens exhibited characteristics of the Eurasian marriage pattern (Goody, 1976); stratification and group endogamy preserved control over resources. Although there were clearly situations when economic resources enabled non-titled but wealthy grooms to take titled brides, we are dealing here with a society where the perception of social differences, of status and its reflection in titles, decisively influenced matrimonial strategies, somewhat independent of wealth. In such a society the marriages of men and women, as sons and daughters, involved different considerations. Women's marriages were significant not only because they carried property in their own right at marriage, but also because they held grave implications for political relations between affines. By contrast men's marriages (especially of second-born *arkhon* sons) were less publicly self-conscious; the status of the groom's family was not necessarily lowered if he took a non-titled bride since she would be incorporated into his household. Had economic considerations been exclusively paramount in this society we would expect to find a similar tendency towards group endogamy among titled brides as we do among titled grooms. The data however indicates that titled sons were permitted to take lower status spouses to a greater extent than titled daughters. In a predominantly viri-patrilocal society the criteria for bride choice were more 'domestic' (that is, whether she would integrate in the husband's and his family's household). By contrast, when a titled family responded to *proxenia* for a daughter's hand, considerations were as likely to be political and status-oriented as domestically oriented (that is, whether the proposing family belonged to the same status group and whether marriage would not imply a lowering of the daughter's social status as a member of a titled social group). Giving a daughter in marriage involved different considerations than those involved when a son was married.

The transmission of titles in Athenian society was not automatic, and it varied according to social origins, the stage in the developmental cycle, sex, and whom one married. Among the *signori* the title of 'Sior' was transmitted to sons, who are referred to as such in the marriage contracts. There was a greater tendency for daughters of this class to be referred to as 'Kiria', possibly because most women in our sample married grooms from the *nikokirei* class and therefore assumed the titles of their spouses. Among the *nikokirei* there appears to have been more variation; in our contracts, some grooms from these families are not referred to as titled. This suggests that the assumption of the 'Kir' title was not automatic or ascribed, and depended upon the assumption of headship in a household and upon independent economic wealth. Daughters, by contrast, appear to have carried their father's titles to a greater extent partly because the giving of a daughter in marriage involved a stronger accounting or consideration of symbolic aspects such as titles, and the status of a family could be gauged by reference to the marriages of the daughters. Adopted daughters, however, did not carry their adoptive parents' titles with them at marriage. The transmission of titles and such marks of social distinction were also influenced by major social changes. By the early 1830s the old *arkhon* class of *signori* had lost most of their traditional privileges and in some cases their wealth. Thus in 1796 a titled family of the *nikokirei* class gave their daughter to a groom from the *arkhon* group in marriage. The couple was registered as Sior Angelakis Kangeleris and Kiria Evdokia. By 1825 when their own daughter was married, the father, Sior Angelakis, was referred to as Kir Angelakis in the contract. His daughter, however, retained her 'Kiria' title and she was married to an untitled Mytilene merchant who promised an antenuptial gift of 1,006 groshia, a substantial sum. This example illustrates the social demotion through the use of titles, the creation of a homogeneous group, and social mobility through marriage. The *arkhontes* may also have been anxious to camouflage their identity by posing as members of the *nikokirei* class.

We now examine the transmission of resources within the family. Significantly, the marriage contracts devoted more detail and attention to what the bride was to receive at marriage from her parents, and as a dower from her spouse in case the marriage should be dissolved or she should be widowed, as opposed to what the groom received at marriage from his parents. This is consistent with a pattern of pre-mortem settlement upon daughters at marriage, and a post-mortem inheritance for sons.

An analysis of the 'matching contributions' of the spouses is thus problematical because we are dealing with different time-scales and different rationales for sons and daughters. Although a married daughter was not excluded from inheriting parental property, pressure from unendowed siblings was likely to encourage her to desist from asking for her share. Similar practices appear to be in operation in the contemporary village of Pouri (Thessaly) where Handman observes that 'it is very rare for a daughter to claim the remainder of her inheritance' (1983; 241). By contrast a son's, i.e. a groom's, contribution to the marriage depended very much upon his ultimate inheritance prospects. With a dominant pattern of viri-patrilocality it is, furthermore, understandable that the contracts should specify the bride's contribution in greater detail. Nevertheless we shall be able to discover the dominant marriage patterns, and what was expected to be given at marriage.

We begin with the transmission of resources to daughters at marriage and their interrelationship. Fields, cash, vineyards, olive trees, livestock, trousseaux, household goods as well as bridal costumes, were all transmitted at marriage. Yet there were major differences between brides. Titled brides received major cash-producing resources rather than domestic ones, which were expected to be provided by the groom. Thus they were very unlikely to be provided with a house (14 per cent versus the average of 19.2 per cent) and even more unlikely to receive a part of a house (5.6 per cent versus an average of 18 per cent). Titled brides expected to move at marriage to the groom's household. Nor did they appear to have retained residual rights in their parental house to return in case of separation or divorce, as occurs in North Africa. Apart from the relatively low incidence of divorce for which figures are unavailable (although counter views suggest that divorce was relatively easy to procure by means of payment to the Church of a suitable amount of money, a system thus likely to favour the wealthy), early death was a major dissolver of marriages. In addition the dower (*progamiea dorea*) was designed to protect women on divorce by providing them with a certain sum of money if the husband died or the marriage was dissolved. In contrast to Northern Europe it appears that the cash was not actually handed over to the bride at marriage, but paid out of the husband's estate or by his kin if he died.

Titled brides were unlikely to receive land unless it bore a cash crop. Table 10 indicates that 66.7 per cent of titled brides did not receive fields versus an overall average of 52.6 per cent. Furthermore, it indicates that

Table 10. *Endowment of fields to titled and untitled brides at marriage*

	No fields received	1–5	6–10	11–15	16–20	21–25	over 25	Row total
				Stremmata				
Titled brides								
Number	24	7	4	0	1	0	0	36
Percentage	66.7	19.4	11.1	0	2.8	0	0	7.0
Non-titled brides								
Number	247	165	32	15	9	5	6	479
Percentage	51.6	34.4	6.7	3.1	1.9	1.0	1.3	93.0
Column total								
Number	271	172	36	15	10	5	6	515
Percentage	52.6	33.4	7.0	2.9	1.9	1.0	1.2	100.0

'Titled brides' refers to brides of the *arkhon* and *nikokirei* groups. It also includes their adopted daughters.

Table 11. *Parental transmission of livestock to titled and untitled brides at marriage*

	None	1–10	11–20	21–30	31–40	Over 40	Row total
			Livestock (usually sheep)				
Titled brides							
Number	30	0	3	2	1	0	36
Percentage	83.3	0	8.3	5.6	2.8	0	7.0
Non-titled brides							
Number	418	37	14	3	2	5	479
Percentage	87.3	7.7	2.9	0.6	0.4	1.0	93.0
Column total							
Number	448	37	17	5	3	5	515
Percentage	87.0	7.2	3.3	1.0	0.6	1.0	100.0

'Titled brides' row refers to brides of the *arkhon* and *nikokirei* groups. It also includes their adopted daughters.

titled brides were generally even more unlikely to receive large areas of fields. If titled families owned arable land most was not given to daughters at marriage. Yet the majority of non-titled brides who received fields (34 per cent) received very modest amounts (1–5 strem-mata). Most of this land was owned and worked by Turks. This pattern is repeated in the transmission of animals: the majority of titled brides (83 per cent versus an average of 87 per cent, table 11) were unlikely to receive livestock. Similar practices prevailed between 1890–1900 in the Peloponnesian village of Dimitsana. There only 4 per cent of brides received livestock, although Kalpourtzi correctly notes that this tendency may have been greater among the poor, who did not use matrimonial contracts (1987; 93).

The modest amount of land and livestock which non-titled brides received at marriage suggests that a new couple was hardly likely to be economically self-sufficient at marriage, and their non-access to cash crops such as olives and vines suggests that these families practised a subsistence-oriented economy, often within the ambit of the bride's family. By contrast olives and vineyards exhibit a different pattern. Titled brides generally received more, rather than less areas of vineyards than non-titled brides (11–30 stremmata versus 11–20 stremmata, see table 12). It is the olive tree, however, which is the most highly stratified in its distribution and transmission. Only 2.8 per cent of titled brides did not receive some olives, versus 20.7 per cent of non-titled women (table 13). Among the latter 45.1 per cent received up to 40 trees, whereas over 86 per cent of titled brides received over this amount. Olives are of course an ideal crop for those who do not have to physically work the land.

The picture that emerges from this pattern of transmission of resources indicates the existence of marked social differences in Athens which tended to exhibit themselves at marriage. Non-titled young women generally did not receive many resources at marriage in so far as immoveable property and animals were concerned; such property as they received was not enough to grant a newly married couple economic independence from kin unless complemented by substantial amounts brought to the marriage by their grooms, and this was an unlikely situation. Titled brides, by contrast, received enough to maintain a comfortable lifestyle. In addition they received cash settlements, apart from their bridal costumes. Our analysis would not be complete without reference to the geographical origins of the brides. Athens was not only a stratified society; it was also geographically differentiated. Peasants were moving to the town attracted by new possibilities; such migration was especially prevalent among the so-called 'Arvanites' (Albanians) living in the surrounding villages. Sixty-six or 12.5 per cent of all brides in our sample lived on the fringes of the city, partaking of both urban and agricultural employment opportunities. This group is identified by a specific bridal costume, which we call 'Type B'. Unfortunately the contracts do not give much information on them. That they are clearly countrywomen is borne out by research on costumes (Bada, 1983) worn at that time. They also appear to have come from surrounding villages due to their tendency to receive fields. These brides generally tended to receive even smaller dowries. In table 14 we compare the dowries of

Table 12. *Endowment of vineyards to titled and untitled brides at marriage*

| | \multicolumn{10}{c}{Area of vineyards in stremmata} | |
	0	1–5	6-10	11–15	16–20	21–25	26–30	31–35	36–40	41+	Row total
Titled brides											
Number	8	0	1	9	8	6	2	0	0	2	36
Percentage	22.2	0	2.8	25.0	22.2	16.7	5.6	0	0	5.6	7.0
Non-titled brides											
Number	124	66	115	73	49	27	15	1	4	5	479
Percentage	25.9	13.8	24.0	15.2	10.2	5.6	3.1	0.2	0.8	0.8	93.0
Column total											
Number	132	66	116	82	57	33	17	1	4	7	515
Percentage	25.6	12.8	22.5	15.9	11.1	6.4	3.3	0.2	0.8	1.4	100.0

'Titled brides' row refers to brides of the *arkhon* and *nikokirei* groups. It also includes their adopted daughters.

Table 13. *Endowment of olive trees at marriage to titled and untitled brides*

| | | Olive trees | | | | | | |
	0	1– 40	41– 80	81– 120	121– 160	161– 200	200+	Row total
Titled brides								
Number	1	4	6	9	7	5	4	36
Percentage	2.8	11.1	16.7	25.0	19.4	13.9	11.1	7.0
Non-titled brides								
Number	99	216	115	37	5	3	4	479
Percentage	20.7	45.1	24.0	7.7	1.0	0.6	0.8	93.0
Column total								
Number	100	220	121	46	12	8	8	515
Percentage	19.4	42.7	23.5	8.9	2.3	1.6	1.6	100.0

'Titled brides' refers to brides of the *arkhon* and *nikokirei* groups. It also includes their adopted daughters.

untitled brides, of countrywomen marrying into Athens, and of adopted girls.

Table 14 compares these general figures to a more detailed control group defined by receipt of particular amounts of resources. It indicates the percentage of brides who received immoveable property and cash and examines how many of these received more than a specified amount. Thus whereas 75 per cent of untitled brides received vineyards, only 4 per cent of that number received over 5 stremmata. In the case of olive trees, while 58 per cent of migrant countrywomen to Athens received olive trees, none received as many as 80 trees. Of particular interest at this stage is the comparison of dowries of countrywomen with untitled brides long resident in Athens. The major differences lie in olive trees, ordinary fields, and to a lesser extent, cash. Countrywomen had even less access to olive trees than did untitled brides. Not one obtained more than 80 trees, versus 10 per cent of untitled Athens resident brides (table 14) and 69 per cent of the Athenian aristocracy (table 13). By contrast more countrywomen tended to receive fields (73 per cent versus 50 per cent for the untitled Athenian residents, table 14), and they tended overall to receive large amounts indicating a greater dependence on agricultural employment.

A greater dependence on agricultural employment did not, however, imply that most new couples expected to set up an autonomous household at marriage in so far as production was concerned. The relatively modest amount of basic resources transmitted at marriage (land and animals) implied that most couples expected to rely on wider kin networks for access to land, from both the groom's and the bride's side. In

Table 14. *Comparison of dowries between all untitled brides, migrant countrywomen and adopted daughters*

	Untitled brides total: 448			Migrant country women to Athens Total: 66			Adopted daughters Total: 42		
	Number	Percentage	Comparison	Number	Percentage	Comparison	Number	Percentage	Comparison
Vineyards	338	75.0	4% >5 stremmata	53	80.0	5% >5 stremmata	27	64.0	7.0% >5 stremmata
Olive trees	350	80.0	10% receive>80 trees	38	58.0	0% >80 trees	33	78.0	7% >40 trees, but 0% > 80 trees
Fields	223	50.0	7% receive>10 stremmata	48	73.0	30% receive>10 stremmata	18	45.0	4% >10 stremmata
House	171	38.0		24	36.0		19	45.0	29% >½ house
Cash	265	59.0	7% >500 groshia	40	62.0	0% >500 groshia	22	53.0	0% >200 groshia

most cases this was an informal arrangement, especially in the groom's parental household, but 79 or 15.1 per cent of our total sample of grooms were formally endowed with parental property at their marriages. Our contracts are silent on the amounts or nature of the property concerned, which leads us to the view that these were not intended to be grooms' dowries, that is, the groom's contribution to the marriage. Rather they were a means to register an endowment which had taken place earlier (for example inheritance of a share of the property of a deceased parent). The actual purpose of registering the fact of endowment was therefore to ensure that the property would revert to the groom's agnatic kin should he die issueless.

Our discussion on the transmission of property at marriage has so far concentrated on presenting a general synchronic analysis by grouping together all the matrimonial contracts between 1788–1834. We wish however to demonstrate that such patterns were not static. By the end of the 1820s the old *arkhon* class of *signori* had merged with the *nikokirei*; this was exhibited through greater intermarriage, the loss of political privileges among the *arkhon* group, and in the adoption of a new bridal costume common to both groups.

Social mobility became increasingly common as the city began to lose its pronounced agrarian character and Athens became the capital of the new Greek kingdom. Land previously held by the Turks was released for purchase and exploitation by Greeks, often at low prices, although continuing uncertainty over legal titles and the continuing heavy dependence of the new state upon agricultural taxes did much to discourage economic development (McGrew, 1985). Numerous merchants settled in the city and intermarried with the old ruling groups; they were characterised by the possession of large amounts of cash, rather than land, and it was often pledged as a dower as in the case of the Mytiline merchant referred to above. But by far the most significant change in the long run was the growth of a top-heavy bureaucracy which decisively influenced the perception of suitable marriage partners. So extensive was this pattern, noted by Friedl (1962), that it had already begun to extend to the countryside by the late nineteenth century. By 1890 in the Peloponnesian village of Dimitsana urban-oriented dowries had already made their appearance. Houses in Athens were already being built by villagers to attract Government employees (often teachers); they were in Kalpourtzi's words 'a completely different matter than rural house transfers' (1987; 94). Cash endowments, too, increased.

Our contracts indicate that these social changes were reflected in and embodied by the nature of dowries. We have chosen 1830 as our base line because of its historical significance for Athens and Greece. The

Table 15. *Transmission of olive trees as dowries before and after 1830*

Year	None	Number of olive trees						Row total
		1–40	41–80	81–120	121–160	161–200	Over 200	
Pre-1830								
Number	98	209	117	44	11	8	7	494
Percentage	19.8	42.3	23.7	8.9	2.2	1.6	1.4	94.5
Post-1829								
Number	3	14	6	3	2	0	1	29
Percentage	10.3	48.3	20.7	10.3	6.9	0	3.4	5.5
Column total								
Number	101	223	123	47	13	8	8	523
Percentage	19.3	42.6	23.5	9.0	2.5	1.5	1.5	100.0

conference of London involving a number of the Major Powers had begun its deliberations to decide the fate of Greece. Although we are dealing with a relatively small sample (5.5 per cent) of our total number of contracts, which cautions against excessive generalisations, we believe that the dowry was becoming more cash-oriented and less agriculturally based after this period. Livestock, which had never been a particularly significant resource since 1788, further declined as a transmittable item. The percentage of contracts which included livestock declined from 13.5 per cent prior to 1830, to 3.4 per cent after that year. The amount of transmitted arable land increased slightly, but as we are dealing with relatively small areas, this is not particularly significant. Vineyards too decreased in significance. Of all marriages contracted after 1830, 37.9 per cent did not include vineyards, versus 24.9 per cent for the pre-1830 period. With olive trees the pattern was slightly different; the number of brides who did not receive olive trees prior to 1830 decreased from 19.8 per cent to 10.3 per cent after 1830 (see table 15).

Significantly the incidence of olive tree transmission increased when modest amounts were concerned. For larger amounts (over 81 trees), likely to have been the preserve of the wealthy and titled groups, the percentage remains static: 14.1 per cent of all brides received over 81 trees in the pre-1830 period which rose to 21.6 per cent in the post-1830 period.

While the agricultural component of the dowry decreased in the post-1830 period, its monetary component increased. Although we discuss cash endowments more fully in the next chapter, we include table 16 here to demonstrate the increasing importance of cash. Of particular significance is the growth of brides endowed with large amounts of cash (over 300 groshia). Prior to 1830 only 17 per cent of brides were en-

Table 16. *Cash endowments as dowries before and after 1830*

Year	Endowments in groshia No cash given	1– 100	101– 200	201– 300	301– 400	401– 500	501– 600	Over 600	Row total
Pre-1830									
Number	195	90	73	52	27	20	12	25	494
Percentage	39.5	18.2	14.8	10.5	5.5	4.0	2.4	5.1	94.5
Post-1829									
Number	12	1	4	5	0	1	0	6	29
Percentage	41.4	3.4	13.8	17.2	0	3.4	0	20.7	5.5
Column total									
Number	207	91	77	57	27	21	12	31	523
Percentage	39.6	17.4	14.7	10.9	5.2	4.0	2.3	5.9	100.0

dowed with over 300 groshia at marriage; after 1830 this increased to 24.1 per cent. The increase is even more striking when one takes the top range into account; 5.1 per cent of brides were endowed with over 600 groshia prior to 1830, this increased fourfold to 20.7 per cent in the post-1830 period.

Dowry inflation in Athens and in Greece generally was certainly not a post-1830 phenomenon, although the concentration on cash after 1830 is significant. Indeed throughout the latter part of the eighteenth century dowry inflation appears to have been particularly widespread in Greece, extending as far as the Zaghorokhoria in Epirus (Maropoulou, 1985), and was sufficiently acute to have troubled the Orthodox Church and the dominant groups in various communities. The Church certainly did not subscribe to an egalitarian view of society and dowry inflation tended to blur the differences between social groups. In addition some families were experiencing major difficulties in marrying their daughters. The Church therefore attempted to regulate the amounts of property transfers according to the social group through encyclicals which threatened excommunication (*aphorismos*), an indication of the seriousness with which it viewed the situation. In 1737 the Patriarch Neophytos wrote to the Metropolitan Bishop of Athens on the 'conditions of the dowry', stating,

Because the Christians of Athens have arrived at high dowries to a general misfortune and suffering, because they have begun giving to their unmarried children [i.e. daughters] not only cash [*aspra metrita*, literally 'silver coins'], but also with these other things and fields, olive trees, vineyards, gold, pearls and clothing, and these are not of a little value, and moreover because of this, the evil is increasing all the time, and parents who are obliged to give all their wealth to their children [i.e. daughters] thus leaving their sons improvident and ungoverned.

(Vretos, 1864; 233–34)

This was a serious situation which was to have far reaching effects on Athenian and Greek society and it was paralleled in other parts of the Mediterranean (notably Renaissance Tuscany). The wording of the letter is significant in terms of what was left unsaid. The letter was clearly written with the interests of the *arkhontes* in mind and referred to the increasing tendency of the up-and-coming *nikokirei* group to heavily endow their daughters, which subverted the domestic power arrangements of the *arkhon* group and their pattern of reproduction. A massive introduction of resources (especially cash) at marriage subverted the relations between social groups and tended to create a new hierarchy. Even more important, it caused problems for the marriages of *arkhon* daughters. Their parents were obliged to increase their dowries, thus deflecting resources from sons. The *arkhontes* were organised in houses with a heavy patrilineal bias; within this largely endogamous social group (especially *vis à vis* daughters), resources (especially immoveables) tended to be transmitted to males. The threat of deflection of resources to daughters from sons not only diminished the potential power and wealth of sons onto whom rights traditionally devolved, but also threatened to overturn the distribution of power within the agnatic household. Second or younger sons who had previously accepted a lower profile within the patrilineal household and depended on the household head, often elder brothers, were now tempted to break the ranks of agnatic solidarity by the promise of large dowries. A new and dangerous mode of free competition threatened the previously more structured pattern of authority and power transmission.

The choice of words 'leaving their sons improvident and ungoverned' was thus particularly apt. Sons certainly tended to become 'improvident' as resources increasingly had to be diverted to daughters. Furthermore the up-and-coming *nikokirei* had greater access to cash, which was still a scarce resource, and this facilitated the circulation of daughters to a greater extent than immoveables had done. 'Ungoverned' was also a particularly suitable description. For the traditional system depended upon the control of the older generation of the same group over access to women and resources and this created its own particular tensions between the older men and their sons who had to assume a subservient position. In the new system, access to the women folk and resources was increasingly controlled by the older generation of another group; a group which, moreover, was increasingly vociferous and resentful of its exclusion from political power within the community. With the resources brought to marriages by dowries, sons could establish separate and independent households. Small wonder, then, that the older generation of *arkhontes* exhibited a degree of paranoia at this impending 'betrayal' by the younger generation. The effects were not limited to a transformation of the family, its ethics and the transmission of property, and the construction of personhood. They also had wider implications for the political system. The traditional schema of geographically discrete localized groups of elite power holders, relatively endogamous and patrolling their borders, was particularly suitable for the Ottoman millet system of government. The new social order heralded a much more fluid power field with different characteristics. The increasing circulation of cash and the concentration on cash as a major source of wealth by the *nikokirei* facilitated their mobility and that of their children (both sons and daughters – the former in dispersed trading activities and the latter through marriage), integrating them into the previously discrete local elites, and paving the groundwork for that remarkable transformation in Greek society in the late eighteenth century that was to result in the War of Independence. It was not merely the circulation of new liberal ideas from Europe that paved the way for the Greek uprising, it was also an increased mobility of a new social group with extensive networks and a common set of beliefs and experiences both within Greece and overseas.

Greece was not unique in this regard. Similar processes occurred in late medieval central urban Italy and heralded the changes in power structures that emerged in the Renaissance. Almost identical words were used to describe dowry inflation in Tivoli where 'nobles and commoners were crushed by "the enormous and unusual dowries that they must pay for their daughters, nieces or sisters" (quoted in Klapisch-Zuber, 1985; 243), characterised as an "evil custom and abuse". Such parallelisms raise important questions about commoditisation in urban Mediterranean contexts and their effects upon marriage and the transmission of resources.'

Yet one must not see this increasing commoditisation in stark contrast, as pushed by the *nikokirei* and resisted by the *arkhontes*, and thus as heralding a conflict between two different 'models' of the family. Ultimately resistance was expressed by most social groups, rich and poor alike, although those who had greater access to cash, such as the *nikokirei*, must have found such attitudes more irksome than alarming. Resistance to commoditisation was not solely due to the effects upon the organisation of the family group, its power structures and property transmissions, as among the *arkhontes*. In the countryside the commoditisation of the dowry and its inflation was feared just as strongly, especially when it involved the introduction of cash. Skouteri-Didaskalou quotes a report of the Eparchos (District Commissioner) of Skopelos in 1824 where villagers revolted against the dowry:

Because of the existence of an old custom in the island of Skopelos, according to which the parents must give to their daughters when these latter marry a ready-made house, the inhabitants of Glossa, a village of 130 houses, came to an agreement and decided to give an end to this custom; they signed a contractual agreement stating that, if anyone would either promise a house to his daughter, or give her one, the rest of them [the Glossiots] will burn the dowered house and banish the giver from their village; they called this contract *nomos* [Law].

(Skouteri-Didaskalou, 1976; 124)

Such resistance continued well into the twentieth century. In the village of Taifyrio in the Kallipolis region,

at the first quarter of the century, during an engagement [when] the negotiating parties tried to introduce a dowry paid in cash, the priest refused to write the dowry-contract and the Taifyriots forced both the parents of the bride and the groom to cancel the engagement and withdraw the promise.

(*ibid.*, 1976; 68)

We thus find ourselves in disagreement with Parry and Bloch when, in reinterpreting Bohannon's account of the effects of commoditisation among the Tiv, they state:

it always seems to be the elders who are deploring the situation. Although we can find no direct evidence that the young men invoked a different discourse about money, we rather doubt that they were so unanimous or unequivocal in their condemnation.

(1989; 14)

In Greece, by contrast, resistance to commoditisation of the dowry was expressed not just by the urban *arkhontes* but also by villagers often at the lower levels of society, because it affected most sectors of the population. Indeed there were even situations when the committee of elders (*dimogerontes*) overestimated the *prika* of poor girls 'in order to help the weak' (Mammopoulos, quoted in Skouteri-Didaskalou, 1976; 121). Whilst the young men certainly benefited from receiving more resources at marriage, the benefits were somewhat ambiguous for they too had to supply their sisters with dowries.

In Athens and in Greece generally the Church appeared to have had little success in halting this inflationary spiral. An encyclical was circulated in 1737 by the Patriarch Neophytos 'after he had been informed of the situation by the Elders (*kotzabashides*) and people' (Vretos, 1864; 233–37). This fixed dowries into three groups:

and for this we have decided that the first class is fixed at 1500 groshia, including all goods, that is *mulkia* [landed property], pearls, jewelry, brass items, and including clothes: 10 shirts and not more; 10 headkerchiefs; 2 beds, up to and including the smallest items. All these goods have to be valued by persons appointed by the Metropolitan Bishop. Following this group there are the second and third classes of dowry gifts, less in monetary amount . . .

(1864; 234)

The encyclical continued in the same vein.

The workings of this system were observed by Lord Charlemont who visited Athens in 1749. The Archbishop sat as the President of the Council of Elders (*epitropi*)

holding in his hands the power of excommunication the only punishment with which the tribunal is armed, or which is allowed by the Turk to inflict; neither is the penalty to be decried a slight one when we consider that it is sometimes carried so far as that no person is permitted even to speak to the excommunicated party under the penalty of equal excommunication.

(Stanford and Finopoulos, 1984; 112)

He further noted the pressure by the *arkhontes* to impose their will:

Not long ago the assembly of the Archonti sent a memorial to the Patriarch at Constantinople praying him to ratify by his supreme ecclesiastical authority a sentence of excommunication issued by them against any Athenian who should for the future give as his fortune with his daughter in marriage more than the sum of 2050 piastres. This sentence was accordingly ratified and the order has since been religiously observed.

(*ibid.*; 113)

Yet in 1760 the Church felt obliged to repeat the encyclical. This time the Patriarch Samuel Hatzeri in Constantinople widened dowry into six groups, the top one having a maximum value of 3,000 groshia, double the amount permitted in 1737 (Valetas, 1948; 76). It appears that the Church was unable to control dowry inflation and merely regulated an existing situation. But the reasons given bear closer scrutiny. The encyclicals refer to the 'accidental [*atychima*] growth of the dowry', that 'all want to become equal', that such practices are 'noisy [*thorivodhes*] and cause sadness'. It also expressed the fear that women would remain unmarried because of high dowries and the Christian population, therefore, did not multiply (under Ottoman rule) or that girls would enter into cohabitation under the Turkish type of Kepin marriage. Kepin or *kiambin* was civil marriage recognised by Ottoman Law. Christian Greeks often resorted to this form of marriage when it was not possible to marry according to the rules of the Church, either because of the prohibitions on close marriage, which were much more extensive than in the West at this time, or because of fourth marriages (according to the Orthodox Church one can marry not more than three times – a somewhat rare occurrence itself), or more importantly because of the rising cost of the dowry. Although the Orthodox Church came out strongly against Kepin marriage, branding the children of such unions as illegitimate, the institution appears to have been quite widespread. Kepin marriage was also resorted to in cases of marriage between Greek women and Turkish men (Zolotas, 1926; 277).

Attempts by the ruling *arkhon* group and the Church to cap dowry inflation were also subverted by the fact that appeals could always be made to the Turkish *cadi* or judge. When unfavourable decisions were made by the Committee of Elders and acted upon by the Bishop, appeals could be lodged with the *cadi*, as these were matrimonial matters: 'thus . . . the power of the Archontes is, by the folly of the people extremely limited' (Stanford and Finopoulos, 1984; 113). The same observer (Lord Charlemont) noted that in spite of this *de facto* limited power, aspirations to join the ruling group were high: 'yet is this dignity, the highest to which an Athenian can aspire, coveted and sought with the most greedy avidity and, upon a vacancy, every possible means is made use of by the leading men to obtain it for themselves, and for their families' (*ibid.*; 113).

The Church also devoted much attention to the stratification of matrimonial costumes. In a social context where dress indicated social origins and status as well as possessed great monetary value, this is hardly surprising. An 1803 encyclical specified that 'every woman should not wear gold embroidered clothes if they belong to this class, but the women of the first class should wear, and be given as dowry the usual gold embroidered clothes; women of the second and middle class (i.e. craftsmen) should wear only silk clothes, *Leipsianika* [silk from Leipzig], amoria, and others . . .' (Kalinderis, 1951; 100). What is significant here is that while all dowries were reduced to monetary terms for regulatory purposes, primarily because heavy investment in clothing was often an attempt to subvert the regulations, clothing and costumes also possessed a strong symbolic element. This symbolism was not only tied to status but also to the presentation of self.

By the late 1830s two major changes had occurred to the encyclicals. In essence they indicate that while the Church was still concerned with regulating matrimonial transfers, the old social order had been effectively superseded. First, there was a decrease in emphasis on costume and a corresponding increase in emphasis on cash dowries: the encyclicals began excluding costumes as the major component of the dowry for estimation purposes, and concentrated instead on referring to dowries of a certain fixed monetary value. We outline the changing relationship between costumes and value in the next chapter, but at this stage it is worthwhile to emphasise that this trend is consistent with the increase of the cash component of the dowry discussed above.

The second major change which occurred slightly after the period we are considering (1838 for Epiros, and roughly similar dates for other areas, such as 1985 for Maropoulou) was that the amounts of permissible dowries were fixed not in relation to the bride's social origins, but rather to that of her future spouse. In other words, a girl's dowry was pegged to the social origins of her prospective groom. Thus a girl of the second intermediate range could offer a dowry equivalent in amount to the high first range if her prospective spouse belonged to this group (Maropoulou, 1985; 107).

Taken together these changes amount to a veritable revolution of the matrimonio-political system. The abandonment of the regulation of costumes was not only due to the fact that their monetary value was decreasing relative to other resources. It was also due to the fact that costumes were too strongly associated with the old Ottoman system and in the brave new world of the independent Greek kingdom were somewhat suspect. Costumes associated with different social groups represented in a most tangible form the *ancien régime* of permanent and formalized social differences. They conflicted symbolically with the aspirations to social mobility and with the new equality in a common ethnicity of the young nation-state, and their removal permitted the emergence of a greater ambiguity (certainly less specificity) in claims to status. Their replacement by a common matrimonial costume facilitated the manufacture of statements about a common transcending ethnicity, expressed in the presentation of women at marriage. A single type of costume increasingly came to symbolise not just a common synchronic ethnicity, but also a common diachronic set of customs. It also had implications for the construction of gender identity.

It is not difficult to see the effects of these changes. The previous system encouraged group endogamy and the lateral circulation of spouses by means of visible markers of social distinction, such as clothing. The new system, by contrast, heralded cash as the major dowry component and permitted gradual but definite social mobility from one group into another by blurring the distinction between contiguous social strata. The differences in the mobility permitted by the two systems are brought out in the following list:

Eighteenth century
1. Group endogamy predominant (especially for women).
2. Horizontal competition.
3. Various resources transmitted at marriage (land, cash and trousseaux).

4. Trousseaux and cash as major resources to attract grooms from higher social groups.

Nineteenth century (post-1830)
1. Tendency towards group exogamy.
2. Horizontal and vertical competition.
3. Uniformity in resources transmitted at marriage (cash).
4. Cash as major resource to attract grooms from higher social strata.

In the post-1830 matrimonial system a girl's dowry could be increased to compete and obtain a groom from a higher social group. Conversely with urban bureaucratic employment becoming a major social resource such cash dowries could be used to obtain grooms from previously lower social strata. In the old system a groom's social origins determined the nature and type of dowry his spouse was expected to bring at marriage; in the new system the amount of the dowry became increasingly the determining factor in marriage. It heralded the change, well brought out by Skouteri-Didaskalou, from the equation 'good groom→wealthy dowry' of the old system to the equation 'wealthy dowry→good groom' of the nineteenth century (1984; 158).

Apart from its concern to maintain social hierarchies intact, especially in the eighteenth century, the Church's attempts to restrict dowry inflation appear to have been also motivated by institutional concerns. Under the Ottomans the Church appears to have been more concerned to ensure the growth of its flock generally than to attract primarily poorer recruits to its monasteries and nunneries. Girls entering nunneries were expected to bring a dowry with them which was eventually added to that institution's holdings. Endowments by wealthy individuals to nunneries functioned in the same way as *habous* land in North Africa and *waqf* in Ottoman territories. The will of one Ioannou Deka drawn up in Venice in 1757 specified '500 ducats to be given per annum as a dowry for 5 poor girls to marry or to enter the Church' (Philadelfeus, 1902; 372). However in other parts of Greece, such as some of the Cycladic Islands, unigeniture prevailed and non-endowed children entered the Church. Although we do not disagree with Goody's assertion (1983) that the Church certainly benefited materially from celibacy either directly through recruitment or indirectly through endowments, nevertheless the Church's specific policy in Greece on these matters was heavily influenced by the overall political framework within which it found itself. As an intermediate group, allied at the top with a resident indigenous seigneurial class, but under Ottoman overlords, its policy reflected the concerns of the dominant groups. At the same time, by being relatively decentralized and possessing strong-grassroots, its policies could be gradually influenced by changes in the articulation between social classes.

Cash did not merely figure in a unidirectional manner transmitted from parents to daughters; it also appeared in the dowers promised by grooms. While clothing and land-producing cash crops were the major means for female social mobility in the eighteenth century, the promised dower was the main vehicle for male social mobility through marriage in this period.

Moveables in their various forms were more economically, and perhaps symbolically, significant than immoveables. In our next chapter we examine the circulation of these goods and their associated meanings. We group cash, trousseaux, and costumes together not only because their circulation can be seen as constituting a system, but also because they raise important questions regarding the material and symbolic significances of gifts and gift exchange in a matrimonial context. Furthermore an analysis of these goods and their shifting meanings can help shed light on the evolution of the significance of the *prika* (the dowry) in both its material and symbolic aspects. For while the dowry can be seen in terms of the vertical transmission of goods from one generation to the next, such a view does not exhaust its symbolic significance, nor whether individuals within this society perceived the dowry in these terms.

4

Gifts and commodities, cash and trousseaux

Introduction

In addition to land and other immoveable resources Athenian brides in the eighteenth century also received other more mobile goods at marriage in the form of cash endowments and trousseaux. Such items were far from insignificant both symbolically and economically; indeed they were more important than land, olive trees and the like, and their importance was to increase in the nineteenth century. We treat the two together because they can on one level be seen as heralding the beginning of a specifically urban and modern form of dowry endowment in Greece – a movement away from immoveable agricultural resources towards a more mobile, alienable, form of dowry enabling, theoretically, a fuller separation of the new conjugal couple from parental ties, especially when combined with neolocality. Only an actual examination of the resources transmitted will establish whether the new conjugal unit constituted an independent unit of production and consumption, and there are many indications that this ideal was far from universally subscribed to in the early part of the nineteenth century. Children, especially sons, were still likely to be dependent upon resources held jointly with other siblings. However, the gradual but definite shift from agricultural land certainly opened up the possibilities for greater separation (physically and economically) of the new conjugal unit from the preceding generation; this was further reinforced through the increase in employment possibilities for men outside the home.

We also wish to test the hypothesis advanced by Skouteri-Didaskalou (1984) and explored by Kalpourtzi (1987) that where an agricultural income predominates, clothes and household goods rather than cash and land are transferred at marriage; whereas when a non-agriculturally based income predominates, cash is the main resource transferred at marriage. As we shall demonstrate, such distinctions have perhaps dubious validity for Athens in the late eighteenth and early nineteenth centuries, partly because its economy cannot be reduced to such ready and exclusive categories. Although household goods are somewhat less important, clothing, cash and land were freely transferred with major differences between the various social groups. Nevertheless the growing commoditisation of the dowry is clear in Athens during this period.

There is further significance in the transmission of cash and trousseaux. To begin with, they appear in inverse proportion to each other across time, for example trousseaux appear more important in the eighteenth century, whereas by the 1830s they had declined in favour of cash endowments. This heralds a shift from a hierarchical agrarian-based social order to a more mobile, cash-oriented, specifically urban society. Second, both cash and trousseaux were the two resources which lent themselves to strategic manipulation. Cash figured both as dowry and as dower and it was utilised strategically to further social mobility in a way which land and immoveable resources could not. Likewise bridal costumes, which formed a significant part of the trousseaux, reflected socially recognised claims to pre-eminence in a way titles did not. We therefore examine the transmission of cash (in the form of dowries and dowers), and trousseaux (in the form of bridal costumes) with the aim of introducing a greater degree of precision in our analysis of social mobility.

A third significance of cash and trousseaux is that they do not correspond to the traditional anthropological categories which identify cash with capital and commodities, and trousseaux with symbolic items and gifts. Rather, cash possessed a heavy symbolic (as well as an ultimately ambiguous) significance while trousseaux had a strong economic value. We explore these meanings not only with reference to the nature of the economy, but also with reference to the process of class formation.

Finally a concentration on moveables and their circulation at marriage raises important questions. The fact that women at marriage tended to receive moveables to a greater extent than immoveables poses a number of problems. Should we see this as an attempt to exclude daughters from access to immoveables, most of which went to sons? Or should we see it as an expression of a cultural logic that assigned certain goods to women and others to men? To reduce all these goods to their monetary value is one way of resolving the first question. But in some cases the value of moveables was actually higher than that of land, etc. Should we therefore conclude that sons were disinherited to a greater extent? There is perhaps a certain absurdity in discussions of 'equality' between sons and daughters, although the question remains important. But the issue of 'equality', expressed as it is in a logic of commodity exchange, may be particularly unsuitable or crude when applied not only to that most gift-oriented of 'exchange' relationships, marriage, but also to a society that was not fully enmeshed in a commodity economy and which responded to it in a distinctive way. In short the concentration on 'equality' does not address the question as to why some resources were given to daughters and others to sons, and even much less so on the effects of such a pattern both on perceptions and on the constitution of personhood. Finally a discussion of these issues can shed light on the whole status of the notion of the 'dowry'. On one level the term *prika* (dowry) is legally unambiguous – it signifies a daughter's share of her inheritance given her pre-mortem at her marriage. On one level this is certainly the case – anything that is given to children *inter vivos* belongs *ipso facto* to the class of goods that are potentially inheritable and thus shares a common 'property' with all these goods. But whether dowry goods are perceived as *one* or *the* share of a daughter's inheritance is another matter. Certainly it is normally a right activated prior to the death of the parents, but the time lapse between the two events creates difficulties and ambiguities in estimating what is actually due to her as the legitimate share of her inheritance, at the time of marriage and in the form of a dowry. This is further compounded when different (often not strictly commensurable) resources are transmitted. Furthermore while the dowry may be viewed in a *post-facto* legalistic sense as a pre-mortem activation of a potential inheritance right, and indeed may actually be viewed theoretically in this way by the actors themselves ('she got her dowry and that is her share of the parental goods'), the actual sentiments when the dowry is given may be quite different. The dowry may not be immediately conceptually linked to the inheritance when it is given. Rather it may be primarily perceived that it is a daughter's right to receive certain goods at marriage, or these goods may be perceived as a necessary condition enabling a daughter to marry, a type of endowment. It may only thereafter be linked conceptually to inheritance: having obtained parental property at marriage, it is only 'right' that this be taken into account when the division takes place and others obtain parental property first. Furthermore while *prika* (dowry) is normally associated with daughters, the word *prikizo*, to endow, can be used in conjunction with sons as well as with daughters. Its meaning is therefore in some cases much closer to an endowment which is not gender specific, rather than to the meanings associated with the English word 'dowry', often associated, as in Italian, specifically with daughters and conceptually linked to inheritance.

We raise these issues because the formula 'dowry=part of the inheritance', while undoubtedly valid, eliminates these important nuances. It also renders the notion of 'equality' more tenuous, as it bypasses the rationality and motivation of all property transfers to children and reduces the sum total of these transfers to whether, finally, they were equal. In modern Greece *prika* (dowry) is often primarily perceived as what is given by the parents to the daughter at marriage – it is seen as a 'gift' which is a daughter's right to claim (primarily as a daughter and therefore as an heir) and the parent's obligation to supply, not primarily as her pre-mortem inheritance but in order to get her married. Only secondarily is it conceptually related to inheritance, when accounting takes place. Indeed in discourse it is often said that 'the bride received . . .' and 'the groom received' (or 'took' – both terms are covered by the word *pire*). The fact that the 'dowry' is nowadays presented as something which men 'receive' by virtue of marriage, although it is of course legally not their property, indicates something about the matrimonial culture and probably the legal culture which influenced it. Furthermore, the fact that individuals do not consciously go about giving or demanding dowries as a strictly exclusive pre-mortem inheritance indicates the operation of a different rationality from that encapsulated in the legal concept which collapses all exchanges to their end result. It thus renders the notion of 'equality' even more interesting because the dowry's actual operation may well be institutionalising an unequal system in spite of the fact that legally, the emphasis is on equality. Whether the system actually favours sons or daughters is, of course, an empirical matter.

A consideration of these points is important when analysing dowries in nineteenth-century Athens. We suggest that the notions encapsulated in the contemporary expressions that a groom 'took' or 'received' a dowry via his wife are relatively modern, a by-product of a specific matrimonial culture not fully developed in early nineteenth-century Athens. Although we do not have direct information for everyday linguistic usage in this period, the wording of the matrimonial contracts provides some clues. Matrimonial contracts of this period refer to the bride's dowry not just in the contemporarily recognisable form of *prika*, but also often as her *meridhio*, or her share of parental property. There is a slight but important difference in nuance between the two terms. The term *meridhio* is 'used of land inherited by *children of both sexes*, without further qualification' (Herzfeld, 1980; 230 our italics) and it is thus explicitly linked to the notion of inheritance (*klironomia*). In this respect some Athenian marriages resembled Ambeliot marriages until 1966 studied by du Boulay (1983). There, brides often had to sign an agreement of disinheritance on receiving their dowry. We have found little evidence of this specific practice in Athens, yet the reference to *meridhio* in our contracts may well have served this purpose. *Prika*, by contrast, although certainly linked to inheritance in a legal sense, has more the primary notion of a gift given a daughter by her parents at marriage. It is only in a secondary sense that it is viewed as an activation of rights to inheritable property.

These may appear as slight semantic differences, but the slippage between the two terms suggests a different matrimonial culture. In early nineteenth-century Athens, dowry was linked more strongly in a performative sense to inheritance. This is congruent with a system of status group endogamy. Because individuals inherited their status and a specific position within society, they inherited certain goods which enabled them to enter status-specific types of marriage. Such a system is also congruent with a matrimonial culture which views the marriage of daughters in a 'collective' corporate sense rather than as a series of discrete individual strategies. As we shall show, the modern system which began to emerge in Athens in the 1830s possessed a different rationality. Dowries increasingly became conceptually separable from inheritance, seen as an obligation imposed by 'society' which men had to 'satisfy', rather than as the expression of a right which individuals possessed as members of a determinate status group and which gave them claims to a specific type of marriage, as it had been in the past. Dowries thus became disembedded from status, that is as expressions and manifestations of specific statuses within society, but became much more a means to acquire prestige by a series of individual cumulative and negotiable steps, or to paraphrase Simmel, as an expression of a 'rationally calculated [matrimonial] egoism' (Simmel, 1971).

Cash endowments at marriage

Money figured prominently in many areas of matrimonial, literary and national life in nineteenth-century Greece. Parents donated large sums to daughters at marriage; husbands promised it to their wives; popular literature dwelt almost obsessively on the contrast between fabulous wealth and abject poverty; peasants recounted stories of buried caches of gold coins, often contrasting them to 'useless statues' (*ahrista agalmata*); and national political debates revolved around the national debt, which assumed alarming proportions by the latter part of the century. Even in present-day Greek culture money has an ambiguous status. One of the most desirable possessions, it is also believed to be corrupting, though significantly it is not held to be inherently corrupt. 'Corruption' in the public domain is defined as 'eating' (*efaghe* – 'he ate') – and it is usually brought about by the temptation of easy money which results in 'feasting' (*hortaze* cognate with *horta*: grazing grass).

These metaphors themselves are interesting and significant: why should a largely urbanised society perceive something which is in itself a good thing (money) as corrupting someone through 'eating', an active and transforming process, and one moreover embedded in a rural imagery ('grazing')? At issue here is a specific attitude towards money, evil and the effects of the metropolis on the construction of personhood. But it is fitting to begin our discussion with an analysis of the circulation of money at marriage, for parents increasingly began to donate the essence of commoditisation and the commodity *par excellence* as the highest gift to their daughters. Can the imagery of money being 'eaten' provide any insights into the process of commoditisation of dowries?

We begin by observing that money marked both the beginning and the termination of marriage in Athens. Athenian women received cash at the commencement and termination of their marriages in the form of cash dowries from their parents, and dowers from their husbands or his male kin. We begin by examining cash dowries. The incidence of cash transmission at marriage was much lower than for other goods. Nearly 40 per cent of all brides did not receive cash dowries, compared to 19.3 per cent for olive trees, 25.6 per cent for vineyards and 52.6 per cent for fields. Yet cash, together with the trousseau, was perhaps the most significant symbolic and economic resource transmitted at marriage either as a dowry or dower, and it was far more important than land and other immoveable resources. Why was this the case?

To begin with, in the late eighteenth century, cash was a restricted resource. In his memoirs Kolokotronis recounts that 'in my time commerce was very limited, money was scarce . . . It was thought a great thing if a person possessed a thousand groshia [then worth about £22]. Anyone with such a sum could command as much service for it as he could not procure now [1836] for a thousand Venetian florins' (Edmonds, 1969; 128). To an even greater extent than the olive tree, cash was the prerogative of the Athenian aristocracy. By contrast, by the late nineteenth century cash had made its appearance as a significant component of women's dowries even in the villages. Out of the 130 contracts examined by Kalpourtzi for Dimitsana between 1890–1900, 104 or 80 per cent contained cash endowments (1987; 96) compared to 60 per cent for Athens during our period. Our figures also indicate that overall, 27.8 per cent of titled brides received cash payments of 600 groshia compared to 4.4 per cent of non-titled brides (table 17). For sums below this amount the differences are largely negligible.

The table also conceals some important features of cash transmissions. Many of the cash endowments are clustered around the thresholds set by the Orthodox Church (100, 200, 300, 400, 500 groshia)

Table 17. *Cash dowries to titled and untitled brides at marriage*

	No cash received	1–200 groshia	201–400 groshia	401–600 groshia	over 600 groshia	Row total
Titled brides						
Number	12	5	6	3	10	36
Percentage	33.3	13.9	16.7	8.4	27.8	7.0
Untitled brides						
Number	193	160	76	29	21	479
Percentage	40.3	33.4	15.8	6.1	4.4	93.0
Column total						
Percentage	39.6	32.1	16.1	6.3	5.9	100.0

Table 18. *Cash endowments to daughters at marriage according to status of grooms, in comparison*

		No cash received	1–200 groshia	201–400	401–600	600+
				in per cent		
A.1	'Sior' grooms	50.0	0	0	0	50.0
A.2	'Kir' grooms	30.6	19.4	19.4	8.4	22.2
A.3	Untitled grooms	40.1	33.0	16.2	6.3	4.4
B.1	'Kir' grooms marrying daughters of titled fathers	11.1	44.4	22.2	11.1	22.2
C.1	Athenian grooms	38.4	32.0	16.6	6.4	5.7
C.2	Non-Athenian grooms	72.2	11.2	0	5.6	11.2
Percentage received by brides		39.6	32.1	16.1	6.3	5.9

and some contracts specify very large amounts; one case is for 6,000 groshia, a fabulous amount. The mean is 211 and the standard deviation is 444 groshia (median=100 groshia).

Although cash was a restricted item, particularly in eighteenth-century Athens, its possession was a prerequisite to the pursuit of a fully urban lifestyle; control over cash was one of the main markers of social and political distinction. Table 17 merely indicates how titled and untitled brides were endowed at their marriages, yet it does not relate to their grooms, which is perhaps more significant. Table 18 examines the transmission of cash according to the various categories of grooms (i.e., who these women married) and it indicates more clearly how cash transmissions were stratified and concentrated in the top layers of Athenian society.

Of particular significance in table 18 is the large number (22.2 per cent) of grooms from the *nikokirei* class who married brides bringing large amounts of cash with them (A.2), compared to the small number (4.4 per cent) of untitled grooms (A.3). The tendency increases even further with group or class endogamy; nearly 22 per cent of titled grooms who married into titled families 'received' over 600 groshia at marriage (B.1). Of equal significance are those grooms whose wives were not endowed with cash at marriage; by far the greatest number are non-Athenian grooms (72.2 per cent, C.2). Some were migrants from surrounding villages, but others (accounting for the 11.2 per cent who 'received' over 600 groshia) were wealthy merchants attracted there by new opportunities, such as Kir Angelakis' groom discussed earlier.

Cash was not only required by parents to endow a daughter at her marriage; it was also required by the groom. We are referring here to the dower (*progamiea dorea*, literally pre-marriage gift) probably of Byzantine origin (Skouteri-Didaskalou, 1976; 119). The dower was an important institution which brought together the various rights and obligations of kinship. In essence it was a gift from the groom and his family to the bride. In Athens the dower consisted of the specification of a sum of money by the groom and his family at marriage (at the drawing up of the contract) which was to be handed over to the bride in the case of divorce, upon the dishonouring of the matrimonial contract, or in the event of the husband predeceasing his wife. This cash was to be obtained at such time from the husband's parents, if they were alive; from the husband's estate if the parents were dead; from the husband's property held in common with siblings. The dower appears to have been expressly designed to protect widows. There appears to have been some variation in Greece in its manner of transfer and terminology (Couroucli, 1987). For example in the Eubean village of Ambeli studied by du Boulay the groom traditionally was obliged to give his bride jewellery (1983; 248), a clear indication of the scarcity of cash and of the desire to prevent the dower's realisation for cash. In Northern Greece where the *agarliki* (a type of brideprice) was given, Skouteri-Didaskalou suggests that this was given to the father or mother of the bride before the marriage and 'it committed all the bride's family to the fact that the marriage will take place. In other words it ensured the right of the groom to take the bride' (1984; 225).

Such a practice does not seem to have been followed in Athens, and an examination of the sources used by Skouteri-Didaskalou suggests that this was indeed more prevalent in the more pastoral north where women appear to have retained even fewer secondary or residual rights to parental property after marriage. In Athens, by contrast, the dower was handed over after the dissolution of the marriage and it had the force of law to be transferred between three months and one year after the dissolution. The matter of the dower was not, therefore, taken lightly by the groom and his kin. Clearly, the dower held brothers together in a series of mutual obligations. Sisters were usually excluded from these obligations in the same way as they were usually excluded *de facto* from sharing in the residue of the parental property once they had been married with a dowry, especially when this dowry was their *meridhio* (share) of inheritance. Thus, although daughters were often excluded from a share in the residual parental estate after marriage, they were often also free from such obligations to their brothers.

The effects of this system are obvious. Daughters would be endowed but often would lose *de facto* claims upon the parental estate; sons would be linked together by a series of mutual obligations, not only through property held in common upon the death of their parents, but also through dower undertakings. The accumulation of dowers served to promote agnatic solidarity. Marriage for a man was not an individual undertaking, for the specification of the dower required the concurrence of male kinsmen, usually brothers, who would be placed under obligation at a later date. As we shall demonstrate, the greater the social gap between groom and bride – that is, the higher the bride's status – the greater the tendency and requirement for the groom to pledge a large dower. Thus a man's marriage, even if a spectacularly good example of social mobility, had its own obligations which certainly rendered it a common sibling concern.

In spite of the differences in the timing of its transfer and its terminology, the dower appears to have been remarkably consistent throughout Greece in two respects. First, it appears to have consisted mainly of cash rather than land, across a territory running from Athens to present day Albania (Vernikos, 1979). Second, it appears to have been a virtual requirement for a man's marriage. In 97 per cent of our total sample grooms pledged a dower, reflecting perhaps a pronounced tendency for grooms to predecease their spouses. Similar figures emerge from the Albanian village of Mouzakia in the early nineteenth century, where 85 per cent of grooms promised a cash dower. Although we lack figures for marriage ages of men and women, the apparent obligation to promise a dower does not suggest early or equal ages at marriage for men and women. Rather it suggests late marriage ages for men, at least in the towns, and/or significant differences in marriage ages for men and women.

Table 19 gives details on promised dowers. Rather than breaking up

Table 19. *Cash dowers according to status of grooms, in comparison*

	0	1–100	101–200	201–300 in groshia	301–400	401–500	501–600	over 600
A.1 'Sior' grooms	0	0	0	0	0	0	25.0	75.0
A.2 'Kir' grooms	0	2.8	16.7	11.1	25.0	2.8	22.2	19.4
A.3 'Mastros' grooms	0	0	80.0	20.0	0	0	0	0
A.4 Untitled grooms	2.7	9.7	39.3	21.6	12.4	4.2	4.0	6.1
B.1 'Kir' grooms marrying daughters of titled parents	0	3.7	14.8	14.8	25.9	3.7	18.5	18.5
B.2 'Kir' grooms marrying daughters of untitled parents	0	0	22.2	0	22.2	0	33.3	22.2
C.1 Untitled grooms marrying daughters of titled parents	0	11.4	34.3	5.7	8.6	5.7	14.3	20.0
C.2 Untitled grooms marrying daughters of untitled parents	2.9	9.5	39.7	22.9	12.7	4.1	3.2	5.0
D.1 All grooms marrying 'Kir' brides	2.8	13.9	13.9	13.9	2.8	25.0	27.8	0
D.2 All grooms marrying untitled brides	2.7	9.6	39.9	21.1	12.7	4.2	4.0	5.8
E.1 Athenian grooms	2.2	8.9	38.6	21.6	13.3	3.8	5.0	6.7
E.2 Non-Athenian grooms	11.1	11.1	16.7	5.6	11.1	16.7	27.8	0
Total: dowers promised by grooms as a group	2.5	9.0	37.8	20.7	13.1	4.0	5.4	7.5

Table includes adopted daughters and all figures are percentages.

our data into separate tables, we have identified a series of key variables and grouped them together in order to facilitate a more comprehensive appreciation of the way dowers were pledged according to various categories of grooms and brides. Although our 'Sior' (or *arkhon*) sample is too small to warrant any meaningful conclusions, it is nevertheless significant that all pledged a dower of over 500 groshia (A1). More important are the differences between the *nikokirei* group and non-titled grooms (A2, A4). Among the former only 19.5 per cent pledged less than 200 groshia, whereas over half (51.7 per cent) of non-titled grooms promised a similar dower. 19.4 per cent of 'Kir' grooms pledged over 600 groshia whereas only 6.1 per cent exceeded this amount among non-titled grooms.

A further significant difference, reflecting the town–country divide in access to resources such as cash, as encountered in other tables, relates to the distinction between Athenian and non-Athenian grooms (E1, E2). Like non-Athenian brides, non-Athenian grooms appear to have had little access to cash, and 11.1 per cent could not provide a dower at all. Indeed these grooms constituted by far the largest group unable to provide a dower. The group also includes wealthy individuals (usually merchants), and 27.8 per cent committed themselves to a dower of over 600 groshia.

Considerations of prestige and self-respect (*aksioprepia*) appear to have influenced the setting of the dower, at least among the titled groups of Athenian society. Titled grooms and their families were all equally likely to pledge large amounts, irrespective of whether their brides were titled or not (i.e. were of the same social origins). One reason for this phenomenon may be the substantial differences in marriage ages between titled grooms and non-titled brides, which may have had the effect of pushing up the value of the dower. A similar phenomenon is evident in the present-day Ionian island of Meganisi, where the wealthiest men appear to take the youngest available brides (Just, 1985), as well as in Lefkas in the first decades of the nineteenth century (Tomara-Sideri, 1986; 154–5). Figure 1 recasts the data to provide an indication of how dower flows figured in their matrimonial contexts. Immediately striking is the fact that over 37 per cent of all titled grooms pledged dowers of over 500 groshia; 37 per cent to similarly titled brides, and 55.5 per cent to brides from a lower social class.

The question arises, why should a greater percentage of titled grooms have offered large dowers to non-titled brides (55.5 per cent) than to titled brides (37 per cent)? Here we must refer to the patterns of group endogamy and exogamy among titled grooms discussed above. The

figures for dower flows closely parallel the figures for group endogamy/
exogamy (47.5 per cent endogamous, 52.5 per cent exogamous). Thus
titled grooms were all equally likely to offer large dowers irrespective of
whom they married. This suggests that at issue here was the expression
of collective status. Men generally offered certain amounts as dowers
because they belonged to determinate social groups, rather than necessarily because their spouses belonged to their social class. By contrast,
among marriages contracted between non-titled spouses only 8.2 per
cent promised a dower of over 500 groshia. Figure 1 brings out one
further striking feature. Non-titled grooms hoping to marry into the
Athenian aristocracy had to be prepared to promise a large dower.
Eighty per cent of these offered a dower of over 500 groshia.

The dower was not merely an economic resource; its significance
varied depending upon its matrimonial context. Among titled Athenian
families it was a symbol and index of wealth and of the 'family's' (i.e.
the men's) *aksioprepia*, or self-esteem. It indicated the 'value' which the
groom's family placed upon the match and it proved that they were
intent on maintaining the bride in a manner to which she was
accustomed. It was also consistent with church ideology, which
emphasised the *prikosymfono* (marriage contract) as the correct means
for entering marriage. Pledging a dower was part and parcel of church-
approved marriage which prohibited cohabitation prior to the signing of
the *prikosymfono* and made material provision for widows. A 'good'
family offered a 'good' dower irrespective on one level of whom its
potential recipients were, because a marriage, once contracted, was in
theory indissoluble and the bride was considered to form part of her new
household symbolically and materially. By obliging the groom, or his
kin, to supply this cash the dower institutionalised the links between a
bride and her affines. By contrast among the urban poor and peasant
migrants to the town, where marriage was often uxorilocal (table 3) and

Figure 1. Dower flows from titled/untitled grooms to titled/untitled brides
above 500 groshia

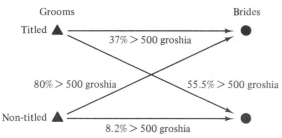

'Titled brides' excludes girls adopted by titled parents, none of whom
received over 300 groshia as a dower.

where cohabitation often preceded the signing of the *prikosymfono*, dowers were less in evidence. This was not merely a matter of possessing less cash (which was indubitably the case), but also a matter of such uxorilocal and less formal domestic arrangements having less need for the safeguard of the dower. Husbands usually predeceased their wives, but they did so in her natal household, or in her dowry house, thus unlikely to unduly disturb the surviving spouse's situation.

In the early years of the period we are discussing, cash held other important significances as well. A scarce resource available only to a few having access to a restricted market, its possession indicated not only wealth but power. It was associated with consumption (initially with rent capitalism and administrative privileges, later with government employment), rather than with production. Paradoxically, the more one offered or gave, the more one demonstrated that one did not need to work, rather than how much one had worked.

The dower and dowry were complementary. While the dowry was a type of pre-mortem endowment of women as sisters by men (fathers and brothers), the dower was a type of post-mortem settlement upon the widow as an affine by the husband's male kin. Indeed at least on a theoretical level the amount of cash promised via the dower was much higher than that actually given via the dowry, and it is also significant that while the Church and the *arkhontes* made strong attempts to control dowry inflation, nothing similar was attempted for the dower. Table 20 compares the two institutions.

As the table indicates, dowers figured to a much greater extent in matrimonial contracts and the amounts promised were consistently higher. How should we interpret this? To begin with, this system ensured that financial burdens did not fall only on the parents of daughters but also on the husband's male kin. Obligations were distributed between both kinship groups which clearly shared a stake in the prosperity of the union. Thus while one group contributed to the establishment of the marriage, another group had to pay if it did not succeed. Everything in this society operated to link men and women and primarily groups together in a series of reciprocal rights and duties; initially between brothers and sisters, fathers and daughters, and later between men and women as affines. Thus, although daughters can be said to have been 'paid off' at marriage by their male kin, to whom the property would return in the case of childlessness, at marriage these sets of obligations were replaced by other obligations. In another respect the dower took the place of residual undivided property rights which women retained with their brothers in North Africa. Although residence in Athens was viri-patrilocal as in North Africa, women could

Table 20. *Dowries and dowers compared*

	0	1–200	groshia 201–400	401–600	over 600
Percentage of cash dowries	39.6	32.1	16.1	6.3	5.9
Percentage of cash dowers	2.9	46.8	33.8	9.4	7.5

not easily return to their natal households on the dissolution of their marriages through divorce or widowhood, as occurs in North Africa, partly because, by having been endowed as brides by their male kin, they retained only secondary rights in their natal household. Instead the dower theoretically took on the function of 'widow insurance' by enabling her to maintain herself in an independent household.

There is an added dimension to the operations of the dowry and dower. For the society was utilising money not in its fully commoditised and commoditising sense. Cash linked groups, and not individuals; the 'exchange' was not immediate but delayed, and a 'counterpayment' (the dower) was only demanded if the 'spirit' of the initial gift (cash dowry to establish a marriage) was not recognised and accepted (through dissolution of the marriage, for example). Something similar seems to have occurred in Renaissance Tuscany where marital gifts by the husband to his bride replaced the *donatio propter nuptias*, a close equivalent to the Greek *progamiea dorea*. Klapisch-Zuber notes that these gifts often represented 'between one- and two-thirds of the promised dowry [in holdings or in cash], trousseau included' (1985; 220), a situation not dissimilar to early nineteenth-century Athens, when all the dowry goods are taken into account. She suggests that while the marital donation (*donatio*) declined, these gifts 'expressed the need ... to establish a reciprocal and almost equal exchange between the two parties' (*ibid.*; 233), and even goes so far as to suggest that marriage gifts represented a 'clandestine counterdowry'.

Societies such as Renaissance Tuscany and late eighteenth- and early nineteenth-century Greece thus attached a very specific rationality to marriage. While the dowry may seem to have had a continuity across time, as indeed it did as a means of transferring resources vertically, nevertheless its rationality and significance to the people concerned was highly specific. For the dowry was enmeshed in a system of alliances between families; as a gift it was countered by a return gift which was given as much as an expression of group status as well as for the purpose of pursuing individual familial prestige. Marriage gifts were as much attempts to express (at least symbolically if not materially) the desire for some form of equality which amounted to none other than a socially accepted claim to belong to a similar status group. The dowry was not a means to establish a separate household from both familial groups, as it is in many parts of present-day Greece; it thus did not represent so much of a burden requiring immediate and total satisfaction in marriage. Yet it was, perhaps even more so than in modern Greece, conceptually linked to inheritance, manifested in the use of the word *meridhio* (a share which is not gender-specific). Women activated their rights to inheritance at marriage primarily as heirs; rights which took a particular form (dowry) and which they, as daughters, were entitled to receive. As members of specific status groups they possessed rights to specific types of dowries, and it was through this membership that they activated their claims. In the contemporary Greek system, by contrast, women activate their rights to dowries as daughters, a transformation which has important implications for gender identity.

The similarities between the matrimonial systems of Renaissance Tuscany and early modern Greece should not blind us to their differences. While in Tuscany many of the gifts and counter gifts were expressed in symbolic items such as clothing (which nevertheless had a strong monetary value), Greece was distinctive in that gifts and counter gifts were increasingly expressed in cash. In a society suddenly thrown into the modern world system on Europe's periphery, this is hardly surprising. But the use of cash and its inherently ambiguous characteristics in the manufacture and reshaping of desires, and its disposable, liquid, and transforming nature had particular effects on marriage and matrimonial culture. In terms of its universal and levelling nature it contributed to a specific notion of the dowry; it redefined the categories of 'daughters' and 'dowries', making them appear inevitably compatible, and it transformed the matrimonial system making it appear to the participants as a 'matrimonial market'. Its dissolubility contributed to a heightened sense of fear that it could be disposed of by husbands (i.e. 'eaten'), a metaphor carried over to everyday political life where corruption ('eating') is used to denote someone who appropriates goods he is entrusted to protect. Finally, the use of cash created specific tensions when it was expressed in that most gift-oriented of relationships, marriage, and had particular implications for the family and its emotional life.

An indication of the functioning of the dower during our period of concern comes from the memoirs of the merchant Panayis Skouzes: 'In April 1794 my father, Dimitriou, died. After this my uncle Ierotheos [the father's brother] was informed and he came to Athens from Hydra, paid my stepmother her dower of 100 groshia . . . and she left our house for she had not borne my father any child' (1975; 100). Skouzes explains elsewhere why his stepmother left his father's house. Apart from not having borne his father any children, she was from a 'lower family' (*katoteri ikoyenia*) and none of his father's family had been keen on the match. Indeed there had been a long history of conflict between the father and his kin over this second marriage. When Skouzes' mother had died and his father had indicated his intention to remarry, his brothers had insisted that a record be drawn up in front of the elders of the community and of kinsmen (the deceased mother's father), listing all the deceased woman's property and based upon the matrimonial contract. The intention was to ensure that this maternal property, brought to the marriage as a dowry, devolve upon the children of the first marriage, for there was the risk that it might be dissipated or that it might be transmitted to the future issue of the second marriage: 'these things [household goods and costume] were then given to my Uncle [father's brother, Ierotheos] to keep on behalf of the orphans. Ierotheos also asked for my mother's land [also brought to the marriage as dowry], and my father objected saying: "If you are even taking all this land, then take the children too." Thus they left these lands to my father' (Skouzes, 1975; 113–16).

Of interest here are a number of features which bring together various points made so far: dower must be paid by a man's kin to a widow who has not borne any children; there is a desire to remove this woman from the deceased father's house, which can only be effected if the dower is paid; a man's second marriage is objected to by his male kin both because the bride is from a lower social group and because of the risks it may entail for the future inheritance prospects of the children; the widower's brother and his father-in-law join together to preserve these goods, primarily mobile items (clothing and household goods); and finally the widower considers that his wife's dowry constitutes 'all his property' and he objects to his brother's attempts to assume control over it even if it is for the sake of the orphaned children. Indeed he manages to retain control of his wife's dowry land perhaps because his children remain with him.

Cash and gender

We now wish to consider the relationship between cash and gender. Although cash was 'male dominated' in that it was men who gave or promised cash either as fathers, brothers, grooms or grooms' brothers, women were nevertheless its recipients either as daughters at marriage or as widows upon the dissolution of marriage. Yet why should this society have decided to give women cash rather than immoveable resources? More precisely why should cash have figured so prominently, especially among the higher social groups, as dowries (also accompanied by other resources, such as land), and even more so as dowers? Would land not have served such a purpose? Indeed, on one level land was a more secure resource as a dower.

Although purely pragmatic and economic reasons can be advanced to explain why dowers consisted of cash, we do not believe that they were the sole reasons and there were specific cultural reasons why the dower took this particular form. One reason, though certainly not the main one, is the desire by men to retain control over the residue of the parental estate in much the same way as *ancien régime 'lignages'* and contemporary North African kinship groups attempt to invest men with control over family property. As sisters, brides were certainly endowed with land but their claims to the residue of the parental estate subsequently took second place to their brothers. As we have seen, land settlements upon daughters at marriage were relatively modest. The aim appears to have been to endow a daughter with enough land to maintain a relatively modest lifestyle. Even among titled groups land took second place to cash endowments and to trousseaux which had a strong monetary value and component. Most women were expected not only to reside viri-patrilocally at marriage, but also to bring resources which would complement a husband's holdings and income, rather than substitute them. And although property held jointly by brothers was eventually divided, clearly the death of any one of them could never be predicted. Pledging a dower of immovable property implied that brothers held no permanent control over their holdings. A death of a married brother could thus activate a sudden claim on land which would be severely disruptive. It would also involve a complex series of realignments and reorganisation of work patterns, as well as potentially alienate land away from the kinship group. Cash, although a scarce resource, had the advantage of at least permitting the surviving brothers to reorganise their resources without interference from third parties; most importantly it enabled men to satisfy their obligations in a clean-cut, definite and immediate way.

A second reason, related to the first, is that the dower was most often paid when the husband predeceased a wife who had borne him no children. In a predominantly viri-patrilocal environment where outside or 'foreign' (*kseni*) women were primarily accepted through motherhood, childless widows were an embarrassment to agnatic sensibilities. As in the case of Dimitros Skouzes' widow the pressure was clearly to leave the household. A cash dower enabled her to be 'paid off' to leave the house. Cash dowers also enabled women to pursue a relatively untroubled semi-independent life in an urban context and was perhaps preferable to land, which required organisation and still left them dependent on others. Some widows doubtlessly were less fortunate and left with no dower.

In cases of separation dowers were often not paid and women who did not retain rights in their parental household were obliged to rely on their own wits to survive, as evidenced by the memoirs of Georghios Psilla, an early nineteenth-century minister: 'We had family problems and my mother was obliged to remove herself from our father's house and several times to reside in the rooms of the church [set aside to provide shelter to the poor and homeless]. Later through a decision of the Synod she separated from our father [*apo trapezi kai kitis*; literally, 'from the table and the bed'] and took up employment, taking care of an old man, a father of a Kotzabashas, Spiridonas Kapetanakis, and lived in his house . . .' (1974; 6). Of note in this example is that Psillas' mother did not appear to have retained rights in her parental household, once she married and moved to that of her husband. Legally separated but not divorced, she was not granted her dower (*progamiea dorea*).

A final reason has more to do with the symbolic associations of cash and trousseaux. Here we believe that the traditional anthropological distinctions between gifts and commodities, and between the private and public worlds, break down or at best have limited explanatory validity. Cash in early nineteenth-century Greek society had a number of associations and circulated between kin to a greater extent than in the wider economy. Kinship obligations were expressed in, and through cash, whereas other obligations such as, for example, those between sharecropping tenants and landowners were expressed through products, patronage and respect. Cash, which was essential to the process of commoditisation and was the commodity *par excellence*, was not a full commodity in this society because it mediated relations between kin to a greater extent than between unrelated free-acting agents in the society. It is therefore much closer to the anthropological notion of a gift than to commodity because of its manner of circulation, in spite of its formal properties.

Furthermore, the possession of cash in this society and its transfer to kin, especially women, indicates that one did not have to work, to sell one's labour in the market, or to dispose of one's resources, such as land, in order to obtain it. More precisely, it indicates that one possessed resources which were worked by others, which enabled men to acquire *nikokiris* status. A *nikokiris* was a man who had risen from humble origins and was concerned to distance himself socially from those origins. A whole range of meanings contained within the linguistic term express this opposition: an urban consumer, master of his own household (*niko*: household, *kirios*: master) whose womenfolk do not work for others, in contrast to a peasant life characterised by cashless, subsistence-oriented production where both the men and women of the household are obliged to work for others. Clearly *nikokirei* modelled themselves closely on the *arkhon* class who in turn differed only in degree from their Ottoman overlords; in time the *nikokiris* model of the family was to become widespread in Greek society.

The full significance of cash endowments cannot be fully understood unless trousseaux are taken into account. Cash and trousseau complemented each other in their flow and in their associated significances. Together they contributed to the manufacture of *nikokirei* identity as well as to a specific concept of the family. Traditional Athenian marriage involved a complex interplay of gifts and counter gifts in an exchange relationship between families. Individuals transacted as group, that is, as a family, expressing and achieving their individual identities within that context. Yet because the types of goods exchanged were diverse and the transactors (donors and recipients) were both men and women, it is important to examine the relationship between 'persons' and 'things' in greater detail. In this manner we could thus identify the relationship between things and persons in their gender-specific contexts and hence the components in the construction of personhood.

It has been established that women received goods at marriage primarily as members of specific status groups, and secondarily as daughters. While these goods were a necessary precondition to their marriages as representing their family groups and providing links with other groups, this was not a sufficient precondition to marriage. Apart from the dowers promised by their husbands, women also brought trousseaux which were essential for their married life. The goods women received as 'dowries' consisted of both modest amounts of immoveables and much larger amounts of moveables – consisting of cash. Immoveables – land and houses – were conceptually linked to males, especially in the top layers of society. Thus women's receipt of these goods was 'symbolic' in two senses. From a Western egalitarian perspective they can be seen as 'token' transfers to women permitting the men to retain control and ownership of these resources. Yet they were also symbolic in the sense that the receipt of these modest amounts of land (especially in their different forms – arable, olive groves, etc.) symbolised membership of a specific status group. This 'disinheritance' of women was accompanied by their receipt of large amounts of cash, often more economically significant than land. While donations or transfers of immoveables were conceptually embedded in group membership obligations, cash transfers were much more strategically manipulable and had more of the nuances of gifts. Although the amounts given were certainly linked to social group status, nevertheless the liquid, mobile, and totally transferrable characteristics of cash rendered it much closer to the notion of a gift from men to women. Wealthy men (as fathers and brothers) endowed women (as daughters and sisters) with cash dowries, necessary qualifications for marriage. Even more so the groom and his agnates endowed women (as wives and widows of their brothers) with the cash *progamiea dorea*, literally the pre-marriage gift. Cash was thus a valuable dominated by men, but funnelled by them to women.

In modern Greece, cash remains gender specific. Hirschon notes that it is 'seen as an integral aspect of masculine competence' (1989; 100). In Piraeus, husbands made over most of their wages to their wives, a situation paralleled in Malta as well as in Cairo (Watson, 1989) and doubtless other parts of the Mediterranean. Hirschon notes that 'a woman's economic role lay within the home' (Hirschon, 1989; 100), a particularly apt statement when it is recalled that Xenophon defined *oikonomia* as 'the art of household management', yet this was a text written to guide the behaviour of men rather than women.

Women, however, were not passive recipients of the system, recipients of goods and persons exchanged between groups. They too were heavily involved in the exchange system, and in the words of Marilyn Strathern, in the 'genderising of valuables' (1984; 166). For they endowed themselves, and were endowed by the womenfolk of their natal group, with trousseaux (costumes, costly lacework, linen, etc.), all goods which defined them as brides and as daughters rather than merely as heirs. The appearance of such goods in the matrimonial nexus transformed the structural fact of group membership, where individuals were identified as members of a collective, to the personalised individuation of women as brides and ultimately as wives and mothers. The production of trousseaux established relations of support and solidarity among women, in contrast to the divisive and differentiating exchange world of cash dominated by men. Yet in contrast to cash it was a valuable arranged by women as an expression of individuality, collective discreteness and personal incommensurability. Trousseaux enabled women as individuals to give a specific expression to their femininity, distinguished them collectively from men, and enabled them to assume their roles as brides, wives and mothers within the differentiating bond of marriage. Trousseaux can also be seen as women's response to men's domination of cash. For the 'subversive stitch' also contributed to the production of wealth in a material sense. Costumes, lace and linen were costly items in their own right which could be given a price and sold, although their sale was not surprisingly, vigorously resisted due to these important symbolic associations.

Goods given and received at marriage thus had a specific gender valuation and identity. The situation would be analytically simple if we could identify those resources that were male dominated as commodities and those that were female dominated as gifts, as seems to occur in a number of societies. But what renders analysis even more complex is the fact that these valuables could function both as gifts and commodities. Cash, which was male dominated, achieved its fullest significance not through its deployment in capitalist enterprise, in production for production's sake, but in expressing kinship obligations and in the establishment of a new conjugal unit. Cash was also rare enough in an imperfectly monetised society to have the symbolic nuances of a gift, and it was given by men to women. Because it was often hoarded, saved for a rainy day, when given it retained, like gifts, the 'spirit' of the giver. It was associated with consumption and a lifestyle characterised by the absence of the need to work outside the home for others. Yet because of its inherent liquid nature it could be disposed of more easily than land by independent-minded husbands, leaving daughters without security – a source of increasing disquiet to those groups who had invested most heavily in cash for the endowment of daughters, as the society became progressively monetised.

Conversely, trousseaux represented and embodied the productive use of time by wives and daughters which the possession of cash permitted. A *nikokira* was a mistress of her own household because she was a mistress of her own time. And it was time spent not in directly productive activity outside the home (such as agricultural work, which could be risky for the family's honour), but in the production of good. which embodied and glorified the use of leisure time in the seclusion and safety of the home. From that a whole set of associated meanings emerge: the connection between the production of textiles in the home with restrained sexuality, as encouraged by Christianity (Schneider, 1980). Similar processes appear to have occurred in other parts of Southern Europe (for example Sicily). In exploring the role of textiles as trousseaux in Western Sicily, Jane Schneider excavates the normative message conveyed by the term *casalinga*, a message which could equally be conveyed by the term *nikokira*: 'a housewife who "loves to stay in the house, living in the bosom of her own family, occupying herself with domestic affairs, with the education of children, seeking refuge from rowdy entertainment"' (1980; 338).

Similar views were expressed in texts which began circulating in early nineteenth-century Athens, initially through translations of foreign (often French) books, and later in Greek contributions. Kitromilides has summarised the dominant model proposed in these texts for women's expected behaviour: 'the woman ought to avoid the "illustrious" virtues and confine herself to the simple and peaceful ones which compose the cycle of modesty. She should be reserved and avoid laughter and noisy company. She should guard against vanity and limit her natural curiosity to decent and proper subjects' (1983; 48).

These are models of behaviour which can find their fullest expression in urban contexts, and which are oriented towards self-control, the interiorisation of norms, and an increasing separation of the public and private domains with gender-specific spaces to enable the fullest expression of the 'inherent natures' of men and women. Such models increasingly came to influence behaviour and gender construction in Greece. Perhaps nowhere more clearly was this brought out than in the concentration on trousseaux as the symbol and physical embodiment of virtue, and carried over in the education of girls at school whose purpose, in the words of a popular journal of the time, was 'to educate girls as virgins, mothers and wives' (Efimeris ton Kirion, A20. 19/7/1887).

In the metropolitan urban context the management and manipulation of time is even more closely linked to gender roles, to virtue and honour. Married women's time has to be fully occupied in domestic chores; indeed 'free time' has to be stolen surreptitiously from work seen as 'obligation' (Hirschon, 1989; 144), whereas men's time is spent, and visibly so, in the *cafeneion* (coffee shop). The locus for the expression of female virtue has also shifted. In traditional Athens virtue was primarily demonstrated prior to marriage in the production of trousseaux, for a woman's virtue was intimately linked to her natal family as a daughter. At marriage her movement to a viri-patrilocal context ensured that her virtue was closely monitored and controlled by the other women in the household. In the modern context, by contrast, with neolocality or uxorilocality, virtue as a wife and mother is proved to neighbours and non-kin primarily within the marriage through effective household management, especially in labour-intensive cooking and food preparation (Hirschon, 1989; 151).

Yet trousseaux were also the embodiment of wealth and the expression of leisure. Although they were intimately tied-up in the manufacture of women's identity, and although their sale on the market implied an abdication from the roles of bride, wife, and mother, nevertheless they were also commodities. They could be bought and sold in the market and increasingly became evaluated in monetary terms as the society became progressively monetised.

Here a distinction formulated by M. Strathern for the symbolism of valuables in exchanges may be useful. She draws a distinction between the metaphoric and metonymic symbolism of valuables. In the former, 'wealth or assets . . . stand for an aspect of intrinsic identity, for agnatic status or "name" for example. They cannot be disposed of or with-drawn from the exchange system without compromising that identity' (1984; 165). Within that class of goods we can locate land and houses for men and trousseaux for women. In metonymic symbolisation, by con-trast, 'people exercise proprietorship to the extent that they have per-sonal rights of disposal' (*ibid.*; 165). Within this class we can locate cash gifts as dowries and the *programiea dorea*. Yet the equation only applies up to a point. For the metaphoric identities of valuables in early nineteenth-century Greece (land, houses and trousseaux) were pro-gressively subverted. Land ceased to have a strong linkage with men, houses were increasingly given to daughters, and trousseaux became increasingly commoditised, losing in the process that essential role in the manufacturing of female identity. They became increasingly 'metonymic' in their symbolism – in Strathern's words 'although dispos-able they are not "alienable" in the way that commodities are alienable' (*ibid.*; 165). What we are suggesting here is not that dowries are not alienable as commodities in modern Greece; indeed they clearly are. Rather the sentiments and symbolism associated with dowries encour-ages their separation from the rest of commoditisable goods. Disembed-ded from the complex interchange of gifts and counter gifts which were symbols of group membership in the traditional system, dowries now symbolise the ability to attract a suitable groom rather than reinforce the complex ties between family groups. Furthermore, the progressive and cumulative intervention of the state on legislation and the evolution of a monetised economy has contributed to the notion of the dowry as the activation of a pre-mortem inheritance right for daughters as daughters. Dowries reduced to a cash estimation derive their symbolism from their monetary value, not from the symbolic nuances of their various goods, and have to be protected from a groom's potential depredations.

Conversely the metonymic symbolisation of valuables such as cash has become progressively 'metaphorical'. Cash has become an aspect of the 'intrinsic identity' of a family's worth which cannot be 'withdrawn from the exchange system [the dowry] without compromising that iden-tity'. As Strathern has observed 'the same valuables may operate as now one type, and now the other' (*ibid.*; 165). Table 21 summarises the complex interplay of valuables.

The relationship between cash and trousseaux was not static across time. While the two coexisted they appear in inverse proportion to each other across time. In the early part of the late eighteenth century trousseaux appeared as more important; by the early 1830s trousseaux had begun to decline in importance and a new standardised bridal costume was beginning to replace the hierarchical organisation of dress. Conversely, cash endowments increased in importance and the dowry became even more monetised and mobile. In the next section we discuss changes to trousseaux and bridal costumes across time.

Trousseaux as social stratification

As marriage required a cash dower of men in eighteenth-century Athens, it required a trousseau of women. As in other parts of Southern Europe, such as Southern Italy (Davis, 1973), Sicily (Schneider, 1980) and Spain, Athenian women could marry without land, cash, animals or a house, but a trousseau was an absolute necessity to qualify her as a bride. In late nineteenth-century Dimitsana Kalpourtzi's figures indicate that 98% of all brides received a trousseau (1987; 91).

Whereas in the previous section we examined the trousseau within its wider context as a member of the class of moveables, we now examine it in greater detail from a number of perspectives. We begin by discussing the role of trousseaux (and especially of bridal costumes) as markers of social differentiation not only in content but also in their transmission patterns. We then explore the trousseau's monetary significance and its symbolic value. By analysing the trousseau we suggest that rather than adopting the public–private division of gender and social space, the distinction between formal–informal is more suitable for understanding. Athenian society of the eighteenth and early nineteenth centuries. We then discuss how a growing homogenisation of national culture in the nation-state, shaped mainly by the *nikokirei* group, was reflected in the adoption of a new style of bridal costume which became universal in Athens. The model of kinship, the family and of marriage itself became increasingly standardised in the new Greek kingdom, receiving its imprint from the urban Athenian *nikokirei* group. Finally, we conclude by discussing Jane Schneider's characterisation of trousseau as 'treasure' (1980) and suggest some modifications to her thesis.

An indication of the importance of the trousseau is provided by the structure of the contracts themselves. Inevitably, the trousseau heads the list of the bride's goods, and this is followed by the dower, as if once having set the scene by specifying what type of bride was being married

Table 21. *Features of cash and trousseaux in matrimonial exchanges*

	Immoveables	Moveables		
	Land and houses	Cash		Trousseaux
		Dowry	Progamiea Dorea	
		Men to women		
Given by	(Land): Parents collectively (Houses): Father primarily (especially in top strata) Mothers (in lower strata)	F, B to D, Z	H to W HB to HW	Supplied by women themselves and purchased among top strata Supplied by women themselves and by grooms in lower strata
Claimed by	(Houses): Sons majority (Land): Major part by sons Minor part by daughters	Daughters/sisters as 'right' expressed as a 'gift'	Men on behalf of their women folk as their 'right'. Women on their behalf as their 'right'	Daughters as their 'right' as women to get married

Represented by/as	(Houses/land): Sons at death of father. Men carriers of 'family name' in public domain	'Gift' as sign of group membership	'Right' as sign of alliance	
Obtained by/through	(Houses): Inheritance (Land): Inheritance and purchase	Men through participation in wider society	Men/women from men	Women's labour
Possession signifies	(Houses): Lineal family identity (Land): Membership of status group (sons)	Leisure, non-manual work, consumption, mastership of one's own household, seclusion of women		Membership of a specific social group rather than family identity
Symbolism	(Land): Membership of family group (daughters) (Houses): Metaphoric (for men)	Metonymic (for fathers) Metaphoric (for daughters)	Mainly metaphoric; metonymic in extreme cases	

B = brother, D = daughter, F = father, H = husband, W = wife, Z = sister, FB = father's brother, DZ = daughter's sister, etc.

it was necessary to indicate immediately afterwards how the groom's family responded. As we shall demonstrate, this counterposing was natural; a trousseau demonstrated status as well as wealth, and required a counter demonstration of the groom's equal status.

The Athenian trousseau (*prikia*) consisted of two distinct sets of items: the bride's clothing and items of personal decoration (*rouha*), and household goods and furnishings (*prikia*). During the eighteenth and early nineteenth centuries the former was more important than the latter. While the contracts devote a great deal of attention to the clothing brought by the bride, specifying them in great detail, household furnishings when referred to, are not given the painstaking attention of the former. The contrast with modern Greece and other Southern European societies is striking. For these societies appear to give more detail to household furnishings such as furniture, linen, sheets, blankets, kitchen utensils and the like,[1] than to the bride's dresses and clothing. We do not believe that this is due to a lack of such goods, or to poverty, for costly dowries were involved; nor necessarily to a correlation with agricultural or non-agricultural incomes as Skouteri-Didaskalou suggests (1984). The difference between the two is not as slight as might be supposed. Eighteenth-century Athenian trousseaux emphasised the bride's status, and ultimately her origins; modern and contemporary trousseaux emphasise the household's wealth. Why should this be so? Four reasons can be advanced. First, an emphasis on clothing is consistent with a society which gives great importance to status and permanent hierarchies. Second, a de-emphasis on household furnishings can be attributable to a pattern of co-residence. Athenian brides did not bring many household articles with them because many expected to reside viri-patrilocally, rather than neo-locally. Third, in many Western European societies the trousseau as household furnishings constituted the legitimate share of a daughter's patrimony (the so-called *legittima*), leaving the sons to inherit the bulk of the immoveable property. Fourth, there are practical and symbolic reasons specific to Ottoman Greece: on the practical level clothing was not a taxable item and was eminently portable. In times of crises clothing was more easily and compactly bundled and transported than were diverse and cumbersome household goods.

A fifth and final reason has to do with the arrangement of space and the organisation of household activities. If Athenian houses of the early 1800s bear any similarity to houses in the provinces in the mid-nineteenth century, it is likely that furniture was relatively scarce and rooms were not functionally specific. In other words, a lack of furniture enabled people to use rooms in a more flexible manner, for example in various sleeping patterns (Pavlides and Hesser, 1986). This phenomenon is consistent with other areas of the Mediterranean. In the contemporary Djerid, Tunisia, poor people do not traditionally sleep in specifically designated rooms, but adapt to the changing seasons. The same authors also introduce a distinction for the use of space in mid-nineteenth century Eressos, Lesbos, between the formal and the informal. We find this concept more useful in highlighting the basic principles for the organisation of space and gender in eighteenth- and nineteenth-century Athens than the more anthropologically popular concept of public and private which we believe is a relatively recent phenomenon.

In one sense the transfer of a trousseau made a marriage, conferring social and familial legitimacy to a new matrimonial alliance. The accumulation of the goods over many years – their estimation and final transfer to the bride's new residence – involved a wide network of kin and affines. Indeed the monetary evaluation of the trousseau and its transfer to the bride's new household were an essential part of the matrimonial preparations, ceremony and celebrations much as the passage of *kiswah* goods in North Africa marks the social recognition of a marriage. In this sense marriage was not only marked by the signing of the *prikosymfono* and the religious ceremony, but also by the public estimation and passage of such goods from one household to another.

The marriage celebrations consisted of a number of discreet events which together made a marriage a social event involving the wider society. Indeed the church ceremony (the *stefanosi*), while certainly important, constituted only a small part of the celebrations. Athenian marriage linked family groups together in public statements of alliance; it was not confined to the vows of the ultimate rationale of a church ceremony. Once the match had been agreed the *ksofili* (temporary agreement and statement of intent) was signed by the two male family heads. This was normally a confidential agreement between the parties concerned and was similar to the Tuscan *scritta*. Sometimes a considerable period elapsed between the signing of the *ksofili* and the signing of the *prikosymfono* (dowry agreement), either because the betrothed were especially young or because the dowry had yet to be amassed. The marriage celebrations, however, were initiated by two public events: the signing of the *prikosymfono* and the display of the bride's trousseau at her home. Three days before the church ceremony the notary evaluated the bride's dowry, checking that the items listed in the *ksofili* were indeed being given to the daughter. This was a public affair, and the priest, the fathers of the bride and groom (or their closest male relatives if the fathers were dead), the godfather, the groom and three witnesses were present. This was certainly a male affair and denoted that the alliance was sanctioned and witnessed by the wider society. Significantly the bride herself did not appear in this ceremony, a situation paralleled in Renaissance Tuscany (Klapisch-Zuber, 1985; 187) and contemporary Tunisia (Sant Cassia, 1986b). By contrast, the display of the trousseau at the bride's home was a female affair. The goods were displayed with care and artistry in the antechamber of her natal home, and included the groom's presents. The display of the trousseau testified to the bride's industry and virtue and the value placed by the groom's family on the alliance.

On the Saturday the bride's trousseau was transported by the bride's female kin to the groom's house, often accompanied by musicians. This was the most boisterous event in the marriage celebrations; like the North African *kiswah* procession it demonstrated to the community that the marriage and its consummation was imminent. On that day, too, the bride together with her friends visited the baths, the expenses being paid for by the groom.[2] Should we see this as a symbolic expression of the 'Griselda complex' where the groom clothes his bride? Perhaps; certainly it symbolises the new responsibility of the groom towards his bride. From this point on the groom would assume the responsibility for her presentation in society from her father and her male kin. His honour was intimately tied to her new role as his bride.

The following day the bride and groom proceeded from the church liturgy to the groom's house. Yet even at this point the procession emphasised the separation of bride and groom and their enclosure in respective kin groups. The bride came first, supported by two female kin and followed by the groom in the rear. In the Peloponnese, Wyse observed that the wedding procession was heralded by muskets let off by the bride's male kin; she appeared 'with a strong escort of fustinella friends, all armed. She was mounted, cavalier-fashion, on a strong horse, and carried before her, at the saddle-bow, a gigantic circular loaf' (1865; 280). In Athens by contrast, the bride was presented with a loaf of bread by the groom's female kin which she then proceeded to divide, as in the Peloponnese, among those present.

Leaving aside these differences, the symbolism is clear. While the formal alliance was initiated and publicly initialled by men, the alliance still involved two separate kin groups as yet unratified. Both ratification and the practical and symbolic expression of the union were dependent upon the involvement and cooperation of the women. It was the female kin of the groom who welcomed the bride into her new household; significantly, it was they who greeted her on the threshold. The presentation of bread, a sacred food (Hirschon, 1989; Campbell, 1964), signified commensality, common household tasks, and its division among those present indicated that it was through the participation of women that the household could offer hospitality to guests. It was the participation of the women which completed this rite of integration. And by most accounts the presentation and the celebrations were a serious and formal event. Wyse observed that 'the whole was conducted with imperturbable gravity and sobriety, provoking no unrestrained laughter, wild antics, or other explosions of mirth, such as might be looked for on so exciting an occasion' (1865; 280).

Although there were significant differences in the monetary value of trousseaux and in the nature of the goods which a trousseau might comprise, trousseaux differed also in their manner of provenance. Among the wealthy and titled families of the *nikokirei* and *arkhon* classes, and among all native Athenian families, the trousseau was provided by the bride's parents (and to a lesser extent by kin), by the labour assistance of adopted or fostered girls in the household, and by the bride herself through her industry and labour. By contrast, among villagers settled in Athens the trousseau supplied by the bride was rarely purchased and a considerable portion of the bride's trousseau was provided not by her natal family but by the groom and his kin. While the bride gave her groom a Fustanella (the 'Albanian skirt'), he gave her jewellery. These may have served the function of love gifts. The trousseau thus travelled both laterally and vertically as an 'indirect dowry' or 'brideprice' from the groom to the bride via her parents. Such practices, which exist in contemporary North Africa and in Northern Greece, are consistent with agropastoralism and are associated with *de facto* agnatic control over critical resources such as land and flocks.[3] Non-Athenian brides also tended to receive items of personal decoration (jewellery, necklaces and rings, though of a lower quality) to a greater extent than Athenian-born brides (table 2). They also received smaller cash endowments from their parents (table 3), and their spouses, some of whom were grooms of village origin, tended to promise cash dowers to a lesser extent than did Athenian-born grooms. Nearly 10 per cent of these grooms did not promise a dower versus the 2.2 per cent of Athenian-born grooms who did not pledge a dower. The dowers of country girls were also relatively small. The maximum was 301 groshia, with the mean at 96 groshia and the standard deviation (STD) at 58 groshia (calculating the dower as an average of all country brides, including the 9.1 per cent who did not receive a dower).

Thus the trousseau of a non-Athenian bride was heavily weighted towards jewellery rather than clothing, and was in effect a type of substitute for a cash endowment. The value of jewellery purchased by the groom for the bride could always be realised through sale, and in contrast to the *trahoma* (the bride's cash endowment), which remained with the groom in the event of the dissolution of the marriage, this was a gift from the groom which could not be reclaimed. It was thus a measure of security for the bride. Significantly, this jewellery consisted of a number of items which individually held relatively low monetary value.

For the majority of Athenian brides, however, the trousseau consisted of items of clothing of all sorts. We therefore examine the significance of costume and the role of clothing as markers of social classes.

Late eighteenth- and early nineteenth-century Athens offers a remarkable opportunity to observe how an outpost of the Ottoman Empire, admittedly with strong Occidental links, eventually became incorporated in the European sphere of influence with the establishment of an independent Greek kingdom. Clothing patterns both symbolised and spearheaded this change. Speaking of clothes and fashion, Braudel draws a distinction between those relatively stable social orders such as China and Islam where 'everything stayed put' (1974; 227) and where 'no changes took place ... except as a result of political upheavals which affected the whole social order', with Western societies heavily involved in the use of fashion as an internal political strategy between social groups: 'the future belonged to societies which were trifling enough, but also rich and inventive enough to bother about changing colours, material and styles of costume, and also the division of the social classes and the map of the world' (*ibid.*; 235–6).

To what extent did this 'future' belong to Greece and Athens of the eighteenth century? The answer must be that this future was already present in Athens, in an embryonic form. Whereas the seventeenth and early eighteenth centuries demonstrate a fixed and hierarchical Ottoman-imposed system of stratification, by the late eighteenth century Athens possessed a more flexible, mobile and complex social structure. Although clothing indicated social status and regional origin, as in any hierarchical pre-industrial agrarian based society, distinctions between different types of costumes were becoming dim. Our contracts indicate that three distinct types of clothing were in use in Athens, each closely but not exclusively associated with a particular social group. We have labelled these costumes Types A, B, C; a fourth, which we call Type 'D' will be discussed later. Type 'A' was worn mainly by non-titled native Athenians, Type 'B' was worn by villagers settled in Athens, and Type 'C' was worn by titled families and the upwardly mobile bourgeoisie. We have here a city-society which distinguished itself internally between those who wore costumes of the wealthy and titled and the rest, and externally between native Athenians and recent migrants to the town.

These costumes also indicated a woman's position in the social development cycle. Costumes were worn on major occasions such as Easter, Epiphany (*Phota*), religious feasts and for the first years after marriage. Significantly, for most social groups they tended to be put away and worn less frequently when the bride had become a mother, indicating that motherhood eventually subsumed other roles derived from civil society. This was particularly pronounced among townswomen but was less common among countrywomen, reflecting a different emphasis placed on motherhood and its presentation.

Large amounts of clothing accompanied brides of all social classes at marriage. The following is a typical endowment of a non-titled bride; it is an ensemble of specific items of clothing which made up the Type 'A' costume:

> 5–30 long shirts of linen or silk (*vrakopoukamisa*)
> 5–10 long undergarments
> 5–10 long coats (*tzoubedes*) embellished with ermine for the summer and fur for the winter
> 1–2 headdresses (*fezes*)
> 1 veil (*feretzes*)
> 5–10 headkerchiefs
> 3–5 belts (cloth)
> belts, slippers and stockings

The copious amount of clothing indicates that brides did not likely supply all their clothing through their own labour; assistance from mothers and other female kin was probably received. Among the wealthy and titled families who endowed brides with larger amounts of clothing whose preparation was also more labour intensive, it is likely that clothing had been commissioned in part mainly from women from lower-status families, and through the labour of adopted or fostered daughters. Textiles in Ottoman Europe were important trade items and domestic embroideries such as kerchiefs, towels, tablecloths, pillow cases and embroidered shirts were products of cottage industry (Gervers, 1982; 7). By the 1840s such goods had already begun to be purchased from overseas, and especially from Europe, the source of new models for the Athenian elite. Liata (1984; 87) cites a case of a merchant purchasing clothing for his niece from Marseilles and Venice.

The frequency of items of clothing and jewellery among the various social groups is outlined in table 22. Some items were particularly associated with certain social strata (such as the silk *anteri* with titled families), and the *grizos*, a plain rough cotton dress, associated with migrant villagers. Such brides wore this dress externally, whereas the

Table 22. *Incidence of items of clothing and jewellery transferred with different types of costumes (1688–1834)*

	Costume type, in per cent		
	Type 'A' (worn mainly by untitled Athenians)	Type 'B' (worn mainly by villagers settled in Athenian suburbs)	Type 'C' (worn mainly by titled families and the upwardly mobile bourgeoisie)
	(total number: 475)	(total number: 74)	(total number: 93)
Clothing			
Vest *(anteri)*	0	0	100.0
Coat *(grizos)*	0	83.8	0
Short waistcoat *(zipouni)*	0	98.7	0
Longvest *(zipouni)*	91.8	0	0
Belt *(zostra)*	59.8	77.0	75.3
Sigouna	0	100.0	0
Headkerchief *(kefalomandila)*	90.0	94.6	95.7
Coat *(tzoubes)*	66.0	0	76.3
Plain blouse *(poukamisa)*	0	100.0	0
Blouse decorated with breeches and lace *(vrakopoukamisa)*	100.0	0	100.0
Veil *(ferethe)*	67.2	0	89.2
Fez hat *(fezi)*	86.7	0	89.2
Jewellery			
Necklace *(yiordani)* with pearls	10.5	0	39.8
Necklace *(yiordani)* with beads	0	32.4	0
Ring *(dachtilidi)*	9.0	79.7	16.1
Necklace *(kordoni)*	0.6	40.5	1.1
Metal bell *(louri)*	55.4	0	56.9
Bracelets *(belerikia)*	2.3	70.3	20.4
Head decoration *(kapoutsali)*	39.6	0	11.8
Pearls	16.2	0	18.3
Earrings *(skoularikia)*	55.8	41.9	67.7
Head decoration *(tepeliki)*	1.7	0	12.9

Bada (1983) conducted independent historical research on costume transfers; the figures here include data drawn from our contracts.

anteri, its equivalent among the titled families, was always worn under another dress, usually a type of coat (*tzoubes*) which was heavily decorated with coins and professionally embroidered. Undergarments were also a distinguishing feature. It appears that they were common among urban brides but not among women originating from the countryside, a point generally explored by Schneider (1980) for Sicily and Northern Europe. The veil (*feretze*) was another feature of urban life, as were hats, a clear indication if ever one was needed, that urban families secluded their womenfolk, at least symbolically, as a means of maintaining prestige. In 1749 Charlemont commented on the differences between the Aegean islanders, whose womenfolk seemed much 'freer', and the Athenians: 'at Athens in particular, whether from an imitation of the Turks, or, as I am rather inclined to believe from a more perfect retention of ancient manners, the women are very reserved. Girls are never seen till married, not even at Church . . . They are seldom met in the streets and go very little abroad' (Stanford and Finopoulos, 1984; 126). But while both Greek and Turkish women were veiled and generally secluded at least among the wealthy classes in the late eighteenth century, by 1821 the veil had disappeared among the Greeks. So complete was its disappearance by the mid to late nineteenth century in a climate of national identity construction that the *feretze* began to be associated with such concepts as Turkish 'barbarism'.

Table 22 also indicates that rural brides generally received jewellery at marriage to a greater extent than did other brides; necklaces, rings and bracelets were customary among brides of rural origin, whereas pearls and earrings were more common among urban and titled brides. Furthermore, brides of rural origin tended to receive jewellery which was of lower value, such as silver rather than gold.

Social differences thus tended to manifest themselves in types of clothing and jewellery and their relative value, their manner of wear, their provenance, and their numbers. Wealthy brides received more numerous, higher quality, and more varied goods than did rural brides, such goods travelling vertically rather than laterally. The wealthy also wore more layers of clothing, which was often heavily embroidered. As in Sicily, embroidery was associated with seclusion and high status (Schneider, 1980) yet the extent of embroidery involved could hardly have been supplied by brides through their own labour and must have represented the pooling of labour or the use of cash for purchase.

At this stage it is worthwhile to move away from formal markers of group membership and social status (such as titles) and concentrate on claims to social status. The endowment and wearing of costume represented not so much a bride's social origins as her matrimonial destination. In most cases this did not involve a radical departure from social origins. Nevertheless costume types, although closely identified with specific social groups, were not identical. The endowment of a bride with a specific costume was the end result of a complex process of negotiation and renegotiation of status between the two affinal groups. As brides were in most cases incorporated in their husband's households, the presentation of the bride in public was the culmination of a process of status negotiation.

By status in this context we mean not just the relationship between titles and the transmission of resources, but the way in which these were socially estimated, and the histories, aims, and strategies of the groups involved. We are interested here in the social manipulation and presentation of the transmission of resources within the context of matrimonial politics. Marriage in Athens was not only the manifestation of social status but its creation and transformation across time, through alliances between family groups. Some families could move upwards by a careful marshalling of resources while others slid down the social ladder. Thus while Type 'A' costumes for example were mainly worn by non-titled Athenian brides, 10.4 per cent of all brides wearing this costume came from titled families. Clearly these marriages were hypogamous on one level, in terms of claims to status. Conversely Type 'C' costumes were worn by brides of both titled families and wealthy non-titled ones who had managed to marry hypergamously and successfully claim elite status through the endowment of the bride with a suitable costume.

Table 23 recasts some of our data to reflect the Athenian presentation of the connection between status claimed and accepted, as manifested in costume, and resource transmission.

Some explanation of the tables may be helpful. Table 23 groups together various resources which accompanied brides at marriage; these brides are, however, classified according to the costume they wore at marriage (A–C), rather than by their titles (which are dealt with in tables 10, 11, 13, 17). Thus rather than merely dividing brides into two categories (titled/non-titled), brides are divided into the three costume categories associated with different criteria (the fourth, costume Type D, is a new post-1830 costume which we discuss below). The brides wearing the costumes traditionally associated with wealthy and titled families were even more unlikely to be endowed with animals (96.2 per cent, table 23) than brides referred to as titled in the contracts (87.3 per cent, table 11), an indication that these families aspiring to an elite lifestyle were even more unlikely to endow their daughters with animals, a case of being *plus royaliste que le roi*. By contrast migrant brides were particularly likely to receive livestock in contrast to Athenian natives (57.6 per cent versus 7.6 per cent, table 23) and to receive fields.[4]

Conversely 12.8 per cent of brides wearing the wealthy or titled costume (Type C) did not receive olive trees (table 23) whereas only 2.8 per cent of brides who were actually titled (in the contracts) did not receive olive trees (table 13). Those actually titled were also likely to receive larger amounts (25 per cent received over 161 trees, table 13), whereas only 10.2 per cent of those with claims to belong to this social group received over 161 olive trees (table 23). Thus a number of brides were presented in society as members of an elite group but did not receive the olive tree which was so strongly associated with the core of this elite group. Olive trees were particularly unlikely among migrant brides (42.4 per cent did not receive any olive trees at all, versus the 17 per cent of ordinary untitled Athenians wearing costume Type A).

Although the differences we are dealing with may appear slight, they do enable us to pursue a more complex understanding of the dynamics of Athenian society. They permit identification of those resources which were associated socially with particular groups, costume being a more subtle indicator of constructed and manipulated social differences than the largely transmitted differences of titles. Thus animals and land were largely the resources transmitted to migrant brides, and the possession of animals was a positive liability to qualify for elite status. Olives were the preserve of native Athenians but brides could be accepted as belonging to the elite even if they possessed less olive trees than titled brides. Far fewer differences in cash were permissible to qualify for elite status. In other words, the possession and transmission of cash dowries to daughters was the single most distinguishing feature of elite brides (wearing costume Type C). In time this was to become even more important in Athens and ultimately a source of particular tensions within matrimonial culture. There are basically no differences between the percentages of titled brides receiving cash endowments and the larger group of brides wearing elite costumes (33.4 per cent vs 34.6 per cent, tables 17, 19). Although titled brides tended to receive larger cash endowments than elite-costume brides, the difference between the latter and ordinary Athenians was far more substantial (table 23).

The same pattern is exhibited when dowers are examined. Table 24 breaks down the dowers promised to brides wearing different costumes; these brides are further differentiated by titles. There were major differences in the dowers promised. Grooms marrying migrant brides (costume Type B) were the most unlikely to promise a dower (9.1 per cent, table 24) mainly because they themselves were of similar origins (tables 16, 19). The brides most likely to be pledged a higher dower were titled brides wearing the elite costume Type C (57.7 per cent were pledged a dower of over 500 groshia), followed by non-titled brides wearing the same costume Type C (19.2 per cent were pledged a dower of over 500 groshia). The latter and titled brides wearing the ordinary Athenian costume Type A tended to merge together as far as high dowers were concerned.

The data in tables 22–24 give little insight into the monetary and symbolic significance of the trousseau. Costumes very clearly represented embodied wealth, as evidenced by the Church's encyclicals on the dowry, which devoted much attention to the detail and materials used. The matrimonial contracts indicate that close interest was also expressed

Table 23. *Transmission of resources to brides according to costume type*

Cash endowments	0	1–100	101–200	201–300	Groshia 301–400	401–500	501–600	Over 600	Total
Costume A									
Number	142	56	55	42	22	15	9	12	353
Percentage	40.2	15.9	16.6	11.9	6.2	4.2	2.5	3.4	67.5
Costume B									
Number	25	26	10	3	1	1			66
Percentage	37.9	39.4	15.2	4.5	1.5	1.5			12.6
Costume C									
Number	27	8	9	8	4	4	3	13	78
Percentage	34.6	10.3	11.5	10.3	5.1	5.1	3.8	19.2	14.9
Costume D									
Number	13	1	3	4		1		4	26
Percentage	50.0	3.8	11.5	15.4		3.8		15.4	5.0
Total									
Number	207	91	77	57	27	21	12	31	523
Percentage	39.6	17.4	14.7	10.9	5.2	4.0	2.3	5.9	100.0

Fields

	0	1–5 stremmata	6–10 stremmata	11–15 stremmata	16–20 stremmata	21–25 stremmata	Over 25 stremmata	Total
Costume A Percentage	54.7	37.4	4.8	1.1	0.8	0.3	0.8	67.5
Costume B Percentage	28.8	25.8	16.7	10.6	9.1	6.1	3.0	12.6
Costume C Percentage	64.1	24.4	7.7	2.6	1.3			14.9
Costume D Percentage	52.6	33.3	7.1	2.9	2.1	1.0	1.5	100.1
(Total excluded)								

Olive trees

	0	1–40	41–80	81–120	121–160	161–200	Over 200	Total
Costume A Percentage	17.0	43.6	26.1	9.3	1.7	1.1	1.1	67.5
Costume B Percentage	42.5	56.1	1.5					12.6
Costume C Percentage	12.8	23.1	32.1	15.4	16.4	5.1	5.1	14.9
Costume D Percentage	11.5	53.8	19.2	7.7	7.7			5.0
Total percentage	19.3	42.6	23.5	9.0	1.5	1.5	1.5	100.0

Animals

	0	1–10	11–20	21–30	31–40	Over 40	Total
Costume A Percentage	92.4	2.5	4.0	0.6	0.3	0.3	67.5
Costume B Percentage	42.4	43.9	4.5	1.5	3.0	4.5	12.6
Costume C Percentage	96.2			2.6	3.0	1.3	14.9
Costume D Percentage	100.0						5.0
Total percentage	87.0	7.3	3.3	1.0	0.6	1.0	100.0

Costume A = Untitled Athenians; Costume B = Villagers; Costume C = Wealthy titled families; Costume D = New Athenians.

Table 24. Cash dowers according to costume types worn by titled/untitled brides

		Groshia								
	0	1–100	101–200	201–300	301–400	401–500	501–600	Over 600	Row total
Costume A of untitled Athenians									
Number	6	21	134	81	39	39	12	11	316
Percentage	1.9	6.6	42.4	25.6	12.3	3.8	3.5	3.8	60.4
Costume A but worn by titled Athenians									
Number	0	5	13	6	5	1	5	2	37
Percentage	0	13.5	35.1	16.2	13.5	2.7	13.5	5.4	7.0
Costume B worn by untitled migrant villagers									
Number	6	17	39	2	2	0	0	0	66
Percentage	9.1	25.8	59.1	3.0	3.0	0	0	0	12.6
Costume C worn by wealthy but untitled Athenians									
Number	1	4	7	15	12	3	5	5	52
Percentage	1.9	7.7	13.5	28.8	23.1	5.8	9.6	9.6	9.9

Costume C worn by titled Athenians								
Number	0	0	4	0	5	2	5	10	26
Percentage	0	0	15.4	0	19.2	7.7	19.2	38.5	4.9
New Costume D worn by untitled Athenians								
Number	0	0	1	5	5	3	1	7	22
Percentage	0	0	4.5	22.7	22.7	13.6	4.5	31.8	4.2
Costume D worn by titled Athenians								
Number	0	0	0	0	0	0	1	3	4
Percentage	0	0	0	0	0	0	25.0	75.0	0.7
Column total								
Number	13	47	198	109	68	21	18	27	523
Percentage	2.4	8.9	37.8	20.8	13.0	4.0	3.4	5.1	100.0

'Titled brides' refers to brides who possessed a title ('Kir', 'Sior') within their immediate family (father, mother, or the bride herself).

by the transacting partners. In all contracts, but especially those involving Type C costumes worn by the wealthy and titled brides, great detail is devoted to the number and types of coins attached to the costumes. Many of these costumes bore coins of various origins, a clear indication of the primitive accumulation of cash and the multiplicity of currencies circulating in Athens. Such detail indicates a certain wariness among affines and a means to forestall tension, possibly because while cash endowments to the bride were often retained by the groom upon the dissolution of the marriage, the costume and dresses belonged to the bride. They were either transmitted to the orphaned children or to the deceased bride's kin if she died issueless, as occurred with Skouzes' mother.

Tension among affines in estimating the value of the trousseau was often resolved by the use of neutral third parties, a situation paralleled in Sicily through the use of the *stimatrice* (Schneider, 1980), a female valuer whose job was to give a monetary value to highly labour intensive and ornate works of embroidery and lace. In Athens, by contrast, value lay not only in labour input, but also in the actual coins embedded in the costumes themselves, and it was such costumes that received more attention in the contracts. A variety of currencies was then in circulation (including the Turkish piastre and the Spanish dollar, for example) and cash was in relatively short supply. Indeed 'in some parts of Greece money was not generally accepted [and] its use was restricted to some kinds of exchanges only' (Loules, 1985; 85). Clothing was thus a prime vehicle for the primitive accumulation of capital and equally important, for its display in a form which could hardly be realised except through its disintegration.

Costumes and jewellery thus represented and indeed embodied a considerable portion of the value of a bride's direct or indirect dowry. As in contemporary North Africa, coins and the clothing to which they were attached could be pawned as security against a loan. Even more significant were unforeseen crises. In 1787 during the tyrannical rule of Hadji Ali, Panayis Skouzes records that in order to save the lives of their husbands, womenfolk gave up their dowries: 'And they went weeping to the *arkhons* who told them, "Give whatever you have – everything – to save your husbands" . . . They sold their jewellery and their farmlands and paid up' (Andrews, 1979; 121–2). In more recent times a similar pattern appears to have been transmitted by Asia Minor island refugees who settled in the island of Amouliani in 1926 (Salamone and Stanton, 1986). The population had lost all their belongings in the Graeco-Turkish War and the land in their new island home was useless for agricultural purposes. Settlement was neolocal and a lack of employment opportunities meant that brides could not be supplied with cash dowries. The refugees responded to their new straitened circumstances by upgrading their traditional patterns of bride endowment: *rouha* (trousseaux and household furnishings) became the most important resource transmitted at marriage. In their original Marmaras island home and in Amouliani, *rouha* was carefully enumerated by the mother of the bride, and '. . . was often equal to or greater than the value of inherited property and capital' (*ibid.*; 109). Such ritual wealth 'considered as capital just as was land or gold, was sold by families, painfully, piece by piece, as they struggled to survive the years of exile during the Graeco-Turkish War (1919–1922)' (*ibid.*; 109). Similar patterns are likely to have occurred in Athens during the War of Independence.

The trousseau was considered capital in eighteenth- and early nineteenth-century Athens, but it was also highly symbolic. To reduce it to its capital functions would be to deny its highly emotive and social significance. The higher up the social scale, the greater was the tendency to restrict its realisation as productive capital. Coins were ultimately jewellery, constituting part of a costume designed to be worn and displayed and not put to productive use, nor to be exchanged for other goods except at the cost of the loss of prestige, and ultimately of social position. The trousseau was also an essential constituent of gender identity. While men derived their identity through their control of houses and land (and increasingly through cash), women's identities as daughters, brides and mothers were inextricably tied to the trousseau, which combined statements about social status and femininity. Pawning a costume literally implied the forfeiting of the most visible marker of social position. As in traditional African economies we are dealing with a multi-centric economy. The value of clothing and jewellery, which were increasingly linked as one moved higher up the social scale, were realised by being worn; more precisely they indicated the *timi* (monetary value and social estimation) placed by the donor (usually the bride's family) upon the recipient (the bride herself). Yet at the same time because it accompanied and marked the establishment of marriage, it was clearly a sign of the esteem with which the proposed match was held. If women gave up their trousseaux they lost that most visible marker of their *timi*, in both its monetary and virtuous senses. This rebounded back on to their husbands and menfolk. It is significant that Skouzes' account links both money and virtue in a scenario likely to strike his readers as the nadir in moral and political degradation brought about by Turkish rule. For the womenfolk who are 'manless' and 'protectorless' have to give up their trousseaux to save their menfolk whose role it was to protect them, thus reversing the moral order.

Jane Schneider (1980) has aptly described the significance of the trousseau as 'treasure'. She has suggested that in Sicily 'until very recently items of trousseau were produced simultaneously for use and potential exchange; their content was at once ornamental and, when stored for emergency conversion, essential' (1980; 351). While we agree with her general argument, we wish to explore this phenomenon from a slightly different perspective. Now the 'value' of treasure lies precisely in its potential for actualisation rather than its realisation. If it is realised its 'value' is lost, or rather its value is realised, but in monetary terms. Although the conversion of the trousseau in emergency situations was certainly envisaged in this society to satisfy particular needs, clearly trousseaux were not put together and given to brides for this purpose. Rather they were given to, and collected by, women as an expression of their role as brides of a determinate social class. The analogy can best be pursued with reference to heirlooms such as paintings and other items of decorative value. Just as the function of a painting is to grace a house and denote something about the occupants and their social origins, so too the function of a trousseau is to denote something about the status and history of the parties to a marriage. Clearly paintings and trousseaux may be sold, and indeed may be purchased with an eventual sale or investment in mind, but they have a determinate and lengthy existence and use between their collection and sale or disposal.

The word 'treasure' contains a multiplicity of meanings, but in its most basic sense it denotes the storage and preservation of precious items, rather than their exchange. If trousseaux were 'treasure' this is because they were accumulated and stored as precious objects to a specific group of people, and because their potential monetary conversion was less 'precious' (in its symbolic connotations) than the value attached to the items themselves by the owners. The exception of course is the holding up of human life for ransom. It is significant that Skouzes linked treasure and human life and he clearly sees it as an inversion of the moral order. It is these two aspects which we wish to explore.

Eighteenth- and nineteenth-century Southern European societies such as Sicily and Greece were market economies and most goods could be given a cash value. But some resources, such as land and trousseaux, did not often enter the market. Land circulated more through appropriation or through sale in straitened circumstances, for example after the plague when the market collapsed; otherwise it was circulated less frequently. Furthermore these economies were far from fully monetarised and cash itself was a scarce resource. Trousseaux, while certainly possessing a determinate monetary value and evaluated in monetary terms, were not pure commodities in the classical sense. Significantly, they were heavily invested in for the purposes of social mobility. They circulated between kin, were put together in determinate 'packages' which carried different messages about the status of the conjugal couple, and achieved their significance in the matrimonial context. They functioned both as gifts, circulating between kin and affines, and as commodities sold on the market between strangers. Although they could be exchanged for cash, cash was itself a relatively scarce resource and was often hoarded. The possession of both cash and a large trousseau in this society conferred prestige because they denoted specific lifestyles characterised by the absence of the need to work. Trousseaux were half-way between 'gifts' and 'commodities'; they were neither fully one nor the other. They were never fully 'gifts' in the anthropological sense, embedded in the matrimonial context, because they were given a monetary value which entered calculations on the size of the dowry, and because they could be sold on the market. They were never fully commodities because they were often transmitted from mother to daughter, and because their sale on the market implied not so much the realisation of their value, but an explicit admission of a fall in social status and circumstance. Significantly, the trousseau decreased in importance when the economy became fully commoditised; it became, in J. Davis' words, 'a poor sort of investment; it does not carry interest, nor does it have great liquidity; it is hard to sell it and impossible to secure a loan with it' (1973; 36).

Trousseaux in late eighteenth- and early nineteenth-century Athens were 'treasure' because they embodied labour, symbolically and materially. It is as if this society sought its inspirational model from an inversion of the labour theory of value. Trousseaux were valuable symbolically and hence materially because their production and accumulation embodied and glorified the productive leisure use of labour. In short they embodied and celebrated the labour of those who did not have to work. A sale of a trousseau as an 'emergency conversion' (Herskovits, 1962) indicated in a clear manner that the owners had lost not only wealth but also social position. At the same time they symbolised the inherent irreducibility of the honour of 'being' rather than 'doing' of the *arkhon* (and to a lesser extent of the *nikokirei*) families. The following description of 'The Nobility' by Simmel could equally apply to the symbolic significance of trousseaux:

The nobleman is occupied, but he does not labor ... War and the hunt, the historically typical occupations of nobility, are not, despite all the toil involved, 'labor' in the true sense. The subjective factor has decisive dominance over the objective factor in them; and unlike the case in labor, the product is not an object severed from the personality from which it has absorbed energy; rather the emphasis lies in the preservation of the powers of the subject himself.

(1971; 210)

It is not hard to see why the *nikokirei* class and wealthy families invested heavily in trousseaux. They symbolised the ability to maintain the womenfolk in the leisure and safety of the home. The costumes themselves indicated the high status of the womenfolk, and they were security items which could be realised in emergencies. Furthermore under the Ottomans such items were not subject to taxation, as land was, and were ideal 'investment' opportunities. By the mid-nineteenth century this model had become legitimated and diffused throughout the wider society.

By the early 1830s the trousseau had undergone a number of transformations. First, the monetary significance of the trousseau decreased with respect to cash endowments. Table 16 indicates that the value of cash dowries increased after 1830. Second, with the establishment of an independent Greek kingdom, closer contact with Western Europe as well as the decline of the traditional *arkhon* class, a new costume emerged, which we call 'Type D', and which was universally adopted throughout Athens. In design, materials and colour this costume was closely modelled on Occidental fashion, replacing Smyrna and Constantinople as the source of inspiration. In its ceaseless striving for new modes of expression we have here strong proof of Greek elite aspirations to model itself on Western European culture. New items of clothing such as the *contoguini*, *kontosi*, *kozaka* and *biccotto* (some of which are of romance origin) replaced the *tzoubes*, *zipounes* and *anteria* of the past. We see here a confirmation of Gellner's thesis (1983) that nationalism aims towards the creation of an equally accessible and standardised culture and language, extending nationally often by reinterpreting or creating new traditions. In the new Greek nation-state the creation of a national language, culture and folklore (Herzfeld, 1982) was also accompanied by the standardisation of the language of clothing both for women, who wore what became known as the first Queen Amalia's costume, and men, who increasingly wore the *foustanella* (the Albanian 'skirts'). Significantly, while the urban costumes (A and C) merged into a single, modern one, the Type B rural costume remained largely static until its eventual confinement to the countryside, a clear indication of the separation between town and country. Henceforth men and women would not wear radically different and identifiable costumes, but rather would follow the same type of costume 'grammar' arranged in various ways as a mark of social distinction, especially in the towns. Indeed as cash became more readily available, costumes began to be decorated with false coins suggesting wealth and pedigree rather than embodying it. The growing homogenisation in dowries and trousseaux is brought out in table 25. This correlates the costume Type (A–D) with other components of the dowry (cash, olive trees, vineyards, fields and animals). With the introduction of the new costume Type D, donations of cash increased, but certainly did not reach the level of that previously given by titled families (an indication that the endowment of brides with expensive costumes by the latter held a largely symbolic value). Indeed the amounts of the various goods which accompanied Type D costumes reads like an average of the goods transferred with the other three costume types, an indication of growing homogenisation in the form of the dowry in all its aspects.

This discussion on cash and dowry endowments leads us to the conclusion that in such contexts it is difficult to talk of the matching contributions of the spouses. Men and women carried different resources at marriage; these resources held different semantic loads, were organised according to gender-specific rationalities, and were realised in different time-scales. We are, therefore, in partial agreement with Comaroff (1980) that marriage payments have a particular political and semantic meaning embedded in the strategies of the participants which cannot be reduced to a crude translation of monetary value. Yet this does not mean that economic values were not attached to resources transmitted at marriage, nor that the spirit of economic calculation was absent. The detailed concern and meticulous listing of such items indicate a society keenly aware of their monetary value, of the privileges and duties attached to status in a hierarchical society, and concerned to maintain – and in some case to challenge – those boundaries. Jewellery and trousseaux did not disappear overnight in Athens; they continued to retain their importance. A visitor to the Court and its balls in 1845, Felicia Mary Skene noted that the 'wives and daughters [of the capitani] . . . generally carry their whole fortunes on their persons, sometimes wear their red caps, with the tassel, composed entirely of real pearls, while diamonds and jewels are lavishly disposed on the most conspicuous parts of their dress' (Andrews, 1979; 239). Nevertheless, it appears that their significance did change – they were now just one resource among many in an economy and polity which was becoming increasingly diversified. Their display was not pegged onto religious ceremonies or stages in the developmental cycle but to the complex demands of an evolving civil society, and their accumulation was not a substitute for cash but rather an indication of the possession of cash and other resources.

Juliet du Boulay, who has written on the 'meaning' of the traditional

Table 25. *Relationship between costume type and other components of the dowry*

Costume type	Total number in sample	Percentage receiving cash		Percentage receiving olive trees		Percentage receiving vineyards		Percentage receiving fields		Percentage receiving animals
		Some cash	Over 300 groshia	Some trees	Over 80 trees	Some vineyards	Over 4 plots	Some fields	Over 4 plots	
Type A	353	58.8	16.3	83.0	13.2	74.8	11.9	45.3	3.0	0
Type B	66	62.1	3.0	57.6	0	80.3	9.0	72.2	28.9	57.6
Type C	78	65.4	33.2	87.2	32.0	73.1	9.0	35.9	3.9	0
Type D	26	50.0	19.2	88.5	15.4	65.4	7.6	50.0	15.3	0

dowry in the Evvian village of Ambeli, has suggested that the function of the traditional dowry 'was not so much to confer, as to reveal, wealth' (1983; 259). While we are in general agreement with this stance we have difficulties with her analysis on a number of counts. First, her account of 'wealth' is somewhat economistic; for us 'wealth' in this context is also symbolic capital. Individuals and families used markers of wealth (such as cash or trousseaux) in highly symbolic ways. Second, while in Ambeli daughters clearly received less than sons, this was not necessarily the case in Athens, for their cash endowments and trousseaux were often quite substantial. Finally we have difficulty with the reasons which du Boulay advances for this inequitable division of property: in her view, men 'are superior in intelligence' (*ibid.*; 253) and 'anything given to girls was thought of as being given away to a strange house, while anything given to boys was thought of as being preserved still within the family' (*ibid.*; 255). In the case of girls, moral reason is an *ex post facto* rationalisation and appears too heavily enmeshed in village categories to be of much analytical use. In Athens, 'things given to girls' were not necessarily seen as detracting from resources to be preserved in the family through transmission to sons. By giving resources to daughters Athenians were making statements about themselves often in highly symbolic ways. It was expressed in the way men and women presented themselves, in the way they promised resources at marriage, and so on. In metropolitan Athens, in contrast to rural Ambeli, the name of a family and its reputation depended not merely on how much land or resources it preserved down the male line, but on whom it incorporated within its ambit and with whom it gave its daughters in marriage.

Therefore, while du Boulay's account marks an important advance in the treatment of the changing significance of the dowry across time, it tends to suffer from the problem of working backward analytically to explain the specificity of the present situation and why it differs from the traditional pattern. Ultimately her analysis rests on moral concepts of the person and how the commercialisation of the dowry has tended to devalue women by giving them a 'price' although she does not use this word. By contrast traditionally when women had little or no 'price', their 'value' within marriage was universally understood. This approach is appealing but it is perhaps too unilinear and evolutionist. For what is at issue is as much the equation of whether women had 'value' but no 'price' in the traditional system, and a 'price' but 'little value' in the contemporary one. In the traditional Athenian marriage system individuals and families often used dowries (that is, 'prices') in a strategic fashion to confer material and symbolic 'value' on themselves. The traditional 'dowry' was a collective statement and an index of how much and in what way a family as a corporate group valued and esteemed itself both materially and symbolically within determinate and specified social relations with other family groups. The dowry consisted of a composite set of obligations and rights expressed by different individuals, men and women, who presented different resources. It was not, as is often the case nowadays, the amount demanded of a family by a threatening 'other' (the groom), to 'take' the daughter off a family's hand in marriage. Certainly in modern Greece the dowry appears to give women a 'price', precisely because cash and commodities form the bulk of the dowry. But as Goody has observed, 'price can only be defined in terms of exchange, normally some form of market; that is not at all the case with wealth, which may be without actual or potential exchange value' (1990; 466). What is significant about marriage in modern Greece is that it appears as a 'market' to the participants (and sometimes to outside observers) because of the massive donation of cash and commoditisable resources. Hence the notion that 'today money is everything'. But what is perhaps even more significant about contemporary Greek marriage is that because the field of potential partners is so great the moral qualities of a potential groom or bride are difficult to ascertain, with significant implications for the estimation of 'price'. Money thus acts to filter potential spouses. In the traditional system, by contrast, with a much smaller and known circle of potential affines, women did not only achieve their identity in marriage. They came to their new family at marriage with a definite identity as members of their natal families and with determinate resources which indicated how their natal families wished to present themselves and to be perceived by their affines.

We conclude our analysis of the transmission of property by taking some specific examples into account. We offer two cases. The first concerns the transmission of property within a family which had access to certain resources, but which did not form part of the Athenian elite. Here the endowment of daughters is relatively egalitarian, the brothers contribute to their sisters' dowry and there is a pronounced corporate attitude towards their marriages. Yet while the brothers contribute substantially, they also collect from their own spouses.

Of interest in this example are the transmission of responsibility across time and the general equality between the resources given to daughters and those received by their brothers from their wives as dowries. In 1817 the eldest daughter, Kouzia, was endowed by her parents and her two brothers (see Fig. 2). Her husband Spiros brought a dower equivalent to her dowry. Two years later when her sister Agathi was due to be married, one of the brothers, Christos, did not contribute

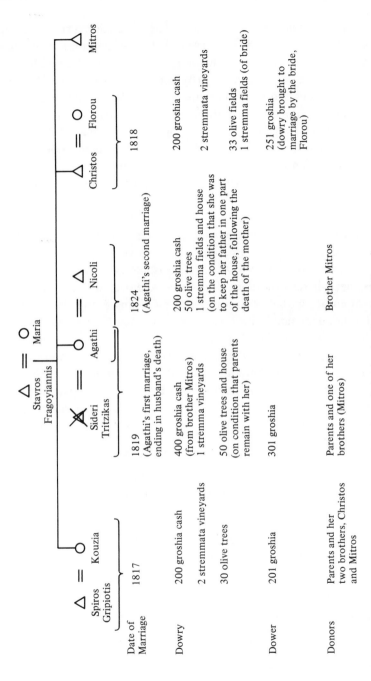

Figure 2. Marriages and the transmission of goods in the family Fragoyiannis

to the dowry since he himself had married a year earlier. The burden of providing Agathi with her dowry was carried by the parents and her one remaining unmarried brother. This daughter received more cash than her sister (double the amount), partly because of her brother Mitros' active involvement and partly perhaps because she was obliged to live with her parents – requiring her groom to forego his own parental home. On her second marriage she brought another 200 groshia with her; it is unclear whether this was the residue of her first cash endowment. Finally of significance is the brother Christos' marriage in 1818, for his wife brought in almost exactly the same amount of goods with which he and his family had endowed their sister Kouzia one year previously.

In the second example, by contrast, there is a marked difference between what the daughter Anetitsa, received at marriage and what her brother's bride, Sevastiani brought to that marriage (see Fig. 3). Yet, both siblings married into the Athenian aristocracy. What is significant here is that whereas the daughter, Kiria Anetitsa, was given a large dowry to ensure an easy transition into the ruling group, her brother received (i.e. demanded) much less from his spouse's family in order to make that social transition. Daughters, in short, were heavily endowed while sons demanded less. Of equal interest is the fact that endowments were unrelated: the brother, Ioannis, did not contribute to his sister's dowry, highlighting the point made earlier that the *nikokirei* possessed a more contractual and individualistic, less commensal and matrimonial ethic.

Figure 3. Marriages and the transmission of goods in the family Karoris

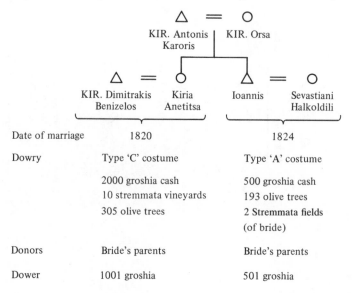

Date of marriage	1820	1824
Dowry	Type 'C' costume	Type 'A' costume
	2000 groshia cash	500 groshia cash
	10 stremmata vineyards	193 olive trees
	305 olive trees	2 Stremmata fields
		(of bride)
Donors	Bride's parents	Bride's parents
Dower	1001 groshia	501 groshia

Conclusion

The changing articulation of cash and trousseaux endowments, as well as the transformations in the nature of trousseaux themselves, indicate a change from an agriculturally based pre-industrial hierarchical and status-bound social order to a more mobile, urbanised and contractual type of society as Athens moved into the nineteenth century and the modern world. The variety of bridal costumes and cash endowments were increasingly replaced by the adoption of a single, universal Athenian costume, by a shift towards household goods as the main constituent of the trousseau, and the general overshadowing of the trousseau by cash endowments as the main economic component of the dowry. What are the implications for our understanding of traditional Mediterranean societies?

On an obvious level we are witnessing a shift from status to class in the new social order generated by the nation-state, but we are also in the presence of a society which traditionally defined and organized itself not in terms of a private-public regulation of social affairs, of the roles of men and women in society, but in terms of a formal-informal distinction predicated upon status. We wish to suggest here that this distinction is more useful towards an understanding of traditional Mediterranean society than of the private-public dichotomy, which we believe is the end-result of a long process of a specifically burgher, or urban middle-class, culture which eventually came to dominate the Greek countryside in the twentieth century. We wish to elaborate on this.

The formal-informal distinction has more to do with the presentation of the self to others in specific social contexts, than with the effects of the inherent properties of space upon action. This is not to say that the formal-informal distinction cannot be reduced to the public-private one; indeed the latter evolved from the former and clearly possesses elements of it. But we believe that such a reduction would obscure the subtle differences between the two. For the formal-informal distinction which ran through the organisation of social life was on the one hand wider in its implications, less physically embedded in the organisation of gender, and intimately linked to social status. Costumes, rather than visible and permanent markers of social status such as houses, the ownership of goods, and so on, indicated status in this pre-capitalist, pre-nation-state society. In other words, people wore their status in this society. This encompassed not only dress, its colour and materials, but also hair styles, the presence or absence of beards and the covering of the head and the feet. This was due in part to the structure of the Ottoman pre-industrial state which rigidly differentiated the population according to religion and occupation, rather than in terms of language-use. For example an Imperial Firman of 1806 divided the Greek *rayah* into three 'classes' which rigidly specified the dress suitable for each group. Members of the third 'class' were not permitted to wear shoes and they were only allowed the privilege of wearing stockings on movement to the second 'class' and the payment of a tax of between 75–100 groshia.

Such regulations did not merely impose a specific form on the presentation of social reality, but also reflected a specific hierarchical organisation of society. They denoted a society which devoted as much attention to the presentation and markers of power, prestige and social status, as to their actual possession by legal rights and privileges. This could give rise to contradictions, as when an Ottoman overlord group in economic decline jealously guarded its outward signs of privilege from the encroachment of their Christian subjects in Athens, Cyprus and other parts of the Greek world. Such markers could also be consciously played upon and manipulated in what may now seem to be eccentric ways. The foreigner Sieber described Sfakian wealthy merchants 'who in their homes wore cashmir turbans, but who when they went out into the streets wore a humiliating blue one because, if they were seen by the Turks they ran the risk of paying a fine of 500 to 3,000 groshia for contempt of the Muslims' (Simopoulos, 1975; 436).

This example enables us to further explore our assertion. For here we have an example of individuals wearing the most highly formal and privileged dress in the privacy of their own homes. Formality and informality depend upon context to a greater extent than the more spatially constituted and irreducible concepts of public or private. And such a context is socially defined as much by the company present as by its physical location. Thus individuals in traditional Athens, men and women, could either be formal or informal in the home; paradoxically, in the case cited above, they could don the most formal costumes in the informality, that is the privacy of their homes. We are not suggesting here that the formal-informal distinction is opposed to the public-private one; they certainly overlay each other but they are not reducible to each other. The public-private distinction seems to us to be defined more in terms of actual physical space and in terms of occasions, which determines whether, for example, women should wear proper shoes or slippers in public, as in Vasilika (Friedl, 1962; Herzfeld, 1986). For example it has often been noted that the 'public face' of the contemporary Greek rural house is the *saloni* (living room) where the family receives visitors and entertains guests. Characteristically it tends to be utilised less by the family for domestic everyday occasions, and kin or close persons are normally entertained in the *kouzina* (kitchen) or elsewhere. In the traditional Athenian house there was much greater flexibility in the use of space partly because rooms were less functionally specific and also because the nature of the company determined the presentation of self (in formal or informal terms). In other words, in traditional Athenian houses the social context determined the presentation of self; in modern Greek society the physical context determines the presumption of self. In both cases strategic manipulation can occur but it is predicated upon different principles.

The differences between the two systems, although subtle, are nevertheless significant. The 'modern' use of space and its gender determination is perhaps less flexible and more domestically based, drawn around the family rather than around the social status of individuals. We see this change as being due to the process of urbanisation in Athens, and to the emergence of the *nikokirei* model of kinship and the family which gradually but definitely renegotiated the definition of what womanhood constituted, through (among other things) the production of elaborate household artefacts within the home, and by implication of what manhood constituted.

The formal-informal distinction can be seen not so much as a repertoire of roles, as that of the performance of a socially determined identity. Marriage in Greece provides a key insight into the construction of personal identity because it involves an exchange, admittedly of a complex sort. One of the seminal features of the Maussian legacy is that the nature of exchange is related to the concept of the person. Marriage in Greece in the late eighteenth and early nineteenth centuries can be seen as a series of gift exchanges establishing relationships between the subjects (family groups, husbands and brides, parents and children, brothers and sisters), rather than a relationship between the objects of a transaction (as in commodity exchange). Indeed what is distinctive is that this society attempted to use goods as gifts; goods which also had a commodity value outside the matrimonial system. The identity of men and women was inextricably linked to the manner in which they utilised different goods to satisfy their various obligations across social groups. The identity of men was linked to the receipt of houses and to the donation of cash dowries to daughters among the upper social groups, and linked to the donation of items of jewellery to their brides in the lower ones. The identity of women as mothers, daughters and brides was linked to the production of trousseaux and costumes, which denoted both their social status and their position within the developmental cycle. And because men and women received different resources and exchanged them in qualitatively different ways and according to different rationalities, their identity was 'composite' and could only be realised in and through an exchange system which was primarily a gift system. Hence the attempts at the stratification of dowries to prevent marriage from appearing like a market exchange. This is not to say that economic criteria were absent in such marriages; they indeed were present and considerations of gain and loss were important and increasingly viewed in these terms. But economic criteria of good matches had to follow certain rules that were not related to the criteria of supply and demand. They were tempered by considerations of status, social origins, and claims to prestige and self-esteem.

Hence the notion of a formal-informal dichotomy containing the presentation of self may be particularly useful in explaining this society. The self was presented in terms of a performance of a socially determined identity. To pursue the theatre metaphor more closely, if the 'play' had been 'written' (by some of the actors who arrogated key parts for themselves), individuals were formally obliged to act out their socially determined parts/identities. If they wanted to extemporise or change their parts/identities, they had to do so cautiously so that the situation appeared to remain the same and the 'play' could continue. They were not characters in search of a role, but 'roles' in search of characters to be acted out. As a result one was either 'on stage' or 'off stage', 'formal' or 'informal', except that the 'identity' portrayed formally 'on-stage' became increasingly discrepant with that notion of self experienced informally 'off-stage', in the market, and so on, especially for the *nikokirei* group. Simmel has noted that in the pre-industrial age 'a man did not depend so much upon the purposive, objective content of his associations [as a result] his "formal personality" stood out more clearly against his personal existence: hence personal bearing in the society of earlier times was much more ceremonially, rigidly and impersonally regulated than now' (1971; 133). He goes on to contrast this with the modern notion of sociability and its interaction of equals, accompanied by a courtesy applied equally to the strong and weak (what has been called 'The Civilising Process'), and which is 'a game in which one "acts" as though all were equal, as though he especially esteemed everyone' (*ibid.*; 133–4). In other words the two systems can be seen as analogous to a 'theatre' and a 'game'. It is perhaps significant that Mauss in his essay on the gift emphasised the theatrical element of gift exchange systems which in a post-Malinowskian way we sometimes misrepresent as 'game-like'. Indeed if there is a common 'Mediterranean aesthetic' it may well lie in a juxtaposition of the two systems – that is, men and women attempt to strategically utilise a repertoire of roles to struggle against socially determined identities.

The introduction of cash and the increasing tendency towards the commoditisation of dowries within a nation-state undergoing rapid urbanisation had a number of far-reaching effects. It subverted the traditional alliance system of marriage, transformed the perceptions of the role and significance of the dowry and affected relations within the family. It also affected the boundaries between the family and society by redefining the nature and significance of spiritual kinship. In the next chapter we examine changes to the moral and political economy of spiritual kinship as Athens lost its agrarian, hierarchical, pre-industrial character.

Plate 1. An Athenian bride

Royaume des environs d' Athènes

Plate 2. Costume of a migrant villager settled in the Athenian suburbs

138

Plate 3. Family grave of the *arkhon* Kantzillieri family; First Cemetery, Athens (Section A)

Plate 4. Grave of Maria Kassimati, a member of the *nikokirei*; First cemetery, Athens (Section A, 115)

140

Plate 5. Nationalist poster, 1913, depicting Mother Greece flanked by her sister and daughter regions and linked by the banners of *eleftheria* (freedom) and *enosis* (union)

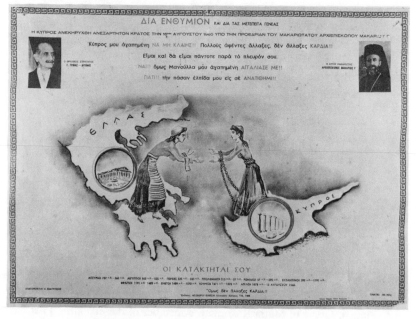

Plate 6. Nationalist poster, Cyprus, 1960, depicting Mother Greece and her enslaved daughter, Cyprus

Plate 7. Annunciation Icon by the artist Loverdos Stelakatos, 1851

Plate 8. *Liberaci Maria da ogni male*: Italian oleograph of a type which circulated in Athens in the 1930s and 40s

Plate 9. Popular religious poster depicting Christ blessing the daily family meal

Plate 10. An Athenian couple

5

'For one's soul': adoption, fosterage and the growth of *koumbaria*

Introduction

Thus far our analysis has concentrated on the changing patterns in the transmission of property at marriage and their relationship to social classes in Athens. We know that settlement at marriage was likely to be viri-patrilocal in the top strata and uxorilocal among the poorer Athenians, that the household was normally an extended one, that women received the bulk of their share of parental property as dowry at marriage, while sons received their share as post-mortem inheritance, and that there were significant variations between the various social classes in the nature of the flow of resources they transmitted at marriage. We now wish to examine the interrelationship between two questions. First, how did the change in the political economy of Athens from a relatively minor administrative outpost of the Ottoman empire to the capital of a new nation-state affect the family, the composition of the household and the significance of kinship? Second, were there any significant differences between the old *arkhon* elite and the new rising bourgeoisie in the way they utilised kinship (especially spiritual kinship) as a political strategy and as a means of recruitment?

Fosterage and adoption

Our sample of marriage contracts includes 42 brides (or 8.6 per cent of our total sample) who had been 'adopted' and a much smaller number of grooms of the same origin. We believe that this merits particular attention partly because marriages of adopted girls exhibit certain distinctive features, and partly because adoption has received particular attention in recent years as a strategy of heirship (see for example Goody, 1983).

There are a number of questions which need to be tackled here. First, were these girls fully and legally adopted; that is, did they actually have full and unequivocal rights to their adoptive parents' property? Or did they resemble fostered children? Second, was there any pre-existing relation between these children and their 'new' parents, such as god-parenthood (*koumbaria*) which might help explain why they had been adopted (such as the death of their biological parents)? There are additional questions. How was adoption legitimised? Was it a purely secular form of adoption which was followed or a purely religious one? Were these differences expressed in different rites?

We begin by observing that adoption in Christian Europe has tended to merge with godparenthood, which fell under the general category of spiritual kinship. The fourteenth-century theological tract, The Exavivlos by Konstantinou Armenopoulos, noted that both 'Baptism and Adoptive Kinship have the same degrees of prohibited marriage to the 8th Degree'; the same degrees which apply to adoptive kinship apply to kinship by blood (*eks ematos*), as was determined by the 53rd Canon of the Holy Synod in Trullo, which states that spiritual kinship is 'higher than "physical" [*somaton* – literally 'of the body'] kinship' (Armenopoulos, 1872). In the eighteenth century a Patriarchal letter repeated the great importance attached to adoption: '*pnevmatiki singenia* [spiritual kinship] is more worthy and purer than the real kinship of blood' (Roilos, 1966; no. 2579 A.L.). It is considered purer because *pnevmatiki singenia* is modelled here on the Holy Family where Mary retained her purity and virginity, and Joseph was Christ's foster father. Adoption is parenthood without concupiscence. The words used (*pnevmatiki singenia*) can mean both godparenthood and adoption, both of which are classified as spiritual kinship (through the Holy Ghost: *Ay. Pnevma*); it is thus unclear whether the Patriarch intended to emphasize adoption rather than godparenthood. Yet the tract is called *peri iothesias* which means 'on adoption' and thus suggests that he was referring to the former. It is, however, well documented that the two institutions tended to merge and that godparents came increasingly to assume the functions of spiritual guardians should the parents die. By the late eighteenth century there are indications that adoption had lost some ecclesiastical support. A Venetian edition of Armenopoulos of 1774 noted that 'the ancients had another type of kinship of adoption which took place in the Church through ritual [*ierologia*]. This prohibited marriage to the same degree as blood kinship, but because such rituals do not anymore take place within the Church, we shall not write widely on it.'[1] It appears, however, that adoption in some form or another continued at the grassroots level in many parts of Greece, including Athens.

But what type of 'adoption' was this? One way to answer this question is to explore the following issues: first, how were the care of and responsibilities to spiritual kin expressed? Second, what rights did spiritual kin (especially 'adopted' children) have to adoptive parental property? In Western Europe full legal adoption was discouraged and so these issues hardly arose, whereas Greek Orthodoxy was slightly more elastic in these matters, reflecting a greater interpenetration of grass-roots practices and a more decentralised and restricted authority structure of a great Church in captivity. In Orthodoxy it appears that adoption (*iothesia*) was a ritual which was considered to be legally, linguistically, and ritually distinct. In this ritual the duties and obligations of the new adoptive parents and the rights of the adopted child were assumed through a particular religious ceremony which was then registered with the Civil authorities. The adopted child was dressed with a shirt or blouse of his or her adopted parent who then carried the child into another room, where a notary, the Bishop and the elders of the community were waiting. The ritual clearly symbolised a birth. The child dressed in this way was passed through the neck opening of the adoptive mother's dress and withdrawn from underneath the dress (D. Kampouroglous, 1896; 75). The notary then took down all the details in his codex and registered the act with the Turkish authorities. It is probable that because the author is referring to the presence of a churchman he was implicitly dealing with *arkhon* practices. The adopted child, called a *nomimo pedhi* (literally 'legal child'), was subject to the same marriage rules and prohibitions as a biological child, as the issue of a legally recognized marriage, and had full rights to assume his or her adopter's name and to inherit property.

Our sample of 42 brides does not suggest that these girls were originally adopted through the full ceremony and registered with the authorities in the prescribed manner. Although the contracts refer to *psikhokore, psikhothigatera* (literally, 'spiritual daughters'), the term most commonly used in conversation, they do not include the term usually prescribed in situations of adoption, which is *nomimo pedhi*. In a notarial culture where great attention is given to details, this is striking. Furthermore there is evidence to suggest that this was no mere oversight.[2] Legally, therefore, such brides did not have full rights to inherit adoptive parental property; the contracts themselves employ some formula to justify and legitimate the transfer at marriage (such as 'a dowry for her domestic services'). They were therefore more like fostered children. Indeed Greek does not distinguish between a fostered and adopted child; the same words, *psikho, psikhothigatera, psikhoyious* are used for both adopted or foster children and parents. Nevertheless we believe that in a good number of cases the brides can for most purposes be classified as 'adopted' children in some sense inheriting parental property. We believe that grassroots practices differed from the legally and religiously sanctioned means for transferring property to adopted children. In many cases 'adoption' appears to have been informal, in the sense that it was not registered with the religious and civil authorities. Kolokotronis recounts that on 7 March 1804, in the village of Turkokerpeni, he had given his clothes to an adopted son when they were suddenly surrounded by Turks and his recently adopted son of a few hours 'got eight balls [bullets] fired into him' (Edmonds, 1969; 94). Similar practices appear to have occurred in other parts of Greece, though not usually in such dramatic circumstances. In Mani 'adoption conventions were not observed . . . The position of adopted children was very good and the Maniots believed that such children often had a better life than ordinary children' (Alexakis, 1980).

In analysing our data it is clear that we are dealing with two social strata which appear to have adopted children for different reasons, and pursued different 'adoption' strategies which had different effects. Girls were more popular as adoptees than boys; indeed marriage records show that only a handful of grooms were adopted. Furthermore titled families adopted to a proportionally greater extent than the mass of ordinary Athenian citizens. Table 26 indicates that the tendency of titled parents to adopt was very significant. The data suggest that other factors than the problem of childlessness must have influenced the tendency of titled families to adopt to a proportionally greater extent. Indeed, if wealthy Athenian families bear any similarities to local elites elsewhere in the Mediterranean (for example western Sicily; see J. and P. Schneider, 1983), they probably tended to have larger, rather than smaller, families. Some evidence for this view comes from the visitor John Hobhouse who noted in 1810 that 'the Codja-bashees, to whom the municipal control of some districts, particularly the Morea, is entrusted, support an enormous household, the members of which are dignified with titles, not attached to the dependents of an English Duke' (Andrews, 1979; 157).

Most girls appear to have been adopted at a young age. Some contracts refer to long periods of service and residence (up to twenty years) in the 'new' parental home. We also know that at least half of these girls were not orphans, as reference is made in marriage contracts to their biological parents (father or mother or both) who often also contributed to their dowry. Many came from surrounding villages and they retained the names of their biological parents.

Adoption held different rationalities for the wealthy titled families and the rest of the Athenian population. Among the former, adoption

Table 26. *Correlation between adoption and titled families*

	Titled fathers	Untitled fathers	Row total
Adopted daughter			
Number	20	22	42
Percentage	47.6	52.4	8.0
Natural daughter			
Number	55	426	481
Percentage	11.4	88.6	92.0
Total			
Number	75	448	523
Percentage	14.3	85.7	100.0

Chi-square: 38.27908 D.F. 1 (before Yates correction).
The correlation between titles and adoption is significant at the 0.0000, which is
very high. Min. E.F. 6.023.

was unlikely to have been due solely to the problems of heirlessness.
Indeed titled families were less likely to legally adopt a child, by
registering the act with the civil authorities and thus endowing them
with inheritance rights to familial property at their death, although such
girls certainly received property as dowry at marriage. This supports our
assertion in previous chapters that what was important for the *arkhon*
families was descent through which individuals claimed rights. As we
shall demonstrate, dowries of adopted brides did not fully reflect parental wealth, being generally rather small. Rather, such girls received a
dowry not as *nomima pedhia* (legal children) whereby they retained
legal rights in the residue of the parental estate, but as 'labour for her
services', as specified in the matrimonial contracts. Fosterage is thus
perhaps a more correct description than adoption, since girls appear to
have been sent to Athenian titled families at a young age by poor village
families unable to maintain them and to provide them with a dowry. In
return for labour services in their new home, wealthy titled 'foster'
parents arranged a marriage with a suitable groom, and supplied the girl
with a dowry. Yet within wealthy titled families such girls were not
strictly maids (*douleftres*) and were generally not referred to as such.
Only three examples exist in our records in which they are referred to as
douleftres – two of them are in 'Sior' families. Rather, they appear to
have occupied a position somewhere between family servants and full
children. 'Family retainers' is perhaps a more suitable description;
certainly they addressed their masters as 'effendis' (my lord). The relationship was long-term and did not necessarily end at the bride's marriage. Nor does it appear to have been entered into by wealthy families

merely as a means of cheap labour recruitment. For a considerable period of residence such girls, especially if taken in at a young age, were more likely to have been consumers than producers of wealth. Maids (*douleftres*) were inexpensive and in large supply, and the wealthy appear to have 'adopted' children even when they had their own children. Similar practices appear to have been followed in nineteenth-century Lesbos. There, the ruling '*afentika* had the moral obligation of supporting the marriage of their female domestic servants and contributing towards their dowries' (Papataxiarchis, 1985; 24) a situation paralleled in the Peloponnesian village of Dimitsana (Kalpourtzi, 1987; 89). In Renaissance Tuscany, *fantine*, or young girls taken into middle-class urban families, were provided with a dowry when they reached marriageable age (Klapisch-Zuber, 1985; 106). Yet these were more properly servants 'who often had difficulty preserving their virtue [in their new families]' (*ibid.*; 107). By contrast, among Athenian *arkhon* families it appears that ties between adoptive or foster parents and biological parents were retained. The famous revolutionary, General Makriyiannis, had two *psikhyious* (boys, as befitting a military man likely to be on the move due to long campaigns) to tend to his personal domestic needs, even though he had his own children. 'Adoption' was a meritorious act, entered into *yia tin psikhe*, for one's soul and salvation, a phrase paralleled in Renaissance Tuscany where godparents baptised children *per l'amore di Dio* (*ibid.*; 1985; 90).

A concern for future salvation, however, did not necessarily result in magnanimity, nor did it exclude political considerations. Although we explore the politics of kinship below, it is worthwhile mentioning that we are dealing here with a traditional hereditary elite within an agrarian regime whose power was mainly domestically based. As in other parts of the Mediterranean prior to the establishment of the nation-state, such elites derived their power not primarily from individualistic semi-contractual wheeling and dealing, but from the stage management of domestic resources: household, semi-incorporation of outsiders into the family (such as through fosterage/adoption), and the circulation of food, sustenance and protection. The son of Papatsonis, the revolutionary hero, noted the large expenses involved in maintaining such large households: 'although we had a lot of property so too were the expenses of our house . . . Apart from this there were at least 10 other families from our village Naziriou, also in our house we entertained 500 guests, Turks and Christians every day' (1960; 47). Similar practices existed throughout the Greek world. Salamone, who studied the traditional social organisation of the Marmara islands dominated by *nikokirei*, shipowners and merchants, quotes an old villager who recalled: 'all the houses had big warehouses next to them . . . Even the poor in those days stored their provisions; the *nikokiris* had to store the most of all – because he had to give to the other households as well!' (1987; 66).

From Sevres the *arkhon* Papasinodinos described his father's (d. 1635) patterns of hospitality and redistribution:

And so hospitable [*philoksenos*] was he that he did not lack friends who visited him every day, Christians and Turks alike. Two or three times he offers his visitors meals, he greets them graciously, he gives them to eat and drink and the best wine he lays before them, and in the evening he offers them beds to sleep on. And if there were not enough blankets he took off his coat to keep them warm. Of every type of food he offered them, and when he had bid them goodbye he gave them gifts. On Wednesdays and Fridays they did not eat fish; and he did not hold back from attending Church functions. A friend of the Church, a friend of the poor and of strangers, charitable [*eleimon*], wise, he helped the churchmen collect their rights [i.e. rents] with the utmost gentleness, whilst he kept nothing for himself, neither from the High Priest nor from the family [*familia*] concerned. And some of the Higher Clergy, or the people who were fugitives [from Ottoman laws] escaped to his house where he kept them, feeding them and their horses . . . And many Christians and Turks knew his house and had eaten at his table. With everyone he was a friend. Judges, tax collectors, beys, he welcomed them all and set them on their way. Worthy he was to converse with the Clergy and the Pashades, and to everyone who asked him for money, either Christian or Turk he gave some – to some as a loan, to others as a gift, and every Sipahi who came to the area could do nothing without his blessing because he did not permit them to extract more taxes than was due to them, or to cause injustices, and all the unjust sipahis were terrified of him.

(Asdrachas, 1984; 97)

The close concern with redistribution, with breaking bread together as a means to create allies, with the incorporation of outsiders, with blessing and with 'justice' based on magnanimity, are all features of a traditional interstitial rural-based elite secure of its power, and have been noted for other areas of the Mediterranean (although the notion of hospitality and the like is no monopoly of the powerful). Fosterage, or the incorporation of semi-family members, was a natural extension of this ideology. Similar practices appear to have existed in the central Italian town of Colleverde prior to 1860 as reported by Silverman (1975). There, the old landowning town-based aristocracy concerned itself with both production and reproduction; it was customary for the *padrone* and his family to supply his client's daughters with dowries. As in Athenian adoption the relationship, although initially contractual, became a long-term one linking families together as collective entities over generations, such that a strict accounting of exchanges became impossible, becoming buried, as it were, under collective sentiments of belonging to a particular powerful family. Adoption, a concern with reproduction, the close matching of religious concerns for salvation and social obligations, and the payments of dowries are aspects of a traditional elite secure of its power. We show below that as this traditional elite was replaced by a new up-and-coming middle class within a context of elective politics, adoption tended to be replaced by *koumbaria* (godparenthood), to which it is related in Church ideology, but which is more contractual, individualistic and leaves the child in its natal family. Where adoption survived among the urban middle class it became increasingly a means of labour recruitment as well as a means of resolving the problem of childlessness. Significantly too it was children of kinsmen who became increasingly adopted, as opposed to girls from humble rural origins. Fosterage and adoption also could extract penalties in extraordinary contexts. Kolokotronis had at least one other adopted son, after he had just acquired and lost one in the village of Turkokerpeni; these young men accompanied their adoptive fathers in the most dangerous conditions. In recounting one particularly difficult situation he had found himself in Kolokotronis says 'I went forward alone, not even having my adopted son with me' (Edmonds, 1969; 169).

It also appears that foster sons in the mountain captains' service during the war of liberation were not only taken in merely as personal assistants, but also to tend to their sexual needs, a practice which Count Capodistrias tried to control, for 'he recalled G. Kleovoulos from Syra in whom he confided the education of the one hundred foster sons (*psikhyious*) he had with many difficulties saved from the corruption of the camps' (Dragoumis, 1925; 211). Similarly the boundaries between foster girls and concubines could be slight, given long periods of cohabitation; in his novel *O Komis Alibrandes*, G. Ksenopoulos refers to 'maids' among the Ionian aristocracy in a somewhat ironical vein. Indeed the renowned poet D. Solomos was born in Zakynthos in 1798 out of a union between an elderly Count and a very young mother, Angeliki, who was a servant of the house, and probably a *psikhokore* of the family.

In late eighteenth- and early nineteenth-century Athens, where status was primarily defined in hereditary terms, dowries of adopted girls tended to be determined not by the status of their patres-familias but by their social origins. In other words adopted girls tended to receive small to average dowries (table 14) irrespective of whether they were adopted by titled families or not. Yet they were slightly better off than countrywomen who married in Athens. In one respect, therefore, fosterage or adoption of a girl from humble rural origins was advantageous for the girl concerned, for she was provided with a dowry slightly more substantial than her natal circumstances would normally have permitted. Such girls differed from the majority of other brides in that they were often supplied with a house (45.3 per cent of all fostered/ adopted girls at marriage received a house compared with an overall inclusive average of 38 per cent). Does this indicate that it was difficult or 'risky' for them to be integrated in agnatically based households, perhaps because their virtue had been compromised? Often they received half a house at marriage; this incidence was substantially higher than for the average bride. The relationship thus lasted for at least two generations, sharing the household with their foster-adopter parents and bringing their *esogambros* (in-marrying and uxorilocally residing groom) with them. From other correlations in our data we know that such grooms often came from surrounding villages. Indeed a substantial number of such endowments specifically link the donation of a house (and more often half a house) with the condition that the bride take care of the foster/adoptive parents in their old age.

Among non-titled families adoption was particularly important as a means of old-age insurance. *Psikhokores* were taken in to care for the new adoptive parents in their old age, provided with a dowry and often resided in the same house or in part of the parental house, thus resolving the problem of childlessness. Although such girls, not being registered as *nomima pedhia* (legal children and heirs) with the civil authorities, had no legal rights to the residue of the parental estate as inheritance, reality may have proven otherwise. Some indication of the inheritance prospects of adopted girls comes from The Codex of P. Poulou (No. 693). In this case an issueless father died leaving his property to his heirs – his sisters – who undertook to give his widow the *progamiea dorea* (dower) of 251 groshia as well as a sum of money (600 groshia), a not insubstantial amount 'as a salary for past work' to his adopted daughter (*psikhothigatir*) for her dowry. In effect adopted girls, like all other brides, received the main portion of their share of parental property at their marriage. There was usually little left of the parental estate once all children had married, and if there were sons these took priority.

We thus believe that in spite of the differences in the wording of the matrimonial contracts between adopted girls and ordinary brides, real differences were in effect less significant than legal ones. Adopted girls among non-titled families received their share of the parental property at marriage, like all other brides. As such girls were not legally adopted, the phrasing, 'a dowry as a wage for her services' could legitimate the transfer of most or part of the parental estate at marriage, thus prevent-ing the risk of sequestration of heirless family land by the Porte at death. Here the actual differences in the dowries of 'adopted' girls of non-titled families and other (non-titled) daughters was less significant than amongst titled families. Finally the careful spelling-out of obligations guaranteed that the adoptive, issueless parents, had some form of old-age insurance, while retaining control of their property until their death. Often such brides retained the name of their genitor rather than their pater and both contributed to the dowry.

Adoption in late eighteenth- and early nineteenth-century Athens thus had different rationalities according to the social group concerned. Because it was often an *ad hoc* arrangement which was not fully legalised, it tended to merge with fosterage. Among titled families who tended to adopt to a greater extent than the mass of ordinary Athenian residents, the relatively small dowries involved, the absence of legal rights to the residue of the parental estate, the emphasis on inherited status which could not be transmitted except to male sons, all suggest an inward-looking elite keen to patrol its borders and to maintain its political privileges in the Turkocratia. Adoption was consistent with, and an aspect of, traditional forms of patronage in a hierarchically fixed society. It provided the family with trusted retainers, linking patron and client families over a number of generations and it was legitimated by religious ideology. Yet it was clear that such girls could never be fully integrated into their adoptive families. The example of the poet Dionysios Solomos is instructive here. Shortly before his death in 1807 his father Count Nicolas 'legalized his relationship with Angeliki [Dionysios' mother] making their two children legitimate' (Dimaras, 1985; 227). Yet 'the guardians of Dionysios, undoubtedly wishing to remove him from the influence of his plebeian mother hastened to send him to Italy' (*ibid.*; 228), and the poet was later obliged by his agnatic kin to appear in court against his mother in a case over property.

Among ordinary Athenian residents adoption was much more a 'strategy for old-age insurance' among childless couples. Our data do not overtly suggest that adoption was *prima facie* a 'strategy of heirship', as Goody (1983) has suggested, although adopted girls certainly inherited parental property at marriage. The absence of their registration with the civil authorities suggests that either such registration was difficult or costly to effect, or else that heirship in its full legal sense was viewed as less significant or less realisable at the grassroots. In contrast to ancient Greece, Rome and tribal Africa, ordinary Athenians were more concerned with the problems of old-age insurance than with heirship as such, which was not viewed as a religious and existential imperative.

Finally it remains to discuss whether such adoption was due to anomalous conditions in Athens during this period. Some children may have been war orphans or offspring of parents who had been displaced by the war. However, we do not believe that the Athenian situation during this period can explain these patterns. Adoption was common in Greece until recently, although the identity of the adopted child has changed. Furthermore many of these children's biological parents were alive at the time of their endowment at marriage. Adoption at least among the higher social groups was grounded in other realities, and it underwent a number of changes through time. It is to these aspects that we now turn.

Spiritual kinship: blood brotherhood, spiritual brotherhood, godparenthood

Traditional Greek society possessed a number of institutions to turn non-kin (*kseni*) into fictional kinsmen. These included blood brotherhood, also called foster brotherhood (*adelfopiia*), spiritual or soul brotherhood (*psikhoadelfosine*), adoption (*iothesia*), and godparenthood (*koumbaria*). Most of these practices, especially those involving spiritual brothers, appear to have been folk practices not officially sanctioned by the Church. Although there were significant variations between them, they nevertheless possessed a cluster of similar characteristics. For example blood brotherhood and spiritual brotherhood were alike in the following ways: they were often collective and linked together two kinship groups rather than individuals; the relationship was transmitted across generations; and they were often used to prevent an outbreak of hostilities in situations where the vendetta and relations of hostility threatened to disrupt social life. In Mani 'in the past [blood-brothers] were obliged to support each other in "bloody conflicts"; it often happened that a man's bloodbrother was killed in his place [i.e. in a vendetta]' (Alexakis, 1980; 262). Soul brotherhood, by contrast, provided a counterweight to this. It was activated 'where justice had not yet been done' (*ibid.*; 262) to bring about peace between two feuding groups: 'Peace was called *aghapi*, "love", and was accomplished by the ritual called *psikhiko*, which could even result in the "adoption" of the last killer by the family of the last victim' (Andromedas, 1962; 93).[3] The relationship of *adelfopiia* (foster or blood brotherhood) was long-lasting, apparently quite common, and could link Greeks and Ottomans. In certain cases it appears to have had the function of *koumbaria* in that it provided a man with allies in the form of adopted spiritual brothers. Kolokotronis, the Kleft-armatole turned revolutionary hero, mentions adopted brothers twice in his memoirs. Once when fleeing from the machinations of his *simpetheros* (affine) he and others escaped to the village of Pasava 'and got to the house of an adopted brother of mine, where we stayed two days' (Edmonds, 1969; 107); however he does not consider it important to mention the man's name. On a second occasion Kolokotronis went to Zante where he met the Botzares 'and took Markou for my adopted brother' (*ibid.*; 127).

Links forged between adopted brethren could be renewed across generations and could transcend ethnicity. Kolokotronis recounts: 'my grandfather, Gianni Kolokotronis, and the grandfather of Ali had been friends and adopted brethren. My grandfather was killed, but the friendship had continued between my own father and the father of Ali; and we also were sworn friends. Remembering this friendship, and counting upon it, Ali wrote a letter to me [warning of certain plans to capture me]' (1969; 113). The key word here is 'sworn'; Kolokotronis, while keen to show that the relationship had lasted for three generations (and hence possessed a certain gravitas), nevertheless emphasises that both he and Ali had renewed the relationship through ritual. Kazantzakis also mentions a similar practice in Crete. The sixth and the lowest grade in the Philiki Etairia (The Friendly Society), the famous revolutionary organisation, was also organised in terms of blood brothers and sponsors.

It appears that the Orthodox Church, especially in the Turkocratia, silently disapproved of such practices. Armenopoulos' text appears to have tried to pretend that blood or soul brotherhood did not exist: 'The so-called *adelfopia* is considered to be unrecognised and doesn't forbid any marriage because such a practice does not copy nature because a brother does not beget brother' (Armenopoulos, 1872; 260). The thrust of the argument here is that *adelfopia* is no impediment to marriage, a belief which appears to have been particularly strong in areas such as the Mani, where even nowadays elderly informants appear to treat the relation as a type of *koumbaria* where the children of *psikhadelfia* are not encouraged to marry (although their own children may do so).

By the end of the eighteenth century the Church had begun to take a stronger line on the issue. Amantos refers to a Synodical letter of Constantinople which states, 'that which is Christian above all, genuine and first is only that spiritual brotherhood which emerges from the Holy Font [i.e. where children are baptised]' (1927; 281).

The institution of foster or blood brotherhood in Greece was partly related to the desire and need to provide security and trust, especially in the countryside, where centrally imposed law was often absent. It was thus particularly important even in the nineteenth century among bandits, just as it had been among the earlier Klefts. (Klefts were bandits in the Turkocratia who became identified with the spirit of national resistance to the Ottomans, and were thus seen in a positive light). Koliopoulos notes that

Banditry was so much identified with foster brotherhood that intelligence of young men united in brotherhood made the authorities suspect the imminent formation of a band of brigands. It is interesting to note that, in contrast to the official Greek Orthodox Church, which condemned the practice, the lower clergy and monks in particular, seldom denied their services in officiating over the particular ceremony, which involved the mixing of the blood of the foster-parents and their swearing on the Gospels.

(1987; 163)

The Church attempted to ban both spiritual and foster types of brotherhood:

Blood brotherhood as an institution was found in all of Greece and the Balkans. Because previously it linked men and women who were as a consequence not permitted to marry, the Church had strongly opposed both the custom and those so linked through it who were threatened with excommunication. The Church and the Patriarchate generally did not consider blood brotherhood an impediment to marriage.

(Alexakis, 1980; 262)

An 1853 Encyclical by the Athens Archbishop Neophytos V warned that 'you are obliged to beware . . . against the total phenomenon of *adelfopia* and similar practices which go against the Holy Law, the Sacred traditions and the Synodical Regulations' (Encyclical 8th, 81B, Athens 11 July 1853). The 'similar practices' to which the warning refers was the tendency to treat religious engagements as *de facto* marriage which often resulted in cohabitation.

One reason why the Orthodox Church condemned such practices was that it opposed the accumulation of an inordinate amount of power and wealth within kinship groups. Blood brotherhood strengthened the collective and 'lineage' character of Maniot and other kinship groups, and blood brothers could pursue the vendetta and be killed in consequence. Blood brotherhood strengthened the hold of the past upon the present by continually aligning individuals in determinate configurations of hostility and alliance. The Church by contrast was concerned to steer a mid-way course between the individual and the group through its insistence on the free choice of matrimonial partners and by imposing an ego-centred system of degrees of prohibited kinship.

Blood brotherhood and soul brotherhood generally disappeared in Greece by the early decades of this century with the decline of strong enduring agnatically based kinship groups. Also, such institutions are examples of popular justice and they declined with the state's increasing although slow appropriation of the monopoly of violence. Alexakis (1982) writes of the disappearance of the former in Mani by 1935; Andromedas (1962) cites examples of the latter dating from 1912.

Similar decline occurred in Epiros (Nitsiakos, 1985) and in other parts of Greece. Adoption also transformed into a more middle-class phenomenon and came to involve kinswomen, rather than humble, unrelated rural girls recruited for domestic services.

Correspondingly, the institution of *koumbaria* appears to have achieved a higher profile in the nineteenth and twentieth centuries. Available data suggest that in Byzantine times *koumbaria*, especially in the use of non-kinsmen as baptismal sponsors, had been important as a strategy for turning the powerful into patrons (Macrides, 1987). However, it is perhaps significant that such examples date from periods when both the ruling group and the subject population possessed the same religion and were relatively ethnically homogeneous. According to Macrides (1987) *koumbaria* was particularly significant as a political strategy among the elite in court patronage, but she gives no examples of it transcending the great divide between peasants and the elite.[4]

By contrast during the Turkocratia the overall politico-religious climate was different. To begin with, the ruling Ottoman group practised a different religion from their Christian subjects, it was keen to maintain its privileges and its separation, and the Church did not look favourably upon the selection of Muslims as baptismal sponsors responsible for the Christian education of children (although this did occur, most links between Christians and Muslims were expressed in terms of spiritual brethren – *psikho adelfosine* – as between Kolokotronis and Ali, above). We have found few references to *koumbaria* in Athens and Greece generally during our period, both in our sample of matrimonial contracts and memoirs. Wedding sponsors were not necessarily baptismal ones, and it is likely that adoption as practised by the Athenian elite held roughly the same patronage functions as *koumbaria*, that is, assistance to poorer families in the form of relieving them of the burden of providing a daughter's dowry. Some *koumbari* were remembered in wills. Furthermore, we believe that in hierarchically stratified pre-Independence Athens, and in Greek society generally, there were less structural inducements to the operation of a free-wheeling transactionalist mentality necessary for the operation of *koumbaria*.

One reference to *koumbaria* during the eighteenth century, at least in its negative aspects, comes from Mani. Interestingly, what is portrayed is a reversal of the attitude normally associated with *koumbaria*, which involved support, mutual respect, equality and formality. This poem can be seen as a denial of the spirit of *koumbaria*, to turn a stranger into a victim rather than an ally, all in the name of 'friendship' – a triumph of regional insularity over individual linkages to the outside.

> When strangers chance to go to their region
> They make of them *koumbaroi* and invite them to eat
> And when the foreigner wishes to depart, they hold him
> And like friends they speak to him and give him advice.
> '*Koumbaros*' they say, 'we wish you well
> And that which we say to you, mark well.
> And take off your gown, your waistcoat and your belt
> And your trousers lest some enemy take them from you:
> Lest enemies strip you, and others take them
> This brings damage to us and great shame.
> For this reason, dear *Koumbaros* truly we say to you
> We would like you to leave your fez and shirt
> And take off your shoes, what use are they to you?
> And now you are safe, you are not frightened of anyone'.
> And thus they strip the naked stranger
> The cruel ones run to leave him naked.
>
> (Quoted and translated by R. Clogg, 1976; 26–7)

Another example of the ambiguous significance of *koumbaria* is illustrated by the revolutionary hero Fotakos, who recounted the myth of the snake and the crab to his soldiers perhaps in order to advise that they should not rely on anyone: in the myth, the snake and crab became friends and *koumbari*, but ultimately betrayed each other (Fotakou, 1960; 132). Yet because *koumbaria* was a discrete dyadic link it was particularly suitable for subversive activities. In anticipation of the uprising Lambros Katzonis visited Preveza in 1789 to recruit some men into the army of irregulars; there he met Kapetan Androutzos and recruited him by baptising his son, Odysseas Androutzos (Vasillas, 1956; 439).

Some memoirs written during this period are singularly silent on *koumbaria*. Although we know from other sources, especially from his *vaptistikos* (baptised child), that Theodore Kolokotronis, the Kleft-armatole turned revolutionary hero, had baptised over fifty children, all of whom were named Theodorakis and often accompanied him as secretaries (Rigopoulos, 1979; 12), Kolokotronis himself hardly mentions *koumbari* in his memoirs. This is surprising for a man who relied heavily on kinsmen to execute delicate and responsible tasks, and whose physical safety depended upon complete trust. In spite of his laconic and highly unemotive style, Kolokotronis was a man who kept close track of his kinsmen, whom he mentions a number of times. He also considered second cousins important enough to mention them specifically. For such a man, therefore, the apparent lack of reference to *koumbari* is perhaps suggestive that he viewed it less as a link between adults than one between adult and child.

The only time Kolokotronis mentions *koumbaria* is when he visits his godmother, who had baptised him. She only appears once in his text and he visits her when he is on the run from Turkish soldiers. He does not hide in her house and thus prejudice her safety, but asks for food. She gives him three *okas* of bread, but he is careful to repay her, and indeed overpays her generously: 'I gave her a Venetian florin' (Edmonds, 1969; 104), hardly a case of delayed or generalised reciprocity. Here Kolokotronis may have been concerned to demonstrate his honour; that is, to demonstrate that in spite of his pressing need for food, a basic item which any Khristianos would offer freely to his neighbour or to any stranger, he actually repaid his godmother – who by virtue of this relationship had an added obligation to assist him – and he repaid her with an even more rare and valuable item: a Venetian florin. The god-mother does economically well out of this transaction forced on her, but Kolokotronis emerges as the honourable man *par excellence*, by generously assisting a woman in all probability likely to have been a widow (he does not mention her husband), and poor (she lives at the edge of the village).

We believe that as the number of institutional strategies available to turn non-kin (*kseni*) into fictional kinsmen narrowed in modern Greece – owing to Church objections, the growth of elective politics, and struc-tural transformations within the society – *koumbaria* became increas-ingly important. Not only did it have to carry a number of structural 'loads' previously carried by a number of different institutions, but it was also more functional for modern contexts. These include:

(i)   *Koumbaria* was more family, small domestic-group centred rather than based on large agnatic groups, as with blood and soul brotherhood.

(ii) The obligations between the contracting parties, while strong, did not commit and expose individuals to potentially risky enterprises and alliances, such as with blood brotherhood.

(iii) The obligations were entered into freely and were different for each generation.

(iv) In contrast to soul brotherhood, it was future-oriented rather than past-determined. It was legitimated by reference to the needs of the subsequent generation (the godchild) rather than by reference to the 'sins' of the ancestors.

(v)   It enabled individuals to possess a discrete, identifiable, and particular set of fictional kin different from all others, and the obligations are not transferrable to other agnatic kin.

We do not wish to suggest that the patronage aspects of godparenthood were unimportant in eighteenth-century Athens and in other parts of Greece, or that it was non-existent. Ottoman overlords, for example, baptised Christian children in spite of church prohibitions. But Ottoman-controlled Greece was organised in such a way as to minimise the full exploitation of godparenthood, as was subsequently to occur in the new Greek kingdom. This was a hierarchical, stratified society with relatively restricted social mobility and the ruling groups were small and keen to patrol their borders. Social mobility was achieved through the possession of cash and the occupation of key administrative posts. Links between town and country were not particularly well developed or complex and the town did not fully dominate the countryside. Landlords and Ottoman overlords collected rents and taxes from whole villages rather than from individual farmers (Vergopoulos, 1975), a situation which did not encourage the development of individual dyadic ties of godparenthood and patronage. *Arkhon* concern with adoption reveals the interests of a traditional landowning elite involved in all aspects of production and reproduction, as opposed to the individualistic wheeling and dealing of a mercantile-oriented urban middle class. Indeed some indication that individual transactionalist dyadic ties between different classes were not particularly well developed and that *koumbaria* was not heavily invested in for the purposes of social mobility especially by the poor, especially in the Turkocratia, comes from the fact that children of the poorer classes were often baptised collectively in the same font and anyone present could become a godparent. In other words there lacked a spirit of premeditation, of long-term recruitment and the continuation of links across time which would be closely nurtured by the participants. The Church in the early nineteenth-century came out heavily against this practice, emphasising the importance of the 'proper choice' of the godparent, the exchange of gifts, individual baptism, and so on (Gedeon, 1889; 459–63).

At this point it is important to clear up a potential puzzle and a possible source of misunderstanding. We have to ask whether *koumbaria* was actually concealed by 'adoption' (*yiothesia*); that is, did *koumbari* 'adopt' their godchildren, transposing them to their homes and finally supplying them with a dowry? For the following three reasons, we do not think that this was the case.

First the contracts make no references to *nunnos* or *tatas* (godparent), the terms usually employed in such cases. Second, godparenthood (*koumbaria*) is an institution which links three parties; the natural parents, the godfather (*koumbaros*) and the child. The Latin terms for such relationships are *compaternitas* (natural parent/godparent relationship) and *paternitas* (godparent/baptised child relationship). Today the normal, church-supported, practice is for the godparent/baptised child relationship to become activated especially if the child is orphaned; but it certainly does not require the godparent to incorporate the godchild into his or her household. Furthermore, many of these girls were not orphans. Third, in most cases cited above, adoptive parents were not religiously and legally recognised proper adoptive parents, but were rather 'foster' parents. In Justinian's terms the girl was an *alumna*, 'best translated as a "foster daughter"', since she was not a ward [*pupilla*] in the legal sense but was being protected and raised by the man in question' (Lynch, 1986; 224). Marriages between a legally adopted girl and her adoptive parent or a parent's natural children were not permitted in Orthodox Canon law and were to influence subsequent regulations over spiritual kinship.

Conclusion

In early nineteenth-century Greece the growth of *koumbaria*, and the decline and transformation of adoption, which was an increasingly middle class phenomenon, and which involved kinswomen rather than humble rural girls for labour-recruitment services, appear to be structurally related. While references to adoption in its various forms, to blood brotherhood, and to soul (or spiritual) brotherhood, appear abundant in early modern Greek society in the first decades of the nineteenth century, references to *koumbaria* are perhaps too sparse to be purely fortuitous. While the former all gradually declined in importance, the latter gained in social prominence. In contrast to adoption, which was the modern and more socially visible form of spiritual kinship (*pnevmatike singenia*), *koumbaria* left the child in its place but strengthened links between the coparents, that is between godparent and natural parent.

Such links were particularly significant in the new society being formed after Independence. Athens underwent a huge population increase from the middle of the nineteenth century. Many wealthy merchants and landlords moved to the capital and *koumbaria* became increasingly important, both politically and economically. Politically, the fluid nature of nineteenth-century Greek politics, the absence of a traditional elite, and the formation of new political classes and ruling groups drawn from various regions and held together by an increasing dependence on control over state patronage and bureaucracy, encouraged the development of *koumbaria* as a 'traditional' means of recruitment at the grassroots. Mouzelis has observed that

in the pre-capitalist Greek economy, the linkage between State and 'civil' society was not in terms of classes or rather of secondary organizations represen-

ting class interests, but in terms of purely personal clientelistic networks. This
was due to the overriding dominance of patronage politics during this period.

(1978; 16)

Support for this view comes from the study of the political scientist K.
Legg, who noted that nineteenth-century Greek politics was dominated
by specific, often interrelated, families: 'the new [post-Independence]
elite was largely descended from the old competing leaders but tied
more closely together because of similar education and intermarriage'
(1969; 300). He also notes that 40 per cent of all ministers and 21 per
cent of all political leaders between 1843–78 were children of politicians
(*ibid.*; 307) and concludes that the state institutions 'were used more for
patronage purposes than as instruments of central Government control'
(*ibid.*; 311).[5]

There are numerous accounts of the use of clientage and of armed
groups of men in the Greek countryside during the first decades of
independence. In 1840, J. A. Buchon observed, 'à tous les habitants
reguliers d'Athènes, il faut ajouter bon nombre des anciens militaires et
clients qui arrivent des provinces pour témoigner leur allègeance à leur
chets ou solliciter leur appui' (Andrews, 1979; 212). In the Peloponnese
armed retainers of rural notables were common:

notre hôte est chef de parti, chef de clan. Il a ses hommes, nombreux et
dévoués, qu'il entretient, qu'il arme, qu'il loge ou établit dans ses terres . . .
Cette vie est un singulier mélange de féodalité et de démocratie. Kaponitza est
le seigneur; son autorité est sans limite et sans partage. Sur son ordre on donne
la mort et on la reçoit. Entre ses mains l'honneur et la fortune de tous. Cet
homme est plus qu'un roi. Mais en voyant cette vie en commun sous le même
toit, ce sommeil côté à côté sur la même planche, ce partage égale des fatigues et
des dangers, le faste et la servilité nulle part, cette union de coeur à coeur, ce
respect réciproque, on cherche un maître et l'on ne trouve que des frères.

(A. Grenier, in Andrews, 1979; 242–3)

In conclusion we turn to that inimitable chronicler of early Greek
political life, Makriyiannis, for some indication of the use to which
koumbaria was put in the new Greek state, its ethos, as well as its risks.
He recounts the overtures made to him by the politician Koleti: 'At first
he wanted to baptise a child of mine and God gave me twins. As I had
promised, I agreed to this . . . I made preparations and he came
together with ambassadors and their wives. I welcomed them and we ate
and drank together. I had all the important and powerful people as my
guests' (1947; 184, n. B). Yet later 'when Koleti discovered that he was
to gain nothing from his koumbaros, he sent soldiers . . .' (*ibid.*; 187).
Makriyiannis' moral is clear: interested trust, trust based on expediency
even if between spiritual kin, can lead to betrayal.

6

The family and emotional life

Introduction

By their very nature, matrimonial contracts give very little direct information on the nature of emotional life within the family, on relations between men and women, and on the expression of love within the family. Indeed in contemporary Greek society the *prikosymfono* (the matrimonial contract, but literally and significantly the 'dowry agreement') and the dowry have become important political issues symbolising the domination and commoditisation of women. The *prikosymfono* (pl. *prikosymfona*), especially in middle class and liberal contexts, is now viewed as a denial of the free expression of love between men and women, of free choice, and of the individuality of women, turning them into items of transaction between groups. Often a distinction is drawn between marriage *ya aghape* (for love) and *me prikosymfono* (through a matrimonial contract). But how did urban Greeks of various social classes in the late eighteenth and early nineteenth centuries view the ethics of marriage? If they viewed marriage differently how did this attitude change across time? In this chapter we examine emotional life within the family by drawing upon memoirs and a symptomatic reading of contracts and popular literature from the nineteenth and early twentieth centuries. We begin by analysing the different significances of the *prikosymfono* for the various social groups and for the Church. For the latter it was an instrument to control 'custom': the 'scandalous' practice of cohabitation among the urban poor. For the higher social strata the *prikosymfono* was important as a 'rite of literacy' in a context of restricted literacy. With the progressive changes in the resources transmitted at marriage and the creation of a 'free matrimonial market' the *prikosymfono* assumed even more significantly the function of a secular contract as a means to achieve trust, and it became both law and custom. Hence we examine the dialectical relationship between writing and social organisation: on the one hand, the use of written formulas reflects changes in the organisation of family life, and on the other hand these formulas themselves influence the way that emotions within the family are expressed and perceived. This enables us to analyse how certain dominant groups in Athenian society redefined the boundaries of the family and its emotional life in a nationalistic literacy-dependent state context. We demonstrate this by reference to popular literature of this period and conclude by examining the way in which literacy and literature influenced the perception and significance of motherhood in urban contexts.

The ethics of marriage
A discussion of the ethics of marriage has to begin with an examination of the meaning of that most visible marker of marriage for the historical anthropologist: the matrimonial contract or *prikosymfono*. For certainly not all marriages were recorded and marked by *prikosymfona*. On one level the meaning of a *prikosymfono* is obvious and self-evident; it is a legally recognised means for the devolution of property from the preceding generation to the next at marriage. Yet this was far from its only significance. The *prikosymfono* as artefact underwent considerable change in meaning across time. Let us start by observing that in a context of restricted literacy and uncertain land tenure, as was the case in the latter period of the Turkocratia, it had as much to do with the claims of the donor to having 'owned' that property as it had to do with the rights of the recipient to its exploitation. In spite of the restrictions imposed by the Ottoman system there was a substantial growth of private holdings (*mulk*), both Christian and Muslim, in the seventeenth and eighteenth centuries (McGowan, 1981). Some of it was clearly obtained at the expense of peasant cultivators:

In the more fertile lowland districts, private holdings, some of them large in extent, increased despite the formal prohibitions of the law. One motive for the surreptitious conversion of fiefs to private domain was the desire of holders to evade the legal restrictions protecting peasants on entailed land. Once the land was characterized as *mulk*, the owner could dictate the terms of labour and residence . . . Semipublic and state lands became vulnerable to moneyed persons who could persuade compliant local officials to legitimize illegal conversions . . . The increasingly lax application of once-strict property laws enabled not only Muslims but also Christians to acquire property ownership to a greater extent than previously . . . where Turkish authority was weak or indifferent Greeks found ways to circumvent Ottoman legal procedures. They might trade previously issued deeds, or in transactions among Christians, *rely upon sales documents signed before bishops or village elders*.

(McGrew, 1985; 28–9, our italics)

We have quoted this passage at length because, although McGrew does not mention it, *prikosymfona* possessed the institutional framework and preconditions necessary to camouflage the steady increase of private property: the transfer of a property to another person, registration in a written form, and 'reliable' witnesses. The high number of registered *prikosymfona* and the fact that they appear to have become more frequent during the latter part of Ottoman rule would tend to support the hypothesis that at least some contracts had the purpose of either disguising the appropriation of entailed lands, or else of ensuring that private property in tumultuous times could not be sequestered. In other words, by being formally registered they implicitly registered claims to property in a system which legally prevented the accumulation of property. In this respect *prikosymfona* had as much to do with property accumulation as with its devolution.

Our main concern with the *prikosymfono* is however with its religious significance, its ritual connotations, and as a statement on the nature of trust within Athenian society. In eighteenth- and nineteenth-century Greece it was primarily a formal statement of a marriage sanctified by the Church and sanctioned by the community's elders, much as the *'aqd* functions in North African society. In eighteenth- and nineteenth-century Athens it appears that very different practices were followed by different groups in the signing of the *prikosymfono*. Among the wealthy and titled Athenians *prikosymfona* were signed immediately prior to the Church ceremony (*stefanosi*) or very soon thereafter, and it formally celebrated an alliance between the two groups. Among the poorer members, especially migrants and ex-peasants, they were often signed quite some time after the couple had begun to cohabit, and after the marriage celebrations had taken place, sometimes even after one of the parents (usually the father) had died. In fact many of these contracts refer to the bride as *neonymphos* (recently married), and not *melonymphos* (future bride); others did not refer to the bride at all, as would be the case had the contract been signed before the church ceremony, which sanctioned the marriage in the eyes of the Church. It was thus on one level a post-mortem inheritance (in those cases where the father had died in the interval), although it was formally registered and presented as an *inter-vivos* or pre-mortem gift. Why should there have been such differences in practice? What was the significance of this?

Family interests and Church prescriptions appear to be the two main keys here. Among wealthy and titled families a *prikosymfono* was a means to clarify the respective rights and claims of the children upon the parental estate. More precisely, it enabled the legal endowment of daughters with their share of the parental property, though not necessarily likely, in most cases, to amount to a share equal to that inherited by sons. It was also a statement of position between the two contracting family groups. In addition it coincided with Church approval, because as E. Papataxiarchis (1985) points out for other areas of Greece (Lesbos), the Church waged a campaign against non-sacramental and legally recognised cohabitation, which it viewed as scandalous and sinful.

Something similar to this latter practice appears to have occurred among the poorer members of Athenian society, such as migrants and ex-peasants. As in Lesbos they appear either to have entered into long and unofficial periods of cohabitation a considerable time before the signing of the *prikosymfono* or, even more frequently, they appear to have viewed their engagement as a virtual marriage and to have anticipated their conjugal rights.

By the 1840s this practice appears to have disappeared in Athens, yet it was still common in the countryside. About, a perceptive observer, noted that

Betrothal, another religious ceremony has almost as sacred character as marriage. In certain districts, Missolonghi for instance, the betrothed enjoys all the privileges of a husband. Before celebrating the marriage they wait till it gives promise of the first fruits. If the bridegroom, after having conscientiously performed the betrothal withdrew from the 'sacrament' his refusal would cost him his life.

(1855; 134)

Similar practices occurred in eighteenth-century France. Segalen notes that this was 'basically a working class phenomenon, a feature of the lives of agricultural labourers whose only asset was not a family patrimony but the labour force of a group of young people' (1986; 131). As in Lesbos such a phenomenon appears to have been present in areas of large-scale land-holding. Because settlement was often uxorilocal among the poor, the implications for female inheritance of parental property were less radical than might be expected. A girl assumed formal and legal rights to her dowry some years after cohabitation had begun, usually on the birth of a child, which would provide the impetus to register the marriage in the legally and religiously approved manner as well as to baptise the child. Because the dowry often included a house or part of a house, signing the contract also ensured that the bride and her groom would remain to care for the elderly parents if relations had been commensal and had prospered. Yet by the very fact of being written down, these were the successful longlasting unions. In reality while 'most marriages in the lower socio-economic groups will be unregistered whatever their constitution' (Goody, 1986; 139), we do not know how permanent all such unions were. As Goody (1986) and others

(Segalen, 1986) have pointed out, major differences existed between normal lower 'class' rural marriages (which tended to be as permanent as any other) and similar urban ones (where unions tended to be more flexible). However, we believe that given the 'rural' nature of the Athenian economy in the late eighteenth century, as well as the patterns of migration, marriages among members of the lower socio-economic groups were more akin in spirit to rural marriages and were likely to be permanent. As in contemporary Cypriot villages, an engagement was tantamount to a marriage; this included the anticipation of conjugal rights and in some cases cohabitation. They certainly were not 'associations of individuals', a situation unlikely even in contemporary Greece.

Similar practices in anticipating conjugal rights occur in contemporary Crete (Herzfeld, 1983) and rural Cyprus (Sant Cassia, 1982) where villagers often joke that the *papas* is not marrying two people but three. As Herzfeld (1980) has pointed out the word *gamos* is polyvalent. It can mean the two families' celebration of the match; the engagement; the religious ceremony itself, that is the *stefanosi* (literally the 'crowning'), and the word is also related to sexual intercourse. He suggests that this polyvalence enables villagers to assert that 'no sex before *gamos*' is practised without falling into contradiction and maintaining the semblance of following an honourable code. However the similarities between contemporary Cyprus, for example, and nineteenth-century Athens should not blind us to their differences. In early nineteenth-century Athens poorer couples cohabited after their *gamos* (the family celebrations and/or the engagements) but often before drawing up the *prikosymfono*. In contemporary Cyprus, while many couples anticipate their conjugal rights after the *gamos*, this is always after the *prikosymfono* has been drawn up. In short the *prikosymfono* has become a precondition of trust, a clear indication of a reliance on legal formulas to regulate relations between family groups.

In the new state the Church, which had long been concerned with grassroots practices, attempted to tighten control. A Holy Synod decree of 1835 aimed at rooting out simony, as 'the right time has come to stop this evil wherever it exists' (Frazee, 1969; 128); bishops were ordered to see that each parish kept a strict record of baptisms and weddings and funerals. Even more significant was an attempt to check on marriages and on the participation therein of the grassroots clergy: no wedding was allowed to be solemnised without the permission of the local bishop, and any priest who solemnised a marriage without proper permission might be suspended for three months (Frazee, 1969; 129). Finally engagements (*mnisties*), which until 1835 had taken place in a church and were accompanied both by ritual and the exchange of gifts between parties, were banned from taking place in the church. In this way the Church hoped to eradicate the practice whereby the poorer members of society viewed such rituals as tantamount to marriage and legitimating cohabitation.

Thus far we have discussed the *prikosymfono* from the perspective of Church prescriptions and family interests and practices, and mainly in terms of its timing. However, the *prikosymfono* was also a social contract between two parties – the groom's and the bride's families – and this was to become increasingly important in the course of the nineteenth century. Briefly put, with the development of a more complex civil society the *prikosymfono* became increasingly important not just to legitimate a cohabitation in the eyes of the Church (as among the poorer classes), nor merely as a means of reducing ambiguity between heirs and of retaining control of the bulk of the parental estate in male hands (as with the wealthy and titled); it became socially required. By this we mean that the requirement to marry legally became a social requirement in addition to a church requirement. No social group was more insistent on this than the *nikokirei* and the petit-bourgeois, due mainly to a radical change in the political and economic implications of marriage. Indeed the Church banned engagement rituals (*mnisties*) precisely because they were being treated as proper or legitimate marriages by the poorer members of society.

In the new Greek kingdom the stakes of political office increased, vastly overshadowing commerce, agriculture, and industrial production as a means to acquire influence and power. With the progressive dismantling of dowry regulations set by the Church and the ruling *arkhon* class, a new nationally extending field of matrimonial competition was created. Marriage became one of the major means of social mobility in a monetarised economy which possessed few genuinely large capitalist enterprises. Matrimonial alliances and the accompanying extension of spiritual kinship became one of the main avenues for the accumulation of political capital in the form of votes, clients, and contacts in the right places (that is, in the vastly expanding state bureaucracy), which in turn permitted the accumulation of commercial capital. Clearly the particular evolution of the Greek state and economy shaped this character of marriage and kinship, but in turn the state and the economy were shaped by marriage and kinship.

Corresponding to these changes the *prikosymfono*'s significance became transformed. Previously the *prikosymfono* accompanied the establishment of matrimonial alliances within largely homogamous groups. Although we are not dealing with watertight social classes, and although social mobility was clearly possible, movement upwards for both men and women was regulated in certain ways. On one level the *prikosymfono* served to control social mobility, especially when the scribes were Churchmen. Although the Church's strictures on dowry inflation were often ineffectual, they nevertheless had the function of setting limits to what was permissible and of identifying deviants who ran the risk of excommunication and social disapproval. Even more significantly they oriented matrimonial competition in certain directions by identifying those resources whose possession eased and legitimated the transition of a groom or bride from one social group to another (cash for men; costumes and trousseaux for women). Clearly although one of the main functions of a *prikosymfono*, and indeed of all written contracts, is to fix an agreement and to establish a set of legally binding, unambiguous and permanent obligations, this did not necessarily imply that trust was lacking between the two parties. Athenians did not record their agreements on *prikosymfona* merely because trust was difficult to achieve between the heirs at a later date. This function was in any case guaranteed by the Ksofili. They were on the one hand an expression of formality, an acknowledgement of the importance of the marriage which required formal recognition in a permanent written form. They established and regularised a set of obligations between the two contracting parties, involved a whole range of witnesses and were marked by religious formulas at the beginning of the contract (for example, IC.XP.NI.KA. – Jesus Christ Victorious or Doxa Christou, 'By Christ's Glory'). Such formulas were not mere rhetorical devices; they constructed the importance of the occasion. *Prikosymfona* were religious artefacts. We are dealing with a context in which religion is literate, of 'The Book', and in which literacy is 'sacred' because it is restricted; in effect with the use of writing by a largely oral culture.

Hence a *prikosymfono* was entered into precisely because of the sacredness of marriage (not necessarily in the Church's sense as a 'Sacrament'), because it was the means to achieve full adulthood and to satisfy a moral imperative where men and women reached their full potential as married members of society (in contrast to the Church's dogma, which viewed married life as the next best thing to chastity). *Prikosymfona*, in short, were rituals of literacy which elevated a social occasion, not just legal safeguards over the distribution and endowment of property (although they certainly had this function). Registering a marriage through a *prikosymfono* was an expression of the symbolic importance individuals attached to the marriage; it was a *timios* (honourable) marriage, not necessarily a 'good' marriage in economic terms. This helps to explain why so many of our contracts are drawn from the lower levels of society, where the amounts of resources transferred are often pitiably small, though not necessarily unimportant to the protagonists.

A further function of the *prikosymfono* was to identify and reassure the contracting parties that they belonged to the same social group. One of the main functions of the identification of certain resources with certain social groups was that it created a semblance of belonging to the same cultural world in the way that dialect and intonation function as group markers in the contemporary world. It was a mark of formality and the formalisation of relations between family groups. We are dealing here with a society which gave particular symbolic value to material things as markers of social status, where the right to belong to a certain social group was expressed in, and pursued through, the use of material symbols.

With the creation of a new nationally extensive arena of matrimonial competition as well as the creation of new resources which entered the matrimonial market, the significance of the *prikosymfono* changed. To begin with, the dowry and the matrimonial contract entered the Civil Code. They moved from the domain of custom to national law, imposing as a result a type of national uniformity which transcended regional variations. More significantly, as literacy became more widespread in society *prikosymfona* began to assume the characteristics of a national (or Greek) tradition which had the force of law. Many Greek villagers ask foreign anthropologists whether they have *prikosymfona* in their native country. They do not merely ask whether it is the custom to endow daughters with a dowry, but rather whether men have to enter the painful and crippling world of obligations 'to society', which the 'tradition' of the *prikosymfono* represents and embodies. In the new geographically and occupationally mobile social order which accompanied the establishment of the Greek state, *prikosymfona* became the only recognisable, standardised and legal means available to dilute the suspicion and caution which inevitably grew in the brave new world of modern Greece.[1] It standardised social intercourse at marriage, transforming the complex process of matchmaking, *proxenia*, to become merely the preliminary step leading to the drawing up of a contract, in contrast to the past when a *prikosymfono* was drawn up as the ritualistic and religious culmination of a process of achievement of trust and alliance. Indeed one of the first laws passed by the Revolutionary Government was designed to place the registration of notaries on a sounder footing (the so-called *kathikonta ton notarion*, or 'duties of the Notaries', Dimakopoulos, 1966; 89). Until recently in modern Greece a *prikosymfono* was a social requirement for marriage, rather than of marriage, as it had been in the past. Consequently, especially in urban contexts, what became important was how many and what type of resources were being transmitted at marriage, rather than how both contracting families were expressing their obligations to each other, to their respective children, and as members of determinate social groups. In Greece there has been a movement from the old equation of alliance→dowry/marriage→*prikosymfono*, to the new equation of *prikosymfono*→dowry→alliance/marriage. Indeed so pervasive has this model become that when attempts or overtures at matchmaking fail in Cyprus, it is often said that the two families 'did not agree on the *prikosymfono*', meaning that they failed to agree on the goods to be transferred. Of course this situation is somewhat rare as efforts are made to ensure beforehand that the family receiving the proposal would be amenable to the match, yet what is significant is the strategic use made of the *prikosymfono* to legitimate (and all that it embodies – writing, permanency, finality) a refusal as well as a strategic withdrawal to save face.

It is clear that we are in the presence of a society that has increasingly tended to fetishise the written word. The written word gives knowledge, power and certainty and can pin down an elusive trust in an uncertain world, in contrast to mere *loyia* (words) which leave no trace. This uncertain world is not beyond the confines of society, in the domain of spirits (*eksotika*) who tempt men and lead them astray, but rather in the domain of other people (*o kosmos*), or non-kin (*kseni*), who are potentially untrustworthy and dangerous. We examine the implications in our conclusion. But what is important is the visualisation of fate or destiny (*mira*, or *moira*, which also means one's 'rightful portion' and which applies equally to property as to death and destiny). Now while there is a continuity of some sorts in Greek culture in the notion of *mira*, how it has been visualised has tended to change across time. In the Classical world, fate (*mira*) is personified by three female deities (the Fates) usually spinning or weaving men's fates (thus holding a spindle or distaff). Although the notion of fate as written emerges with Lucian, it remained somewhat rare until the modern period. Nowadays Greek villagers explicitly link fate with writing (*ine grammeni*, it is written), and Krikos-Davis observes that 'the notion of one's destiny written down at one's birth is encountered in modern Greek tradition more than that of spinning it' (1982; 128). In other words there exists not only the emergence of writing as a more powerful metaphor and symbolisation of fate, but also a transformation in the nature of the fetishisation involved: from a fetishisation of persons/deities to a fetishisation of objects/writing, or more precisely of objectification and hence calculability.

The parallelisms are worthwhile pursuing: in modern Greek culture individuals receive their share of property (*mira*) at marriage as well as their life-chances, and they receive these things through something written, the *prikosymfono*. 'Fate' is to be found within the world, and is therefore more akin to the notion of luck, *tyche*, which many villagers often find difficult to distinguish except in extreme situations, a this-worldly view increasingly subscribed to by the up-and-coming *nikokirei*.

In such a modern context where there is a fetishisation of the written word, it is hardly surprising that the *prikosymfono* has now become identified with a denial of the spirit of 'modern marriage', or 'free choice' (as villagers often somewhat disdainfully say of 'the West', which implies to them that if unions can be entered so easily, then they can just as easily be terminated) and paradoxically that most attempts to weaken the hold of the 'custom' of dowry transmissions have not had much success. The tendency to transform the *prikosymfono* into a legal secular contract and an expression of social relations anchored by the law, was particularly subscribed to by the *nikokirei*. But at the same time, owing to the Church's strictures against lower-class forms of marriage practices, marriage began to assume in the public eye the character of a sacrament in the Church's sense, that is, bounded by Church defined and imposed rites. In short we are moving from a situation where the contract was embedded in a rural type of alliance and was sacred because it was written, to a situation where the contract became disembedded and transformed into a pre-mortem division of property to establish separate households, or urban type descent. By establishing agreement and enabling definite calculations to be made it became unalterable and thus sacred. Centuries earlier a similar process was noted by Ibn Khaldoun, who identified the shift from rural *assabiya* (solidarity) to 'genealogy' in the North African town. In Renaissance Tuscany, too, the dowry as written agreement achieved an unquestioned authority: 'From the top of Tuscan society to the bottom, families ran to the notary to establish to establish a dowry, and marriage without a dowry seemed more blameworthy than a union unblessed by the Church. The dowry penetrated to the very heart of the social ideology of the time' (Klapisch-Zuber, 1985; 214). By the sixteenth century, in Greece, too, the provision of a dowry marked the distinction between honour and dishonour. Icons of St Nicolas, the patron saint of merchants, depicting him providing dowries for the three daughters of an impoverished noble and thus rescuing them from prostitution were common from Ioannina to Crete (*From Byzantium to El Greco*, in *Exhibition Catalogue 1987*; 186). Marriage without a written dowry was inconceivable.

Thus far we have established that the use of matrimonial contracts had different attendant meanings in the past than in contemporary times. We now wish to examine in greater detail how *prikosymfona* were constructed in the past and who they involved. Were they primarily a parental endowment of the bride, an alliance between two families established through the marriage, or a collective family endowment of the bride involving kin other than parents?

The contracts do not merely refer to the bride, groom and their respective parents. A significant percentage (nearly 30 per cent) also often explicitly refer to the bride's brothers, who are also registered as 'giving' her a dowry.[2] Part of this is certainly due to the high proportion of fatherless brides. However, another reason was that a dowry was not merely a gift from the parents to a daughter, or a means of transmitting wealth across generations at the point of marriage. It was also a collective statement of wealth, prestige, and position within society, but even more specifically of the interrelationship between two kin groups. Brothers figured in the contracts for two reasons. First, they held a direct interest in the proceedings, as the dowry was a pre-mortem devolution of parental property, and hence their agreement was necessary to pre-empt disagreements and difficulties in the present and even more so in the future when the residue of the parental estate was to be divided. Second, they often contributed to their sisters' dowries; their labour and efforts went into amassing the various goods necessary to build up the parcel of goods termed the dowry. The family was thus collectively involved in any of the marriages of the daughters. Brothers and sisters entered a long period of exchange, involving different types of goods and different patterns of action. Prior to a sister's marriage, the brother would be expected to give freely of his labour, protection and income. She would not be expected to ask this of him, but would receive and claim this by virtue of being a sister. After her marriage, the sister would be expected to give up all claims to the parental estate, having moved to her new home and removed herself from her natal family, although relations might still be strong. Finally, in this society it was men who made alliances with other groups and women who served as bridges or links between the two, a point we explore below.

When property was given, rights were always retained residually. The reference to brothers 'giving' their sisters a dowry indicates not a sibling solidarity, but an agnatic one. For if a woman died issueless, her dowry property reverted back to her nearest surviving male kin, not to all her nearest surviving kin. This explains why, when sisters appear in the contracts, they are noted as merely 'giving their agreement' to the endowment. It was the nearest surviving males whose obligation it was to endow the bride, even when she had sisters but no brothers.

Such practices and terminology indicate more precisely the nature of solidarity within the kin group. Women had claims upon the men who retained both ideologically and legally the right to dispose of property, a clear indication of the important role of agnation in traditional Athens. Sisters might contribute through their labour to one another's dowries, but they did not give as autonomous free agents; indeed as sisters women appear in only 2.7 per cent of the contracts. They therefore did not retain residual rights in that property. Links between sisters were de-emphasised in favour of links between a sister and a specific set of brothers, which have differed for each sister as each brother matured and married, to be replaced by other unmarried brothers.

We are thus dealing with a society which was ideologically predisposed to treating the endowment of women at marriage as a type of male 'problem'; one monopolised by men both in its construction and its resolution, either through symbolically conferring status on the men as givers of property, or through ensuring that such property reverted back to them if the union was childless.

If relations between brothers and sisters were marked by a certain possessive responsibility by the brother, how were relations between husband and wife expressed? And what was the social position of the widow?

In a dominant viri-patrilocal settlement pattern at marriage, women must have initially found it difficult to gain full acceptance by affines. In many cases because the groom's father was dead and they had to contend directly with his mother. Indeed women were characterised as an unrelated corner or hearth (*ksenogonia*) of their own natal household. R. Mandel (1983), who has analysed the symbolism of the ballad 'The Bridge of Arta' found throughout Greece and the Balkans, suggests that the theme of a master craftsman's wife who has to be sacrificed and then immured in the foundations of a bridge in order for it to stand, brings out the liminal position of women in Greek society. Yet the position of brides must have differed considerably according to the social group. Among the small tightly knit Athenian aristocracy, marriage certainly heralded a change but it was unlikely to have involved a radical culture shock. In addition brides were sufficiently endowed to be somewhat isolated from the awkwardness of their situation. Some indication of the domestic culture of the *arkhon* and *fanariot* families is furnished by the visitor J. A. Buchon. We quote his observations at length as they indicate the cosmopolitan orientations of the *arkhon* class, its sense of social difference, the suspicion that surrounded them after Independence (especially by the *nikokirei* group), their tendency to isolate themselves from the rest of the Athenian population, and finally their intermarriage with the new political class of the ex-Klefts:

Les familles fanariotes avaient, longtemps avant la révolution grecque, adopté les habitudes occidentales. Presque toutes étaient opulentes, car tour à tour les dignités d'hospodar de Valachie et de Moldavie, et celles de drogman de la Porte et de l'Arsenal et autres hauts offices des principautés, avaient passé entre leurs mains. Leurs enfants apprenaient en naissant la langue française; toutes leurs relations étaient avec les Occidentaux, et surtout avec la diplomatie, et chaque famille se rangeait sous une bannière particulière. Au moment de la révolution grecque, les familles fanariotes riches et puissantes prirent la part la plus active à l'affranchissement de la Grèce. Mais, en général, les Fanariotes étaient suspects au reste de la population grecque. Leurs habitudes étrangères, leurs distinctions aristocratiques éveillaient la méfiance de ce peuple d'une nationalité jalouse et d'un sentiment complètement démocratique. A Athènes, où toutes ces familles se sont retirées, elles vivent beaucoup entre elles et s'allient entre elles. Cependant peu à peu elles se mêlent davantage au reste de la population. Ainsi la brune et belle Rallou Karadza, petite-fille du vieil hospodar Karadza, le type le plus pur de l'antique aristocratie fanariote dans son beau temps, épouse un fils du chef de montagnes moraite Colocotroni, le jeune Constantin Colocotroni, élevé à Paris et parlant français comme nous.

(Andrews, 1979; 211)

By contrast among the rising middle class, initially hemmed in by a rigid political structure which offered few possibilities for political expression or office, the position of brides was more complex and varied. Matrimonial strategies also held a greater significance. Upwardly mobile bourgeois brides, accompanied by cash and trousseaux while acceptable, were unlikely to have been fully integrated by their affinal groups. Most accounts of the *arkhon* class of *signori*, admittedly written by bourgeois writers, suggest that they were intensely jealous of their privileges and origins, a situation unlikely to have been conducive to full incorporation of a bride from socially inferior origins. However for the majority – those who married within their own social group – marriage tended to separate the bride from her natal family to a greater extent than among the tightly knit aristocracy and the neighbourhood-bound ex-peasants and migrants. Indeed the tendency towards neolocality and more monetarised cash dowries was to a large extent initially an urban middle class phenomenon. We refer to two examples. First there is the case of Mihalis Melos, the prospective merchant suitor discussed above who desired a house away from his parents-in-law. The second is taken from the codex of P. Poulou (1957; no. 189, [1827]). Kirios Anagnosti Papa Michael asks from the parents of his bride Kirias Elizaveth Danili that they purchase for him a building plot for a 'middle sized house and in a good location'. Yet in many cases conflict emerged between sons and fathers over the issue of a separate household. Yorghios Gazis from Epiros, secretary of Karaiskakis during the War of Independence, recalls in his memoirs how his father Kostas strongly opposed his plans to establish a separate household with his fourteen-year-old bride. So strongly expressed was the father's view that the son was obliged to abduct his wife from his paternal home in 1836. Relations between the agnatic group headed by the father and Yorghios plummeted and were only restored when the latter agreed through a written contract to give his father 300 drachmas per annum to support him in his old age (*ya ta yiratia mou ke ya ta eksoda tou spitiou*). Furthermore he could only claim his inheritance if he returned to the bosom of his family, that is, to reside with his father (Gazis, 1971; 272, 274).

There were a number of reasons for the tendency towards neolocality and more monetarised dowries. To begin with we are dealing with a much larger group, wealthy merchants and individuals of all sorts, who increasingly came to settle in Athens, initially from other regions of the Greek kingdom and after the 1870s from Greek-speaking Ottoman territories. Given such diverse origins, suspicion between potential affines must have been more difficult to overcome than it would have been among groups who had interacted all their lives. Furthermore, marriage became riskier in terms of the security of dowry goods. In the Turkocratia land was less of a commodity and did not enter the market to a great extent. In the new Greek state land became a full commodity and it began to be supplanted by cash as the main dowry component. Although this clearly belonged to the bride its very liquidity made parental concern more acute.

The family itself was home-oriented; daughters were more home-bound than migrants, busily producing textiles, embroidery and so on for their trousseaux. The shift to a *kseno spiti* (foreign house) must therefore have been most traumatic for both mother and daughter; less so for the males who increasingly worked outside the home in bureaucratic employment. Perhaps even more important, and in contrast to rural 'aristocratic' families in other parts of the Mediterranean, such as southern France (Maresca, 1980), resources were not necessarily in the hands of the older generation but were monopolised by the young in the form of pen-pushing jobs in the vastly expanding Athens-based state administration. Neolocality was a natural solution to these predicaments, a solution encouraged by the Church.

A further reason is that with the opening up of the matrimonial market, the spread of a cash economy, and the growth of cash endowments at marriage, the urban middle class became increasingly disposed to perceive marriage in economic terms. Here we do not just mean that the marriage of a daughter involved a considerable expense for the family; we also mean that the urban middle classes perceived the successful marriage of daughters as the satisfaction of a debt imposed by society and as a means to acquire salvation. Paraphrasing Weber, this was the matrimonial ethic of the urban middle class. It structured the way fathers worked, accumulated wealth and retired once their daughters were married, and it also structured the concerns of mothers and the comportment of daughters. All the members of the family were socialised to maintain this ethic from a young age. For daughters this involved the emphasis on chastity and its exploration through the production of *kendimata*, ornate lace items and clothing, within the safety of the home, producing not the 'utilitarian' goods of country women, but 'symbolic' items for home decoration. Collectively it produced a social world with a certain degree of homogeneity and was expressed in areas such as the home and comportment which were characterised by what Weber called the 'stylisation of life'.

The concern with security and with symbolic manifestations of purity in an urban context was heavily grounded in the life-chances of the city. Perhaps more than anything else employment by the state in its bureaucracy represented the difference between security and despair, well brought out by Edmond About: 'Toute cette bourgeoisie est triste et souffrante. La difficulté de vivre, le manque du nécessaire, l'amour-propre éternellement froissé, et surtout l'incertitude de l'avenir, empêcheront longtemps encore la naissance de cette intimité sans laquelle nous ne concevons pas la famille' (Andrews, 1979; 252).

A further feature of the matrimonial ethic of the urban middle class was the increasing tendency towards homogamy in economic or universally calculable terms. Such concerns were most clearly brought out in the Lessons of the well known and somewhat progressive religious preacher, Kosmas o Aetolos (d. 1779, Sanctified 1961). In his 'Advice to Married Men' (Lesson B1, no 42B) he advises that the bride be 'suitably imbued with a sense of *pudeur* . . . Have you taken a poor woman as your wife? You have taken in a slave. Have you taken a rich woman for your wife? Then you yourself have become a slave and you have earned a cudgelling on your head' (Menounos, 1979; 195).

Ithografia and anthropology
In this section we wish to explore the ethics of marriage and the family by reference to the popular literature of the late nineteenth century. This is necessary for a number of reasons. First, we are dealing with a historical society where perhaps, more than anywhere else in Europe, the concept of nationhood depended upon the strategic manipulation of both texts and time. Second, we are dealing with a period of nascent nationalism pursued through the written word which had radical impli-

cations for wide areas of social life. Third, this was and is a society acutely conscious of the power of the written word over the spoken word, of *grafi* (writing) versus *foni* (speech); many novels of this period attempt to explore this opposition, often using them as metaphors for national identities (Politi, 1988). As Mario Vitti has pointed out for this period: 'everyone, educated or illiterate, recognises the superiority and prestige of writing as an institutionalised weapon against time and distance. This can be seen from newspapers, broadsheet pamphlets, books of poetry and speeches, and memoirs. Kolokotronis dictates his memoirs to Terzetti, Makriyiannis teaches himself to write: both have faith in the written word' (Vitti, 1988; 3).

The genre of literature with which we are concerned is known as *ithografia*, or 'popular' literature. This literature was often serialised in newspapers. We are aware that there is a long and learned debate as to whether this genre was 'realist', and we are not competent to tackle this issue except in an elliptical way. Yet we hope to demonstrate that anthropological analysis can benefit from the use of such texts, though not in the sense of taking such literature as an accurate reflection of reality. Our point of departure is not so much a concern with the actual intentions of authors, or whether or not such literature was realist; rather, we are interested in the conditions which gave rise to a certain problematic, and to the effects of a specific type of circulation of these texts upon the Athenian elite reading public and how it echoed some of their concerns.

As various observers have noted, the attempt to develop *laografia* (folklore) in Greece was intimately linked to the construction of national identity (Herzfeld, 1982; Alexiou, 1984/5). Briefly, the *laografic* enterprise was designed to distinguish Greece from its Oriental (i.e. Ottoman) heritage and to discover the true sources of Hellenic identity, rooted in the past and manifested in the countryside, which would make Greece more European than the European nations, as the font of Western Culture. In some respects it was as much 'anti-West' as 'anti-Oriental', though the former was paradoxically more a byproduct of the latter. In Greece the West was often uncomfortably close, in the shape of foreign and unpopular monarchy, and as Mario Vitti has pointed out, echoing Drosinis, the attempted discovery of national traditions was linked to an anti-West and anti-monarchist tendency (1987; 283).

It has been suggested that the movement towards *ithografia* stemmed from the same source as did *laografia*.[3] Indeed the renowned folklorist N. Politis encouraged authors to document popular life. Yet we wish to suggest that while the stimulus may appear to have been the same for both *ithografia* and *laografia* the two enterprises were radically different.

G. Jusdanis has written, 'the demoticists . . . defended the language of the people and foregrounded the popular tradition; they wished to foster the development of an indigenous literary culture, one reflecting Greek reality and not mimicking western models' (1987; 83).

There are two problems here: what was 'Greek' and what was 'reality'? More precisely what type of 'Greekness' and what type of 'reality' were involved? If we are dealing with writing, and literature, then we are presented with a triple process of construction: of 'Greekness', of the perception of the situation of 'ordinary' people and the construction and presentation of such perceptions in texts, and in artifice; for as Barthes (1974) has pointed out writing is never innocent.

This genre has been called *ithografia*: 'a form of realism devoted with much precision of external details, to the life of peasants in the Greek countryside, described either with sentimentality or with a strong emphasis on its brutal and unpleasant aspects' (Beaton, 1982; 105).

Yet this was not folklore; it may have appeared to be *laografia* in a different guise, and although both *laografia* and *ithografia* may appear to have addressed the same problem (that of constructing a Greek identity), the enterprises were different. To begin with, as Mario Vitti has pointed out, 'whilst in Russia, France and Italy, realism was concerned only secondarily with the agricultural environment, in Greece such an environment was its main concern' (1978; 292–3). Second, many of these writers were often not writing about mainland Greece, but about areas which had just been freed, or were still under Ottoman rule. In this respect we differ from Beaton, who appears to view *ithografia* as the pursuit of *laografia* by other means:

> the science of folklore itself turned out . . . to have grown up not from an objective spirit of enquiry but from a cultural need to find support for a theory; and in a parallel way the new literary genre of ethography was more or less *consciously* cast in the role of creating the 'reality' of a cultural tradition which would link present with past in a distinctively Greek sense of identity of a kind that had not previously existed.
>
> (1982; 120 our italics)

The key word here is 'consciously'. We do not dispute this motivation for which there is strong historical support, but we doubt whether this exhausts the significance of *ithografia* in Greece. Even if we grant that neither folklore nor *ithografia* were 'innocent' enterprises, in that both were ideologically informed, both were 'non-innocent' in different ways and at different depths. And *ithografia* was perhaps not 'innocent' at a greater depth because we are dealing with an artifice which played upon conscious verisimilitude rather than upon the more largely unconscious selectivity involved in Greek folklore, where folklorists at least had customs to document and select. For while *laografia* was a more conscious enterprise in the sense that it was the visible tip of the iceberg of national identity construction (and hence more subject to unconscious selectivity in that conscious artifice construction would more obviously conflict with the purpose of the enterprise), *ithografia* as 'fiction' was also shaped, perhaps to a greater extent, by the undercurrents of the internal concerns of class and social status than folklore could ever be (which aimed at greater 'permanence' by claiming to 'be objective', and was thus perceived as more 'truthful' by the consumers of texts – the urban reading public).

Thus while we agree with the general statement of the informing of *ithografia* by national identity concerns, we are interested here in its largely internal aspects. Beaton has himself observed that

most of the Athenian reading public throughout the 19th century was only a generation away from its peasant origins, and towards the close of the 1860s [*interestingly enough, not before*] the cultural elite of that society began to look back on its rural origins in search of a stable national identity. The rediscovery by the middle class of the way of life of the Greek peasantry was . . . motivated by the . . . desire . . . to lay claim to a tradition that would consolidate the identity of Greece as a nation.

(1982; 198–99 our italics)

However, this was not a rediscovery of a *terra incognita* for construction it was. Nor was it a rediscovery in an 'antiquarian' sense, for the 1860s heralded the massive and growing influx of peasants to the city. The peasant way of life was not confined to the countryside, picturesque relics to be moulded in new ways; it was also uncomfortably present inside the city, where it reminded a relatively new bourgeoisie, heavily dependent upon state patronage and employment, of the origins from which it wished to distance itself. Much the same phenomenon appears to have occurred in North African cities, where ex-*fellahin* continue to adopt a more formalist scriptural Islam in order to distinguish themselves from their more exuberant ex-villagers (Gellner, 1985). This helps to explain the ambiguous treatment of the countryside in popular Greek literature. It was not just concern to discover a world of rural origins which the urban elite had lost (for it is doubtful if it ever did); it was equally a concern to distance themselves from such origins and it was pursued paradoxically through the use of local particularisms such as dialect rather than through the equally restricted *katharevousa*. It is significant, as Mario Vitti points out, that this was the first time that nationalism and cosmopolitanism were opposed. In one respect *ithografia* was more 'subversive' in Greece than *laografia* (the reverse situation from other societies) in that it betrayed the internal concerns of an urban middle class to a greater extent than was permissible in folklore. If folklore is analogous to statements read in court, *ithografia* was analogous to the discussions between the lawyer and the client before the court hearing.

Further support for our contention comes from the work of J. Politi (1988). In a highly stimulating analysis of the novel *O Archeologos* (The Archaeologist) by Karkavitsas, she attempts to show how the hidden tensions between *laografia* and *ithografia* emerge in the text, pointing out that while *laografia* was consciously backward-looking in order to be meaningful to the present, *ithografia* desired to be forward-looking (often by positing an ideal state) in order to transform contemporary reality. In this essay she indicates how the author constructed an opposition and tension between the pen (*écriture*), concerned with an atemporal rurality, and the voice (*graphe*) concerned with class-struggle, temporality, change and urbanisation. The novel revolves around two brothers, the first-born Aristodimos and the younger Dimitrakis, and their attempts to recover their patrimony. It is clear that the brothers represent two differing modes to the acquistion of national identity. We summarise the oppositions which Politi brings out:

	Aristodimos	Dimitrakis
Represented by the	pen	voice
Associated with	Classical Pagan inheritance	Byzantine and Christian inheritance
Symbolised by	Sterility and death wish	Eros and living force
	books	physical work
	'Affiliation'; 'belonging to culture and society'	'Filiation', 'belonging to nature'
Language used	Katharevousa	Dimotiki
Linked to the	Father	Mother

Politi suggests that while the lesson which Karkavitsas wishes to teach, 'that the ethnic group should cease rummaging through the past in the hope of discovering its national identity and should look to the present in the hope of forging for the future a *new*, affiliative, rather than filiative identity' (1988; 48), the conclusion remains indeterminate. Indeed she believes that the text 'supports the ideology of parenthood and filiation' (*ibid.*, 49), precisely by the indeterminacy of its conclusion.

Although Politi does not explicitly say so, we believe that the linkage between these two alternatives and their transcendence is provided by the heroine, Elpida (Hope). The solution to this predicament is almost mythical in Lévi-Straussian terms: the heroine, partly kin partly affine, enables the hero to discover his identity.

Elpida embodies a number of oppositions: she belongs both to the inside and the outside, to kin and to affines, to filiation and affiliation, to writing and to speech, and so on. In this respect she acts as a type of operative translator of oppositions. While she is the offspring of the antithesis of marriage, a rape of her mother Archondo, she nevertheless offers the possibility of renewal through her own marriage. While she is the product of a most dishonourable act, a type of Original Sin, she represents purity through her practice of her embroidery. While she is a kinswoman of the hero, she is also his bride. She represents the silent narration of knowledge transmitted from mother to daughter, down the female line and free of tension, in contrast to the knowledge transmitted down the male line, full of tension and the desire for patroctony.

That Elpida should have been selected by the author to represent the transcendence of the hero's dilemma is no mere literary device. For, as we shall suggest, women and the cult of motherhood became particularly significant in late nineteenth-century Greece as a means to unify the society. As Politi remarks:

Nationalist discourse is perhaps the only male discourse which collapses gender inequality and assigns to woman a principal code. In the nationalist code the female prototype combines both male and female virtues and becomes almost androgynous . . . In her role as motherland and mother-tongue it is she who inspires her male children to heroic action and is made to speak the aggressive, expansionist discourse.   (1988; 50)

Nationalist discourse in Greece was intimately related to the emergence of the *nikokirei* middle class. Perhaps nowhere are these middle class concerns brought out more closely than in the life and works of Alexandros Papadiamantis, born in 1851 on the fringe of the Greek state in the Aegean island of Skiathos. One of the central features of his work is the manner in which an enlightened ex-villager views his island home with a mixture of deep sensitivity and nostalgia and horror. As Elizabeth Constantinides points out, Papadiamantis felt a deep suspicion of Western ways: 'His country's noble traditions were being corrupted, in his eyes, by "European" ideas and habits, from political institutions to matters of dress and comportment. On one occasion he goes so far as to deplore (or at least he seems to deplore) the abandonment of the veil by Greek women' (Constantinides, 1987; xv). Indeed many of his short stories deal with the ambiguous 'benefits' of modern civilisation. In 'Fortune from America' a young consumptive brother returns from South America with a large sum of money to provide his suitorless sister with a dowry. This vastly increases her matrimonial prospects. The introduction of such wealth gnaws away at intimate kinship and affinal relations, introducing an element of distrust, deceit, suspicion and betrayal. In 'Civilisation in the Village' a poor alcoholic father searching for the doctor to tend his seriously ill child is seduced from his purpose by card-playing and grasping outsiders (petty Government officials) who ply him with drink and take his money while his child dies.

What makes Papadiamantis' work great literature is the way he can enmesh the concerns of an urbanite sensitivity and his own rural background with an intimate knowledge of the countryside. Yet this sensitivity, born out of long and intimate contact with his island home and personal circumstances (poverty and celibacy in Athens), is urban-based and informed, and ultimately ambivalent. The novel concentration on women in the countryside, which makes him Greece's early equivalent of a Lorca, and the sublimated religiosity which has echoes in Conrad, is a perspective guaranteed by the distance of an urban-based sensitivity towards recent rural origins. It is for this reason that we believe, from an anthropological perspective, that a great deal of *ithografia* can be seen as the working out of tensions inherent in the construction of a specific model of the family and of gender roles in the town, transported to and expressed in another semi-mythical plane, that of the countryside. In this respect we differ from D. Ricks, who suggests that 'Papadiamantis looks to an Eden of national innocence' (Ricks, 1988; 28) because that Eden is flawed. We quote a significant passage from Constantinides:

Though Papadiamantis defends the traditions and beliefs of his Greek island, with its strict moral code, scrupulous observance of religious rites, rigidly hierarchical society, patriarchal family, and suspicion of foreign manners, his stories nevertheless illustrate the dark side of that life as he perceived it. Females are the victims of their male kinsfolk and husbands; males, in turn, are blighted by poverty, lack of opportunity, and their own fecklessness. For women there is no escape, or adaptation to circumstances; for men the principal escape is seafaring or emigration.

(Constantinides, 1987; xvi)

We have quoted this passage at length because these features are also found in certain urban contexts. From the accounts of anthropologists who have worked in the Aegean islands (Dubisch, 1986; Kenna, 1976; Dimitriou, 1989) it is highly doubtful that social life there is 'patriarchal' and 'hierarchal'; indeed most accounts emphasise social equality and the relative power of women. One recent work on the Aegean island of

Fourni goes so far as to suggest that the dominant social actors in these societies are women (Dimitriou, 1989). The above quotation bears close similarities to certain accounts of urban life in a context of deprivation and uncertainty (for example Hannerz, 1969) and there is a strong element of pessimism in the work of Papadiamantis, or what Vitti has called 'un pessimismo naturalistico' (1971; 278). Yet what constitutes the distinctiveness of the world portrayed by Papadiamantis is its specific mixture of intimate knowledge of a rural area peopled by individuals who act according to a sensitised urban perception of the author. The contrastive use of the Skiathos dialect for dialogue and *katharevousa* for the author's narrative casting of the scenes and sketches further reinforces the impression of intimacy and hence of authenticity.

We do not wish here to suggest that we have exhausted the significance or the greatness of Papadiamantis' work; there are indeed many other aspects which concern fundamental moral questions such as the meaning of evil, or salvation, and so on. Rather, we have been concerned to show under what conditions such literature was produced, how an author from a rural background treats his material, and how urban concerns and perspectives inform his treatment and presentation of the countryside.

We are not in the position to explore further the possible implications of how internal concerns surfaced in *ithografia*. Rather, we wish to touch briefly upon a small and selective segment of this literature which deals with marriage and the matrimonial ethic. Our analysis may be general but it may nevertheless indicate some general lines for more refined research.

The close interweaving of economic concerns and marriage are clearly brought out in the novel *Loukis Laras* by Dimitrios Vikelas. R. Beaton (1982) has pointed out that this text is problematical in that the author takes a distinctively uncharacteristic line in refusing to idealise the War of Independence. It is also difficult to distinguish between what the character, Laras, and the author Vikelas are actually saying. The market-place appears to replace heroic patriotic self-sacrifice as the main means for self-expression. Beaton suggests that

Laras' prudence in business and his example as a patriot who served his country not by heroic exploits but by creating its wealth, are never presented at a distance, and there is nothing in the novel to counterbalance the narrator's clear admiration for the world of finance and commercial free enterprise.

(1982; 113)

Barthes has suggested that in modern literature (what he prefers to call 'writing'), to decipher the author's message is not important: 'no one, no "person" says it: its source, its voice, is not the true place of writing, which is reading' (1977; 147). In other words we should be concerned with the destination of a text rather than with its origin. But what precisely was the destination of mid to late nineteenth-century texts? How did the mainly urban petit-bourgeois reading public (the destination of these texts) invest them with meaning? Two passages (and there are others) are particularly likely to have been invested with a whole set of attributable meanings by this public in a manner likely to have held affinities with their world views. We quote them because they draw upon a whole set of resonances which illustrate the way the matrimonial ethic is embedded in, and structures, labour:

God nevertheless blessed our labours. The 'balance' [*isozygeion*] was better [*pachiteron*: literally 'fatter'] every year than the previous one and our trading reputation grew and grew, becoming stronger in the market of Smyrna.

(Vikelas, 1967; p. 11)

From that time on I made a great deal of money, and lost a great deal. By God's grace *receiving* (*lavein*) made up a greater total than *giving* (*dounai*) so that today I have the satisfaction of seeing the untroubled future of my children secure through my labours.

(Quoted in Beaton, 1982; 113)

These passages could be read as a panegyric on the Protestant Ethic, but they are not. The author/narrator is not suggesting here that because of God's grace he was done well. Rather, he has laboured for his children, and God, like *tyche* (luck) was largely accidental. There is no 'rational' order to the accumulation of wealth and grace in the northern European capitalist manner. On the contrary, capital accumulation is more akin to gambling: one makes, and loses, a great deal of money. There is no 'rational' manner to capital accumulation because it is dependent upon too many imponderable external factors. If one does well that is because God's grace, like *tyche* has smiled upon one almost turning it into fate, but this has very little causal relationship with the way one has accumulated wealth. Furthermore the whole enterprise ends when his children are assured of an 'untroubled future'.

The subterfuge is pursued through other means. 'Debit' and 'credit' could be seen as an expression of rational long-term accounting, but the words used (as Beaton points out) are biblical as well as mercantile, further reinforcing the suggestion of the aleatoric nature of capital accumulation.

We do not wish to suggest that such an attitude was prevalent in Greece in the nineteenth century. Rather we believe that it was perhaps only well developed in urban, commodity-oriented cultures like Athens. Indeed the link between capital accumulation and the family is strong even in certain religious tracts which take a distinctly opposed view, i.e. against trade, and in favour of agriculture, as the following quotation from 1817 indicates:

After you have reached the age of 13 years take great care as captains of a ship until you marry. Keep your body pure and unpolluted, that is to say, as The Temple of God. I do not say this just to those who know the sacred writing, but also to the illiterate young believers. And also to those of you whose parents have property, vineyards, fields, gardens and other things that bear fruit and not to buying and selling (*alisiverisi*). Buying and selling of products is always theft from the smallest to the biggest thing. From those who sell wild weeds, herbs and vegetables to those who sell gold and indigo, all these people are thieves and proud, and neither in this life nor in the hereafter will they be saved. I see our Lord, who in The Bible, says: 'The worst people are the merchants', and those who enter big business leave the Orthodox faith because they have fallen into error and will end in the earth. And so much does this evil sin take them over that they take ten groshia and only give one groshia as thanksgiving . . .

Gardens (by contrast) give an income for living free from any scandal, and neither do they engender falsity, nor are they endangered in the sea or in shops. But instead you depend upon the rains from the heavens and when they bear fruit they bring good fortune and happiness to your home. In the mornings you leave your homes to return in the evening to be greeted by your children, as well as your parents and wives. Spend of these things which God has given you, from the labour of your hands and with the sweat of your brows. [If you do this] you will live well and at peace.

(in: S. Asdrachas, 1984; 92–125)

In a number of novels unmarried daughters are metaphorically likened to *grammateia* (promissory notes or I.O.U.s). In Andreas Karkavitsas' novella *I Lygeri*, a father's predicament is brought out graphically if somewhat artlessly:

The father of Vasiliki felt like a debtor with a heavy mortgage. Pantellis had of course other bills of exchange [*synallagmata*], his five other daughters, but Vasiliki was the only one falling due to the present. A seventeen-year-old daughter, my friend!

(Karkavitsas, 1978; 121)

This passage encapsulates a number of key concerns: the idea that men have to labour to satisfy an obligation imposed 'by society', and early marriage ages for daughters. Above all it indicates a world where everything is viewed in monetary terms, where social and familial obligations can only be satisfied through the possession of cash and where the dowry is likened to a mortgage. Yet if daughters' marriages are perceived as an economic problem, they also ideally required a political, or status-oriented, solution. Daughters are also viewed metaphorically as 'bills of exchange' (*synallagmata*) to establish alliances; interestingly the word is also used for 'foreign exchange'. So too, from the perspective of men, if marrying a daughter or sister is viewed as satisfying an obligation imposed by society, then one's sons are expected to collect at a later stage. The situation is cunningly highlighted by Edmond About:

If marriages are contracted rather hastily in the country, it is not always so in the town. A residence in Athens accustoms the mind towards speculation: there are more wants to be supplied, more resources to be sought for. A young man looks out not only for a wife but for a portion. Unfortunately marriage portions are rarer than brides. A girl with six thousand Francs ready money, and who is used to wear feathers, is not a bad match.

(1855; 136–7)

In such a context it is hardly surprising that the *prikosymfono* became purely and simply a contract, and a contract moreover wrought out by two sets of unrelated men. For the groom it became the means to extract the greatest possible wealth to accompany his bride; for the father it signified not only that he had redeemed his debt to society in an honourable fashion, but that the groom was now obliged to marry his daughter. The problem of *prikothires*, dowry hunters or men who manage to extract the maximum possible dowry from an unrelated family, was certainly not new in nineteenth-century Greece, but with the transformation of marriage, it became more acute. One novel which highlights the problem is Papadiamantis' *I Fonissa* (The Murderess).

For further insights into the position of women in nineteenth-century Greece we must turn to popular literature. According to G. Jusdanis, such texts, which circulated widely in Greece, were 'consciously ideological' not merely in form, that is in the demotic language they employed, but also in content, in the world they depicted (Jusdanis, 1987; 82). The settings are almost invariably described as a world devoid of love. Papadiamantis' characterisation of the condition of womanhood is well known and much quoted:

when she was a child she served her parents; when she married she became a slave for her husband although, due to his character and his weakness, she was at the same time his guardian. When she bore children she became the slave of her children. When her children married and had their own children, she became again a servant of her children's children.

(Papadiamantis, 1964; 417)

In another novel we are afforded the response of a wealthy aristocrat, the Count Alexandros Oxiomahos Filaretos, to *proxenia* for his daughter's hand:

'that person?', [the Count] Oxiomahos said angrily and proudly; 'that one, Dimos' son, wishes to marry my daughter!' . . .
    'He has unmeasurable wealth, effendi! . . .' the matchmaker replied with a curious smile and closing his eyes. 'Wealthy! (How lucky she is!) Today money

is everything . . . Isn't that so, effendi? . . . And after all what has the blessed Kir Dimitros, the groom's father, got to do with this? How does he come into this? Mr Aristidis, is or is not, a young man as is required, honourable, good, and . . .? But even if he had nothing else other than his profession [doctor], with all the customers he has, he would still lead a very wealthy life . . .'

The old man listened silently and deeply grieved for quite a while . . . but he tired, looked all around him, and his gaze fell on his genealogical tree: the names that were written in little blue circles were the names of his lineage (*tis yenias tou*) who for so many generations had stood as the first of the city, the highest of the high born! . . . And now he himself, one of their descendants, had to savour every insinuating word . . . How the times had changed! The son of Dimos Sterioti who had arrived from Epiros wearing only one sandal, who used to sell scraps of roast meat in his brazier from the streets and who had later opened up a small grocery store which he developed gradually, and amidst his poverty lent money by the week at usurious interest to become rich quickly . . . That son of Dimos, a dissolute and arrogant upstart, that puffed-up doctor, had the effrontery to ask to become his son in law . . .!

(Theotoki, 1981; 53–55)

The reference to money ('today money is everything') is clearly rhetorical but is nevertheless echoed in ordinary conversation amongst villagers (cf. du Boulay, 1983; 256), indicating a fall from grace. If money is 'everything' (*ola*), it is always in short supply as well as a source of corruption, and in this sense it carries a moral: those who are exposed to it in great quantities are corrupted and fall. Hence the inverted message of this passage – for here the previous generation of powerholders, the *arkhontes*, have fallen on bad times, but there is a backhanded sense of sympathy for them. The *arkhontes* had been corrupted by money and power, they had 'eaten', but then fallen from power retaining merely their pride and an inordinate sense of their exclusiveness and distinction. This exclusiveness is threatened in a most direct way by a potential marriage with a lower status groom. A delight in laying bare the pretensions of the old ruling class is nevertheless accompanied by a realisation that fortune can only be obtained by dubious means, and the passage thus appears to legitimate a society from which one can be saved only by participation in it.

Yet on another level such colourful portrayals reveal the concerns and fears of petit-bourgeois culture: an 'unjust world' (*adiki koinonia*), faceless and oppressive, which can only be resolved 'by law' (*me nomos*); a concern with maintaining a precarious social position which can often be threatened by a 'bad marriage'; a fear of social upstarts who can subvert the order of power and authority in the home while at the same time delighting in the overturning of an old aristocracy, whose titles they envied without contesting their authenticity (highlighting the ambiguous attitude of the middle class to a foreign monarchy); cautionary tales about incorporating 'outsiders' into the family, and the obligation of young girls to sacrifice their affections and sentiments to uphold the family honour, that is, the honour of their fathers. In Karkavitsas' *I Lygeri* the young Anthi, daughter of a wealthy Peloponnese merchant, is married to Nikolas, a servant. She is horrified but acquiesces because of her family interests. In the *Lygeri* the presentation is seemingly from the perspective of Anthi the daughter. She secretly hopes to marry a *levendis* from her natal village. Her parents decide otherwise and although she contemplates suicide she eventually complies with her parents' decision. Eventually her husband, Nikolo, takes over the household. She becomes entrapped when she refuses to escape with the young man of her dreams after she has been married. Finally, not only does she accept her fate but ultimately views herself as a 'Kiria'. This is particularly pronounced after the birth of a son; in short, motherhood transforms her: 'she was his wife; she belonged to a man and for every action; for every thought she had to give an account to him' (Karkavitas; 3, 110). In *Sklavi sta desma tous* it is aristocratic pride which suffers a grievous blow. The upstart groom is always introduced with a number of rhetorical devices. He comes from elsewhere and is of humble origins (abandoning his unproductive land for the town in *I Lygeri*, from mountainous and bandit-infested Epiros in *Sklavi*); in both cases he arrives wearing a *miso tsarouhi* ('half a pair of sandals', even today Greek Cypriot peasants use the word *ksypolitos* (barefoot and barebacked) to indicate desperate and suspicious social origins); he is often incorporated into the household through fosterage or as a servant, but eventually takes control by usurping the position of the elderly father and abrogating power to himself. The moral is multi-faceted: fear the enemy within your midst; charity beyond direct kinsmen is misguided and dangerous; maintain your social position; and marriages across social boundaries, especially to people of more humble origins, are devoid of love and affection even if they possess certain economic benefits. The younger generation can also be seen as a metaphor for the new intakes of social classes into Athens.

We do not believe that such moralistic projections are an accurate portrayal of emotional life within the urban Greek family of the mid nineteenth century. Rather, they must be seen on three different levels. First, they reveal the concerns and fears of an Athenian-based petit-bourgeois culture which was certainly not applicable to all of Greece. Second, they must be seen in terms of their effects. The circulation of such texts in the cities and their presentation in weekly extracts in newspapers helped to forge a certain universal urban petit-bougeois cultural perspective. It also helped to socialise young urban girls in terms of accepting their matrimonial fate and submitting to male *prov-lepsis* (insights) in much the same way as Anthi resigned herself to her father's organisation of her marriage. An increased interiorisation of norms in the city replaces the diffuse multiplex means of social control found in villages. We deal with this below. Finally, popular literature of this sort as a phenomenon, and in its subject matter, must be seen within the context of national identity construction within which folklore played a significant part (Herzfeld, 1982). Although popular authors were encouraged by folklorists to document domestic life (N. Politis, 1883), the two enterprises were opposed on another level. Whereas folklore attempted to construct an ideal model of Greek culture and identity, drawing selectively on rural customs which were portrayed as indicators of the essential continuity of Greek civilisation, popular literature betrayed the apprehension of the middle classes in having to come face to face in an urban milieu with the very symbols of the countryside and of their own social origins which they were eager to leave behind.[4]

Among the main productive population, including ex-peasants and migrants, evidence suggests that many were strongly tied to their homogeneous neighbourhoods. Migrant girls to Athens worked as maids and in other capacities of urban employment to obtain their dowries. In the case of migrant families, daughters often married migrant grooms and settlement was frequently uxorilocal. This was a more commensal arrangement and probably a less authoritarian one than existed within other groups. The paucity and nature of resources transmitted at marriage did not make for the establishment of economic self-sufficiency, in part because resources were often handed over at a later stage, after cohabitation had begun, and was purposely designed to attract grooms and their labour contribution to the extended household. Nor did it make for the seclusion of women in the home; women worked alongside their husbands, tending the animals and engaged in urban employment.

The number of young men and women from poorer strata engaged in employment away from home appears to have grown in the nineteenth century. There are reports of 2,000 maids, 2,000 male servants and 3,200 women shop attendants in Piraeus in 1882 (Kampouroglous, 1883). For example an Athenian merchant reported that between 1839–46, fifty-two persons passed through his employ, many of whom came from the Aegean islands of Tinos, Sifnos and Syros. Because of the dominant system of unigeniture, many were probably younger daughters (Liata, 1984; 50). As the tendency towards adoption decreased the number of maids grew corespondingly (table 27).

There were thus very different rationalities and types of family

Table 27. *Distribution of maids in the total female working population,
Athens, 1853–79*

Year	1853	1856	1861	1870	1879
Maids	?	?	7,724	10,808	15,593
Total working female population	?	1,300	8,556	12,037	21,774

? = Unknown.
Source: Petrinioti-Konsta, 1981; 51.

organisation in late eighteenth and early nineteenth-century Athens.
Table 28 summarises some of the differences between the various social
groups. Any discussion on the position of women must take into account
the state of widowhood. At least 30 per cent of all mothers of the brides
in our sample were widows, suggesting significant differences in marriage ages between men and women or particularly high rates of adult
male mortality. Many women were thus faced with the prospect of
having to spend a considerable portion of their adult lives as widows.
The dower (*progamiea dorea*) was therefore a particularly important
institution. Men were apparently in short supply, a factor which
undoubtedly further contributed to dowry inflation. Of our total sample
of 523 brides, only 16 or 3.1 per cent were widows entering their second
marriages. We know that their grooms were bachelors, and the figures
are extremely low when compared to the data assembled by Segalen for
various districts in eighteenth- and nineteenth-century France (1986;
34–5).[5]

In the nineteenth and early twentieth centuries men were apparently
marrying late and there were two unsuccessful attempts in the Greek
parliament in 1887 and 1928 to create a special tax for unmarried males
(Kairophilas, 1982; 157). Not surprisingly, many widows entered their
second marriages possessing their own houses; 69 per cent of widows
brought a house or part of a house with them at their second marriage
compared to 35 per cent of first-time brides. However, widows were
more unlikely to be endowed with cash and with olive trees than were
first-time brides. The picture that emerges indicates that most widows
entered their second marriages with subsistence oriented items such as
animals, fields and houses, rather than prestige goods. They were not,
therefore, particularly good matches on the economic level, which suggests that they probably married widowers rather than bachelors. In
addition widows marrying first-time grooms had to make over some
property and cash to the groom which was known as the *agarliki* (or
pallikaryiatiko) (Skouteri-Didaskalou, 1984). Given the types of

Table 28. *Differences between Athenian social groups in terms of family and social organisation*

	Aristocracy (*Arkhon* class)	*Nikokirei* and wealthy Athenians	Migrants and plebeians
Prikosymfono	Drawn up as an integral part of the marriage process. To maintain social position, to endow daughters with family property and hence identify the resources to be inherited by sons, and because of its ritualistic significance	Drawn up to maintain social position but increasingly to protect bride from potential depredations by groom	Drawn up often after cohabitation had begun; to legitimate marriage and offspring and as a type of *de facto* inheritance to ensure that daughter receiving house is bound to care for elderly mother
Settlement at marriage	Viri-patrilocal	Virilocal but increasingly, neo-local	Matri-uxorilocal
Division of parental estate	Tendency for daughters to receive somewhat less than sons, but still usually substantial amounts	Tendency towards equal partible inheritance but daughters increasingly receive different resources	Tendency for daughters to receive houses but possibly less than sons
Social organisation	Tightly knit, emphasis on male *yenia* (agnatic group or lineage), heavy inter-marriage	More diffuse in its geographical origins, formed mainly by development of state bureaucracy (after 1831)	Neighbourhood bound
Role of fosterage/adoption	As a means to recruit family retainers, as an aspect of traditional patronage	As a means to keep property within the family; increasingly replaced by *koumbaria*	As a means to ensure old-age care and insurance

resources to which widows had access, this would have been particularly difficult to accumulate, further reinforcing our suggestion that widows married widowers.

By most accounts widowhood was not a happy state. Although the dower was intended to give economic self-sufficiency to women, in certain cases it was not forthcoming. Nor apparently was support from kin or affines, as the memoirs of Georghios Psillas, a member of the Athenian middle class, indicate:

[Upon the death of my father] my mother found herself in awful poverty and because she was obliged to collect the straw after harvest in the village of Markopoulos, she stayed in one of the rooms of our Church having rented out our paternal home after the death of my father ... [later she returned to our house, where] she set aside a small room below the ground in the cellar and she remained there for a few years together with my sister, living through her work and that of my sister. However our lodger left ... and she went again to lodge in another Church's poor rooms in the parish of St. Athanasiou in Psyrri taking me away from the house of Marmarotouri in a huff where I was a servant at 11 years old because, being a relative, he gave me nothing but food.

(Psillas, 1974; 8–9)

Love and marriage in the Athenian family

We now wish to discuss the nature of emotions within the Athenian family. What was the status of love within the Athenian family and how was it expressed? Does the Athenian marriage pattern approach the 'companionate' marriage which Macfarlane (1986), for example, claims had evolved in North Western Europe but especially in England from at least the sixteenth century? Like most of the historians of the family we shall be forced to rely on two types of sources: travellers' and observers' accounts, and popular literature. Clearly the two are widely different and caution is particularly required when utilising the latter. Yet an analysis of popular literature should prove particularly useful, especially when we lay these accounts alongside other analyses of the significance of emotions within the Victorian family as manifested through literature.

Alan Macfarlane has observed that

one of the major lessons to be learnt from the anthropological discussions of marriage is that the Western concept of 'companionate' marriage is unusual. Elsewhere marriage is not entered into for the sake of companionship; it is not the marriage of true minds ... This does not mean that the relationships in such societies are shallow and that affection is absent, but merely that love and affection run towards kin by blood. Yet the Malthusian marriage system is based on the premise of a deep bond between husband and wife.

(1986; 154)

Many modern-day Greeks and Cypriots would agree with Mac-farlane's characterisation that marriage for 'companionate' motives is a hallmark of North Western Europe; indeed many village leftists in Cyprus and Greece, for example, would widen this premise to include 'developed' countries, such as Russia. Yet while they contrast this to the Greek situation, in which a dowry is still often required, the ideological point of their statement should not be missed. For what they are implicitly, and sometimes explicitly, pointing out is that in the absence of economic development, 'the Government' (*i givernisis*) should assume the obligation of providing young couples with housing, thus relieving the parental generation of such crippling debts and allowing the couple to choose partners for companionate motives. In other words they are implicitly contrasting the 'developed' external world of North Western Europe and Russia (according to their ideological preferences) with the 'undeveloped' internal world of Greece.

We must be careful in assuming that this type of evaluation is heartily and unequivocally biased in favour of the Western model. Many Greeks and Cypriots are making a political criticism, not a statement about the desired nature of family life. Indeed on a more fundamental level the notion of marrying for 'companionate' motives would strike most modern Greeks as very particular and restricted, especially if reduced to 'love'. In ordinary discourse when two people marry 'for love' the word normally used is *'eroteftikan'* (from *eros*), and not *'agapithikan'* (from *agape*). It implies immediate passion without much regard for consequences and implications, but above all a jettisoning of the normal and careful collective (i.e. family) processes involved in finding a spouse. In essence it emphasises the short- over the long-term. Indeed as Hirschon (1989) points out, 'love' in contemporary Piraeus is seen as potentially dangerous, since it renders one of the parties vulnerable to exploitation. Yet this does not mean that marriage *yia agape* is not practised, or condemned. In many contemporary Cypriot villages boys and girls regularly fall in love during the latter years of coeducational secondary schooling and later pursue *proxenia* through the normal acceptable channels, that is through the older generation. If this fails consistently the young man may decide to 'steal' the girl with her connivance and thus oblige the girl's parents to agree to the match. Social opinion often favours the suitor because it is said that the girl's parents have not taken the daughter's feelings into account and have aimed exclusively at a status-match, rather than one within which their daughter would have felt emotionally satisfied. In other words, once a child has a particular preference parents rarely go against it. Another reason is that many villagers react with glee when an attempt to solidify wealth permanently through equal marriages is thwarted by such precipitate action. Similarly, it is far from rare for a Cypriot father to proclaim proudly that a daughter of his had married in Australia without the need for a dowry, *yia agape*, 'because her groom loved her' or because 'he wanted her'. What he means is that the normal and acceptable channels for making a marriage involving all the family members as a collective decision had been followed, but that a dowry had not been requested, even though it is the groom's right to request a dowry and the bride's father's obligation to supply one.

These observations should caution us against generalisations regarding the presence or absence of love in conjugal unions in Greece, as in other non-North Western European cultures. Indeed it is dangerous to equate a particular means of linguistic self-expression, and especially literary self-expression within historical literate cultures, with an exclusive monopoly on love. Contemporary Greek and Cypriot examples indicate that it is not so much a matter of the absence of emotion in marriage which is at issue, but rather the means through which it is expressed and pursued. Literary cultures such as England are perhaps more likely to appear to separate companionate issues from pragmatic ones primarily because long exposure to literacy enables further dispassionate discussion and exploration of such issues by the participants themselves. Indeed Greek Cypriot villagers explicitly recognise the subversive power of 'love letters', a theme which also appears in popular engravings. The love letter is viewed as particularly dangerous, often leaving the girl open to exploitation. What villagers are implicitly highlighting is not just the danger that the couple are conducting a secret private liaison outside parental control, but the power of the written word to detach emotions from other familial concerns. Having said this we now wish to concentrate on the nineteenth-century Athenian family. How was love expressed between husband and wife, and by extension, to the children?

We are fortunate to possess an excellent and perceptive account of ordinary Athenian life from the pen of the French observer Edmond About in the mid-nineteenth century. About's account indicates that interest and emotion were closely integrated and that abstract considerations of love were often absent.[6] He begins by noting that an urban life 'accustoms minds to speculation' (1855; 136) and that 'a young man looks out not only for a wife but for a portion' (1855; 137). He also noted that while there were basic differences between the poor and wealthy in Athens, there was nevertheless a striking homogeneity in morals, especially as concerning relations between men and women as husbands and wives. Coming from a Parisian background he was struck by the nature of the peccadillos of the wealthy; there was little of the complex illicit emotional entanglements so well documented by Balzac for French society, but rather political and financial ones:

High society has, as everywhere else, morals of its own. The chronicle of scandal in Athens is rich enough to supply a little Brantome. But these intrigues have a peculiar character; love has little to do with them, all depends on vanity or interest.

(1855; 144)

A main reason for this is that the sacredness of the conjugal tie is sufficiently respected in Greece. The reason is very simple. Love is luxury, especially if illicit . . . There are also very few who have leisure for it.

(1855; 143)

We must be cautious in our evaluation of the term 'luxury'. What About meant was not that once life in Athens had reached a certain level of sophistication, ease and culture, then love would become an accepted necessity of marriage in Greece. Rather he seems to imply that the intermeshing of interest and emotion in the structures of everyday life in Athens rendered love superfluous as the prime motivation for marriage. It is clear from Macfarlane's account that love as a motivation for marriage began to find its clearest expression in England in a context of late age at marriage with no upward limit on the marriage-age and with the necessity of economic independence. In Greece, by contrast, marriage ages were relatively young, there were strong cultural perceptions of what was considered a late age at marriage for both men and women, and economic independence was often partly a consequence of marriage through the dowry, rather than a precondition for marriage to take place. It was not so much the potential economic autarchy of the groom that was at issue but rather the economic might of the bride's father. Furthermore a newly married couple started their conjugal life not only with resources from the bride's family, but could expect resources at a later date as inheritance from the groom's family. A newly married couple could thus expect financial and emotional support for a considerable part of their early conjugal career. A natural consequence of the requirement towards economic independence prior to marriage, as occurred in England, was predisposition, a *habitus*, of emotional independence from natal kin with yearnings towards 'a total communication – physical, emotional, mental – between people' (Macfarlane, 1986; 157), as a means to resolve 'the loneliness which Milton, Donne, Shakespeare and others diagnosed at the heart of love [which had] led many to marry' (*ibid*; 173).

Such conditions were largely absent in nineteenth-century Athens. Loneliness, separation and the fine-tuning of such a lack of contact into the 'institutionalised irrationality' of love through letters, serving to objectify emotions and produce a 'discourse of love' (which is often in fact written and pursued through the silent and private experience of reading), and which separates and distinguishes between private and public discourse, had very little grounding in Athenian realities. It is hardly surprising, therefore, that About labelled love a 'luxury' in mid-nineteenth-century Athens. But wisely, pursuing a line of enquiry which was to trouble many twentieth-century linguistic philosophical debates concerning the nature of knowledge, he decided instead to sketch in the social framework which rendered emotional life in the Athenian family both similar and highly different to that obtaining in the Northern European family. He observed:

The Greeks marry young. Marriage is a subject of conversation among young people of sixteen; they marry rather rashly and without any certainty as to the future.

(About, 1855; 134)

Open discussion and exposure to the implications of *proxenia* predisposes individuals not only towards a semi-collective and semi-public evaluation and pursuance of marriage, but also highly sensitises them to possibilities and chances in the 'matrimonial market'. A central feature of *proxenia* is that it is both public, involving as it does more than simply the two individuals to the match, but also extremely private, involving an individual's perception of a chance on the take which has to be grasped suddenly. Rashness does not imply carelessness, and certainty does not exclude shrewd calculations of probable endowments and inheritance prospects. In this respect Athenians were merely adapting rural patterns to an urban setting.

About was also struck by the equality between sons and fathers, as well as between husbands and wives; such patterns were markedly different to those obtaining in his own natal environment. We give here some of his observations, accompanied by our comments in square brackets identifying the models to which he is implicitly contrasting the Athenian pattern:

Marriages are contracted and broken off freely [as in North Western Europe]; woman is neither a slave [as was presumed to be the case in the 'East'], nor shut up [as among French bourgeois families]; unions are fertile [more an 'Eastern' than a North Western European feature], and that is the principal, if not the sole object of marriage [in contrast to North Western European, especially English, patterns following Macfarlane]; the brothers are equal among one another [in contrast to the North Western European primogeniture system] and to their father; relations give one another help and assistance, whatever may be the difference of their conditions of life [an ideal rarely achieved in urban contexts such as Paris, where class and status transcended kinship loyalties as documented by Balzac]; the husband and the wife herself, are jealous of their rights and defend energetically the sacredness of marriage.

(1855; 148)

Equality has so much a part in their morals that the sons are almost equal to their father. They have for him respect and deference; they do not obey . . . The father of a family was a friend to his son, more wise and more respectable than others; he was not as at Rome, a master, and at need an executioner.

(1855; 147)

Similarly, patterns of marriage and divorce exhibited a curious mixture of features which About found somewhat contradictory from a Western European perspective:

If it be difficult to break off a marriage [i.e. an engagement which was considered to be tantamount to a marriage], nothing is easier to undo it when it has been performed [in contrast to Catholicism]. The papas, I have said, are by no means incorruptible, and, if one only knows how to set about it he will discover in the most regular union 5 or 6 irregularities which necessitate the nullity of the marriage.

(1855; 134–5)

Yet while the dissolution of marriages appeared much easier to effect than in North Western Europe, its frequency was low, a feature which may appear to contradict the earlier observations about 'rash' decisions to marry 'without any certainty as to the future', especially if viewed from a North Western European perspective:

Divorce is a luxury which middle class people never allow themselves; the country is peopled with exemplary couples.

(1855; 135)

We wish to further explore the implications of About's observations of love as a 'luxury' in nineteenth-century Athens by reference to Greek literature produced during this period, comparing it to Victorian novels. If 'love' was not the initiate of conjugal unions, which in any case could be easily dissolved, what kept unions together? The system of property transmissions, as well as the reality of continuing emotional and financial support from natal kin, goes some way towards an explanation. But other factors were also at play, involving relations with the Divine, the social origins of the moralists who influenced perceptions of relations between men and women, and popular conceptions of morality.

Steven Mintz, who has examined the role of emotions within the Victorian family, has suggested that one of the central themes running through Victorian family culture was an attempt to deny the existence of carnality and passion and to transmute it into a purer plane where love was spiritualised:

. . . to spiritualise love was a way to psychologically distance the institution of marriage from sensuality, lust and passion, emotions that were identified with religious impurity, moral weakness and guilt.

(Mintz, 1983; 134)

Such a viewpoint stands in marked contrast to that contained within Greek novels and short stories written during this period. In a number of Papadiamantis' short stories passion is accepted and indeed viewed as integral to a relationship between husband and wife. In *The Homesick Wife* a young dissatisfied bride abandons her home and her elderly husband in the night to ask a young man, highly inflamed by her beauty, to row her back to her natal family in another part of her island home. They are chased by her husband in another boat and in the process the young bride, with seductive semi-innocence, gives up part of her top layer of clothing to make a sail and increase their speed. They are eventually caught up with by the faster boat but there is no showdown, no crisis. The elderly husband, who acts more as a concerned father than a jilted spouse, leads her away with the sympathy and understanding that an enlightened parent would demonstrate towards an errant child. The moral is clear: although the bride feels an obligation towards her husband, the lack of passion between them turns this into an empty, sterile, featureless union. In another short story where a young shepherd secretly spies on a young girl bathing, the author's sympathies are clearly with the former. Running through Papadiamantis' stories is an implicit theme: men and women inhabit different worlds, passion is a source of goodness between spouses, and carnality is an accepted, indeed necessary, feature for the viability of the marriage bond. Sex is neither banished nor spiritualised and transmuted, it is part of human nature and therefore good within its socially approved context.

One reason for this clear-cut, direct characterisation of human nature was that many of the moralists and preachers in Greece up until the mid-nineteenth century who dealt with relations between men and women and with popular morality (in contrast to the theologians who concentrated on high dogma and were more concerned with rejecting Protestant and Catholic proselytising; Maloney, 1976), came from humble social origins and worked mainly in rural areas. This was in marked contrast to the Scottish moralists of the eighteenth century from whom Mintz (1983; 135) claims, the Victorian viewpoint of marriage evolved. Men like Cosmas O Aetolos, who wrote a hugely influential text primarily for an illiterate rural audience, drawing upon homely but restricted examples from the scriptures, phrased their messages in a simple language finely attuned to realities in the countryside. As a result the emphasis lay on highlighting the important role of Orthodox ritual for the Christian faith and in ensuring that the faithful understood the sequence of ritual within the Church. The perspective on human nature which emerged was not an attempt at the transformation of ordinary practices, beliefs and sentiments – a type of mental Counter-Reformation, or even Reformation – but rather at the channelling of those elements into acceptable Church-controlled ambits (for example a concern with sexual pollution and its relation to Church participation). In the view of Cosmas, men and women are inherently different, a point which is illustrated by the use of body and power metaphors:

And man is like a king whilst the woman is like a vezir; man is like the head whilst woman is like the body. Thus God blesses man, his wife and your children . . .

(Menounos, 1976)

If men and women have different natures, they have different rights, and a type of 'contractualism' operates between them in the same way that it operates between men and God. Mintz has pointed out the parallelism between the two for the Victorians, which we wish to contrast to the Greek case. He writes,

As in their relationship with God, men and women were without rights and had no just claim to special consideration. Much as God's mercy was exercised through acts of Grace, kindness in marriage depended on acts of sympathy not on rights that one might claim as one's due. This rejection of 'emotional legalism' and emphasis on the transforming power of sympathy was a way to exclude notions of power from the marriage relationship and to place marriage on a higher moral basis.

(1983; 136)

In popular Greek consciousness, however, marriage has a high moral basis and it is legitimated by reference to the moral duty to produce offspring, as had been noted by About. Furthermore, man 'contracts' with God, and even more especially with the Saints and the Panayia, for special favours through *tamata* (votive offerings), and he is therefore not powerless. In 1810 the visitor Charles Meryon observed the practice in Athens of 'penning a flock of sheep in the porch of the Church, whose plaintive bleatings, it was supposed, would give greater effect to the petition of the people, and move the pity of Heaven' (Andrews, 1979; 146; Meraclis, 1986: 123–26). Similar 'transactionalist' practices are found in other parts of the Mediterranean, such as Sicily (see for example DiBella, in Peristiany and Pitt-Rivers, 1991).

Just as men attempt to cast their interaction with the Divine in a transactionalist mode with aspirations towards contractualism, marriage is a transaction between men and women involving the exchange of different goods, services and responsibilities. This involves not only the direct parties but also their natal families. Increasingly, as we have indicated, the marriage bond became progressively contractual and legalistic in nineteenth-century Athens, as did mentalities of the period. Yet while there was a turning inwards, especially among the *nikokirei* families, this did not involve the moral and psychological isolation that accompanied Victorian marriage. Men and women did not expect to find 'a mirror to themselves' in 'the other', no companionship against the world as appears to have been the case in England (Macfarlane, 1986). Children were still a necessity rather than a luxury; indeed they were the *raison d'être* of marriage, supported by popular belief and religion. Indeed child-rearing became increasingly significant as did the role of mothers as child-rearers, rather than as producers. About observed that 'the mother of a family gives orders to her daughters and obeys her sons. She is a woman' (1855; 148). Paradoxically the 'companionate' element in the family was 'displaced' to relations between parents and children. In our next section we examine the transformation in the role of women in nineteenth-century Athens.

Gender construction in an urban context

It has now become a truism to state that in contemporary rural Greece, as in other parts of the Mediterranean, motherhood constitutes an essential part (indeed *the* essential component) of female gender identity. We know very little about gender construction in the past both for rural and urban Mediterranean contexts, although some excellent accounts are available for certain aspects of gender construction and presentation in Byzantine and Greek studies, mainly based on written sources (for example, Galatariotou, 1984–85). We wish to examine the ideological significance of motherhood in its urban Greek context in the past. This endeavour is fraught with difficulties and as a preliminary exercise we propose to establish two guiding principles. First, we should not necessarily presume that contemporary rural patterns of gender construction have been static and provide accurate insights into gender construction in the past. On the contrary certain contemporary features of gender construction in rural Greece are likely to have been heavily influenced by urban concerns and perspectives in a context of nation-state construction. Second, and conversely, given the particular evolution of Greek culture and society over the past 200 years, urban concerns are likely to have been heavily influenced by rural ones. In other words we must expect to find the city in the countryside, and the countryside in the city. Can we therefore, excavate the construction of gender in eighteenth- and nineteenth-century Athens?

We wish to begin with contemporary accounts and then move backwards in time taking these factors into consideration. We take two accounts from two different contexts: du Boulay's treatment of gender construction in rural Evia, which she has consistently characterised as 'traditional' until the late 1960s (1974, 1986), and Hirschon's account (1989) of gender identity among Asia Minor refugees in a relatively new, highly urbanised, and densely populated quarter of Piraeus. The two contexts could not be more different, yet it would be wrong to see them as opposed and representing quintessentially 'rural' and 'urban' models. Indeed what is interesting is how certain themes are carried over from one context to another, transformed, or given an additional meaning.

We begin with du Boulay's account. Juliet du Boulay has suggested that the position of women in contemporary Greek villages is based on a central paradox consisting of 'a single religious vision that sees women in two aspects – as by nature fallen but by destiny redeemed with marriage as the essential means of passage from this nature to this destiny' (1986; 139). She then proceeds, in a sensitive article, to show that 'two factors, motherhood and age, act over the years not to modify the severity of the code under which women have to live, but to increase the respect which they are accorded within it' (*ibid*; 158–9), and that 'a man realizes the value of his wife in later life' (*ibid*; 159). Du Boulay explicitly rejects the notion of 'muted models' (Ardener, 1975), and a number of authors (e.g. J. Dubisch, 1986) have implicitly criticised her premise by pointing out, for example, that some of their women inform-ants resented having to have had children and to live up to the model enshrined in this religious vision. We wish to address this issue by reference to eighteenth- and nineteenth-century Athens, a city, it must be remembered, with a pronounced agricultural base, and to compare this account with Hirschon's treatment of gender identity in contemporary Piraeus.

There are a number of structural preconditions which underlie du Boulay's depiction of the position of women which seem essential to her argument. These include, first of all, an overarching non-secularised religious system: the perspective of women as 'by nature fallen, by destiny redeemed' is embedded in an overarching non-secularized religious system which is almost Islamic in the sense that it provides a dominant, all-encompassing blueprint for the social order, at least for relations between men and women. A second precondition is equal and structural opposition: the paradoxicality of the position of women relies upon two symbolic elements in equal and structural opposition: Eve as the fallen woman and the Virgin Mary as the Mother of God. Both are models of, but primarily for, earthly Greek women. The culture gives equal importance to both; any change in the relative importance of one would upset the structural balance and hence the model's dynamic vitality. A third precondition is Patri-virilocality. The social context within which this paradoxical position of women appears to find its strongest practical reinforcement is that of partri-virilocality. Both du Boulay and Campbell, who subscribe the most visibly to this view, worked in such environments.

There are a number of problems with this approach, some theoretical, others ethnographic, which create difficulties for the analysis of gender relations in the present and the past. For example, to what extent is this view of women as 'by nature fallen, by destiny redeemed' specific to Orthodoxy? Throughout the Mediterranean, on both its northern and southern shores, one hears countless stories highlighting this essential ambivalence in the way women are portrayed. It is found in Catholic Italy, Malta and Spain as well as southern France. So, too, the gradual acceptance of women by their husbands, the fact that women realise themselves and achieve their destined status through marriage (in 'Greek' terms: 'the conversions of Eve into the Mother of God', du Boulay, 1986; 159) is no monopoly of Greek society. It is found in southern Europe, but especially in many Mediterranean viri-patrilocal contexts where religion has very little to do directly with this phenomenon. Peters (1980) reports a similar situation among the Cyrenaican Bedouin, and it is found also in Tunisia (Sant Cassia, 1986b); both of these are Islamic societies. Indeed in Aegean islands with a dominant pattern of uxorilocality the model upon which islanders draw emphasises the 'Mother of God' pole to a greater extent than the 'Eve' aspect, found in viri-patrilocal contexts. We thus believe that this ambivalent, developmental-cycle perspective which attributes to women a set of diametrically opposed characteristics ('Eve', 'Mother of God' which they pass through and embody), is not directly and exclusively attributable to religion, but is heavily influenced by domestic arrange-ments, although Church-formulated ideologies may orient, reflect, and/ or justify particular conceptions of womanhood on the ground. The compatibility of Church-originating conceptions of womanhood and popular conceptions may also be extremely flexible. It is exceedingly difficult and risky to derive the conception of womanhood at the grass-roots level from Church ideology (Loizos, 1988). Too many variables come into play and at least one anthropologist has plausibly argued that we must also look at the way popular conceptions influence Church-defined dogmas, either directly, or more often through co-option (Loizos, 1988).

What the preceding discussion highlights is the problematic status of discourse in which and through which such models or images are expressed. It is unclear from du Boulay's accounts (1986) to what extent villagers actually directly evoke such models in discourse, but the impression gained from her work and from our fieldwork experiences in the Greek world suggest that this is an implicit model. It is evoked elliptically or exophorically, rather than specifically or directly, when statements are made about 'women's natures'; in other words it is a gender construct which is not overt but implicit. They are symbols of womanhood, derived ultimately or at least legitimated by reference to a theological discourse which contains a particular world vision where women are clearly used as metaphors for the Fall and Redemption. Furthermore, Christian theology holds up the two images of woman-hood not as discrete entities but as integrally related symbols whose ultimate meaning is realised in mutual terms. Yet whereas Christian theology as text is a circumscribed, fixed, self-referential and totalising discourse which maps out the world and experience, social life whatever its degree of predictability and traditionality possesses gaps and lapses and it is usually in these interstices that such images of 'womanhood' are drawn upon in discourse. The 'single religious vision that sees women in two aspects', in du Boulay's words (1986; 139) is not perhaps so much about always 'seeing' women in these terms (and here there is a diffi-culty with the word 'to see', which in Greek can also be expressed in the word *theoro*, related to 'theory'), but rather as evoking a two-dimen-sional set of images from an ultimately theological discourse to deal with tensions in social life and render them meaningful. Such tensions may well be intellectual ones, an attempt to explain why individuals act in certain ways in spite of all culturally imposed attempts to the contrary. What we are trying to suggest here is that just as the study of politics in a nation-state should take into account wider factors relating to the state and its ideology, we ought to be particularly cautious when investigating gender symbolism in a context of a literate mega-religion of salvation with its own discourses and symbolism. They may be used in intellectu-ally strategic ways as vocabularies of justification or as counter-justifica-tion at the grassroots level.

In this section we wish to indicate how the application of a Weberian approach may assist an understanding of gender construction in Greek society. Such an approach requires taking into account both religion and law as two analytically distinct variables in the construction of gender identity. In certain cases, such as Islamic politics, the relationship between religion and law may be particularly close; though of course, however strong Koranic law may be, the question of interpretation remains. In southern European contexts, by contrast, the state as legis-lative agency and the Church as the formulator of dogma are largely separate; though religious beliefs may certainly influence the nature of laws, especially as regarding personal status.

Both religion as dogma and as a corpus of beliefs, and law as the codification of personal status, influence conceptions of gender in complex ways. As a set of beliefs religion may influence the way gender is contructed at the grassroots level; that is, by providing a vocabulary of justification, such as Women as Eves. This is particularly strong in certain Orthodox religious tracts, for example Cosmas. Yet dogma may also be influenced by grassroots practices and beliefs, either by co-option of certain themes (such as popular beliefs in Saints who are then accepted by the Church, as in Lourdes, Tinos and so on) or because the Church's personnel may be drawn from certain segments of the population. Also, in studying the ways in which religion impinges on grassroots conceptions of gender we have to ask who carries the religious message – Papas, Catholic Parish Priest or Imam – because, for example, their sexual status (celibate or not) may influence the way in which chastity is viewed (ideal but unattainable for most, as in many Catholic contexts, or ideal on one level but suspect on another, as in the Orthodox case). The sexual status of religious functionaries may also influence, quite independently, the extent to which the grassroots population responds to Church attempts to intervene and legislate on matters of personal sexuality (abortion, contraception and so on) within marriage. Paradoxically celibacy, as in the case of Catholic priests, may facilitate the Church's insistence on the sinfulness of abortion or contraception because its personnel are not faced with those sets of problems – hence they may more easily make abstract, general and dogmatic pronouncements. They may also claim to have made one of the 'supreme sacrifices' (celibacy), rendering their position less morally assailable in society, though more open to social censure if they lapse. The sexual status of the religious functionary may also influence the extent to which the grassroots population is prepared to confide matters of personal sexuality to them – in contemporary Cypriot villages few go to confession; villagers explain that they feel ashamed to do so and fear that because the papas is married his wife will soon find out the substance of the confession, and hence the whole village. They often resolve the problem by going to confession at a monastery. Indeed popular conceptions and criticisms of clergymen in the Greek world vary according to the status of the functionary. When village priests are criticised it is often because of their failure to act according to popular social canons; and when the higher clergy are criticised it is often because they have failed to act in the popular mind according to the strictures of the faith that they impose and are expected to embody. These are radically different criticisms – the former concentrates on membership of the community, and the latter on religious roles. To a certain extent of course this difference in perspective is determined by the structure of the Orthodox Church.

Other factors which enter the equation of how religion may impinge on the construction of gender identity include the possibilities for the enforcement of dogma at the grassroots level, the compatibility of such dogmas and grassroots practices, and the extent to which the official Church can monopolise and incorporate expressions of religious mysticism. For example, although Catholicism and Orthodoxy are similar in that women have a higher spiritual profile than men (in contrast to Islam; Davis, 1984), the extent to which they have been able to incorporate expressions of religious mysticism is not shared. Catholicism, partly because of the Counter-Reformation, partly because of its more centralised structure and the nature of southern European states – closely allied to the Church – and doubtless because of many other factors, was more able to infiltrate and impose itself at the grassroots level than was Orthodoxy. In this respect there was a more complex and dialectical relationship between the grassroots population and the central Church hierarchy, the two levels mutually influencing each other in belief, religious practices, and incorporation of popular themes, as in Spain for example (Brandes, 1980; Christian, 1972).

In Greek Orthodoxy, by contrast, mainly because the Church occupied an intermediate and ultimately ambiguous position in the Ottoman system of government, the two levels (grassroots and Church hierarchy) remained relatively distinct. The politico-religious implications were: first, extreme religious and ritualistic formalism and hence a reluctance to indulge in theological innovation which would spearhead the Church's drive to culturally transform society and model the state in its own image; second, a reluctance to incorporate localised religious and ecstatic movements at the popular level, which may have had politically destabilising implications (as Catholicism has often had in Third World countries); third, a doctrine of voluntary submission to the powers that be, *ethelodouleia* (Clogg, 1982; 191); and fourth, folk versions of High Religion at the grassroots level.

Consequently, the Orthodox Church was unable and unwilling to incorporate grassroots expressions of religious mysticism. These expressions took two forms. On the one hand there were the illicit and deviant forms of religion (charms, potions, witchcraft) in which Greek Orthodox women participated as in both Catholicism and Islam. But even more important were the 'non-licit', non-sanctioned means of religious expression, as opposed to deviant forms. They could accommodate more individual and private forms which replicated but were not dominated by the central authorities, as in women's devotion to small shrines built by them away from the village, or belief in the evil eye. Indeed when questioned about the evil eye many Greek villagers point out, in order to legitimate, or Orthodoxise, such practices, that 'the Church itself believes in it, because it has been written down in the Sacred Books'. In many cases too, the grassroots clergy, partly because of its humble social origins, often connives and participates in such practices. As Danforth (1982) has suggested, such practices often represent the 'working-out' of tensions inherent in gender and power relations. However, they do not necessarily threaten, or are perceived to threaten, the dominant overt structures of authority in the home, such as occurs in Morocco (Hilse-Dwyer, 1978; Maher, 1974) where women resort to 'illicit', 'deviant' and hence threatening forms of religious activity. On the contrary, women's religious activities are seen as particularly important for the preservation of the family.

The technology of the transmission of the religious message and of the practical steps to salvation are also important. Oral sermons and prayers, church attendance, ritual practices, indulgences, religious chants, icons, or written religious tracts to be explored privately, all influence in different ways how the religious message is received as well as access to the Divine. Oral sermons and indulgences, for example, place the religious functionary at the centre of the religious message and of access to the Divine, as in Catholicism. In Orthodoxy, partly because of its highly formalised chants and partly because the religious message was not simplified by the higher clergy for popular consumption, grassroots participation in religious rituals tended to emphasise other aspects: a single yearly pan-village ritual at Easter which linked up with the agricultural calendar, family pilgrimages and popular devotion to icons. All of these practices bypass extreme formalism (High Orthodox Church), or a heavy reliance on scripturalism (as in Islam), or the oral interpretation of the scriptures by way of examples of spiritual exercises for the laity (as in Catholicism). Ritual practices tied to the performance of family roles, rather than individual conscience or strict adherence to scriptural injunctions or even spiritual exercises, constitute the path to the Divine in Greek Orthodoxy. Even among the contemporary Athenian intellectual elite religion is inconceivable without interaction with icons.[7]

We make such lengthy points in order to illustrate the complexity of the interaction of religion and law upon conceptions of gender. A brief comparison between Greek Orthodoxy and Catholicism in the way the gender components of religious ideals are constructed is useful here.

This will enable us to specify more clearly the position of women as defined in Greek Orthodoxy and ultimately to tackle the issues raised by du Boulay.

To begin with, while both Orthodoxy and Catholicism emphasise chastity as an ideal goal, the extent to which this ideal – as celibacy – was imposed upon and accepted by the grassroots as a practical and realisable goal for both men and women appears to have differed in each faith. Part of the reason may lie in the differing organisation of the two churches. In Orthodoxy religious chastity implied a removal from society and the family into monasteries (the monastic ideal being very strong in Greece); in Catholicism by contrast chastity pursued through religious celibacy in the form of Parish Priest or the monastic life did not necessarily involve physical separation from the bosom of society or from the family, as occurred in the participatory orders of the Dominicans, Franciscans, Jesuits, certain female Orders, and so on. Furthermore, whereas many monasteries in the West were staffed by disinherited younger sons and daughters, often in a dominant unigeniture system, in the East a celibate life was often a direct consequence of poverty. This applied to both men and women, but especially to the latter. Skouzes groups the poor and nuns (women without dowry) together: 'nor did the poor of Athens go elsewhere to beg, since they could keep alive this way. More than a thousand souls lived in the parishes and a great quantity of women became nuns, who did not marry, and the cells were full and the inmates busy at all manner of labour' (Andrews, 1979; 119). Clearly on the formal ideological level both Catholicism and Orthodoxy emphasise the religious primacy of the monastic life. The following Orthodox tract would be equally subscribed to by Catholicism: 'Our Lord loves marriage, yes, but even more so virginity. If you can preserve your virginity [*parthenian*], and want to become a monk, or a woman a nun, you are well fortunate, and thrice blessed, you are free [*eleftheros*] of all worldly things, you are like an angel. And if you wish to preserve your virginity, as the first foundation you have to give up your lands, your money and your goods' (Menounos, 1979; 199).

While a denial of worldly wealth was a necessary and formal precondition for the religious life in Catholicism and Orthodoxy, participation in worldly affairs was as variable as the availability of worldly goods within the monastic context. Partly because of the privileged position of the Church in South Western Europe, and partly because elites there often diverted some of their wealth to monasteries and Orders so as to maintain disinherited children, a religious life was neither bereft of worldly comforts nor necessarily secluded from worldly affairs, and a

Church career for men was a respectable means for social mobility. Religious stratification often paralleled social stratification, or was often influenced by it. Indeed, Catholic religious orders in southern Europe have traditionally drawn recruits from different social strata. In Orthodoxy by contrast, because of the interstitial position of the Church under the Ottomans the general tendency at the grassroots towards equal partible inheritance, and because the monastic life involved a greater removal from society, a monastic career, especially at the higher levels, tended to attract less 'this worldly' aspirants than in the West, as well as individuals less socialised towards the pursuit of politics by religious means. Often recruited from the poorer strata, it is hardly surprising that the acquisition and display of worldly goods attached to High Office in Orthodoxy became a powerful symbol for the Higher Clergy, while at the same time the source of criticism from the grass-roots. A distinctive combination of other-worldly lower monastic recruits and this-worldly Higher Clergy pervaded Orthodoxy probably to a greater extent than in any other major Christian faith.

The alternative was even more stark for women. While the village Papas had to be a married man, clearly accession to religious office was closed to women. Nor did a cloistered life necessarily imply the main-tenance of an original social status while preserving the economic strength of the family corporation, as in the West. On the popular level, and partly also due to the exhortations of the Great Church in Ottoman captivity to multiply the *yenos* (the early word for the *ethnos*, which itself indicates the biological and reproductive aspects of a religiously-defined cultural group), celibacy, or non-reproduction, for women does not appear to have been a realisable or indeed ideal goal for women.

It is worthwhile to explore the structural and psychological frame-works for the pursuit and expression of male, but especially female, celibacy on three levels: at the level of Church organisation in terms of available facilities; at the level of symbolism, as an ideal; and in terms of popular consciousness.

We begin with monasteries. In 1833 593 monasteries existed in Greece, of which 412 were deserted and dissolved in 1834. This decline may have been due to land reform as well as to the law that every monastery had to have more than 30 monks or nuns. In 1897 there were 170 monasteries with 1322 monks, a figure which remains relatively unchanged in the twentieth century. Nor did the Orthodox Church cater particularly to nuns, although increasingly in the nineteenth and twen-tieth centuries Greek nuns brought a 'dowry' to be added to the nun-nery's holdings. In most cases Greek women became nuns because they rejected marriage, for a variety of complex reasons, rather than perhaps because of the compelling religious ideal of celibacy. Indeed in some cases nuns were widows. Orthodoxy is much more like Islam in this respect, where 'to marry is to accomplish half of religion' (*hadith* as quoted in Davis, 1984; 30). Becoming a nun accomplished the other half, by default. In other words, not only was celibacy not perceived as a practical alternative, but it was positively rejected at the grassroots. Even nowadays Cypriot villagers refer to the Old Testament strictures to 'go forth and multiply' as the reason why marriage, rather than celibacy, is religiously sanctioned. In their perspective it is marriage rather than celibacy which ought to be practised.

On the level of religious symbolism, while the preservation of celibacy as a means of religious self-expression and salvation is an ideal in Orthodox thought, it is often not given practical emphasis as a viable alternative for women. Apart from the small number of nunneries, other factors are important. On the popular level celibacy is viewed as a type of 'sin' (*amartia*), especially for women. Clearly virginity was an important stage prior to marriage, but its loss after marriage was not necessarily lamented as tantamount to a displacement to a less exalted sacred state for women. Indeed, as we shall try to show, it was through motherhood that women achieved their highest religious and existential exultation.

Here it is worthwhile to compare Catholicism and Orthodoxy in their perception and visualisation of Mary, The Mother of God, because their significant differences can help to highlight specific Greek Orthodox perceptions. We use the term Mother of God advisedly because certain designations, such as The Virgin Mary, have particular nuances in different faiths. In Greek popular discourse Mary is known primarily by two terms: *Theotokos* (literally, 'God Bearer') and the *Panayia* (literally 'The Most Holy One'); the latter is by far the most popular in discourse although the former is more favoured in 'official' tracts, for example titles of icons, religious tracts and so on. In Catholicism, taking into account the various languages, She is known as *La Beata Vergine* (The Blessed Virgin), The Madonna, The Mother of God or The Mother of Jesus, as well as *Regina Celi* (Queen of The Heavens). It is clear that Greek religious culture does not give particular emphasis to the virginal aspects of Mary, as much as to her maternal role as The Mother of God. This is to a certain extent reflected in painting. Whereas art in Catholicism, especially in Renaissance Italy, has traditionally given particular emphasis to the Annunciation, ultimately highlighting the virginal aspect of Mary ('Behold the handmaiden of the Lord . . .'), Greek Orthodoxy has traditionally concentrated on depicting Mary as The Mother of The Child Christ with Christ sitting on her lap. Indeed with the exception of Veneto-Cretan art (heavily influenced by Catholicism), Orthodox religious painting has generally tended to concentrate less on the Annunciation. Instead the emphasis has been on the symbolism of the human aspects of motherhood with particular concentration on the interaction between mother and child (for example in *glikofilousa* – literally, 'sweet kiss' – paintings). Indeed while Catholicism utilises the symbolism of the body and its postures as the 'royal road' to Divinity, Orthodoxy tended to rely more on the 'theology of the face' (Baudinet, 1989; 155).

The differences can be taken further. Mary is not seen as Immaculately Conceived and bodily assumed into Heaven, as in Catholic theology. Rather, Orthodoxy subscribes to the notion of the *koimisis* (the Dormition). As she is not seen as Immaculate in conception nor in her semi-Christlike Assumption into Heaven, she is on one level nearer to man. In Orthodoxy the virgin remains a human intercessor, certainly with Divine Grace, but she remains an *anthropos*, a human and a Mother, and does not become a semi-deified human as in Catholicism, where, like Christ, she ascends bodily into Heaven, becoming the *Regina Celi* – The Queen of Heaven. Indeed the Encyclical of Anthimos VII of 1894 came out strongly against the Catholic dogma of the Immaculate Conception of the Virgin Mary (1854). In the eighteenth century some monks (for example Ag. Nikodimos O Agioreites, 1749–1809) had tried to develop the cult of the Virgin as a semi-deified human, especially in the hymn 'Kyria Theotokou'. Yet it is significant that not only did he feel that he had to justify himself by claiming that his hymn was not influenced by Protestantism or Catholicism, but also that his works were not republished until the late nineteenth century.

The implication of all this is that there are some striking and deep differences between Catholicism and Orthodoxy in the conception of the Virgin Mary and in the ways women participate in religion. One of the residing features of Catholicism is the progressive and cumulative elaboration of the 'nature' of the Virgin and the Mother of God, in the whole growth of the cult of Marianism. There was an internal dialogue in both text and image in the evolution of Catholicism across time which was largely absent in Greek Orthodoxy. In Catholicism, both the religious image and the religious tract (of a theological and exegetical kind) were elaborated independently in a complex division of labour (secular painters and theologians), whereas in Greece they were largely explored by the same personnel (monks). Text and image interacted in much more complex ways in the West, and from the Renaissance onwards the text provided a framework from which the image could subsequently 'take-off' (Baxandall, 1972). Hence the body became invested with particular meanings and symbolism. In Orthodoxy, by contrast, the religious nature of the text largely restricted the purely pictorial elaboration of images: icons remained a kind of literature for the illiterate. Stylistically, too, Orthodoxy was more interested in exploring oppositions in iconic form which were basically scriptural (Maguire, 1981), than in exploring and developing the internal dialogue and elaboration of both text and image, as in Catholicism. Under the restraining hand of the Turkocratia the emphasis was much more on retaining the continuity and identifiability of icons as the most readily available and accessible aids to the Divine. To use an Islamic metaphor, the image became Koranicized (formalised, fixed and unchanging, but eminently portable). Access to the Divine through icons implies access through private individual rituals, rather than the ability to recite (as in *hadiths*) or to interiorise faith (as in Protestantism).

Indeed popular devotion in Orthodoxy, certainly up until the mid-nineteenth century closely resembled medieval European grassroots practices, especially in the construction of religious value. In both cases material manifestations of holiness were usually discovered within the local community, either as in the West in the form of Saints' bones (Geary, 1986), or in the East more usually in the form of a bible or icon of the Saint (or the Panayia in Orthodoxy) often at the boundaries of the community. Initially this is met by scepticism and the Saint usually admonishes the believer in a dream. In both cases this scepticism is overcome by some negative sanction and in Greek Orthodoxy, as in Medieval Catholicism, the local clergy are often strongly involved in the process. Similarly, these sacred relics are often discovered at a time of political disturbance, as with the discovery of the Icon of the Panayia in Tinos in 1821. The latter case is almost paradigmatic. The icon was discovered after the Panayia appeared to an eighty-year-old man (semi-removed from society by virtue of his venerable age) who tries unsuccessfully to locate the icon. He and the only two believers are directed to a field, where they find a submerged wall and attempt to build an oven with the stones, but it falls down. The Panayia then appears to a nun who betrays greater scepticism than the old man, but the Virgin threatens the island with cholera if her wish is not heeded. The Bishop (a recent appointee eager to make his mark) on being told, believes her and orders excavations. After excavating unsuccessfully for two months the villagers give up and cholera strikes the island. On recommencing work and inaugurating a small chapel, a dry well fills up which is soon followed by the discovery of the icon reputed to be one of the three painted by St Luke. The Icon manifests its power by performing miracles on non-believers who recognise its power to a greater extent than the villagers. The first is to calm the seas after an English ship, captained by a Catholic is about to be shipwrecked. The captain makes a vow and his ship is saved. The second miracle involves a Turkish Aga who is cured of his lameness. Soon after the church becomes a centre of pilgrimage for revolutionary generals, and becomes identified with the new Greek state (Anon., 1985).

The religious apparatus and the paths to the Divine which are available to the faithful in Greek Orthodoxy are thus very different to those found in other parts of the European Catholic Mediterranean. We are thus better able to appreciate some of the points raised by du Boulay in her discussion of the relationship between religion and gender construction; we are also able to place some of her insights into a more dynamic social context. For example the view of women she highlights as 'by nature fallen, by destiny redeemed' is largely an amalgam of early Judeo-Christianity with little intervention of the Marianist development. Mary is certainly less deified in Orthodoxy than in Catholicism; it is a perspective which is largely encountered in an oral culture, or more precisely in a culture where any literary-based elaboration on the divine nature of the Mother of God has had very little impact – mainly because little occurred in Greek Orthodoxy.

This attitude is also likely to be encountered in viri-patrilocal contexts where women own little property and where a transformation in a woman's position is likely to be heavily dependent upon how she performs her matrimonial roles, rather than in the joint manipulation of her own and her husband's resources.[8] If we exclude, purely as an exercise, the religious elements of gender construction in Ambeli, we find the general principle that in the early years of marriage a woman is not granted much acceptance until the birth of her first child, and is only fully accepted through the practice of motherhood: 'a man realises the value of his wife in later life' (du Boulay 1986; 159). This principle is generally found in other contexts, such as in North Africa and Epirus; areas of pastoralism or transhumance where women carry little property.

We are not suggesting here that religious elements are unimportant or mere accretions; nor are we advancing a materialist interpretation which gives exclusive primacy to property rights, though these are certainly important in providing the general framework available to men and women to express their interests in society. If gender is socially constructed then religion is a constituent element in identifying those actions which are socially approved, and even more so in identifying those behavioural patterns which are religiously disapproved. Du Boulay has suggested that 'villagers view Adam and Eve in terms of certain observed behavioural traits of their own men and women, while these traits are themselves defined by their failure to approximate to the prescribed ideal' (1986; 157). She might have succeeded in bringing this out more fully had she been able to give concrete ethnographic examples of discourse and social action where the ideal and real are transacted; as it is her examples make statements which are *post-facto* rationalisations based upon this type of religious framework. They may certainly orient behaviour, but it is a different matter to show how in specific cases men and women move from observed behaviour traits to a discussion of religious ideals, and then back again.

An ethnographic comparison is perhaps useful here. Ambeliot women enter marriage in roughly the same conditions as many North African rural (especially pastoral) women. In both cases they carry little property and move to their husband's households; in both cases, too, acceptance and a realisation of their value is likely to come late in married life. This we take as a general feature of such contexts. But how they achieve this state is largely a function of culture. In North Africa, partly because of the system of property transmissions at marriage where the brideprice is often not fully paid or where women retain residual property rights in their own natal households, wives often return temporarily to their brothers (or fathers) should they be mistreated or in the case of quarrels, and refuse to return unless placated by a gift (Peters, 1980). The relationship is usually solidified over the passage of time through this type of matrimonial feuding. Greek rural women are not permitted this possibility of action, because of the strong disapproval with which divorce is viewed (the North African action being a threat to divorce), because of the centrality of the nuclear family and the conjugal bond, as well as other factors. Instead, women work out their identities in and through motherhood, which is powerfully anchored in religion and religious ideals. Christianity in this case provides as Weber points out 'the railway tracks along which material interests are expressed' (Weber, 1948; 280).

In analysing the position of women in eighteenth- and nineteenth-century Athens and its subsequent transformation throughout the nineteenth century, we wish to accept certain aspects of du Boulay's thesis and to modify some of them. Our data indicate that a certain uniformity existed in attitudes towards motherhood; these were exhibited in the way women from all social strata changed their costumes. After the birth of children women abandoned their costumes denoting social origins, for much less elaborate ones, when they began to achieve that state of redemption (and hence a greater value in the eyes of society), signified by motherhood. Motherhood transcended all differences of social position and origin in early nineteenth-century Greece.

However it is in the area of the second precondition (equal and structural opposition of two religiously defined symbols) that we believe certain changes occurred in Athens, and eventually, by implication, in other areas of Greece, throughout the nineteenth century. In du Boulay's scheme both symbols of womanhood (Eve and the Mother of God) are given equal importance in a largely oral culture. However, throughout the latter part of nineteenth-century Greece the image of the Mother of God began to receive greater importance than the image of Eve; the Mother of God symbol became increasingly secularised. We are not stating that the two symbols can be separated (indeed they mutually presuppose each other), but we are suggesting that a culture can emphasise one aspect more than the other to orient behaviour as well as to explain the nature of womanhood. For the two symbols of a single unitary religious vision are of a different order. Eve is a model *of* the nature of womanhood in a pre-cultural state, whereas the Mother of God is a model *for* guiding the behaviour of women in Christian society and a modern state, and the emphasis on one or the other may change according to context. This is a Weberian argument, viz. changes in social organisation are often accompanied, and dialectically interact with, doctrines of salvation.

In late nineteenth-century Greece, as in other parts of Southern Europe, there occurred a progressive upgrading of the importance and the cult of the Virgin Mary. The causes in Western Europe are complex and have been analysed elsewhere by more qualified observers (for example Zeldin, 1978). In Greece the influence of Western developments must not be discarded; the internal causes were as much likely to have been due to grassroots urban developments as an imposition from the top. Clearly there were significant differences between grassroots devotion in Catholicism and Orthodoxy. Whereas the Virgin has appeared in Western Europe a number of times, it is significant that she still works through her icons in Greece. In Athens until the early 1940s she was always manifest through her icons, for example in shedding tears and so on.

The cult of the Mother of God took various forms in Greece. Although a proper historical and anthropological study of the phenomenon has yet to be undertaken we wish to highlight certain broad features. Analytically it is possible to see the growth of this cult on two levels, possessing a different cluster of images and attributes. On the popular level it took the form of the cult of the Panayia which was an amplification of folk concerns. The Panayia here is an *anthropos* rather than a divinity, a woman and mother rather than a virginal girl as in the Annunciation. Literally 'The Most Holy One', she is less the Mother of God as the mother of the child Christ, an intercessor on behalf of men, other *anthropi*, with her Son in a manner similar to the Madonna del Soccorso in Mediterranean Catholic countries. She is thus an identifiable symbol of motherhood with the attributes of patience, protection and solace for men in an hour of need. On the popular level this cult was manifested in the growth of pilgrimage within Greece to monasteries associated with the Panayia (for example Tinos) as well as to the Holy Land, and the massive circulation of cheap mass-produced icons for consumption within the home, many of which are copies of Western pictures. So complete has been this interpenetration (mostly from West to East), that the iconography of the Virgin Mary, or more precisely the most residing images in the popular mind in Greece, is now a fusion of Western Catholic and Eastern Orthodox imagery which transcends doctrinal differences. Plate 7 is a good example of this. A painting of the Annunciation, executed by Yeorghios Loverdos Stelakatos in 1851, it is clearly heavily influenced by Western models. In many homes of long standing Athenians Italian pictures of the Madonna which circulated in the late nineteenth and early twentieth centuries are common. Indeed from the eighteenth century huge numbers of Orthodox woodcuts and engravings were produced in Venice, Mount Athos, Constantinople and Tinos, many of which by the mid-nineteenth century were copies of folk icons. In Athens during this period many of these prints were heavily influenced by Western models, such as Ide O Anthropos, or Ecce Homo (Papastratos, 1986; 30). The ready availability and growth in circulation of such images should not be rejected as sociologically unimportant, for they provided men and women with images and models to emulate in a pre-electronic age, in much the same way that American television soap operas (such as 'Dallas') influence women's fashions and aspirations in many semi-peripheral societies including contemporary Greece and Cyprus (Crawford, 1984).

Various factors influenced and encouraged the cult of the Panayia in Greece. Yet here there were important differences between Orthodoxy and Catholicism. Because Orthodox theology had remained largely static during the difficult years of the Turkocratia, it was less pre-disposed to innovation. One of the seminal features of Catholicism is the way it can incorporate grassroots sentiments and reflect them in theologised discourse. In Catholicism it is much easier to plot the progressive theological redefinitions of the nature and the powers of the Virgin: councils and papal doctrines progressively redefined issues which partly reflected grassroots concerns and developments. Indeed there has been a tendency in Catholicism to multiply the images associated with different attributes of Mary: Madonna del Soccorso, Mater Dolorosa, Madonna delle Lachrime, and so on; attributes which often emphasise the suffering aspect of the Madonna, with the result that identification with her is usually through these sentiments. By contrast in Orthodoxy there was comparatively little discourse on 'the highly theologised prototype of relations to Jesus, exemplar of celibate chastity, object of subtle and tender *placement* in the economy of salvation, who is the creation of ecclesiastical and usually celibate speculation' (Davis, 1984; 28). Individuals thus identify with her as Mother or intercessor, rather than as a symbol of almost supra-human suffering.

There are two implications of this difference for nineteenth-century Greece. First, grassroots devotion to the Virgin retained much of its folk character, while on the national level much of the cult of Motherhood, which partly reflected the phenomenon, was expressed in the secular political domain rather than in the religious one. In other words, the growth of the cult of the Theotokos (the image of sacred motherhood) in Greece was, as in Byzantine times, linked to the power of the Prince (the nation-state). Indeed, so strong were popular wishes that the National Day in Greece commemorating the Liberation from the Turks was soon shifted to 25 March, the Feast of the Panayia. On the national level the displacement of devotion to the Panayia to the expression of the ideological concern with Motherhood is well documented. The growth of nationalism, the rewriting of history under Ottoman rule, the idea that Greece and Constantinople fell initially to the Turks as a type of expiation of previous 'sins' committed in the Byzantine Garden of Eden (Clogg, 1976; xiii) (and hence the Liberation of Greece from the Ottomans was akin to the promise of the Resurrection heralded by the 25th March), the privileged position of the Church and religion in the new Greek state, the desire to liberate Greek-speaking Christian regions such as Epiros, Thessaly and Macedonia from Muslim oppression, the Holy Trinity of *pistis* (faith), *ikoyenia* (family) and *ethnos* (nation), all contributed to the growth of the cult of motherhood. Greece was *I Mitera Ellada* (Mother Greece) whose family was spread out in different lands striving to be united. Just as mothers sacrificed themselves for their children, so too did *I Mitera Ellada* spare no efforts to unite with her long-lost suffering children in other lands. This matricentric ideology was accompanied with, and pursued through, the production of national images for public consumption showing Mother Greece striving to be united with her daughter regions. In the University Museum at Ioannina an early twentieth-century poster depicts a Mother standing on a map of central Greece leaning over to hand a *stoli* to her daughter in Epiros (Plate 5). Fifty years later a similar type poster was produced for the Cypriot struggle for *enosis* (Plate 6). The central imagery remained the same, it was merely the region which had changed. The text of the poster is itself interesting, structured as it is in a conversation between Mother Greece and Daughter Cyprus:

(Greece): My beloved Cyprus, do not cry! You have changed many masters, but you have not changed your heart/essence [Kardia]. I am and shall always be by your side.

(Cyprus): Yes! However, my dear mother embrace me! Because all my hopes I've placed in you.

The outcome of this ideology is that throughout the mid-nineteenth century and later, homes and public places were saturated with images of motherhood in both its divine and secular aspects.

The growth of literacy was also important on another level, for it helped to separate the two images of womanhood: Eve and the Mother of God. The structural opposition of Eve and the Mother of God is particularly suitable for, and powerful within, an oral culture where the two images are locked in a series of symbolically opposed associations which can be apprehended *in toto sensu*. In a literate context, although their critical oppositions are recognised, further elaboration comes into play. The image of the Virgin Mary is substantiated and defined by her opposition and complementarity to other female figures within the New Testament: St Anne, Mary Magdalene and so on. She becomes more 'real' as, for example, a participant at the Marriage Feast at Cana, the mother standing by her crucified son, the suffering mother receiving the body of her dead son, and as the child-soul in the *koimisis* (Dormition) surrounded by the Apostles rising to be held in the arms of her son-God in Paradise just as she herself held up her son-child at the Yennisis (Birth of Christ). The implication of all that is that motherhood in its divine aspects is accompanied by an embarrassment of examples drawn from the life of the Virgin on earth, embodied in images but more importantly for Orthodoxy, accompanied by texts which circulate widely within society. Thus while the essential polarity of the Eve–Mother of God axis is not lost, there occurs an elaboration in images and texts of the content of Divine motherhood and its implications.

Some indication of the effects of literacy upon the content of religious imagery is provided by M. Alexiou (1975). Examining folksongs and laments of the Virgin in both Byzantine and modern contexts, she notes that 'unlike many other types of folk-song [i.e. earlier ones], [the modern songs] . . . have been exposed to the influence of a non-oral tradition – specifically, to the influence of Holy-Week hymns and

Gospel readings' (1975; 135). The content of these songs also changed. In seventeenth-century vernacular *threnoi* as well as in *The Sacrifice of Abraham* 'Mary desires to go down to Hades alive in order to seek out her forefathers and blame them for what has happened. Adam and Eve, also Cain, are held responsible through their sin and violence' (Alexiou, 1975; 139). By contrast in modern folk ballads the content changes radically; the Virgin is less linked to the past, the transmission of sin and the Fall and its transcendence through redemption and the Resurrection, but rather is more closely identified with her role as an earthly mother:

The [modern] folk ballads scarcely mention the Descent to Hades, or the Resurrection, emphasizing instead Mary's preparation of the *paregoria* [funeral feast]. The ritual feast for the dead, which is of pagan origin, is still performed today by the bereaved family; but here it has been invested with a new significance, since Mary will prepare the meal for all to share, thereby uniting those divided by death.

(Alexiou, 1975; 139)

It is worthwhile to note that *paregoria*, or *parighoria*, literally means 'comfort'; Mary thus provides both food in her role as mother, but also literally comfort for those experiencing bereavement. Alexiou observes that 'the human aspect and dramatic potential of the theme have been exploited to the full, to the exclusion of theological or mystical elements. Thus, Mary addresses Christ not as "my son and God", as in the Byzantine laments, but simply as "my son", and Christ himself is sometimes credited with powers more magic than divine' (*ibid.*, 140).

We wish to suggest that in the urban literate contexts of the new Greek state, rather than the rural oral ones, the image of motherhood in both its sacred and secular aspects thus became emphasised and elaborated in such a way that it began to achieve a semi-sacred state. Such a process was not merely ideological; it was actively encouraged by the Church and vigorously pursued by the rising urban Athenian middle class of *nikokirei*, and it was reinforced by actual changes in social organisation, by the growth of salaried employment outside the home, and by the seclusion of women in the home. The Church favoured equal partible inheritance, the independence of the conjugal couple from extra-kin ties which could be most visibly manifested and pursued through neolocality, and it vigorously condemned the scandalous cohabitation of engaged couples prior to a Church-performed marriage ceremony as occurred among the urban poor and in the periphery, for example Lesbos (Papataxiarhis, 1985).

Yet it was the *nikokirei* group which most consistently pursued and elaborated the ideal of motherhood as the ultimate destiny of women, while at the same time gradually separating this from a concept of woman as fallen by nature. This was accomplished by various means. On the level of social organisation the preference for neolocality, the elaboration of the notion of the *nikokira* as mistress of her own household, and the substitution of the formal/informal distinction by the more physically concrete distinction of private/public, created the physical and cultural space where Motherhood could find its fuller expression in civil society.

Of even greater importance was the socialisation of women and the role of literacy, which we wish to explore in turn. From du Boulay's account, country folk until recently generally subscribed to the notion of the 'natural woman – Eve – a being not evil but prone to evil, less wicked than weak, prone to temptation and triviality' (1986; 152). This is a view echoed in the Yugoslav Macedonian village of Skopska Crna Gora where 'women are held to be evil not in themselves, but in the consequences of the actions that they cause. Household division is the most frequently cited example' (Rheubottom, 1985; 89). Of critical importance here is the concept of evil and its transformation in the Greek context across time. Evil has had a number of different connotations which we do not explore here except to note that certain consequences of women's actions can be considered evil, such as the destruction of a family (*Katastrophi tis mias ikoyenia*) or the connection of women, especially in contexts in which they are outsiders, with illicit magical practices. The former is a powerful concept in rural areas because women are posited as weak creatures (*adinati*). However as countrymen migrate to the town, as occurred in Athens in large numbers from the 1830s, and as they adapt to the realities and difficulties of urban living, some country values become transformed. Pollution beliefs cease to have the structuring principle they possess in rural life, though the body still carries many meanings derived from urban civil society. The evil contained within the 'other', the *ksenos*, becomes potentially more grave in its urban consequences than in the village context where individuals know one another in the round, unless mediated in the city by other forms of association such as common village ties. In this respect a country mentality of suspicion colonises the city.

Even more important is the urban transformation of the socialisation of women. Women become socialised in an intense but narrow way, to further interiorise notions of chastity. These notions are demonstrated and given tangible expression in a large number of activities, both 'sacred' and 'profane', although the ultimate significance of these activities cannot be rigidly classified into these categories. Tending the home and cooking become symbolic practices – the former to create an ideal space where the sacred family can reside, and where the family and domesticity is sanctified; cooking and culinary skills become an essential component of the construction of female gender identity, expressed in the ability to transform 'nature' into 'culture', the 'raw' into the 'cooked'. Plate 9 depicts a popular poster of a genre found in countless rural and urban homes. What is interesting about this picture apart from its obvious modelling on Leonardo's Last Supper (also a common picture found in many homes) is the depiction of the earthly family modelled on the Holy Family. It is through eating together that holiness and grace are attained. Christ appears to bless the midday meal. Interestingly it is not the nuclear family that is depicted, for there are two elderly parents of the couple; the ideal of domestic harmony encompasses a three-generational unit. Yet the picture was possibly influenced by Western models, both in terms of the decor and of Christ's facial attributes. Furthermore a number of structural oppositions underlie the picture relevant to our concerns. The outer circle of the 'family' consists of the oldest generation, which is physically most distant from Christ; the children by contrast are physically closest to Christ. There is a clear hierarchy in generations which are inverted – the hierarchy of earthly authority is counterposed to the inverted hierarchy of divine grace where the youngest are first. In addition while the vine is outside, fruit is inside, both framed in a picture and on the table. The time of man, manifested by the clock is counterposed to the time of the seasons outside; flowers are inside, green vegetation in pots outside. Grace and salvation, in short, are found within the order of the home and family and the ordered nature of domestic tasks.

Time, or rather the creation of time by filling it with the devising of complex culinary dishes also becomes an essential component of women's identity. Hirschon notes that quickly-prepared meals are called 'prostitute's food' (1989; 150). Whilst they satisfy hunger they lack the blessing and grace associated with home-produced food. The metaphor can be further extended by the association of 'eating' with 'sex' in the Greek language.[9] Virtue and modesty, in short, can only be demonstrated through filling time, through activities in the home, expressed in the vocabulary of virtue which women employ to describe their personal obligation to the home (Hirschon, 1989; 144); in striking contrast to the language employed by men, whose relation to the home is expressed in terms of a general duty imposed by society.

Profane activities are also reflected in the sacred domain. Tending the home is expressed symbolically on the sacred plane by tending the family graves, and in the many religious rituals in which women are involved (Hirschon, 1989; Danforth, 1982; Kenna, forthcoming). The sacred and the profane are thus intimately linked – they endow women with a sense of grace in much the same way that Mary was blessed. Their virtue is demonstrated and expressed through the domestic management of time. These interiorised notions thus relieve the social mechanisms operative in the village context, whose function is to help maintain and preserve chastity: postponement of brothers' marriages until their sisters have married and the threat of violence or violent retaliation by male kin. Both are largely unsuitable for urban contexts, although we do not doubt that such practices do occur in the city. By and large however the threat of violence is largely not permissible in urban contexts because of the state's monopoly of violence, middle-class aspirations to propriety (and concealment), the de-emphasis on extended kinship ties concomitant with a nuclear family orientation, and because of the risks involved.

The types of gender mechanisms which increasingly came into play in urban Greek society were largely internal. Until recently daughters were socialised from a young age to the values and perspectives of a *nikokira*, producing *kendimata*, lace and embroidery items of all sorts, which symbolised the independence of their future matrimonial state and demonstrated their chastity and virtue. This was reinforced by national school curricula and the social role of popular novels which upheld the sacredness of motherhood and its critical role for the *ethnos*. Indeed it is not fortuitous that in Karkavitsas' novel *O Archeologos*, the heroine Elpida (Hope) who provides a solution to the predicament of the sources of national identity, is explicitly involved in embroidery. As Politi observes she is the 'prototype of the female national subject' (1988; 50).

Nowhere is this attitude brought out more clearly than in the periodicals specifically designed for women which began circulating in Athens from the 1870s onwards (for example *Ephimeris ton Kirion*, 1887; *Thaleia*, 1867; *Evridikhe*, 1870/73; *I Oikogenia*, 1897/8; *I Pleias*, 1899–1900). Running through these periodicals, which are oriented towards the educated Athenian elite, is a concern with the relative placement of men and women in society and the home, the sacred quality of childcare, and fear of exposure to Western influences which could 'weaken' the *ethnos* and the national character. The following is a sample not just of a specific construction of gender identity, but also of its intimate relation with the *ethnos*:

Man is endowed [*prikismenos*] with strength to meet life's challenges whereas a woman's strength is toward the tending and feeding of the child. Powerful is the man who takes risks; weak and cautious the woman. He is clever and has imposing and sweeping plans. She is a demon and loses herself in details. Thus with this situation begins the creation of a family and therefore of the *ethnos* and culture.

(Evridikhe, 21/11/1870)

Unfortunately our national character threatens to disappear due to the influence of this pernicious culture [from the West]. Because of this we have to be extremely cautious to unite together to bring back the rule [Kingdom] of the woman which has become weakened. This family as a golden throne has to be maintained, giving light, joy and blessing with a sacred enchantment spreading out from the woman. Finally she has to become the solace of her husband, and a guardian-angel of her children.

(Anna Serouiou: 'Our Programme', Oikogenia- Weekly – 4/1/1897)

These passages bring out a number of themes. Woman is the hidden armature or link between *pistis, patridha* and *ikoyenia* (Faith, Homeland and Family); if she does not fulfil her duties, especially those in the home, then the *ethnos* suffers and weakens (*adinatisei*). The religious symbolism is clear; the reference to the golden throne echoes the sacred throne upon which the Panayia is often seated in icons, and she is the guardian-angel, both pure and offering protection, an image which also embodies Mother Greece (Plate 5). As in Papadiamantis' work, salvation for women lay through *engarterisis* – a 'combination of patience, endurance and forbearance' (Constantinides, 1987; xvi), similar to the virtues of Mary. Finally there is the ambivalent attitude towards the West. We believe that such attitudes enable a closer understanding of the significance of *ithografia* – on one level, while the writing of *ithografia* represented the working-out of the tensions inherent in constructing a specific model of gender identity for women, its subject matter was in the town transposed to, and expressed in, another plane, that of the countryside.

It is also clear from these extracts that the dominant image of motherhood in both its secular and sacred manifestations became somewhat loosened from its associations with the image of Eve as representing the fallen nature of woman. Some indication of the transformations to gender identity in urban contexts comes from the work of R. Hirschon among Asia Minor refugees settled in Piraeus. She notes that Mary, Mother of God, was seldom referred to as the 'Virgin' [*parthena*], in striking contrast to Catholicism, where *La Beata Vergine* is a common term. She notes that while Eve 'embodies the dangerous element in woman's nature, its potential for chaos and destruction' (1989; 152), the imagery of motherhood is more developed, expressed primarily in tending the house and in religious activities: Mary 'represents the redeeming power of female qualities, the submission to divine will, the image of purity, of human perfectibility' (*ibid.*). Significantly the 'chaos and destruction' that women are perceived as capable of setting in motion are located within the family after marriage, a clear indication that the symbolism of Eve is of a different, lower order subsumed within the overarching imagery of motherhood. In an urban context motherhood itself becomes the problem that hardly appears in rural contexts. The 'evil' that they are capable of causing is not so much an outcome of women's 'natural weakness' (as Eves), but rather of their failure to successfully perform their duties as mothers. It is a result of their failure to uphold the ideals of motherhood and housewife which the culture expects and which they have internalised according to a private ideal which is not fully resolved, as in rural areas. After observing rural and urban mothers in Greece a behavioural psychologist concluded that:

Rural women were much less inclined to consider parents as solely responsible for the behaviour of their offspring, despite the fact that in their milieu there were few if any environmental factors which might contribute to alienation of the young from their parents. I believe that this exaggerated sense of responsi-bility makes the urban mother feel as if she is under trial, waiting for the 'final judgement', a state of mind that can only cause anxiety in the mother and burden her relationship with her child . . . it appears that the traditional model of the all giving mother, when applied out of context, leads the mother into doing for the child many things he could very well do on his own, losing in the process much of her status and importance and becoming more of an attendant than a care-giver.

(Doumanis, 1983; 102, 104)

Conclusion

Parts of this chapter have of necessity been somewhat speculative, for we have been involved here in an excavation of the mentalities of the past. We therefore wish to retrace some of the steps we have taken to clarify the exercise. In effect, any anthropological history of the Greek family is faced with the following conditions. We possess some excellent anthropological accounts of the position of women in contemporary Greek rural society and a much smaller number of works dealing with the contemporary urban situation. We have no comparable information for earlier periods. There is no valid reason to claim that contemporary rural Greek society represents urban society at an earlier stage. On the contrary they are likely to have been very different. Perhaps more than in most other Mediterranean societies town and country in Greece have been interacting intensively for the past 150 years. Part of this is due to the inordinate influence of the Athenian magnet.[10] Given this it seems reasonable to make the following two assumptions: first, that many of the cultural patterns observed in contemporary Greek rural society have long been heavily influenced by the process of urbanisation, however 'traditional' they may appear to be, in effect what Friedl has called 'lagging emulation' (1964). Second, given the massive migration from the rural hinterland to the town we would expect to find lagging retention of country perspectives in the town. The countryside may have been urbanised for a considerable portion of the past 150 years, but Athens has also become ruralised in the process, long after its agricultural base disappeared in the new Greek kingdom. Already by 1849 Charles-Ernest Beule had observed that in this sense the pattern of the growth of Athens bore close similarity to that of Ancient Rome, in other words the 'ruralisation of the city': 'Songe-t-on que la moderne Athènes s'est formée à peu pres comme l'ancienne Rome? C'était un refuge, je ne dis pas pour les bandits, mais pour les ambitieux, les oisifs, les spéculateurs, les exilés; ils accouraient de l'Orient et de l'occident afin de tenter la fortune' (Andrews, 1979; 263). Clearly, too, the images that townsmen and countrymen have of each other are not reflective of reality. They are idealised, transformed, defined and redefined to suit both exigencies and context.

The question therefore is, can we reconstruct a picture of life and ethics in the Greek urban family of the late eighteenth and nineteenth centuries which is consistent with contemporary accounts and which takes due cognisance of the above facts? Fortunately we have a number of informative sources, including information on how property within the family was divided at marriage, settlement patterns and other measureable areas of family life (dowries, trousseaux, and so on); literature produced during this period, both folkloric and literary; and general information on the overall intellectual and ideological climate in Greece during the nineteenth and early twentieth centuries.

Each of these sources require different approaches and perspectives. Inevitably, studies of this kind are bound to be somewhat eclectic and selective due to our inadequate understanding of the data at our disposal. The result may seem somehow inadequate but it may stimulate further questions about past and present family life in Greece and other Mediterranean societies.

Major considerations in our understanding of the development of the Greek urban family and its emotional life have been that it occurred within the context of a newly formed nation-state attempting to construct an image of a permanent unchanging Greece while retaining, and indeed developing, a model of a Christian family; there was a growing tendency to utilise cash and mobile resources as dowries to daughters; and marriage and the establishment of a separate conjugal unit was accompanied by the use of written contracts. In urban Greece and increasingly in rural areas the growth of literacy was critically important.

In a direct way it indelibly influenced the nature of emotional life within and between families such that any transfer of property from one generation to the other, as well as changes in personal status, were initiated by and accompanied with religious and literate rites. In a more indirect way literacy had wider implications for other areas of family life. National identity construction made heavy use of the metaphor and symbolism of motherhood. Increasing literacy also enabled a richer elaboration of the religious symbolism associated with the Divine Motherhood of God, and the ready availability of popular novels devoted to family life helped to form a specific ideal of the family, strengthened the potency of the image of Divine Motherhood as the royal road to existential self-realisation for urban Greek women, and ensured its interiorisation.

The growth of this symbolism heavily influenced the nature of emotional life within the urban Greek family. It helped legitimate parallel corresponding changes in familial organisation evolved mainly by the *nikokirei* class who increasingly came to dominate the state administration and to be formed by participation in the state bureaucracy.

The *nikokirei* model of family organisation was neolocal, inward-looking and home-centred; by 1874 Henri Belle observed that 'chaque famille a presque toujours son habitation séparée' (Andrews, 1979; 269). It subscribed to a private-public division of space with corresponding roles for men and women, and regulated its affairs and protected its interests by means of written contracts. Women were increasingly segregated in the home, devoted almost exclusively to child rearing, and strong emotional links usually developed between mothers and daughters.

7

Conclusion: exchange, marriage and the person

So, all these parents, all these families, all these widows are under the obligation of marrying off all their daughters – five, six, seven of them: and to provide them with a dowry . . . And what a dowry according to the customs of the islands: a house in Cotronia, a vineyard at Ammoudia, an olive grove at Lechouni and a field at Stroflia! But recently, in the middle of the century another disease has started to spread. The 'counting'. Each parent was obliged to give also dowry in cash. Two thousand, thousand, five hundred, whatever. Otherwise he had better keep his daughters and admire them. He had better place them on the shelf, lock them up in the wardrobe, send them off to the Museum.

A. Papadiamantis. *I Fonissa*
Collected Works. Athens. 1984; 433.

While this study has focused on the transmission of property in Athens in the late eighteenth and early nineteenth centuries, its overall aims have been somewhat wider. For we have been interested in a number of questions that relate generally to the phenomenon of the dowry across time. In sum, how can the study of property transmissions in Athens during this period contribute towards an understanding of the contemporary dowry and of the family in Greece?

It should first be stated that we are dealing with a specifically urban phenomenon. Many of the actions of Athenians during this period, and increasingly afterwards, only make sense when we take into account that they were living in a city which was undergoing rapid social change. This includes not only rapid and consistent population increase (of rural as well as urban migrants), but also a specific type of urban economy characterised by a heavy reliance on the state and its administration for employment, uncertain employment in the fragmented and small private sector, a black economy, scarcity of resources, and an awareness of the hostility of the urban environment. Many Athenians were not necessarily landless peasants, in the sense of having no land back in their villages, but they initially lacked resources and skills to deal with urban life. This did not render them a lumpenproletariat because many possessed extensive kin networks in the city and in their natal villages to which they tended to return regularly, and many did manage to raise their social position.

This set of attitudes was a function of past history and expectations, and it was reinforced by initial experiences of Athens. Migrants brought to the capital city the attitudes of the countryside: a peasant concern with frugality whose expression culminated in the town with dazzling and ostentatious displays of wealth; the desire to possess urban real estate both to compensate for their abandoned or delegated holdings as well as to provide some degree of security in an uncertain world;[1] a peasant respect for the precipitating, sacred and unalterable power of writing, reinforced in the city by the growing and enforceable power of bureaucrats and interiorised in the strong concern to achieve social mobility through education for sons. Even more importantly, many Athenians from the late eighteenth century were ex-peasants rather than long-standing urbanites or 'urban foragers' like Belmonte's Neapolitans (1983; 276), who appeared to put little hope in the future or trust in others, including kin. Already by mid-nineteenth century About had noted this phenomenon: 'Greeks who cultivate the ground feel themselves humiliated . . . The French peasant only thinks of enlarging his field, the Greek peasant is always ready to sell it' (1855; 44).

Property transmissions in Athens become meaningful when placed in their specific historic, economic and geographical contexts. Here it is useful to compare Athenian property transmission systems with those prevailing in other parts of the country and to examine how they changed across time. In continental Greece, as indeed in Western Europe at an earlier period, the flow of goods and services at marriage was exceedingly complex. In many parts of Greece until recently, especially in rural areas, a system of indirect dowry prevailed, the goods being provided by the groom and his parents rather than by the bride's parents (Alexakis, 1984; Handman, 1989). In Western Europe the 'morning gift' was prevalent until the eleventh century and 'the dowry began to re-emerge in Italy, Southern France and Catalonia in about the 11th century in the wake of peace, economic and demographic growth and the establishment of public authority' (Hughes, 1985; 29). The same author has suggested that there was a movement from brideprice to dowry in Western Europe – a view echoed by many observers including Halpern (1958), who suggests that the dowry emerged in his Yugoslav village in the nineteenth century. Clearly the flow of goods and services at marriage in pre-industrial Europe was multi-stranded, from groom to bride as well as from parents to bride. We are interested in the relationship between these general patterns of property transmissions, complex as they were, and the nature of the economy, and the polity, as well as implications for relationships between family groups, the autonomy of the conjugal couple, and so on. The 'morning gift' of early Europe, or the 'sponsalitium' as it was later called, in which the husband awarded a gift the morning after the wedding night 'to the wife as the price of virginity' (Hughes, 1985; 27) may have represented 'a man's formal claim to sexual rights over his wife no longer purchased from her kin, but gained from the woman herself' (*ibid.*; 28); but this was because the Church was veering towards the idea of the free choice of marriage partners, and the strengthening of the conjugal bond rather than continuing vertical links between parents and children. Hence the gift tended increasingly to be given to the bride rather than to her kin, and the emphasis on consummation as the main sign of a marriage, rather than on any agreement entered into between two sets of affinal kinsmen, helped identify the significance of marriage as a transaction between two contracting individuals, rather than two groups. In addition, because men were likely to predecease their wives, the morning gift was designed to give the bride some form of security in case of widowhood, especially when she could not rely on the continuing support of her own natal kin, having already been endowed by them at marriage.

Hughes has suggested that the rise of the dowry 'coincided everywhere with the decline of the customary morning gift, whose nature became strictly usufructual and whose value was ultimately pegged to the dowry' (1985; 29). The rise of the dowry and the decline of the morning gift are thus seen as directly related; on one level they are indeed related, but on another this is a matter of degree, and not a radical shift. In early Europe wives had rights to a share of their husband's estate, with a probable corresponding decrease in their natal family's estate; while in the later European pattern they were more closely linked to their parental estate. However in Europe as in most tribal societies property was a bundle of rights and kin groups were unlikely to give individual men, much less women, great independence of action.

Even more important, we wish to suggest that the shift from brideprice to dowry (if it can be acceptably presented in these terms) is due to major changes in the economy and polity and represents a shift from 'horizontal' to 'vertical' kinship, rather than necessarily implying a radical transformation in the absolute property rights of women. Here the general features of property transfers in Greece, including Athens, and those obtaining in early Western Europe deserve closer scrutiny.

The morning gift in its various forms is a feature of a type of society which has the following general characteristics: strong agnatic links, the incorporation of the wife in her husband's natal group, and wealth linked to control over persons rather than things. It is particularly suitable when groups do not possess a monopoly over resources, where central authority is weak and where capital resources are not heavily commoditised, and thus easily alienable from the group. These marriages are oriented towards alliances. Such societies often require certain strategies to retain control over persons, rather than over the resources to which they have potential access – strategies such as close marriage and the levirate, found in pre-Christian Southern Europe as well as in North Africa. However if the equation is changed, if widows do not qualify as spouses for leviratic marriage, for example, then their rights and control over property become progressively more independent of the residual control previously exercised by kin groups. As Goody (1983) has shown, the Church progressively banned such traditional strategies for the retention of property within kin groups while endowing women with more potential autonomy over the choice of their marriage partners. Yet for whatever the Church proposed, men and kin groups disposed; kin groups made strenuous attempts to limit women's autonomous rights to dispose of their own property. It is hardly surprising therefore that as these traditional strategies became progressively illegal, 'marriage charters of the 12th century [in Barcelona] had begun to stipulate that in the event of the husband's death his kinsmen could repurchase for a specified sum property that had been granted as "sponsalitium"' (Hughes, 1985; 29). The shift from brideprice to dowry, more a matter of differences in the articulation of property transmissions than a radical transformation of the significance of property transmissions, was therefore a product both of the Church's attempts to change the rules of marriage and property transmission, and of the attempts by kin groups to restrict the implications of these changes upon their control of patrimonial resources in a context of growing commercialisation and urbanism.

We have commented at some length on this issue because it has a direct bearing upon the problem we wish to address. In Greece of the eighteenth and nineteenth centuries, and well into the twentieth century, a variety of property transmission systems coexisted. In certain mountainous areas of the Peloponnese, in Sterea Ellada, in Thessaly and Macedonia, as well as what is now Yugoslav Macedonia, a type of brideprice prevailed: brides tended to receive property more from their grooms rather than from their natal kin (Rheubottom, 1980; Alexakis, 1984). In many islands by contrast a *de facto* soft form of primogeniture prevailed; this was a more dotal form of regime favouring a restricted number of children (males and/or females) at their marriages.

A different type of property transmission began to emerge in urban areas such as Athens and Kozani, certainly by the seventeenth century. Initially in the eighteenth century there was little to distinguish the Athenian model of marriage from that of the surrounding countryside, and there was a distinctly rural climate in Athens. We have quoted early travellers' reports in order to indicate that the emphasis lay on alliance or horizontal kinship. As Segalen observes,

> . . . processions in which the young people of both families are matched in the conscious or unconscious hope of further links of the same kind, wedding feasts joining both families and turning strangers into in-laws, the coming and going between the two houses are all rituals symbolising the alliance taking shape and the bride's move from her father's house to her husband's.
>
> (1986; 127)

Although differences between the various Athenian social strata clearly existed, by the 1830s a relatively uniform property transmission pattern had emerged; this included a more egalitarian division of property among the children with a heavy bias towards the endowment of daughters at marriage, an increasing tendency towards cash dowries, the *de facto* exclusion of daughters from inheritance, a tendency towards neolocality among the upper strata or uxorilocality if they could not afford to do so, dowers by husbands to which widows had usufructory rights, and so on. This pattern was preceded by the phenomenon of dowry inflation. Throughout the latter nineteenth century, but increasingly in the twentieth century, such regional and rural-urban differences were largely eradicated, and although differences in emphasis remain, the 'modern' form of property transmission is relatively uniform. Indeed some anthropologists have seen the dowry as a mechanism for the integration of town and country (Friedl, 1963) and the ideal of neolocality and dowry flats in towns is strong even in areas such as Lakonia and the Peloponnese, which maintain an ideological emphasis on agnatic links (C. de Waal, personal communication). What has happened? Changes in the law go only part of the way towards explaining why such changes have come about. More instructive perhaps are examples of similar processes which have occurred in other parts of Southern Europe, such as early Renaissance Italy. There, Hughes has observed, 'where wealth and status were not balanced, the dowry often came to secure for some daughters a larger slice of the patrimony. Nowhere was this clearer than in the Italian commune. In Savona, for instance, patrician dowries had risen strikingly in the first two decades of the thirteenth century as families with new fortunes used the dowry as a mechanism for alliance and the acquisition of status' (1985; 43). In mid-quattrocento Florence so important had the dowry become as an instrument of social mobility that a government sponsored fund, the *Monte delle doti*, was established which became 'a vital organ of Florentine public finance and of vital concern to several thousand families who believed that their social and economic aspirations could be thwarted or furthered by the performance of the fund' (J. Kirshner, 1978; 3). The same author notes that 'jurisprudents of the fourteenth and fifteenth centuries elaborating on the dotal system in lectures and in scientific monographs concurred that the size of the dowry should be more or less commensurate to the social rank and wealth of family' (*ibid.*; 4).

Although difficulties in comparing early Renaissance Italian communes and late eighteenth-century Athens clearly exist, the two societies have, nevertheless, certain common features. Both were urban environments and heavily involved in trade; in both societies, new social groups were emerging and their wealth was threatening the old social order of ascribed and permanent hierarchies; this was accompanied by a dowry inflation as the new up-and-coming civic class viewed marriage as the most available means of social mobility, and this was strongly resisted by the old aristocracy. In both Athens and the Italian communities, political conflict over the spoils of office and administrative privilege emerged between the old aristocracy and the new civic class, and in both Athens and the Italian commune the political struggle was carried out exclusively within the city. Finally in both cases the political conflicts heralded the emergence of a new social order radically different from the permanent hierarchies of the European Middle Ages and the Ottoman empire. The similarities, therefore, are far-reaching, and it is instructive that Hughes notes that 'the cities of Italy, which did not practise primogeniture, which upheld chastity as a feminine ideal, and which maintained the nunnery as a "convenient stowage for their withered daughters" had experienced dotal inflation as soon as dowry became associated with an active marriage policy' (1985; 44). Similar conditions obtained in Greece in the early modern period, yet the problem there was even more acute, since nunneries were hardly a viable alternative for daughters.

It is significant that the passage quoted at the opening of this chapter by Papadiamantis mentions the problem of cash but does not mention the Church as a haven or as a solution to the lack of resources, for it was neither in Greece, especially from the nineteenth century onwards. As in Spain and other Mediterranean countries the state increasingly acted to restrict Church holdings. In 1821 there were 6,000 monks living in Mount Athos (Frazee, 1969; 41), but in 1833 the government acted to close all the small monasteries, and 412 monasteries were subsequently closed. Frazee observed that 'The Government . . . would thus receive considerable land and property; the 2,000 monks of Greece were to be resettled in the remaining 148 monasteries. The lesson taught by the sixteenth-century reforming princes had not been lost on the Regency' (1969; 120). Nunneries shared the same fate. A Royal Decree of 25 February 1834 ordered the closure of all nunneries except three (in the Aegean, the Peloponnese and Attica), and each remaining nunnery had to have at least 30 nuns. The decree also allowed any nun under the age of forty to be easily dispensed from her vows (Frazee, 1969; 127). By 1858 the nunneries had increased from three to four; in 1897 there were nine institutions with 152 nuns and in 1907 a total of ten nunneries had 225 inmates. There was, furthermore, an additional implication for the realisation of 'selfhood', which requires further analysis. Here the avenue for heroic self-expression ceased to be expressed in and through the Church, and instead was increasingly expressed in everyday life and in the market-place, heralded in the novel *Loukis Laras*. As McNeill has pointed out: 'in the 18th century and before, holiness attracted wealth, and by the 19th century wealth sustained idleness more often than authentic spirituality. As a result, when monastic properties were confiscated by land-hungry nation-states, the monastic calling lost nearly all of its devotees' (1978; 21). As in Renaissance Florence the dowry in Greece was increasingly expressed in cash terms, and the subtlety and particular force of Papadiamantis' observations lies in the fact that while he is ostensibly referring to rural areas, these problems were strongly felt in urban areas and likely to have been particularly experienced by his urban readers.

Such similarities are perhaps not fortuitous, nor merely based upon parallel historical contingencies. For we would like to suggest that a very distinctive process is involved in the formation of specific types of family structure, ethics, and property transmission patterns. This has much to do with a specific type of capital and state formation in the context of commodity urbanism. We hope that this has useful implications for the study of the family and kinship in the Mediterranean.

A recent book on urban life in Mediterranean Europe has attempted to answer the question 'as to whether the classic conception of the city as embodying more universalistic values is accurate for this part of the world. Put in terms of the Weberian ideal of modernism, do the people of the cities have a more "modern" cultural orientation? Are they less familistically oriented than rural dwellers?' (Kenny and Kertzer, 1983; 12). Although there are some very important differences between Western and Eastern Mediterranean European towns, the latter fitting more closely Sjoberg's characterisation of the pre-industrial city and urbanised more recently, all contributors stress the common centrality of family life. One reason is the important role of kinship in easing and orienting rural migration to the city and the extensive uses to which it is put in adapting to precarious and uncertain employment and housing situations. In Yugoslav cities, which probably most closely resemble Athens in their patterns of growth, partly because both experienced Ottoman domination 'cities grew almost exclusively through rural migration, bringing about the peasantisation of urban centres' (Simic, 1983; 207). The same author notes that 'in Yugoslavia the traditional concept of kinship corporacy, together with the emergence of a new, relatively unstratified society, has counteracted the centrifugal and fragmenting forces of individual and socioeconomic mobility' (1983; 210).

Yugoslavia is perhaps a special case partly because its new urban-dominated social order was superimposed upon extensive kinship groups, such as the *zadruga*, which had largely evolved in the semi-mountainous areas less subject to Ottoman domination, and also because the high profile of urban life is largely a recent development. Even in Italian cities such as Palermo, which had a longer tradition of complex civic life, and which were centres of elite culture the extended family among the urban poor is critical in influencing the choice of marriage partners, in reinforcing group norms, and generally in providing assistance in the face of unemployment (Kertzer, 1983; 62). Yet while many observers now correctly question the validity of the rural-urban distinction and assert that 'the development of urban anthropological theory must be found on a conceptualisation of the "urban" which goes beyond the margins of a place we call a city or town into the very complexities of Mediterranean society at large' (Kenny and Kertzer, 1983; 10–11), there exists a lingering impression that many anthropologists still search for what they consider to be rural elements in the city. Part of the problem would seem to be that because we have an imperfect knowledge of past urban customs, including the family, marriage and the transmission of property, we tend to view customs such as the provision of dowry houses for daughters, reliance on extensive kinship networks, the strategic uses of godparenthood, patronage, the segregation of men and women, the identification of men with public areas and women with the home, arranged marriages and so on, as somehow rural in origin or at best functionally important adaptations to urban life. In Greece however, and possibly in other countries where the town has recently managed to dominate rural life to a great extent, partly because the ruralisation of the city and the urbanisation of the countryside were roughly simultaneous and recent processes (in contrast to other cities where the processes were separated in time), some of these customs which we now identify as 'rural' evolved within the city as a response to a particular urban way of life, and they eventually went on to fashion, dominate and transform rural customs. The analyst thus finds himself in an unenviable situation in which the genealogy of custom is not clearly perceptible. Indeed in many ways the city acts to reinforce what are presumed to be rural customs. I. Press for Seville (1979; 154–55) and Freeman for a Castilian hamlet (1970; 190–91) suggest that conjugal role segregation between men and women and the visible separation of men and women in public are more rigid within the town than the country. In Athens the same phenomenon has been reported by Hirschon: 'in fact, the separation [of roles] is even clearer here, since in village life women are inevitably drawn into the many tasks surrounding agriculture or shepherding' (1978; 73).

Such observations should alert us to the fact that something distinctive is taking place. What often occurs in many Mediterranean cities is not the retention of rural customs, nor their reinforcement (although from the perspective of migrant actors this may appear to be the case), but rather the elaboration and 'rationalisation' of practices which were themselves urban in origin and had been adapted to the countryside. Nowhere is this clearer than when we are dealing with the family and its transmission of property, fictional kinship, and arranged marriage. In the early modern Greek city, as we have shown, there was a diversity of matrimonial practices: patrilocality among the *arkhon* class with daughters inheriting land and cash at marriage in the form of dowries, though sons received the bulk of the parental estate as inheritance; a tendency towards neolocality among the *nikokirei* with massive cash endowments to daughters at marriage, and a much more uxorilocal settlement pattern among the urban poor and the migrants in which the house was an economically more significant resource. Yet by the 1830s in Athens a more distinctive pattern had emerged, one which tended to emphasise the equal division of property among children but especially oriented towards daughters with sons taking the residue of the estate, an emphasis on cash dowries, and a tendency towards neolocality with the womenfolk becoming increasingly housebound. It was this model whose spirit was enshrined in the Greek Civil Code, and it was this model which, being Athenian and hence more 'enlightened', eventually came to dominate Greek society. To be sure, it did not dominate in the sense of sweeping away all regional variations in the transmission of property; in many areas, such as Lakonia, men still inherit the house, and women in pastoral Epiros at the time of Campbell's fieldwork did not receive much land at marriage, a situation paralleled further north in the

Yugoslav Macedonian villages of Skopska Gora (Rheubottom, 1980). But it dominated in the ideological sense that dowries in some form or another are viewed as essential for daughters, that neolocality is held to be an ideal (Loizos, 1975), and that participation in a fully urban lifestyle is now perceived to be dependent upon the possession of a separate dwelling, ideally in the city. In addition, as migration to the urban areas increased, the dowry in the form of cash and urban real estate became the chief mechanism to resolve the housing situation (Friedl, 1963; Allen, 1979).

What we are suggesting is that it is perhaps in the spirit and rationality of marriage, and of a specific conception of conjugality, that the urban Athenian model has triumphed. Dowries in the past and in rural areas were primarily strategies to conserve resources within the family; in most cases the transmission of resources was selective and rarely oriented towards equality; the emphasis was on the corporate house or the family line, were backward-looking rather than forward-looking. The purpose of the transmission of property, including dowries, was not so much to confer status in the modern sense, but to maintain it and to prevent the dissipation of the patrimony.

Various examples support this contention. In the Aegean island of Karpathos property among the 'Kanakares' was transmitted bilinearly, with the eldest daughter inheriting from the mother and the eldest son from the father; the disinherited younger sons left while the younger daughters often remained unmarried, residing with the eldest endowed daughter 'serving them as maids and agricultural labourers' (Vernier, 1984; 32). The resulting household was certainly not simple or nuclear and more closely resembled the Alpine villagers studied by Cole and Wolf (1974); Vernier sees it as 'exploitative' of the younger children, especially daughters. By contrast among the urban Athenians of the nineteenth century and increasingly in the twentieth century, the marriage of all daughters and their endowment was viewed as the critical component of a forward-looking, somewhat adventurous matrimonial policy, in short for social mobility rather than corporate resource maintenance. In this sense the spirit of dowry transmissions in traditional rural areas in Greece was radically different from the urban Athenian one, and a mere formalist analysis of the differences between systems of property transmission in Greece as if they were of the same general type risks failing to take into account the fact that their rationalities are very different.[2]

Similar processes to those emerging in mid-nineteenth-century Athens appear to have been operating in other parts of Greece. Papataxiarchis has attempted to show how in Lesbos 'the idea of the nuclear household as a residential unit with an autonomous corporate profile is part and parcel of the concept of marriage in general and of conjugality in particular which was proposed by the Church and followed by a traditional land-based elite in Lesbos in the course of the 19th century' (1985; 5–6). In Lesbos a particular form of female primogeniture was practised with the result that very different patterns of marriage were followed by the wealthy and the poor; while the former could supply houses for daughters, the latter could not and practised the scandalous custom of cohabitation, instead of a religiously sanctioned marriage. Many of the Church edicts were designed to end this practice. While we do not doubt that the Church was clearly influential in bringing about this ideal, which Papataxiarchis documents well in his sophisticated analysis, the causation implied is somewhat localised. In a bounded community like Lesbos, with the close interweaving between the local elites and the Church, the latter undoubtedly was able to impose its definition of marriage and kinship, and to be seen to have a high causative and shaping profile. Similar processes occurred elsewhere, though the various emphases of the Church differed in other parts of Greece. However we believe that a more basic process was involved which has much to do with the process of commoditisation and the spread of a monetary economy in an urban environment.

In Athens the Church was not concerned with legislating over the provision of houses, although it was concerned with dowry inflation which may have left some daughters unmarried. But the model of marriage for all daughters, their endowment with dowries, neolocality, a separate conjugal fund for the new couple and so on, was primarily a result of the dissolution of corporate kin ties, developed in Athens as a concomitant of the economic and political reality of the *nikokirei* class. Many were from different geographical origins, and thus had no pre-existing climate of trust to build upon. They thus gave particular primacy to the role of the matrimonial contract to construct trust; they were merchants and traders and therefore likely to interpret, as well as construct, kinship in 'economic' terms. By this we mean that they viewed kinship in terms of an 'interpersonal ideology' (Parkin, 1974) rather than in terms of a corporate group ideology, such as the *arkhon* class possessed. The *arkhontes* were a traditional interstitial elite linked by common ties of birth, kinship and property. They differed from migrants and the urban poor who were more uxorilocally based and held together by ties of commensality and work, in short by need rather than common and familiar origins, as among the *arkhon* group. The interpersonal ideology of the *nikokirei* tended towards semi-contractual relations like godparenthood, and to individual strategies, rather than the group-based fosterage practices of the *arkhon* class, and they viewed social relations in terms of debits and credits, as does the hero of the novel *Loukis Laras*. Yet many of these practices and indeed their expression utilised a pre-existing 'religious' language, such that they appear to be 'traditional'. The *nikokirei* were the group most highly attuned to the value of money. They tended to view the marriages of daughters in terms of a discrete set of 'transactions' in which one marriage of one daughter was theoretically separated from the other, rather than view marriages *in toto* according to a traditional schema, as with the rule-bound universe of farmers or landholders in the island of Karpathos, or as is found with North African families, where there is a careful balancing of different types of marriages. Because each marriage was considered discrete in theory, not collectively oriented towards a specific goal such as the retention of patrimony, but rather to the individual accretions of prestige, it was easier to maintain an ideal of equality between children, at least between daughters. The accruing prestige through self-sacrifice was viewed as the satisfaction of a debt to society, and hence meritorious.

This pattern of transmission often excluded sons from much direct enjoyment of familial property, that is from direct economic benefits, but as the parents themselves derived no such benefits it was easier to impose an acceptance of these practices upon sons. In any case, sons were socialised to expect a large dowry from their wives, and interest and emotion were finely tuned. The reward for acting as a dutiful son was often expected by him upon his marriage, in the form of a large dowry, a type of sublimated revenge upon his father by taking instead from his father-in-law. The *nikokirei* helped to formulate a new social distinction – that between the public and the private – because of the insecurity of town life, because of its status implications where the absence of the need to work could be most readily expressed by removal from the public domain and seclusion in the home, and because it was the menfolk who entered business and trade and were thus away from the home. The fact that the men were absent and that their activities were in different spheres further reinforced links between mother and daughter.

On a more fundamental level, this book has discussed the process of commoditisation in an urban context within a newly emerging nation-state. This is of particular interest because of its direct relevance to the debate in anthropology over 'gifts' and 'commodities' and the 'spirit of the gift'. In late eighteenth-century Greece there appear to have been two distinct processes at play. On the one hand there was an increasing commoditisation of goods entering the matrimonial market as well as a narrowing down of the types of goods transferred at marriage, while on the other hand there appears to have been an increasing personalisation of those transacting.

In the Ottoman period the matrimonial system can be characterised as having consisted of discrete spheres of exchange. Each social group was expected to be roughly endogamous and women generally 'circulated' within their own social group. Generally speaking, the types of resources which accompanied them at marriage were roughly similar, although the amounts varied as did the timing or transfers of resources between affinal groups. The clear function of this system was to maintain the discreteness and powerbase of the ruling group, the *arkhontes*, which was largely domestically based. Hence the matrimonial system served to define women as 'gifts' which circulated within their own social group. Relations between social groups were based on formality, that is the presentation of the self as a member of a clearly defined social group. Marriage was accompanied by the transfer of widely divergent resources; yet because the system of stratification was politically imposed and because these resources were technically available to all social groups in varying degrees, certain markers of social status were necessary to identify individuals as members of a determinate social group, while at the same time embodying wealth. There were two primary resources which served this function: cash, and more significantly trousseaux and costumes. Cash was a relatively restricted resource in eighteenth-century Athens, despite the fact that this was a market economy. Cash had the added significance that its possession denoted one's freedom from the need to work. Trousseaux and costumes on the other hand had a dual purpose: they were stored wealth and could be given a relatively determinate monetary value, and they could reflect social status in situations which counted in this society – formal encounters where rights and privileges could be claimed. However, while they permitted their owners to realise their monetary value in straitened circumstances, they did so at the cost of loss of prestige and social position. In a very definite way they helped resist any tendencies towards commoditisation, and ultimately entrepreneurship, among the *arkhon* group, consistent with Appadurai's observation that 'whenever what Bohannon called conveyances give way to what he called conversions the spirit of entrepreneurship and that of moral taint enter the picture simultaneously' (1986; 27).

Yet such a system depended upon a complex balance between an Ottoman imposed system of stratification and a distribution of administrative privileges which permitted the politically privileged to maintain their economic pre-eminence. The system was too finely tuned to permit any disjuncture between the two, and in the latter eighteenth century the rising *nikokirei* group, heavily involved in new trade opportunities and petty commodity production, had much greater access to cash than did the declining *arkhontes*. The infusion of large amounts of cash threatened the pre-existing matrimonial system precisely because it did not operate as a free market. It is thus possible to see, in agreement with Appadurai, that not only was the attempt to transform surplus cash into trousseaux and costumes an expression of entrepreneurship, but that it also threatened the whole basis of power of the *arkhon* group precisely because the strategic use of costumes confused the formal markers of political privilege. Nor was it simply a matter of the *arkhon* group co-opting the *nikokirei* on an individual basis by a process of osmosis.

To begin with, exposure to new sources of wealth was too sudden to permit necessary adjustments across whole areas of social life, and the 1821 revolution hastened the process politically. But even more important is the polyvalent nature of material symbols. The social markers of prestige defined by sumptuary laws were not arbitrary tokens which were irrelevant to a group's social reproduction and pre-eminence. Instead they lay at the very heart of *arkhon* power, and the higher clergy closely allied to the *arkhontes* made strenuous efforts to restrict their democratisation. It was because costumes and trousseaux were so closely identified with women at marriage, and because such costumes were the most visible markers of the power and prestige allocated to them by their Ottoman overlords that they had to resist such inroads so strongly. As Appadurai has noted 'those commodities whose consumption is most intricately tied up with critical social messages are likely to be *least* responsive to crude shifts in supply and demand, but most responsive to political manipulation at the societal level' (1986; 33).

The following list indicates how various conversions were viewed in late eighteenth-century Athens

1. Trousseaux ⟶ Cash   Moral taint for all groups; to
   costumes   be resorted to only in
       extreme circumstances

2. *Arkhon* $\xrightarrow{\text{marriage}}$ *Nikokirei*   Moral taint for *arkhon*
   women $\xleftarrow{\text{resources}}$ men   group

3. *Arkhon* $\xrightarrow{\text{marriage}}$ *Nikokirei*   More acceptable for *arkhon*
   men $\xleftarrow{\text{resources}}$ women   group. Spirit of
       entrepreneurship for
       nikokirei

Why should conversion 2 have had nuances of moral taint? One reason is that it subverted the powerbase of *arkhon* group and paved the way for infiltration by the *nikokirei*. Conversion 3 was much more acceptable on an individual level because with a dominant pattern of viri-patrilocality, *nikokirei* women could be more easily integrated. On a collective level, however, such patterns caused problems for the *arkhon* group as a whole. In order to marry their daughters they had to supply them with higher dowries due to the *nikokirei*'s heavy investment in daughter endowment with the consequent result that *arkhon* sons were left 'improvident and ungoverned'. The problem was later resolved through the decision to peg dowries not to the bride's social origins, but to the groom's – a clear indication not only of capitulation to supply forces, but also of harnessing the increasing commoditisation of resources transmitted at marriage to social mobility through daughters.

The increasing emergence of cash as the major resource transmitted at marriage and its subsuming of other resources was accompanied by other features – the emergence of neolocality as an ideal; the gradual dismantling of extended kinship and adoption and its replacement by *koumbaria*; and the transformation of the matrimonial contract from a religious commemoration of fertility to a semi-secular, strictly Church-imposed and defined contract to establish trust in an urban environment. We believe that something more fundamental was involved here than the mere commoditisation of resources transmitted at marriage. We believe that a specific process was involved which has much to do with the political construction of value – not just monetary value, but ultimately symbolic value in terms of gender and ethnic identity.

We are after all dealing with a very specific type of exchange – that of marriage, in which women and resources are given to other kinship groups. Seen in one of the more conventional interpretations of Mauss it would be easy to view this process in terms of a movement from the exchange of 'gifts' to the exchange of 'commodities'; but where do women fit into all this view? The commoditisation of women is clearly extremely unsatisfactory as an analytical characterisation. Indeed it could be argued that by investing women with resources, the dowry provides women with a measure of security. On the other hand, seen from the perspective of the southern shores of the Mediterranean, it could be asked; why give one's daughter to a stranger and then give him money to boot? Would it not be more suitable to ask for a brideprice based on the bride's social status, to ensure the groom's sincerity and proper behaviour? In short, why invest daughters with such large amounts of resources, which moreover increasingly consist of commodities in a commodity-dominated economy? What are the implications of these questions for gender identity?

There are perhaps a number of reasons for the situation as it stood. One has to do with the process of urbanisation, with migration to the city, and hence investment in daughters' dowries to achieve social mobility. Cash was the significant factor in nineteenth-century Athens; and urban real estate had the advantage of security against potentially dissolute grooms and satisfied the peasant desire for a tangible symbol of security with links to the past. Another reason has to do with the emergence of a new middle class formed initially by trade and petty commodity production (in short with the greatest contact with the market), and later by salaried government employment (a source of regular cash). A situation similar to the former occurred in Renaissance Italy, where merchants heavily invested their daughters with dowries in order to achieve social mobility. Massive endowments of daughters thus served in both Renaissance Italy and late Ottoman Greece to break down the politically imposed system of discrete spheres of matrimonial exchange where resources circulated more as gifts, in that they bound the ruling groups together and ensured their political supremacy. High dowries also eventually guaranteed the incorporation, and in some cases the replacement, of the old elite by the new. The criticality of this process was due to the fact that these resources were fundamental to the reproduction of social groups.

Where nineteenth-century Greece differs from Renaissance Italy is in the fact that cash in Greece became a means of social differentiation in a rapidly commoditising economy in a manner unprecedented in the Italian situation. Yet we believe that the process of commoditisation of resources entering marriage was not without some resistance. Appadurai has observed that 'marriages may accentuate the commodity dimension of women that in other contexts would be totally inappropriate' (1986; 15). We believe that one manifestation of this resistance to the commoditisation of marriage, and by implication of women was the growth of the cult of motherhood and its glorification in whole new areas of social life and in symbols such as the Proto Nekrotapheio (First Cemetery) in Athens (Plates 3, 4). The emphasis on motherhood as a sacred exalted state can be seen as an attempt to restrict the commodity association of women. To begin with, it is both general and specific in that it was applicable to all women irrespective of actual amounts transferred at marriage, and that the value of a person was achieved in and through marriage and motherhood – a state which cannot be transacted. Its apparent 'traditionality' as a theme also helps conceal the subtle transformations which were occurring in the construction not just of gender but of the moral person. This has implications for the notion of self within gender identity. The 'self' rather than the 'person' becomes something one defines for oneself in and through marriage and parenthood and is not defined by genealogy and descent. If, as Mauss has said, 'far from existing as a primordial innate idea [the category of 'self'] . . . continues here slowly and almost right up to our own time, to be built upon, to be made clearer and more specific, becoming identified with self-knowledge and the psychological consciousness' (Mauss, 1985; 20), then there is no reason to exclude this process from anthropological consideration of Greek society.

The emphasis on motherhood, in spite of its consequent and necessary pollution, helps explain the low practical esteem which nineteenth- and twentieth-century Greeks have held for the celibate life. If the person can realise the self in and through marriage, the celibate life comes a poor second in spite of the higher theological value placed upon it. We thus agree with Herzfeld when he states that '"sexual pollution", the Church Fathers not withstanding, is not absolute. It is a relativity, refracted through the segmentary cleavages of a corrupted social fabric; and it reflects the disemic tension between inclusion and exclusion that characterises the actual conditions of social life' (1987; 179).

The growth of the cult of motherhood could perhaps only have occurred through the powerful stimuli which it received through national political factors, the growth of Greek nationalism, and the circulation of texts – popular literature oriented towards urban middle class women. Nationalism through irridentism strengthened the image of Greece as *I Mitera Ellada*, Mother Greece striving to unite with her Daughter or Sister Regions and could at times legitimate courses of political action which would otherwise have been condemned.[3]

While we agree with Herzfeld that the categories of inclusion and exclusion are variable and defined strategically according to exigency and context, we are unhappy with the general drift of his argument, and this enables us to introduce our final points regarding the economy and civil society. Herzfeld's laudable enterprise, inspired by a reading of Vico, is to introduce an element of introspection into the anthropological enterprise. By basing his account on an analysis of how Greek villagers deal with social reality, including official Statist ideologies and the etymological roots (often Greek) of many 'academic' words, he attempts to show the ways in which the anthropological enterprise is based on the same premises.

The theory-practice conundrum in anthropology is a problem drawn from everyday life. For, like Modern Greeks confronting the complexities of their identity, anthropologists . . . do not have to choose between theory and practice in any irrevocably ultimate sense. The choice is a rhetorical one, and reflects the characteristic professional perplexity of disciplines whose subject is on the same intimate scale as themselves. If what anthropologists study is either exotic or trite – the discussion of segmentation seems an apt metonym for the whole discipline here – then theory serves as an officialising strategy in the social pragmatics in which anthropology is embedded. One cannot say that there is no such thing as theory; but it is a culturally contingent and pragmatically evanescent phenomenon. In this regard, it is not essentially different from the official discourses of other formal systems, including that of the state. Every Greek, caught in the disemic dilemmas of modern Greek life, experiences the same undismissable choices at every moment of every day.

(1987; 204)

It is difficult to disagree with such sentiments, but there are perhaps problems with this approach. First, the metaphorical likeness between the 'Greek predicament' and the anthropological one can easily become over-deterministic and too self-referential. Second, the atemporality of his schemata of oppositions (*Romios* is to *Ellinas* as inside is to outside as female is to male as self-knowledge is to self-display, and so on) renders it much closer to the structuralism which Herzfeld combats, although it must be said that he locates this in a hierarchy of segmentation. Herzfeld suggests that 'these *ideal types are constantly and dialectically parlayed into virtually the entire range of social life.* Both are ideals in that both are stereotypes; but, by the same token, what gives both experiential reality is their *use* in the day-to-day rhetoric of morality. That rhetoric constitutes their reality' (1987; 113, Herzfeld's italics).

One difficulty here is that individuals, Greek villagers and anthropologists alike, can also reject the rhetorical employment of such stereotypes, and often do so. Additionally, the value of classical anthropological accounts such as that of Evans-Pritchard on the Nuer lies precisely in showing that in spite of segmentation, the pattern of ordinary social life often proceeds quite differently and less traumatically than a formalist reading of segmentation would warrant. Furthermore, by suggesting that rhetoric consitutes a great part of the reality of social life and practice, analysis would concentrate mainly but not exclusively on the game-like element of the clash of rhetorical interpretations and presentations of social life. An analysis concerned with the 'progression' or evolution of social life across time would have to consist of the dialectical working-out of these hierarchies of oppositions, with little space for the incorporation of the effects and implications of exogeneous factors, except in so far as they can be incorporated into the pre-existing disemic structure. Finally, the overreliance on etymology as a type of ontological tool can easily lead the researcher astray, for categories such as inside/outside are in a fundamental sense unlike words: they may appear to be self-evident but their content may change across time. And they may change in a way which leaves higher or lower-level categories untouched. In short, the nature of the categories themselves and their intrinsic meanings are also important and any change in their constitution may influence how disemic oppositions at a higher level are employed, or indeed rendered superfluous.

We make these contentions because it is clear from our material that a number of categories have changed across time in Greek society. Many of the disemic oppositions which Herzfeld mentions – inside is to outside as female is to male as self-knowledge is to self-display – were constituted differently in late eighteenth-century Greece and among various social groups, and some did not exist at all. Indeed some of these oppositions were invented. Their gradual formation in the nineteenth century into outlines more or less but not completely recognisable in contemporary Greece was largely the effect of urbanisation, of the transformation of peasants into Athenians under the cultural hegemony of the *nikokirei*, themselves under the tutelage of outside Powers. The movements from formal/informal to public/private; extended kinship (including adoption) to *koumbaria*; costume to cash; virilocality to neolocality; utility items to lace artefacts, and contract as religious occasion to a means to establish trust, all herald a fundamental change which was taking place in Greek society and the way in which Greeks constructed their mental and social universe.

We wish to suggest that what was occurring in late eighteenth- and early nineteenth-century Greece can be approached by reference to two seminal essays by Marcel Mauss ('The Gift' and 'A category of the human mind: the notion of person; the notion of self'), viz. the commoditisation of things and the personalisation of the transactors. This is a long and confused debate in anthropology and we cannot do it justice here. But we wish to note that most discussions on the process of commoditisation, in contrast to what is embedded in the thought of Mauss and Marx, often fail to take into account the nature of the polity and more specifically the nature of civil society as it is refracted in and through the person, as a causative or shaping agent on the nature of exchange.[4]

In both essays Mauss (and Marx) raises a central paradox: while things became progressively commoditised, persons became progressively individuated; while exchanges in primitive societies retain their interested strategies and motivations, objects are nevertheless imbued with the spirit of the giver, while exchanges in capitalist society operating within an ideology of overt calculable self-interest nevertheless permit the notion of the disinterested gift. While gift exchange with others in primitive societies is a means for enforcing and claiming social recognition often in hierarchical relationships, commodity exchange in complex industrial societies appears to deny individuality which can only be achieved through sublimated gift exchange with Divinity or the transformation of commodities into gifts in exchange with others, while upholding equality; and finally, when objects become progressively removed from the giver, transactors become progressively personalised and individuated. In sum, while there seems to be a progressive movement in the evolution of human society towards the emergence of commodity exchange there is nevertheless a progressive evolution of the notion of the self: 'from a simple masquerade to the mask, from a "role" to a "person", to a name, to an individual, from the latter to a being possessing metaphysical and moral value' (Mauss, 1985; 22).

Our sources support the reading of Mauss outlined above. Indeed what is significant about late eighteenth- and early nineteenth-century Greece is that the traditional anthropological formula of clan is to class as gift is to commodity as emotion is to interest makes little sense. For while there clearly occurs an increasing commoditisation of goods and services entering the exchange nexus, there is both a more overt spirit of rational immediate calculation as well as an increased individuation of persons. We would like to suggest that, just as Mauss introduced a triad in his discussion on the *hau*, that so too it is important to introduce a third element in discussions on the process of commoditisation. That element is civil society; ultimately, man in his interiorisation of norms and values derived from civil society. Most discussions on the process of commoditisation, in contrast to Mauss and Marx, often fail to take into account the nature of civil society as a causative or shaping agent on the nature of exchange. The great merit of the work of Mauss and Marx lay in positing man as an active agent in his own transformation, now a premise often lost in many accounts of the nature of exchange. What is significant in all exchange is *the distinction between the self and the other*. That self may be a role, or a member of a collectivity rationally calculating yet giving what may genuinely be felt as a part of oneself, or the self may be an individual, 'a being possessing metaphysical and moral value' (Mauss, 1985; 22) disinterestedly giving a symbol of himself, never to be reunited with the giver, yet forever linked to the recipient and becoming part of that person's identity.

Ultimately of course the person and what that term signifies is moulded by the nature of civil society. And civil society influences both the nature of exchange within determinate social settings, by defining who and what may be exchanged and by defining the boundaries between those areas in which it is licit to exchange according to a certain rationality and those in which it is not. The distinction between the 'inside' and the 'outside' increasingly becomes defined by Civil Society in terms of the 'private' and the 'public'. Civil society increasingly influences through law how and in what spirit exchange may take place. Politics influences the nature of exchange, not just in terms of the manipulative strategies of the Kula or the Potlatch, or indeed merely in terms of defining by law who can exchange (as in Ancient Greece), but also by redefining old boundaries and creating new ones (including mental ones) which establish who, how and what may be exchanged.

Paradoxically, this process is clearly brought out in the marriage exchanges of early modern Greece. It is perhaps entirely apt that marriage – that most classic, paradigmatic and *a priori* basis of exchange – should also have been the exchange most resistant to commoditisation in the early modern world. This would seem to apply as much to the love-orientation which Macfarlane (1986) claims for the English, as to ex-peasants turned Athenians often cast by outsiders and ironically self-presented as cunning calculating *Romei*. In early modern Greece we do not have a context which stratifies types of goods for exchange, as in the multicentric economies of the Tiv and Homeric Greece. Rather, we have a context in which goods function as tokens to restrict access to the womenfolk of strictly defined groups. The particular predicament faced by the *arkhontes* was that such goods were not goods such as raffia cloths, as among the Lele, whose distribution and access could be more or less controlled, but were the ones most likely to be commoditised in the modern world. For this culture chose a scarce item – cash – in an imperfectly monetarised economy on Europe's periphery, as well as items which symbolised the capacity to obtain access to monetary wealth and to leisure, as tokens for access to women and marriage. The introduction of new sources of monetary wealth and its deployment by the rising *nikokirei* profoundly altered society and its manner of reproduction. It was not merely a matter of inflation, it was more of a revolution, politically, socially, culturally and mentally, and it was also bound to provoke a type of resistance at other levels, mainly ideological. This emphasises the point made years ago by Lévi-Strauss (1969), in a challenge to Leach (1961), that marriage is a very special type of exchange, notwithstanding the introduction of counter-presentations of a different nature.

What we are suggesting here is that marriage constitutes a very special type of exchange, in either its elementary or 'complex' forms and that in spite of the transmission of goods and counter-presentations as in dowry systems, and in spite of the inevitable strategic considerations at play at the individual or familial levels, there is nevertheless a tendency to restrict its becoming a market, even though it is indubitably subject to market principles and calculations. The reduction of dowry and other systems to the marriage market conceals a basic truth that society, even in its most highly commoditised form, attempts in various complex ways to restrict the full implications of the process.

Resistance to commoditisation of matrimonial goods in early modern Greece came naturally, but not only, from the *arkhontes* and the higher clergy who wished to preserve their political preeminence. It also came paradoxically from the *nikokirei* themselves, as if having contributed directly to the process of commoditisation they wished to restrict its implications for the institution of marriage itself. For whereas marriage had been a means to continue the *genos*, to ensure a type of salvation predicated upon procreation (notwithstanding the spirit of calculation which certainly entered individual transactions), in early modern Greece it became formally less separable from other commodity exchanges if only because the goods constituting the dowry were ultimately reducible to and calculable in cash terms. Resistance to this process took various forms, but at a higher ideological level: the establishment of the private/public distinction in the home; the increasing seclusion of womenfolk in the household; the reinforced emphasis on leisure, meaning non-monetary work; the circulation of texts exalting the state of motherhood; and finally in making women metaphors for the nation to be secluded and protected, in short 'non-commoditised'. Rather than restricting access to the goods which functioned as tokens to marriage in this society, it was access to women themselves in urban contexts which became increasingly elaborated, a tendency naturally encouraged by the commercially critical resources they carried. Like the Potlatch and art auctions, marriages even in the modern world can be seen as 'tournaments of value' (Appadurai, 1986) where non-monetary factors such as honour (*timi*, significantly but deceptively the same word for 'price' or 'cost' in Greek) came into play; factors which are a complex byproduct of the interaction between material wealth and style.[5] As Appadurai notes, 'what is at issue in such tournaments is not just status, rank, fame or reputation of actors but the disposition of the central tokens of value in the society in question' (1986; 21). Reformulated the equation becomes:

money is to tokens as 'fashion' is to sumptuary regulations.

The morality of exchange also underwent transformation. Marriage ceased to have that circular element where fertility and the continuation of the family were perceived as a manifestation of being blessed, and which consisted of a complex system of exchanges which realised the various fragmented roles of the participants in a unitary whole. Rather, it became for the parents a tangible manifestation of having laboured to establish one's children; the perseverance, ability and struggle to endow daughters 'against all the world' became the main basis of the claim to salvation and exculpated public conduct so long as family interests were pursued and preserved. For the groom, of course, the rationality and morality of the exchange was more in the nature of having succeeded in making a good match 'in spite of the world', while for the bride salvation was increasingly achieved through the practice of motherhood. In short, the spirit of exchange became increasingly delayed, mediated through the world, rather than in the 'simple performance' of roles; as the narrator in one of Papadiamantis' short stories observes: 'what one man sows, another man reaps' (Constantinides, 1987; 19).

It is hardly surprising, therefore, that as many observers have noted, two very different types of morality operate in modern Greek culture: a highly charged and competitive public context in which men try to get the better of one another, especially when legitimated by reference to family interests (*to synferon*) (Campbell, 1964; Loizos, 1975; Peristiany, 1965), and the family context characterised by extreme self-sacrifice, self-abnegation, and disinterested gift-giving. Money, that symbol of immediate exchange and strict equivalence, is embedded in a dual rhetorical opposition. On the one hand it is held up as the highest eroding factor of trust in the outside public world, even threatening relations between kin (especially between brothers and sisters, essentially equals), while on the other hand it becomes the most potent symbol of love, especially between parents and children, essentially unequals.

In a recent collective volume on money and the morality of exchange Parry and Bloch (1989) attempt to go beyond the now traditional anthropological distinction between ceremonial exchange and commodity exchange, and to try to show that the symbolism of money and the uses to which it is put in non-Western society question the received wisdom that money is necessarily disruptive of 'traditional' social orders. Some of their conclusions are directly relevant to this study even if we do not agree with them all. For Greece presents an interesting case which is both part similar to and different from Western society.

It is clear that money is not morally neutral in Greece, as it is in the West, in the sense that in contrast to its meaning in the Western world, money does not signify 'a sphere of "economic" relationships which are inherently impersonal, transitory, amoral and calculating' (Parry and Bloch, 1989; 9). In Greece, cash figures prominently in dowries in the nineteenth century and well into contemporary times. Indeed it mediates relations between kin, and rather than being 'morally neutral' it is morally loaded. In contemporary Greece, as in other Mediterranean societies (such as Malta) it is given by men to women, handed over almost exclusively to them, in much the same way as in Malaysia, although the symbolism of women 'cooking' money (Carsten, 1989) is absent in Greece. Its acquisition is legitimated by reference to the necessity to provide daughters with dowries; once that obligation is satisfied men 'rest' and 'forget' and come closer to God, away from the mundane and divisive world of exchange. But it also has its negative aspects, a feature that Greeks constantly bemoan. Money can set kin against one another, and this view is often much older than most villagers would prefer to admit. Kolokotronis recounts in the early nineteenth century how his *simpetheros* (affine) betrayed him: 'when he looked upon the groshia [he] determined to betray me, for the Maniotes will do anything for groshia' (in Edmonds, 1969; 105). Yet the passage indicates not only the potential fragility of affinal bonds (which he sometimes contrasts to the strength of his agnatic and spiritual kinship bonds), but also the different regional origins of his *simpetheros*. For Kolokotronis this explains the betrayal. In the city, or rather in the image of the city (largely manufactured by peasants who brought their own culture with them), the potential absence of trust is even greater because, as is often said, 'in the city you don't even know your neighbour' (*stin poli oute kseries ton gitonas sou*). Whereas in rural areas evil was traditionally conceptualized in terms of the *eksotika* (semi-supernatural beings who lived on the borders of the village and who turned men's minds and led them astray from their families), nowadays as is claimed 'the *eksotika* don't exist anymore'. Rather, evil is conceptualized as existing within society, especially in the city in the form of the potential harm that the 'other', the *ksenos*, can do. In urban Piraeus Hirschon (1989) records that the statement 'the world/people is bad' (*o kosmos ine kakos*) is commonly heard. Evil is therefore within the 'world' and located in the 'person' or 'people'. As a result a whole set of defensive techniques are developed within the metropolis to reduce the potential harm that intrusion may inflict. Lying is an important technique and it is significant that Hirschon notes that in the city, lies are defensive weapons, rather than the offensive weapons they are in the village: 'lies were more often used to protect one's family privacy or simply to make a fool of someone; they seldom took the form of false malicious stories or slander' (1989; 180) – as was practised in rural Ambeli studied by du Boulay, 1976.

Money becomes both the metaphor and the vehicle for this change, symbolising the break-up of the moral community and the bonds of kinship. As one elderly informant lamented to du Boulay, 'now the kindred is nothing, money is everything' (1983; 256). It is significant that this statement, heard in many parts of Greece, in this case formed part of a discourse about the effects of the introduction of cash into the dowry. Hence the ambiguous nature of money in Greek society: money is a good which all aspire to possess, its acquisition is legitimated by and subordinated to the necessity to provide for children, especially for daughters, but not exclusively at their marriages. Yet where money is acquired for its own sake, either in the form of the rational accumulation of profit and ever more profit (*pleoneksia*), or in the form of dowry hunting (*prikothiria*), it is deplored. Capital accumulation and dispersal is linked to the developmental cycle and closely follows it. Money must enter the household in that it is given to wives and daughters, and thus acquires a more abstract nature.

This discussion indicates that money has come to symbolise the brave new world of modern Greece, a construct sharing common properties with Western societies and indicating that Greece, and especially Athens, is also part of the Western world. On the other hand this image is often upheld in opposition to conceptions of the 'village' and 'traditional' Greece. Both are of course constructs, for Greek society has been involved in trade, exchange and cash almost continuously for two millennia. Money has long been a feature of Greek society, but its insertion into that most basic form of 'exchange', marriage, in increasing proportions since the early nineteenth century, has created particular tensions within society and the family, between individualism and collectivism, between self-interest and collective concerns. Yet the opposition between 'modern' and 'traditional' Greece, rhetorical as it may seem, is a potent one because contemporary Greeks are playing with the very constructs that underlie much of Western discourse about money and its subversive and levelling effects. What is interesting about this particular case is that these images are contained within one particular society. The 'other' or the 'traditional', a world devoid of money and hence 'moral' and 'collective' is not in the domain of 'exotic' societies, but within that society's image of itself and self-presentation. Modern Greek society constructs an internal discourse about itself, contrasting 'traditional' society in which money was scarce yet loyalties are known, and 'modern' society in which money rules and loyalties remain uncertain.

On another level, of course, such rhetorical oppositions are not borne out by reality. Money does not necessarily erode kinship relations; kin groups were never necessarily solidary, and even in modern, Western

Athens belief in the evil eye (a function of traditional small communities according to conventional anthropological theories) seems often stronger than in the villages, at least in so far as the great propensity of urbanites to purchase charms is concerned. Indeed what is interesting about modern Greek society has been its tendency to insert commodities within marriage 'payments', the use of money to express emotion between parents and children and of commodities given as gifts. This seeming inability to distinguish between these categories in practice (perhaps a function of a relatively young society, obliged like Peter Pan to remain young – that is, a continuation of ancient Greece) goes hand in hand with the construction of rhetorical oppositions.

It is hardly surprising, therefore, that in modern Greek society good and evil cannot be rigidly separated; as Hirschon notes 'notions of good and evil are less than absolute moral categories in Greek thought' (1989; 240). But this is not, as Macfarlane claims, due to the intervention of money and the emergence of capitalism: 'capitalism and a money order were fatally intertwined with an inability to distinguish good and evil' (1985; 74), ultimately a type of secular narcissism. Rather it is due to a particular view of human nature and ultimately of society and its transience and the non-secularisation of time. Greek Cypriot men sometimes say: *imaste psemata*, literally, 'we are lies'. By this they mean many things. Like lies, men are transient; they can appear and disappear without a trace except in the memory of others. Men's actions and their meaning are contextual, and these contexts are largely evanescent. Like lies, men may have a purpose in life, but it is often difficult, indeed sometimes impossible, to discover what that purpose may be. And yet lies may also have both good and bad effects; what has begun as bad may have beneficial effects, and vice versa. It is thus difficult to distinguish clearly and absolutely between good and evil. Yet in spite of this difficulty good and evil are found in this world and are largely a function of human actions rather than intentions. If there is an epistemological sin committed by Greeks, it is that they fetishise social interaction, society (*o kosmos*, which also means 'people'), and not money as the source of evil. Indeed, in spite of the apparent similarity between Greek society and Western society, the equation of 'private vices and public good' is reversed: it is society that is flawed, and men must try to struggle in spite of these imperfections.

This opposition runs through much of social life in modern Greece. Transposed to another level it encompasses the world of the village versus the wider society, the honest *horianos* (villager) in contrast to the unreliable and dubious *politis* (town dweller). This opposition is not new. Already in the early nineteenth century, Makriyannis in his memoirs had consciously contrasted the honest *agonistis* with the self-interested politician (Holton, 1984/5; 149), the formerly unschooled fighter like himself and the educated wheeling and dealing politician like Koletis, his *koumbaros*. Yet while these oppositions are held up rhetorically, there is an equally strong and disturbing awareness that these distinctions are often eroded in real life and that money becomes a metaphor in the blurring of distinctions, by being posited as a prime agent. The subtlety of this construction lies in the fact that it is not money as such which is the cause of the fall from grace, but rather its symbolism, a theme explored in popular literature such as Theotokis' novel *I timi ke to hrima* (Price/Honour and Money) and Papadiamantis' *I tyche apo tin Ameriki* (Luck/Fortune from America). This opposition is carried over to other areas of social life. Self-sacrifice in the family context is analogous to *patriotismos* in national affairs. Yet *patriotismos*, which is associated with *areti* (virtue), sincerity, truth, love of honour, is 'a double-edged word . . . often those who profess patriotism use it as a cover for self-interest' (*ibid.*; 156), and sell-out to foreigners (*kseni*) much as occurred in Greece during the Junta and also, but more ambiguously, in Cyprus of 1974 prior to the Turkish invasion.[6]

In this context of public competition and lack of trust, the unity of the Greek nation has to be drawn from the symbolism of the family, especially in that non-commoditised symbol of *I Mitera Ellada* (or the quintessential motherhood), the source of disinterested gift-giving extending back to an indeterminate past.[7] This leads us to suggest that many of the themes raised by Herzfeld (1987) in his discussion of the ambivalent nature of Greek identity can perhaps also be fruitfully pursued by reference to the attempts by a nation-state to come to terms with the process of commoditisation. Many of these attitudes towards identity ('European', 'Asiatic', European-Arab Muslim and so on) are found not only in Greece but also in many other peripheral European cultures (for example, Malta, Finland, South Italy, Andalusia). Components of identity such as democracy, whose birthplace is assumed to be Ancient Greece, become packaged and commoditised and subsumed within other discourses on identity. The significance of the often-heard saying in modern Greece that 'We Greeks gave the light of democracy to the West' should also perhaps be seen as a statement about gifts as opposed to commodity exchanges, about the retention of some form of proprietorship over the gift, a type of wistful modern *hau*, which in spite of the modern world of total alienable exchange, can still return to the descendants of the original donor and confer the essence of European identity. It further points to the paradox to which we can allude but not explore, that nationalism can perhaps also be seen as a reaction against the market; as Clogg (1976; xvii) points out, most of the members of the Philike Etairia, mainly *nikokirei*, were also failed merchants.

The observations we have made have recently been paralleled by other authors. Many have questioned the validity of the Malinowskian heritage to our understanding of simple and industrial societies. Morris in discussing ancient Greece suggests that there is 'no reason . . . [why we should] exclude the possibility of a significant role for gift exchange within class and even early state societies' (1986: 7), and Parry has written that 'the whole ideology of the gift, and conversely the idea of 'economic self interest are *our* invention' (1986; 458. Parry's italics).

Where we hope to have pushed understanding further is in suggesting that many of the transformations occurring in early modern Greece, especially in the process of commoditisation and how it affected matrimonial transactions, not only question some of our basic premises regarding the evolution of society, but also require the introduction of new conceptual tools. A critical one is the notion of civil society and the way it defines exchange and interaction, which is interiorised by members of the *polis* or modern nation-state. In all cases it establishes a distinction between the private and the public and attempts to regulate relations between the two, as in fifth-century Athens, Renaissance Italy and modern Greece, but not in Feudal and Byzantine society.[8] The boundaries vary, as do the notion of self and the morality of exchange, both with men and with Gods, and this explains why most attempts to apply modern concepts (such as capitalism) to the study of other cultures or civilisations ultimately have limited value. Not only are the Greeks not the 'aboriginal Europeans' as Herzfeld justly complains, but many of the contemporary customs and practices often viewed as rural Greek in origin are in fact the flotsam and jetsam of an urban society and polity attempting to deal with the process of commoditisation. This includes their own national official culture for themselves and for outside consumption by other cultures, whose *fons et origo* is claimed to lie in Classical Greece.

Notes

1 Introduction: history, family and the 'other' in Greece

1. Japan is a case in point. The assiduity with which the Japanese are courted and feared in Europe is a symptom of the attempt to discover, or to participate in, this secret 'grace' which has resulted in such efficient production. The fact that in the last century the Japanese did precisely the same thing only points to the seduction of technological capitalism.

2. An example is the Peloponnese, which staffed the state administration; though this is largely a function of the geographical base of the new Greek state.

3. Greeks from Constantinople or from anywhere north of the existing Arta-Lamia border, called *heterochthones*, were officially debarred from holding public office until approximately 1845.

4. Gudas (1986; 99) notes that 'it was not until 1863 that the shadow theatre began to break through its Turkish crust'. Cf. Damianakos, 1987; 183–91.

5. In the new Greek state the legal system governing property relations, especially within the family, appears not to have departed significantly from the previous state of affairs. While the law of 23 February 1835 accepted the Exavivlos of Armenopoulos as State law in so far as property devolution was concerned and excluded all other Byzantine law, customary law was also recognised as having the force of law, under the terms of the law of 23-2-1835 (Skouteri-Didaskalou, 1976; 119). Hence the attempts by one of the Bavarian Regents (Von Maurer) to document local customary law in various parts of Greece as a means to establish a corpus of law. Inevitably such a system created problems and conflicts of interpretation, but the ready availability of the courts and a more streamlined court system to that obtaining under the Ottomans permitted at least speedier resolutions.

6. This is not to say that *topikismos* (localism, or attachment to local identities) is not present in Greece; indeed it is sometimes strongly felt and applied by individuals to explain their own and others' behaviour and actions. But often *topikismos*, as seen from the outside, may be viewed differently by those accused of it, as with Cretan villagers who claim that because they are Cretans they are 'better' (more authentic) Greeks than mainlanders. Few regional Greeks would claim 'we are not Greek', in contrast to the Bretons, Corsicans and so on. This is in contrast to other parts of the Mediterranean

where for example Corsicans have long aspired to autonomy from France, and Sicilian separatists at the end of World War II aimed to establish Sicily as the forty-ninth US State. By contrast the whole thrust of Greek social development has been towards unity and incorporation of territories right up to Cyprus, rather than the separation or shedding of territories from the metropolis.

7. Except codices 13/14 which are insignificant.
8. The contracts contain information on the following topics: the bride's family and its social position; whether or not the bride's parents were alive; the property and goods the bride received at marriage (land, olives, vineyards, house, cash and costume) and whether any conditions were attached to these goods; whether the bride was an adopted girl; the groom's social position, geographical origins and his promised dower. They thus contain a mine of information; this data was coded and computer inputted, on the Cambridge University mainframe computer, and statistical data retrieved under the SPSS package (Statistical Package for the Social Sciences). It should be noted that the concentration is on the bride's resources at marriage rather than the groom's. Hence we do not have strictly comparable and equally detailed data for both parties to a marriage. Nevertheless, we hope to show an analysis of the movement of women and goods at marriage can help towards a better understanding of the wider society.
9. O. L. Barkan, 1956, tables 1 and 2; N. Todorov, 1986; 62; D. Karidis, 1985, table 3.
10. Chandler observed in 1765 that 'Attica probably produces grain sufficient for the natives; but the edict prohibiting the exportation is continually eluded and public distress bordering on famine ensues almost yearly' (in Andrews, 1979; 112).
11. L. R. Matton, 1963; 213; and EKKE Statistikai Meletai 1821–1972. 1974 Table XVIII Vol. I.

2 Men and houses, women and households
1. Eva Kalpourtzi (1987; 91) has suggested that the transfer of immoveables generally, as opposed to houses in particular, may have been linked to old-age support.
2. This compares to 22 per cent for the Peloponnesian village of Dimitsana at a later period (1890–1900) (Kalpourtzi, 1987; 87).

3 Marriage, women and land in nineteenth-century Athens
1. The 'Turkish law' to which Charlemont refers is of course Sunni law. This raises the interesting question as to whether in Greece under the Turkocratia property transmission patterns were in practice influenced by Sunni law, or more precisely, by the cumulative effects of appeals to Sunni law. Most accounts of property transmission in Greece tend to view practices as the adjustment of local custom to state imposed law in the nation state. This is reinforced by the indubitable fact that under the Ottoman millet system communities were largely self-governing, each following their own customs. The tendency is thus to disregard the effects of Ottoman law. However we do know that in cases of dispute over large areas of social life, including marriage, it was open to Greeks and other *rayahs* to appeal to

Muslim *qadis* and place themselves under Sunni law. Further research should help to clarify whether and to what extent Islamic law on property transmissions influenced patterns on the ground.

2. It would otherwise have been bizarre to give a daughter a dowry which was larger than her eventual inheritance and then to insist on a refund.

3. The Church, while insisting on a daughter's right to a dowry and indeed providing the scribal personnel to register the dowry, concerned itself with dowries mainly when customary practices of property division resulted in scandalous practices such as pre-matrimonial cohabitation.

4. So complete and extensive was this desire to break with the past that most of the Byzantine and post-Byzantine churches in Athens were pulled down. Of 134 pre-Independence Athenian churches 72 were destroyed in 1843, most having been built in the Turkocratia, a clear if unconscious attempt to remodel the historical topography.

4 Gifts and commodities, cash and trousseaux

1. For example in eighteenth-century urban Valletta, Malta (Sant Cassia, work in progress), where costume is hardly mentioned in contracts; Vasilika (Friedl, 1962); contemporary Pisticci (Davis, 1973).

2. This is also similar to the North African pattern.

3. Indeed it is interesting to note that this pattern of trousseau-donation by the groom was also found in the Evvian village of Ambeli until recently (du Boulay, 1983) and in Renaissance Tuscany, both areas where daughters were largely excluded from inheriting land. Klapisch-Zuber (1985) labels this the 'Griselda Complex' after Boccaccio's story in the *Decameron*, and she observes that the husband's gifts were temporary: 'once they had placed their role, the husband could repossess them' (*ibid.*; 225). We possess little information on the subsequent destinies of these trousseaux, but it seems reasonable to presume that practices differed somewhat in Athens. Most of the non-native grooms (who followed such practices) resided at marriage not in their natal households but in their brides' households. One third of these brides received a whole house and another third received part of a house at marriage (table 3). They were thus strangers in their new household, a very different situation from Renaissance Tuscany, and therefore unlikely to repossess the jewellery. By contrast in Ambeli, du Boulay notes that the jewellery was sometimes reclaimed by the husband (1983; 249), a situation which was perhaps rendered possible by the fact that the bride was often resident in her husband's natal household.

4. A carry-over of this mentality which associates animals with rusticity and vulgarity was found in pre-World War II Rhodes (Herzfeld, 1980) where *khtima* denoted not just landholding but also pack animals. Older Paphian villagers in Cyprus also use the word in this way.

5 'For one's soul': adoption, fosterage and the growth of *koumbaria*

1. Published by A. Spanos (1774; 497), in a chapter entitled, 'Enchiridion peri ton Synekesion Z: peri tis Iothesias'.

2. For example we have one case of an adopted son who is referred to both as a *psychoyos* and a *nomimo pedhi*, indicating that the notaries were fully conversant with the differences between the two terms. This marriage con-

tract states that he was inheriting his legal share of the parental property and that he assumed his pater's name.

3. Alexakis (1980; 262–65) gives additional reasons; see also P. S. Allen (1985).
4. Ruth Macrides acknowledges that 'it is very likely that the family played a far greater role as a source of baptismal sponsors than the sources relate' (1987; 161).
5. The growth of the *nikokirei* class was also reflected in the expression of organised religion. Until the seventeenth and eighteenth centuries it was mainly the *arkhon* group that had subsidised the building of churches, but by the nineteenth century this was largely replaced by the *nikokirei*-subsidised cult of saints. Many of these new churches in Athens were dedicated to such saints as Nikolaou, Georgiou, Dionisiou, Theodorou and Athanasiou. The growth of the cult of saints and the emergence of a more complex civil society has been noted for other parts of the Mediterranean (for example Boissevain, 1965 for nineteenth-century Malta), and certainly in Orthodoxy, as in Catholicism, saints are viewed as closer to man and more approachable: *To Theo dhen ton vlepeis, ton Aghio ton eheis konta sou* – God you cannot see, but the saint is close to you.

6 The family and emotional life

1. Some indication of the lack of communication between the different parts of Greece is furnished by Kolokotronis: 'The community of men was small, and it was not until our rising that all Greeks were brought into communication. There were men who knew of no place beyond a mile of their own locality. They thought of Zante as we now speak of the most distant parts of the world. America appears to us as Zante appeared to them. They said it was in France' (Edmonds, 1969; 128). Holton (1984/85; 149) has also observed that the contemporaneous Makriyannis also emphasised that group identity also existed primarily at a local or regional, rather than a national, level.
2. Similar practices are noted by Kalpourtzi, 1987.
3. 'Popular' literature is somewhat of a misnomer because such literature was read mainly by an educated elite. Yet it was 'popular' in the sense that Dimotiki was used and it ostensibly dealt with the lives of 'ordinary people' – though as we shall see the constitution of the ideological concept 'ordinary people' is itself highly variable.
4. In the process certain ideological presuppositions seeped through the resistance of the folklorists. We do not consider it 'somewhat surprising [that the folklorists attributed] to the advent of Christianity a liberation of Greek womanhood from its former travails' as Herzfeld does (1985b; 224), because this was precisely the ideological thrust of the new middle *nikokirei* class which subscribed heavily to the Christian reinforcement of its values of seclusion of women in the home, chastity, independent nuclear households, and home-centredness. Similarly, whereas Herzfeld in this article views the model built up by folklorists such as Papadopoulos as a nationalist device to distinguish Greece from 'the benighted communities of the East, where the multiple organization of the family which derives from polygamy and indeed from the subjugation of woman is the principal cause of the animal

degradation in which these peoples live' (Pappadopoulos, quoted in Herzfeld, 1985b; 226) which it manifestly is, we view this in different terms. Rather, we see this attitude in internal terms as a manifestation of *nikokirei* class formation. It is not so much that multiple households are Eastern and hence 'non-Greek'; it is rather that they are not urban Greek middle-class. This is one problem in Herzfeld's otherwise excellent article. In approaching nationalism in Greece and its 'message of redemption' we should take cognisance of the Weberian approach which attempts to link this with the way such messages were carried and formed by determinate social strata. Otherwise the attempt runs the risk of appearing clever but rather shallow.

5. As migration of single men and women to the city grew, the age at marriage must have increased, though we have no figures for this. Employers of maids were no longer under the obligation to provide them with dowries, as in the past. Some figures for Lefkada between 1825–50 suggest that the phenomenon of late marriage was also present in the countryside to a certain extent. There, 85 per cent of men and 43 per cent of women had not married by the age of twenty-five. In the village of Polis the figure for women was even higher, at 70 per cent. Lefkada was under Venetian and then British rule until 1863 and the possible influence of Western European unigeniture systems should not be excluded.

6. These observations clearly do not apply to contemporary Athens.

7. Indeed the Orthodox Church was exceedingly reluctant to 'translate' the Gospels from New Testament Greek into Dimotiki (popular) Greek until well into the twentieth century, and the controversy surrounding the shift from the Julian to the Gregorian calendar in the beginning of this century still has repercussions nowadays as certain families and bishops continue to celebrate Easter according to the old calendar.

8. Du Boulay points out that in Ambeli all the three *sogambri* who had married into their wives' houses and whose wives owned large amounts of land 'were in fact noted for their harshness to their wives' (1986; 159). We do not think that this is an adequate refutation of the above property thesis because these men were in a particularly anomalous position. Their harshness can be attributable to their insecurity.

9. Indeed the food normally served in Greek restaurants is often quite different to that served in the home.

10. Although the interaction of town and country is, as Julio Baroja long ago pointed out, a standard feature of the Mediterranean, Greece has perhaps been uniquely spectacular in this regard. Southern Italy, for example, has had a long history of migration from the last decades of the nineteenth century and although, as in Greece, the 'take-off' took place most visibly after World War II to the industrial triangle in the north, migration prior to this period was more multi-directional than in Greece (Douglass, 1983). Athens dominated the minds, aspirations, pockets and perspectives of its country folk, more than Rome, Madrid or Barcelona.

7   Conclusion: exchange, marriage and the person

1. As Hirschon points out for the Piraean suburb of Yerania, 'numerous and drastic currency devaluations have resulted in a sceptical attitude towards paper assets with a corresponding preference for real estate investment' (1983; 307).

2. Thus pastoralist property transmission patterns are governed primarily by the need to create affinal links which are of a political nature, and the requirement to maintain an adequately sized flock. Fishermen by contrast, have throughout the Mediterranean totally different social organisations and property transmission patterns. Settlement is usually uxorilocal, women inherit the house and men move to sororal clusters at marriage. Women have a high profile in fishing communities; in Symis women owned by far the majority of property, which in any case consisted mainly of housing and small plots, and represented themselves at least since the eighteenth century in contracts; the boats were named after the wives, and men were referred to by their mothers' names (Eleni Zachariou-Mamaliga, 1986; 47). This parallels other accounts of fishing communities in the Mediterranean (Lison-Tolosana, 1976 for Galicia, Spain), and Norman Lewis notes that 'most men could expect to reach the age of 30 before they could afford to marry' (1985; 8). Marriage ages for men tend to be late often because they needed to amass sufficient resources to obtain a boat, and fishing itself required some degree of cooperation on a long term basis with others. The particularly risky enterprise of fishing in which there is always the possibility of premature loss of life encourages the concentration of property in the hands of women.

3. As with banditry as a means to foment unrest in Ottoman-controlled territories; see for example Koliopoulos (1987).

4. One notable exception is Hart (1982). We believe that Mauss' essay on 'The Gift' reaches its fullest potential when read in conjunction with his essay on 'The Person'.

5. This seems to us the essential conclusion to be drawn from the debate between Pitt-Rivers (1977) and Davis (1969; 1977).

6. For who were the 'foreigners' here? For the Leftists it was the 'Americans' and mainland Greeks, for the Rightists it was the 'Turks'. In Cyprus this symbolism is carried even further: *mas ksepoulisan* – not only did 'they sell us', but they 'sold us' in a 'sale', that is, at a cheap price, in other words, 'they betrayed us'.

7. Yet while the world (*o kosmos*) and people are flawed, salvation is still possible within this world. Just as unity is achieved in the family not through egotism but through self-sacrifice, so too in national life unity is achieved through sacrifice, *thiseia*, by shedding one's blood (*aema*) for the *patridha*, a type of baptism by blood to join the pantheon of Greek heroes and commemorated in countless songs, such as those of Sofia Vemvo.

8. This helps to explain why attempts to construct a Greek national identity in the nineteenth century bypassed not just the Turkocratia but also the Byzantine period.

References

About, Ed. 1855: *Greece and the Greeks of the Present Day*. Constable's Miscellany of Foreign Literature. Vol. 9, Edinburgh. Originally published in French in 1854.

Alexakis, El. 1980: 'Τα γένη και η οικογένεια στην παραδοσιακή κοινωνία της Μάνης'. Unpublished Ph.D. dissertation, University of Ioannina, Athens.

1984: *Η εξαγορά της νύφης. Συμβολή στη μελέτη των γαμήλιων θεσμών στη νεότερη Ελλάδα*. Athens.

Alexiou, M. 1975: 'The Lament of the Virgin in Byzantine Literature and Modern Greek Folk-song'. *Byzantine and Modern Greek Studies*, 1, 111–40.

1983: 'Sons, Wives and Mothers: Reality and Fantasy in Some Modern Greek Ballads'. *Journal of Modern Greek Studies*, 1, 73–112.

1984/5: 'Folklore: an Obituary?' *Byzantine and Modern Greek Studies*, 9, 1–28.

Allen, P. 1979: 'Internal Migration and the Changing Dowry in Modern Greece'. In J. Koumoulides, ed., *Greece: Past and Present*. Muncie, Indiana: Ball State University Press.

1985: 'Conflict Management and Conflict Resolution in Mani: Feud in the Modern Context'. Paper presented at the Lesbos Conference on the Anthropology of Modern Greece.

Amantos, K. 1927: 'Επιτίμιον κατά της αδελφοποιίας'. *Annual of Byzantine Studies*, 4, 280–4.

Andrews, K., ed. 1979: *Athens Alive*. Athens: Hermes.

Andromedas, J. N. 1962: 'The Inner Maniat Community Type'. Unpublished Ph.D. dissertation. Columbia University.

Anonymous, 1985: *Περιγραφή της ευρέσεως της Θαυματουργού Αγίας Εικόνος της Ευαγγελιστρίας στην Τήνο κατα το έτος 1823*. Athens.

Antoniadou-Bibikou, E. 1979: 'Ερημωμένα κωριά στην Ελλάδα. Ενας προσωρινός απολογισμός'. In *The Economic Structures of Balkan Lands in the Years of Ottoman Rule 14th–17th cent*. Athens: Melissa.

Appadurai, A., ed. 1986: *The Social Life of Things*. Cambridge: Cambridge University Press.

Ardener, S., ed. 1975: *Perceiving Women*. London: Malaby Press.

Argyriadis, Ch. n.d.: 'Ordres juridiques périphériques et histoire de la codification: L'exemple de la Grèce'. Mimeographed, n.p.

Armenopoulos, K. 1872: *Πρόχειρον Νόμων το λεγόμενον η Εξάβιβλος*. Athens. Originally published in Venice (1774) by A. Spanos.

Asdrachas, S. 1984: 'Η οικονομία και οι νοοτροπίες: Η μαρτυρία του χρονικού των Εερρών του Νεκταρίου Τέρπου του Αργύρη Φιλιππίδη'. Working Notebooks, 7, 91–125. Athens: Hellenic National Research Foundation.

1986: 'La Rivoluzione Greca: Una Sintesi Storica'. In *Risorgimento Greco e Filellenismo Italiano: Lotte, Cultura, Arte*. Rome Edizioni del Sole.

Augustinos, G. 1977: *Consciousness and History: Nationalist Critics of Greek Society*. Cambridge University Press.

Bada, K. 1983: 'Η αθηναϊκή γυωαικεία φορεσιά κατά την περίοδο 1687–1834. Ενδυματολογική μελέτη'. Unpublished Ph.D. dissertation, Ioannina University.

Baloumis, E. 1984: Η λειτουργία του λαογραφικού στοιχείου στο έργο του Α. Καρκαβιτσα. Athens: Bouras.

Barkan, O. L. 1956: *Quelques observations sur l'organisation économique et sociale des villes Ottomanes des XVIe et XVII siècles*. Les recueils de la société Jean Bodin pour l'histoire comparative des institutions, VI, 2, 289–311.

Barthes, R. 1974: *S/Z*. New York: Hill and Wang.

1977: *Image, Music, Text*. Translated by S. Heath. New York: Hill and Wang.

Baudinet, M. J. 1989: 'The Fact of Christ, the Form of the Church'. In M. Feher, ed., *Fragments for a History of the Human Body*. Part 1. New York: Zone.

Baxandall, M. 1972: *Painting and Experience in Fifteenth Century Italy*. Oxford: Oxford University Press.

Beaton, R. 1982: 'Realism and Folklore in Nineteenth Century Greek Fiction'. *Byzantine and Modern Greek Studies*, 8, 103–22.

Beaujour, F. 1947: *Πίνακας του εμπορίου της Ελλάδος στην Τουρκοκρατία (1787–1797)*. Translated by E. Garidi. Athens: Tolidis.

Belmonte, T. 1983: 'The Contradictions of Social Life in Subproletarian Naples'. In M. Kenny and D. Kertzer, eds, *Urban Life in Mediterranean Europe*. Urbana: University of Illinois Press.

Benizelos, J. 1902: 'Ιστορία των Αθηνών υπό Αθηναίου διδασκάλου Ιωάννου Μπενιζέλου'. In T. N. Philadelfeus, ed., *History of Athens*. Vol. 2. Athens: K. Eleftheroudakis.

Boissevain, J. 1965: *Saints and Fireworks*. London: Athlone Press.

Brandes, S. 1980: *Metaphors of Masculinity: Sex and Status in Andalusian Folklore*. Philadelphia: University of Pennsylvania Press.

1981: 'Like Wounded Stags. Male Sexual Ideology in an Andalusian Town'. In S. Ortner and H. Whitehead, eds, *Sexual Meanings*. Cambridge: Cambridge University Press.

Braudel, F. 1974: *Capitalism and Material Life 1400–1800*. Translated by M. Kochan. London: Fontana/Collins.

1975: *The Mediterranean and the Mediterranean World in the Age of Philip II*. Vols I and II. London: Fontana.

Burgel, G. 1976: *Αθήνα: Η ανάπιυξη μιας μεσογειακής πρωτεύουσας*. Translated by P. Rylmon. Athens: Exantas.

Campbell, J. K. 1964: *Honour, Family and Patronage*. Oxford: Oxford University Press.

Caro Baroja, J. 1963: 'The City and the Country: Reflections on Some Ancient Commonplaces'. In J. Pitt-Rivers, ed., *Mediterranean Countrymen*. Paris: Mouton.

Carsten, J. 1989: 'Cooking Money: Gender and the Symbolic Transformation of

Means of Exchange in a Malay Fishing Community'. In J. Parry and M. Bloch, eds, *Money and the Morality of Exchange*. Cambridge: Cambridge University Press.

Christian, W. A. 1972: *Person and God in a Spanish Valley*. London: Seminar Press.

Clogg, R. ed. 1976: *The Movement for Greek Independence 1770–1821. A Collection of Documents*. London: Macmillan.

1982: 'The Greek *millet* in the Ottoman Empire'. In B. Braude and B. Lewis, eds, *Christians and Jews in the Ottoman Empire*, Vol. 1. London, New York: Holmes and Meier.

Cole, J. and E. Wolf. 1974: *The Hidden Frontier: Ecology and Ethnicity in an Alpine Valley*. New York: Academic Press.

Collignon, M. 1913: *Le Consul Jean Giraud et sa relation de l'Attique*. Paris: Imprimerie Nationale.

Comaroff, J. L. ed., 1980: *The Meaning of Marriage Payments*. London: Academic Press.

Constantinides, E. 1987: 'Introduction' in A. Papadiamantis, *Tales from a Greek Island*. Baltimore: Johns Hopkins University Press.

Couroucli, M. 1985 a: *Les Oliviers du Lignage*. Paris: Maisonneuve et Larose.

1985 b: 'Family Structure and Residence Patterns in 19th Century Corfu'. Paper presented at the 1985 Lesbos Conference on the Anthropology of Modern Greece.

1987: 'Dot et Société en Grèce Moderne'. In G. Ravis-Giordani eds, *Femmes et Patrimonie dans les sociétiés rurales de l'Europe Méditerranée*. Paris: Editions du Centre National du Recherche Scientifique.

Crawford, S. 1984: 'Person and Place in Kalavasos. Perspectives on Change in a Greek Cypriot Village'. Unpublished Ph.D. dissertation, Cambridge University.

Cuisenier, J. 1976: 'The Domestic Cycle in the Traditional Family Organization in Tunisia'. In J. Peristiany, ed., *Mediterranean Family Structures*. Cambridge: Cambridge University Press.

Damianakos, S. 1987: Παράδοση Ανταρσίας και Λαϊκός Πολιτισμός. Athens: Plethron.

Danforth, L. M. and A. Tsiaras. 1982: *The Death Rituals of Modern Greece*. Princeton University Press.

Davis, J. 1969: 'Honour and Politics in Pisticci'. *Proceedings of the Royal Anthropological Institute*: 69–81.

1973: *Land and Family in Pisticci*. London: Athlone Press.

1976: 'An Account of Changes in the Rules for the Transmission of Property in Pisticci 1814–1961'. In J. G. Peristiany, ed., *Mediterranean Family Structures*. Cambridge: Cambridge University Press.

1977: *People of the Mediterranean*. London: Routledge and Kegan Paul.

1984: 'The Sexual Division of Labour in the Mediterranean'. In E. R. Wolf, ed., *Religion, Power and Protest in Local Communities*. The Hague: Mouton.

Dimakopoulos, J. D. 1966: Ο Κώδιξ των Νόμων της Ελληνικής Επαναστάσεως 1822–1828. Athens.

Dimaras, K. 1985: Ιατορία της Νεοελληνικής Λογοτεχνίας. Athens: Ikaros.

Dimitriou, S. 1989: 'Gender and Symbolic Systems in an Aegean Community'.

Unpublished Ph.D. dissertation, School of Oriental and African Studies, University of London.

Douglass, W. A. 1983: 'Migration in Italy'. In M. Kenny and D. Kertzer, eds, *Urban Life in Mediterranean Europe, Anthropological Perspectives*. Urbana: University of Illinois Press.

Doumanis, M. 1983: *Mothering in Greece. From Collectivism to Individualism*. London: Behavioural Development, Monographs.

Dragoumis, N. 1925: *Ιστορικαί Αναμνήσεις*. Athens: Stochastis.

du Boulay, J. 1974: *Portrait of a Greek Mountain Village*. Oxford: Oxford University Press.

1976; 'Lies, Mockery and Family Integrity'. In J. G. Peristiany, ed., *Mediterranean Family Structures*. Cambridge: Cambridge University Press.

1983: 'The Meaning of Dowry Changing Values in Rural Greece'. *Journal of Modern Greek Studies*, 1, 1, 243–70.

1986: 'Women–Images of their Nature and Destiny in Rural Greece'. In J. Dubisch, ed., *Gender and Power in Rural Greece*. Princeton: Princeton University Press.

du Boulay, J. and R. Williams. 1987: 'Amoral Familism and the Image of Limited Good: A Critique from a European Perspective'. *Anthropological Quarterly*, 60, 1, 12–24.

Dubisch, J. 1986: 'Introduction'. In J. Dubisch, ed., *Gender and Power in Rural Greece*. Princeton: Princeton University Press.

Dupré, L. 1825: *Voyage. A Athènes et Constantinople. Ou Collection de Portraits, de vues et de costumes Grecs et Ottomans*. Paris: Dondey–Dupré.

Edmonds, E. M. ed., 1969: *Th. Kolokotronis. Memoirs from the Greek War of Independence 1821–1833*. Chicago: Argonaut.

Exhibition Catalogue 1987: *From Byzantium to El Greco*. London: Royal Academy of Arts.

Fabian, J. 1983: *Time and the Other. How Anthropology makes its Object*. New York: Columbia University Press.

Fotakou, 1960: *Απομνημονεύματα περί της Ελληνικής Επαναστάσεως*. Philological Chronicles. Athens.

Frangakis, E. and M. Wagstaff, 1987: 'Settlement Pattern Change in the Morea (Peloponnisos), *c*. A.D. 1700–1830'. *Byzantine and Modern Greek Studies*, 11, 163–192.

Frazee, Ch. 1969: *The Orthodox Church and Independent Greece 1821–1825*. Cambridge: Cambridge University Press.

Freeman, S. T. 1970: *Neighbours. The Social Contract in a Castilian Hamlet*. Chicago: Chicago University Press.

Friedl, Ern. 1962: *Vasilika. A Village in Modern Greece*. New York: Holt, Rinehart and Winston.

1963: 'Some Aspects of Dowry and Inheritance in Beotia'. In J. Pitt-Rivers, ed., *Mediterranean Countrymen*. Paris: Mouton.

1964: 'Lagging Emulation in Post-Peasant Society. A Greek Case'. *American Anthropologist*, 66, 62–86.

Galatariotou, C. 1984/85: 'Holy Women and Witches: Aspects of Byzantine Conceptions of Gender'. *Byzantine and Modern Greek Studies*, 9, 55–94.

Gazis, G. 1971: 'Κώδιξ της βιογραφίας, Εν Αμφίσει, 1841'. In G. Gazis, ed., *Dictionary of the Revolution and other works*. Ioannina: Society of Epirotic Studies.

Geary, P. 1986: 'Sacred Commodities. The Circulation of Medieval Relics'. In A. Appadurai, ed., *The Social Life of Things*. Cambridge: Cambridge University Press.

Gedeon, 1889: *Κανονικαί διατάξεις. Επιστολαί, λύσεις, θεσπίσματα των αγιωτάτων Πατριαρχών Κων/πόλεως*. Constantinople: Patriarchal Publications.

Gellner, E. 1983: *Nations and Nationalism*. Oxford: Basil Blackwell.

 Ed., 1985: *Islamic Dilemmas: Reformers, Nationalists and Industrialization*. Paris: Mouton.

Gervers, V. 1982: *The Influence of Ottoman Turkish Textiles and Costume in Eastern Europe*. Toronto: Royal Ontario Museum Publications in History, Technology and Art.

Goody, J. 1976: *Production and Reproduction*. Cambridge: Cambridge University Press.

 1983: *The Development of the Family and Marriage in Europe*. Cambridge: Cambridge University Press.

 1986: *The Logic of Writing and the Organization of Society*. Cambridge: Cambridge University Press.

 1990: *The Oriental, the Ancient and the Primitive*. Cambridge: Cambridge University Press.

Gudas, R. 1986: *The Bitter Sweet Art, Karaghiozis. The Greek Shadow Theatre*. Athens: Gnosis.

Hajnal, J. 1965: 'European Marriage Patterns in Perspective'. In D. V. Glass and D. E. C. Eversley, eds., *Population in History*. London: Arnold.

 1983: 'Two Kinds of Pre-industrial Household Formation System'. In R. Wall, J. Robin and P. Laslett, eds., *Family Forms in Historic Europe*. Cambridge: Cambridge University Press.

Halpern, J. 1958: *A Serbian Village*. New York: Columbia University Press.

Handman, M. E. 1983: *La Violence et la Ruse: Hommes et Femmes dans un Village Grec*. Aix-en-Provence: Edisud.

 1989: 'Les prestations matrimoniales en Grèce: Vaste champ en friche'. In J. Peristiany, ed., *Le prix de l'alliance en Méditerranée*. Paris: Editions du Centre National du Recherche Scientifique.

Hannertz, U. 1969: *Soulside: Inquiries into Ghetto Culture and Community*. New York: Columbia University Press.

Hansen, E. 1977: *Rural Catalonia under the Franco Regime*. Cambridge: Cambridge University Press.

Hart, K. 1982: 'On Commoditization'. In E. Goody, ed., *From Craft to Industry*. Cambridge: Cambridge University Press.

Herskovits, M. J. 1962: 'Preface'. In P. Bohannan and G. Dalton, eds, *Markets in Africa*. Evanston: Northwestern University Press.

Herzfeld, M. 1980: 'The Dowry in Greece: Terminological Usage and Historical Reconstruction'. *Ethnohistory*, 27/3, 225–41.

 1982: *Ours Once More: Folklore, Ideology and the Making of Modern Greece*. Austin: University of Texas Press.

 1983: 'Semantic Slippage and Moral Fall: The Rhetoric of Chastity in Rural Greek Society'. *Journal of Modern Greek Studies*, 1, 1, 161–72.

 1985 a: *The Poetics of Manhood. Contest and Identity in a Cretan Mountain Village*. Princeton University Press.

1985 b: ' "Law and Custom": Ethnography *of* and *in* Greek National Identity'. *Journal of Modern Greek Studies*, 3, 167–85.

1986: 'Within and without: The Category of "Female" in the Ethnography of Modern Greece'. In J. Dubisch, ed., *Gender and Power in Rural Greece*. Princeton University Press.

1987: *Anthropology through the Looking-Glass, Critical Ethnography in the Margins of Europe*. Cambridge: Cambridge University Press.

Hilse-Dwyer, D. 1978: *Images and Self Images: Male and Female in Morocco*. New York: Columbia University Press.

Hirschon, R. 1978: 'Open Body Closed Space: The Transformation of Female Sexuality'. In. S. Ardener, ed., *Defining Females, The Nature of Women in Society*. London: Croom Helm.

1983: 'Under One Roof: Marriage, Dowry, and Family Relations in Piraeus'. In M. Kenny and K. Kertzer, eds, *Urban Life in Mediterranean Europe*. Urbana: University of Illinois Press.

1989: *Heirs of the Greek Catastrophe*. Oxford: Clarendon Press.

Holton, D. 1984/5: 'Ethnic Identity and Patriotic Idealism in the Writings of General Makriyiannis'. *Byzantine and Modern Greek Studies*, 9, 133–60.

Hughes, D. 1985: 'From Brideprice to Dowry in Mediterranean Europe'. In M. Kaplan, ed., *The Marriage Bargain: Women and Dowries in European History*. The Institute for Research in History and the Haworth Press. Originally published 1978, in *Journal of Family History*, 3, 3.

Iszaevich, A. 1981: 'Corporate Household and Egocentric Kinship Group in Catalonia'. *Ethnology*, 20, 277–90.

Jusdanis, G. 1987: 'Is Postmodernism Possible Outside the West? The Case of Greece'. *Byzantine and Modern Greek Studies*, 11.

Just, R. 1985: 'A hommes plus riches, épouses plus jeunes. Le cas de Meganisi, île ionienne'. In C. Piault, ed., *Familles et biens en Grèce et à Chypre*. Paris: L'Harmattan.

Kairophilas, J. 1982: *Η Αθήνα και οι Αθηναίες*. Athens: Philippotis.

Kaldis, W. P. 1963: *John Capodistrias and the Modern Greek State*. University of Wisconsin Press.

Kalinderis, M. 1951: *Τα λυτά έγγραφα της Δημοτικής Βιβλιοθηκης Κοζάνης 1676–1808*. Thessaloniki.

Kalpourtzi, E. 1987: 'Ίνα πραγματοποιηθή η δια τον γάμου σύζευξις'. *Greek Society*, 1, 81–6.

Kampouroglous, D. 1892: *Μνημεία της Ιστορίας των Αθηναίων*. Vol. 3. Athens: P. D. Sakelleriou.

1896: *Ιστορία των Αθηναίων. Τουρκοκρατία*. Vol. 3. Athens: G. D. Papadimitriou.

Kampouroglous, P. 1883: *Ιστορία τον Πειραιώς από το 1833–1883 έτους*. Athens: D. N. Karavias.

Karidis, D. 1981:'Πολεοδομικά των Αθηνών της Τουρκοκρατίας'. Unpublished Ph.D. dissertation. Faculty of Architecture, Athens.

1985: 'Αθήνα-Αττική στον πρώτο αιώνα οθωμανικής κατοχής. Η σχέση πόλης-υπαίθρου'. *Proceedings of the International Symposium: 'The Modern Greek City'*. Athens: Society for Modern Greek Studies.

Karkavitsas, A. 1978: *Η Λυγερή*. Athens: Estia.

Karoris, A. 'Κώδικας πράξεων του Νοταρίου Αθηνών Αντωνιόυ Καρώρη

(1788–1823)'. Unpublished manuscript, General State Archives, manuscript no. 11. Athens.

Kasdagli, A. 1988: 'Family and Household in 17th century Naxos'. Paper presented to the Special Lectures on Greek Themes. Cambridge.

Kenna, M. 1971: 'Property and Ritual Relationships on a Greek Island'. Unpublished Ph.D. dissertation. University of Kent.

1976: 'The Idiom of the Family'. In J. G. Peristiany, ed., *Mediterranean Family Structures*. Cambridge: Cambridge University Press.

Forthcoming: 'The Power of the Dead. Changes in the Construction and Care of Graves and Family Cults in a Small Greek Island'. *Journal of Mediterranean Studies*, 1, 1.

Kenny, M. and D. Kertzer, eds. 1983: *Urban Life in Mediterranean Europe. Anthropological Perspectives*. Urbana: University of Illinois Press.

Kent, F. W. 1977: *Household and Lineage in Renaissance Florence: The Family Life of the Capponi, Ginoni and Rucellai*. Princeton: Princeton University Press.

Kertzer, D. 1983: 'Urban Research in Italy'. In M. Kenny and D. Kertzer, eds, *Urban Life in Mediterranean Europe*. Urbana: University of Illinois Press.

Kirshner, J. 1978: 'Pursuing Honor while Avoiding Sin. The Monte delle Doti of Florence'. *Quaderni di Studi Senesi*. Domenico Maffie No 41. Milano.

Kitromilides, P. 1983: 'The Enlightenment and Womanhood: Cultural Change and the Politics of Exclusion'. *Journal of Modern Greek Studies*, 1, 1, 39–62.

Klapisch-Zuber, C. 1985: *Women, Family, and Ritual in Renaissance Italy*. Chicago: Chicago University Press.

Kodrikas, P. 1963: *Εφημερίδες (1787–1797)*. A. Angelou, ed. Athens.

Koliopoulos, I. 1987: *Brigands with a Cause. Brigandage and Irredentism in Modern Greece 1821–1912*. Oxford: Clarendon Press.

Kriksos-Davis, K. 1982: 'Moira at Birth in Greek Tradition'. *Folia Neohellenica*, IV, 106–34.

Lambiri-Dimaki, J. 1985: 'Dowry in Modern Greece: An Institution at the Crossroads, between Persistence and Decline'. In M. Kaplan, ed., *The Marriage Bargain*. Haworth Press: New York. Originally published in C. Safilios-Rotchschild, ed., *Towards a Sociology of Women* (1972). John Wiley and Sons: New York.

Laslett, P. 1972a: 'Mean Household Size in England since the Sixteenth Century'. In P. Laslett and R. Wall, eds, *Household and Family in Past Time*. Cambridge: Cambridge University Press.

1972b: 'Introduction: The History of the Family'. In P. Laslett and R. Wall, eds, *Household and Family in Past Time*. Cambridge: Cambridge University Press.

1983: 'Family and Households as Work Group and Kin Group: Areas of Traditional Europe Compared'. In R. Wall, J. Robin and P. Laslett, eds, *Family Forms in Historic Europe*. Cambridge: Cambridge University Press.

Laslett, P. and Wall, R. 1972: *Household and Family in Past Time*. Cambridge: Cambridge University Press.

Leach, E. 1961: *Rethinking Anthropology*. London School of Economics. Monographs in Social Anthropology.

Legg, K. 1969: *Politics in Modern Greece*. Stanford University Press.

Lévi-Strauss, C. 1969: *The Elementary Structures of Kinship*. London: Eyre and Spottiswoode.

Lewis, N. 1985: *Voices of the Old Sea*. Penguin: Harmondsworth, Middlesex.
Liata, E. 1984: *Τιμές και αγαθά στην Αθήνα (1839–1946)*. *Μια μαρτυρία από το κατάστιχο του εμπόρου Χριστόδουλου Ευθυμίου*. Athens: Research Center of the National Bank of Greece.
    1986: 'Τεκμήρια για την αθηναϊκή κοινωνία στις αρχές του 18αυ ιώνα. Η αθηναϊκή αστική φορεσιά'. *Mnemon*, 11, 32–53.
Lison-Tolosana, C. 1976: 'The Ethics of Inheritance'. In J. G. Peristiany, ed., *Mediterranean Family Structures*. Cambridge: Cambridge University Press.
Loizos, P. 1975: 'Changes in Property Transfers among Greek Cypriot Villages'. *Man (n.s.)*, 10, 502–23.
    1988: 'The Virgin Mary and Marina Warner's Feminism'. *London School of Economics Quarterly*, 2:2, 175–92.
Loules, D. 1985; *The Financial and Economic Policies of President Ioannis Capodistrias 1828–1831*. Ioannina: University Press.
Lynch, J. 1986: *Godparents and Kinship in Early Medieval Europe*. Princeton: Princeton University Press.
Macfarlane, A. 1978: *The Origins of English Individualism*. Oxford: Basil Blackwell.
    1985: 'The Root of all Evil'. In D. Parkin, ed., *The Anthropology of Evil*. Oxford: Basil Blackwell.
    1986: *Marriage and Love in England. Modes of Reproduction 1300–1840*. Oxford: Basil Blackwell.
Macrides, R. 1987: 'The Byzantine Godfather'. *Byzantine and Modern Greek Studies*, 11, 139–62.
Maguire, H. 1981: *Art and Eloquence in Byzantium*. Princeton: Princeton University Press.
Maher, V. 1974: *Women and Property in Morocco*. Cambridge: Cambridge University Press.
Makriyiannis, J. 1947: *Απομνημονεύματα*. Y. Vlahoyiannis, ed. Athens: E. G. Bayiakakis.
Maloney, S. J. 1976: *A History of Orthodox Theology Since 1453*. Norland Publishing Company: New York.
Mandel, R. 1983: 'Sacrifice at the Bridge of Arta; Sex Roles and the Manipulation of Power'. *Journal of Modern Greek Studies*, 1, 1, 173–84.
Maresca, S. 1980: 'Grandeur et permanence des grandes familles paysannes. L'essor des organizations agricoles en Meurthe-et-Moselle'. *Actes de la Recherche en Sciences Sociales*, 31, 35–61.
Maropoulos, M. 1985: 'Comportements ecclésiastiques et communautaires face â l'augmentation du montant des dots. Le cas du Zagori en Epire aux XVIIe-XIXe siécles'. In C. Piault, ed., *Familles et biéns en Grèce et à Chypre*. Paris: L'Harmattan.
Matton, L. R. 1963: *Athènes et ses monuments*. Athènes: Institut Français d'Athènes.
Maurer, L. G. 1835: *Das Griechische Volk*. Heidelberg. Privately printed.
Mauss, M. 1985: 'A Category of the Human Mind: The Notion of Person: The Notion of Self'. In M. Carrithers, S. Collins, S. Lukes, eds., *The Category of the Person, Anthropology, Philosophy, History*. Cambridge: Cambridge University Press.
McDonogh, C. W. 1986: *Good Families of Barcelona*. Princeton: Princeton University Press.

McGowan, B. 1981: *Economic Life in Ottoman Europe*. Cambridge: Cambridge University Press, and Paris: Maison des Sciences de l'Homme.

McGrew, W. 1985: *Land and Revolution in Modern Greece, 1821 to 1871*. Kent, Ohio: State University Press.

McNeill, W. 1978: *The Metamorphosis of Greece since World War II*. Chicago: Chicago University Press.

Medick, H. and D. W. Sabean. 1984: *Interest and Emotion. Essays on the Study of Family and Kinship*. Cambridge: Cambridge University Press.

Menounos, J. 1979: *Κοσμά του Αιτωλού Διδαχές*. Ph.D. dissertation, Ioannina University. Published in Research in Modern Greek Philology No. 3. Athens.

Meraclis, M. 1986: *Ελληνική Λαογραφία: 'Ηθη και 'Εθιμα*. Athens: Odhysseas.

Mintz, S. 1983: *A Prison of Expectations. The Family in Victorian Culture*. New York: University Press.

Mirivilis, S. 1956: *Η Παναγιά η Γοργόνα*. Athens: Estia.

Morris, I. 1986: 'Gift and Commodity in Archaic Greece'. *Man (n.s.)*, 21, 1–17.

Mouzelis, N. 1978: *Modern Greece: Facets of Underdevelopment*. London: Macmillan.

National Centre of Social Research (EKKE), 1974: *Στατιστικαί Μελέται 1821–1972*. Athens.

Neris, L., A. Neris and N. Neris: 'Κώδικας πράξεων των Νοταρίων Αθηνών Λ. Νέρη, Α. Νέρη και Ν. Νέρη (1815–1823)'. Unpublished manuscript in General State Archives, manuscript no. 12. Athens.

Nitsiakos, V. 1985: 'A Vlach Pastoral Community in Greece: The Effects of its Incorporation into the National Economy and Society'. Unpublished Ph.D. dissertation. University of Cambridge.

Papadiamantis, A. 1964: *Η Φόνισσα*. Collected Works. Vol. 3. Athens: Domos. 1985: *Tales from a Greek Island*. Translated with an Introduction by E. Constantinides. Johns Hopkins University Press.

Papaioannou, Th. 1984: *Ενθύμιον Αθηνών*. Athens: Gnosis.

Papastratos, D. 1986: *Χάρτινες εικόνες. Ορθόδοξα-Θρησκευτικά Χαρακτικά, 1665–1899*. Athens: Papastratos.

Papataxiarhis, E. 1985: 'The Values of the Household. Social Class, Marriage Strategies and Ecclesiastical Law in 19th Century Lesbos'. Paper presented to the 1985 Lesbos Conference on the Social Anthropology of Greece.

Papatsonis, P. 1960: *Απομνημονεύματα. Από των χρόνων της Τουρκοκρατίας μεχρι της Βασιλειας Γεωργίου Α'*. Introduction and notes by E. Protopsaltis. Athens.

Parkin, D. 1974: 'Congregational and Interpersonal Ideologies in Political Ethnicity'. In A. Cohen, ed., *Urban Ethnicity*. (Association of Social Anthropologists Monograph No. 12), London: Tavistock.

Parry, J. 1986: 'The Gift, the Indian gift and the "Indian Gift"'. *Man (n.s.)*, 21, 453–73.

Parry, J. and M. Bloch, eds, 1989: *Money and the Morality of Exchange*. Cambridge: Cambridge University Press.

Pavlides, E. and J. Hesser, 1986: 'Women's Roles and House Form and Decoration in Eressos, Greece'. In Dubisch J., ed., *Gender and Power in Rural Greece*, Princeton: Princeton University Press.

Pentzopoulos, D. 1962: *The Balkan Exchange of Minorities and its Impact upon Greece*. Paris and the Hague: Mouton and Co.

Peristiany, J. G., ed. 1965: *Honour and Shame. The Values of Mediterranean Society*. London: Weidenfeld and Nicolson.

Peristiany, T. G., and J. Pitt-Rivers. 1991. *Honor and Grace in Anthropology*. Cambridge: Cambridge University Press.

Peters, E. L. 1980: 'Aspects of Bedouin Bridewealth in Cyrenaica'. In J. Comaroff, ed., *The Meaning of Marriage Payments*. London: Academic Press.

Petrinioti-Konsta, X. 1981: 'Οι προσδιοριστικοί παράγοντες της γυναικείας συμμετοχής στο εργατικό δυναμικό στην Ελλάδα, 1961, 1971'. Unpublished Ph.D. dissertation, Law Faculty of the University of Athens.

Petropoulos, G. 1957. *Ο κώδιξ του νοταρίου Αθηνών Παναγή Πούλου (1822–1833)*. Law Faculty of the University of Athens.

Philadelpheus, Th. N. 1902: *Ιστορία των Αθηνών επί Τουρκοκρατίας (1400–1800)*. Athens: G. Bart-K. Eleftheroudakis.

Pitt-Rivers, J. 1977: *The Fate of Shechem or the Politics of Sex*. Cambridge: Cambridge University Press.

Politi, J. 1988. 'The Tongue and the Pen: A Reading of Karkavitsas' *O Arhaeologos*'. In R. Beaton, ed., *The Greek Novel AD 1–1985*. London: Croom Helm.

Politis, N. 1883. 'Προκήρυξη'. *Bulletin of the newspaper Estia*, 333.

Poulos, P. 1957: 'Κώδικας πράξεων του Νοταρίου Αθηνών Π. Πούλου (1822–1833)'. Published by G. Petropoulos, *Ο Κώδιξ του Νοταρίου Αθηνών Π. Πούλου (1822–1833)*. Athens: Athens Academy.

Pouqueville, F. C. H. L. 1820: *Voyage de la Grèce*. Vol. 4. Paris.

   1829: *Storia del Risorgimento della Grecia che contiene la narrazione degli avveninenti del 1740–1824*, 3 vols. Torino: Ghiringhello.

Press, I. 1979: *The City as Context: Urbanism and Behavioural Constraints in Seville*. Urbana: University of Illinois Press.

Psillas, G. 1974: *Απομνημονεύματα του βίου μου*. Monuments of Greek History. Athens: Athens Academy.

Rheubottom, D. 1980: 'Dowry and Wedding Celebrations in Yugoslav Macedonia'. In J. L. Comaroff, ed., *The Meaning of Marriage Payments*. London: Academic Press.

   1985: 'The Seed of Evil Within'. In D. Parkin, ed., *The Anthropology of Evil*. Basil Blackwell.

Ricks, D. 1988: 'Alexandros Papadiamantis and Thomas Hardy'. In R. Beaton, ed., *The Greek Novel AD 1–1985*. London: Croom Helm.

Rigopoulos, T. 1979: *Απομνημονεύματα. Από των αρχών της Επαναστάσεως μέχρι του έτους 1881*. Athens. Privately printed.

Roilos, G. 1966: *Οικογενειακόν Δίκαιον*. Vol. 3. Athens-Thessaloniki.

Ross, L. 1976: *Αναμνήσεις και ανακοινώσεις από την Ελλάδα (1832–33)*. Athens: Tolidis. Translation of *Erinnerungen und nitthe Ilungen aus Grichenland*. Berlin 1863.

Salamone, S. D. 1987: *In the Shadow of the Holy Mountain*. East European Monographs. Boulder.

Salamone, S. D. and B. Stanton. 1986: 'Introducing the Nikokyra: Ideality and Reality in Social Process'. In J. Dubisch, ed., *Gender and Power in Rural Greece*. Princeton: Princeton University Press.

Sant Cassia, P. 1982: 'Property in Greek Cypriot Marriage Strategies 1920–1980'. *Man (n.s.)*, 17, 643–63.

1986 a: 'Religion, Politics and Ethnicity in Cyprus during the Turkokratia (1571–1878)'. *Archives Européennes Sociologie* 27, 3–28.

1986 b: ' "Bloodmoney and Brideprice have no Merit": Marriage, Manipulation and the Transmission of Resources in a S. Tunisian Village'. *Cambridge Anthropology*, 2, 3, 35–61.

Schneider, J. 1980: 'Trousseau as Treasure: Some Contradictions of Late Nineteenth Century Change in Sicily'. In E. B. Ross, ed., *Beyond the Myths of Culture. Essays in Cultural Materialism*. London: Academic Press.

Schneider, J. and P. 1983: 'The Reproduction of the Ruling Class in Latifundist Sicily'. In G. Marcus, ed., *Elites Ethnographic Issues*. Albuquerque: University of New Mexico.

Segalen, M. 1986: *Historical Anthropology of the Family*. Cambridge: Cambridge University Press, and Paris: Editions de la Maison des Sciences de l'Homme.

Sibthorp, J. 1820: 'Remarks respecting Attica'. In R. Walpole, *Travels in Various Countries of the East*. London. Privately printed.

Silverman, S. 1975: *The Three Bells of Civilization: The Life of an Italian Hill Town*. London: Columbia University Press.

Simic, An. 1983: *The Peasant Urbanites. A Study of Rural-Urban Mobility in Serbia*. London and New York: Seminar Press.

Simmel, G. 1971: *On Individuality and Social Forms*. Chicago: Chicago University Press.

Simopoulos, K. 1975: *Ξένοι ταξιδιώτες στην Ελλάδα*. Vol. 3. Athens. Privately printed.

Sjoberg, G. 1960: *The Preindustrial City, Past and Present*. London: The Free Press.

Skouteri-Didaskalou, N. 1976: 'On Greek Dowry: Spatio-temporal Transformations'. Post-Graduate Diploma thesis. University of London.

1984: *Ανθρωπολογικά για το γυναικείο ζήτημα*. Athens: O Politis.

Skouzes, P. 1975: *Απομνημονεύματα. Η τυραννία του Χατζή-Αλή Χασεκή στην Τουρκοκρατούμενη Αθήνα (1772–1796)*. Athens: Kedros.

Slaughter, C. and C. Kasimis, 1986: 'Some Social-Anthropological Aspects of Boeotian Royal Society: A Field Report'. *Byzantine and Modern Greek Studies*, 10, 103–60.

Stakelberg, O. M. Baron v. 1825: *Costumes et Usages. Des Peuples de la Grèce Moderne*. Rome. Privately printed.

Stanford, W. B. and E. J. Finopoulos, eds. 1984: *The Travels of Lord Charlemont in Greece and Turkey, 1749*. London: Trigraph.

Strathern, M. 1984: 'Subject or Object? Women and Circulation of Valuables in Highlands New Guinea'. In R. Hirschon, ed., *Women and Property – Women as Property*. London: Croom Helm.

1988: *The Gender of the Gift*. Los Angeles and Berkeley: University of California Press.

Theotoki, K. 1981: *I Sklavi sta desma tous*. Athens.

Todorov, N. 1979: *''Οψεις της μετάβασης από το φεουδαλισμό στον καπιταλισμό στα Βαλκανικά εδάφη της οθωμανικής Αυτοκρατορίας'*. In *The Economic Structure of Balkan Lands in the Years of Ottoman Rule*. Athens: Melissa.

1986: *Η Βαλκανική πόλη 15ος–19ος αι*. Translated by E. Avdela and G. Papageorgiou. Athens: Themelio.

Tomara-Sideri, M. 1986: Συγκρότημα και διαδοχή των γενεών στην Ελλάδα του 19ου αι. Η δημογραφική τύχη της νεότητας, Athens: Historical Archive of Greek Youth,

Topping Eva, C. 1983: 'Patriarchal Prejudice and Pride in Greek Christianity. Some Notes on Origins'. Journal of Modern Greek Studies, 1, 1, 7–18.

Tsoukalas, K. 1981: Κοινωνική ανάπτυξη και κράτος. Athens: Themelio.

Valetas, G. 1948: Σαμουήλ Χαντζερή. Λόγοι πατριαρχικοί. Athens. Privately printed.

Vaporis, N. 1975: 'The Translation of the Scriptures and the Ecomenical Patriarchate: The Translation Efforts of Hilarious of Tirnovo'. Byzantine and Modern Greek Studies, 1, 141–73.

Vassilas, E. 1956: 'Τέσσερα γράμματα του καπετάν Ανδρούτσου στη γυναίκα του'. Epirotiki Estia, 5, 439–42.

Vergopoulos, K. 1975: Το αγροτικό ζήτημα στην Ελλάδα. Η κοινωνική ενσωμάτωση της γεωργίας. Athens: Exantas.

Vernier, B. 1984: 'Putting Kin and Kinship to Good Use: the Circulation of Goods, Labour, and Names on Karpathos (Greece)'. In H. Medick and D. H. Sabean, eds, Interest and Emotion. Cambridge: Cambridge University Press.

Vernikos, N. 1979: Προικοσύμφωνα και η προγαμιαία δωρεά'. In Proceedings of the 3rd Folklore Symposium of Northern Greece. Thessaloniki: Institute for Balkan Studies.

Vikelas, D. 1967: Λουκής Λάρας. Athens: Grigoris.

Visvizis, I. 1965: Τινά περί των προικώων εγγράφων κατι την Βενετοκρατίαν και την Τουρκοκρατίαν. Athens. Privately printed.

Vitti, M. 1971: Storia Della Letteratura Neogreca Torino: ERI, Edizioni RAI Radiotelevisione Italiana.

1978, 1987: Ιστορία της Νεοελληνικής Λογοτεχνιας. Athens: Odhysseas.

1988: 'The Inadequate Tradition: Prose Narrative during the First Half of the Nineteenth Century'. In R. Beaton, ed., The Greek Novel AD 1–1985. London: Croom Helm.

Vretos, M. 1864: Εθνικόν Ημερολόγιον. Athens.

Wall, R. 1983: 'Introduction'. In R. Wall, J. Robin and P. Laslett, eds., Family Forms in Historic Europe. Cambridge: Cambridge University Press.

Watson, H. 1989: 'Women in the City of the Dead. Migration, Money, Marriage'. Unpublished Ph.D. dissertation. University of Cambridge.

Weber, M. 1948: The Protestant Ethic and the Spirit of Capitalism. London: Allen and Unwin.

Wyse, W. M. 1865: An Excursion in the Peloponnesus in the year 1858. Vols 1 and 2. London: Day and Son.

Xenopoulos, G. 1961: Διονύσης Αλιμπράντες. Collected Works. Vol. 16. Athens: Biris.

Yannoulopoulos, Y. 1981: 'Greek Society on the Eve of Independence'. In R. Clogg, ed., Balkan Society in the Age of Greek Independence. New Jersey: Barnes and Noble.

Zachariou-Mamaliga, E. 1986: Οι ψαράδες της Σύμης. Οικονομική – κοινωνική – πολιτιστική όψη. Unpublished Ph.D. dissertation. Rodos: University of Ioannina.

Zeldin, T. 1978: Histoire des passions françaises. Ambition et Amour. Paris: Eneres.

Zinkeisen, J. 1863: *Geschichte des Osmanischen Reiches in Europa*. Vol. 7. Cotha.

Zinovieff, S. 1989: 'Dealing in Identities. Insiders and Outsiders in a Greek Town'. Unpublished Ph.D. dissertation. University of Cambridge.

Zolotas, I. G. 1926: *Ιστορία της Χίου*. Athens. Privately printed.

Zoras, G. Th. 1972: *Το ημερολόγιον του εν Αθήναις ολλανδού προξένου και η ελληνική επανάστασις*. Athens: Journal des operation consulaires des pays Bas et ce qui c'est passé pendat la gestion du Mr Origone.

Periodicals

1887: *Εφημερίς των Κυριών*. Published by K. Peron. Athens.

1870/3: *Ευρυδίκη*. Published by A. Ktena – Leontias. Constantinople.

1897/8: *Η Οικογένεια*. Published by A. Serouiou. Athens.

1867: *Θάλεια*. Published by P. Lazaridou.

1899–1900: *Η Πλειάς*. Published by Ladies' Society 'Ergani Athina'. Athens.

Index

Adoption (*see also* **Spiritual Kinship, Godparenthood**), 145–55
and dowry provisions, 149–50
and fosterage, 148–49
and godparenthood, 146, 161–62
and patronage, 151–52, 161
different rationalities among social groups, 148–49, 154
of boys, 152
of girls, 148
of D. Solomos, 154
ritual, 147
Aksiocratia (rule of the worthy), 51
Ancient Greece, as source of European Identity, 4–5, 255
Arkhon group, 7–9, 23
adoption practices, 149–51
as dependent on family wealth, 52–3
as representatives of Ottoman rulers, 23–4
decline, 29–30, 60, 72–3, 175–76, 188–89
linkage to dowry inflation, 51–2, 72–3
high dowers, 90
wealth, 24
similarity to Tuscan *case*, 46–7, 53
Asia Minor refugees, 18, 203, 224
Athens, 9, 14
Athenian model of the family, 15
clientage, 163
culture, 48–9, 58, 228–29
effects of incorporation in prebenadal regime, 26
seasonal population, 24–5
matrimonial contracts, 19
under Ottoman rule, 22–32

Beaton, R., 180–81, 185–86

Cash, 84–103
and dowers, 87–8
and gender, 95–103
and grooms, 86
and morality of exchange, 250–51
as dominated by men, 99
as essential to qualify for elite status, 115
as link between groups, 93, 97
as link to trousseaux, 80–3
as metaphor of break-up of moral community, 252, 254
as scarce resource, 123
as symbol, 84–5, 97–8
as tokens for women, 248
at marriage, 84–95
flows, 58
transmission to daughters, 71
resistance to cash dowries, 73–4
Catalan property transmission, 53–4
Cereals, 25
Church (Orthodox)
attitude to adoption, 147, 161
attitude to bloodbrotherhood, 156–57
attitude to engagements, 168–69, 173
attitude to marriage, 200–201
attitude to women, 205–6
compared to Catholicism and Islam, 206–12, 217–28
doctrine of *Koimisis* (Dormition), 212
emphasis on matrimonial contracts, 20–1
Formalism, 207, 213
monasteries and nunneries, 210, 233–34
on dowers, 91, 92
on dowries, 51, 71, 75–6, 78
unable to impose its laws, 13, 207–8
views of time, 4
villager attitudes to Church, 206
Civil Society, 247–48
Civiltà, 11
as contrasted to *politismos*, 12

Clothing (*see also* **Costumes**), **103–20**
    and costumes, 111–13
    standardisation, 124–25
Commoditisation (*see also* **Cash, Gifts**)
    and marriage, 241
    and the notion of the person, 246–47
    of trousseaux, 123
    resistance to, 74, 255–56
Costumes, 111–20
    as figuring in Church encyclicals, 76
    as manipulable resource, 58–9
    as representing wealth/capital, 120–21
    as status, 131–34, 241
    new costume: 77, 124

Dower (*progameia dorea*) (*see also*
    Dowry), **63, 87–92, 96–7, 115**
    relation to dowry, 92–3
Dowry
    and inheritance, 82–4, 94
    brideprice to dowry, 230–31
    changes across time, 78, 102, 177–78,
        192
    complementary to dower, 92–3
    dowry-hunting, 188
    homogenisation, 125–26
    indirect dowry, 229–30
    inflation of in late eighteenth century,
        51–2, 60, 71–7
    meaning, 6, 16, 79, 82–3, 93–4, 127–28
    of adopted/fostered girls, 149, 152
du Boulay, J., 33, 83, 87, 125–27, 189,
    203–8, 214–16, 221, 252, 258n.3,
    260n.8

Education, and wealth, 9
Eghoismos, 51
Engagements (*mnisties*), 167–68
Evil Eye, 208

Family and Kinship, 18–19
    morality and amity, 16
    links between brothers and sisters,
        174–75
Fate (*moira*), 172–73
Filotimo, 51
Folklore (*laographia*) (*see also* **Greek**
    Nationalism, *Ithografia*), **179–82**
Food
    link to gender construction, 221–22
    sharing and *koumbaria*, 158–59, 163
Formal–Informal Distinction, 131–35
    formal relations through matrimonial
        contract, 171, 240
Fosterage (*see* Adoption), 149

Gender Construction, 202–25
    linked to exchange of goods, 98–101,
        133–34
    linked to trousseau, 121–22

    of valuables, 99
    role of cooking, 221–22
Gifts (*see also* **Commodities**)
    and commodities, 97, 239–42, 246–51,
        255
    and gender identities, 100
    exchange and the concept of the
        person, 133–34, 246–51
    Hau, 247
    'metaphoric' and 'metonymic', 102
    to God and the saints, 201, 213
Godparenthood (*koumbaria*) (*see also*
    Adoption, Spiritual Kinship), **158–63**
    in Byzantine times, 158
    increased significance in new Greek
        state, 158–59, 163, 254
Good and Evil, 221, 253
Goody, J., 2, 20, 61, 78, 128, 145, 154,
    167, 231
Greek nationalism, 5
    and folklore, 179, 191
    and gender construction, 183, 223–24
    effects on clothing, 124
    image of Mother Greece, 218–19, 244
    influences, 50
    versus inherited social differences, 50
Greek state, 7–8
    and commoditisation, 254–55
    and restriction of church holdings,
        233–34
    and society, 10, 12
    encouragement of status versus class,
        50, 131
    influence on model of kinship, 55

Herzfeld, M., 3, 6, 12, 14, 17, 18, 83,
    124, 132, 168, 179, 191, 245–46, 254,
    258n.4, 259n.4
Honour and Shame, 6
    chastity and trousseaux, 100–1, 121
    honour and matrimonial contracts, 170
    honour as linked to high dower
        pledges, 90–91
Houses, 33, 34, 37–8, 40–3, 44, 69, 106–7,
    131–33, 153
Households, 45–6
Hughes, D., 229–30, 232–33

Icons, 208, 211–12, 213–14, 216, 217, 224
Ithografia (*see also* **Folklore**), **178–94**
    and folklore, 179–82, 191
    and gender identity, 224

Klapisch-Zuber, C., 3, 33–34, 46, 47, 53,
    73, 93, 108, 150, 170, 258n.3

Land, 10, 55
    and population, 24–25
    as secondary to cash, 96
    circulation, 122–23

growth of private property, 165
property rights under Ottomans, 12
transfers to Ottomans, 24–25
transmission to daughters, 64–65
Law
and matrimonial contracts, 171, 173
customary law (*synetheio*), 12–13
influenced by *nikokirio* models, 236
Lies, 251, 253
Livestock, 64, 70, 114
Love, 195–98

Macfarlane, A., 2, 194–95, 197–99, 202,
248, 253
Maids, 147–49, 191–92
Marriage
as alliance, 107–8
as a distinctive form of exchange,
248–49
as marked by matrimonial contract,
169–70, 172
as presented in popular literature,
185–88
celebrations, 107–8
different settlements at marriage, 65–
66, 83
endogamy between social groups, 59–
60
ethics of marriage, 165–78
homogamy, 178
matching contributions of spouses, 125
strategies, 176, 187–88, 189, 198
transformation in meaning, 249–50
views of Church, 209
Matchmaking (*proxenia*), 56–8, 195
as linked to matrimonial contract, 171
various considerations, 61–62
Marianism, 212, 214
**Matrimonial contract (*prikosymfono*),
19–21**
as condition of trust, 168
as a means to disguise illegal
acquisition of land, 165–68
as religious artefact, 170
differences in rationality between social
groups, 166–68
ksofili, 21, 107
notarial culture, 20–1
significance of land, 165–66
Mediterranean, 2
comparative problems, 2–6, 47
formal/informal versus public/private,
131–35
Morality, 250
'Morning Gift', 230
Motherhood
cult as a means to unify society, 183
ideal as destiny for women, 220–21,
223–24
linked to nation-state, 218–19

Migrants
dowries, 65–8
grooms unable to provide dowers, 90–
1, 115
trousseaux, 109

Neolocality, 44, 177
Nikokirei, **13, 30**
and trousseaux, 98, 100, 123–34
and trade, 31
godparenthood strategy, 163
insistence on notarial contracts, 169
access to cash, 97–98
**model of family and kinship, 32, 53,
177–78, 189–90, 220–21, 227, 236,
238–39**
Olive trees, 25
compared to other resources, 114–15
transmission to daughters, 70

Panaghia (**Mother of God**), **216–18, 224**
Laments for the Virgin, 219–20
Papadiamantis, 183–84, 185, 200, 224,
228, 250
Pastoralism, 25–6, 55
Periodicals, 223–24
Politismos, 14, 48–49
Popular devotion, 213–14
Property transmissions, 62–71
change across time, 16
compared to other Mediterranean
societies, 52–55
differences in transfers of clothing, 113
disinheritance to daughters, 83–84, 88,
98
'equality' between sons and daughters,
81–82, 98, 128–29
to adopted/fostered daughters, 147
variability in Greece, 15–18, 229–33,
237

Residence patterns, 33, 193
viri-patrilocality, 35, 42–44, 45, 46
uxorilocality, 37, 38, 46
Rural–Urban distinction, 234–36, 253–54

Schneider, J., 100, 103, 112, 113, 120,
122, 148
Self, presentation of, 131–35, 244, 245–46
Shadow Theatre, 11, 50
Social Classes, 23–4
conflict, 29–32
intermarriage, 59–62, 69, 72–3, 77, 88,
175–76
mobility through manipulation of
costumes, 114
Social stratification, 49, 50, 110
**Spiritual Kinship (*see also* Adoption,
Godparenthood), 155–62**
as related to trust, 156–57

Spiritual Kinship (*cont.*)
  blood brotherhood, 155
  decline of blood and soul brotherhood,
    157–58, 162–63
  Philike Etairia, 156

Titles, 62
Trousseaux, 103–30
  as important symbolic and economic
    resource, 85, 123
  as 'treasure', 122–23
  change across time, 125
  display of, 108
  linked to cash, 103
  linked to gender identities, 99
  of non-Athenian brides, 109–10
Tuscan family, 34, 243
  similar to *arkhontic* family, 46, 232–33

Urban poor, 49, 60, 173, 191, 209
Urbanization, 14, 18–19

Veil, 113, 184–85

Widows, 39, 192, 194
Women
  as daughters viewed in literature,
    187–88
  'freer' status in islands, 33, 184–85
  gender construction, 98–101, 221–23
  **images of women as Eves and Mothers
    of God, 203–17, 221**
  motherhood, 215–16, 243–44
  position at marriage, 175, 190
  in relation to the commercialisation of
    the dowry, 127–28
  roles in urban contexts, 236
Writing
  effects of, 190–91
  popular novels, 227
  power of writing, 179, 196
  symbolism, 172
  text and image in religion, 212–13

Cambridge Studies in Social and Cultural Anthropology

Editors: Jack Goody, Stephen Gudeman, Michael Herzfeld, Jonathan Parry

1 The Political Organisation of Unyamwezi
  R. G. ABRAHAMS
2 Buddhism and the Spirit Cults in North-East Thailand*
  S. J. TAMBIAH
3 Kalahari Village Politics: An African Democracy
  ADAM KUPER
4 The Rope of Moka: Big-Men and Ceremonial Exchange in Mount Hagen, New Guinea*
  ANDREW STRATHERN
5 The Majangir: Ecology and Society of a Southwest Ethiopian People
  JACK STAUDER
6 Buddhist Monk, Buddhist Layman: A Study of Urban Monastic Organisation in Central Thailand
  JANE BUNNAG
7 Contexts of Kinship: An Essay in the Family Sociology of the Gonja of Northern Ghana
  ESTHER N. GOODY
8 Marriage among a Matrilineal Elite: A Family Study of Ghanaian Civil Servants
  CHRISTINE OPPONG
9 Elite Politics in Rural India: Political Stratification and Political Alliances in Western Maharashtra
  ANTHONY T. CARTER
10 Women and Property in Morocco: Their Changing Relation to the Process of Social Stratification in the Middle Atlas
  VANESSA MAHER
11 Rethinking Symbolism*
  DAN SPERBER. Translated by Alice L. Morton
12 Resources and Population: A Study of the Gurungs of Nepal
  ALAN MACFARLANE
13 Mediterranean Family Structures
  EDITED BY J. G. PERISTIANY
14 Spirits of Protest: Spirit-Mediums and the Articulation of Consensus among the Zezuru of Southern Rhodesia (Zimbabwe)
  PETER FRY
15 World Conqueror and World Renouncer: A Study of Buddhism and Polity in Thailand against a Historical Background*
  S. J. TAMBIAH
16 Outline of a Theory of Practice*
  PIERRE BOURDIEU. Translated by Richard Nice

17   Production and Reproduction: A Comparative Study of the Domestic Domain*
     JACK GOODY
18   Perspectives in Marxist Anthropology*
     MAURICE GODELIER. Translated by Robert Brain
19   The Fate of Shechem, or the Politics of Sex: Essays in the Anthropology of the Mediterranean
     JULIAN PITT-RIVERS
20   People of the Zongo: The Transformation of Ethnic Identities in Ghana
     ENID SCHILDKROUT
21   Casting out Anger: Religion among the Taita of Kenya
     GRACE HARRIS
22   Rituals of the Kandyan State
     H. L. SENEVIRATNE
23   Australian Kin Classification
     HAROLD W. SCHEFFLER
24   The Palm and the Pleiades: Initiation and Cosmology in Northwest Amazonia*
     STEPHEN HUGH-JONES
25   Nomads of Southern Siberia: The Pastoral Economies of Tuva
     S. I. VAINSHTEIN. Translated by Michael Colenso
26   From the Milk River: Spatial and Temporal Processes in Northwest Amazonia*
     CHRISTINE HUGH-JONES
27   Day of Shining Red: An Essay on Understanding Ritual*
     GILBERT LEWIS
28   Hunters, Pastoralists and Ranchers: Reindeer Economies and their Transformations*
     TIM INGOLD
29   The Wood-Carvers of Hong Kong: Craft Production in the World Capitalist Periphery
     EUGENE COOPER
30   Minangkabau Social Formations: Indonesian Peasants and the World Economy
     JOEL S. KAHN
31   Patrons and Partisans: A Study of Two Southern Italian Communes
     CAROLINE WHITE
32   Muslim Society*
     ERNEST GELLNER
33   Why Marry Her? Society and Symbolic Structures
     LUC DE HEUTSCH. Translated by Janet Lloyd
34   Chinese Ritual and Politics
     EMILY MARTIN AHERN
35   Parenthood and Social Reproduction: Fostering and Occupational Roles in West Africa
     ESTHER N. GOODY
36   Dravidian Kinship
     THOMAS R. TRAUTMANN
37   The Anthropological Circle: Symbol Function, History*
     MARC AUGE. Translated by Martin Thom

38 Rural Society in Southeast Asia
KATHLEEN GOUGH

39 The Fish-People: Linguistic Exogamy and Tukanoan Identity in Northwest Amazonia
JEAN E. JACKSON

40 Karl Marx Collective: Economy, Society and Religion in a Siberian Collective Farm*
CAROLINE HUMPHREY

41 Ecology and Exchange in the Andes
Edited by DAVID LEHMANN

42 Traders without Trade: Responses to Trade in Two Dyula Communities
ROBERT LAUNAY

43 The Political Economy of West African Agriculture*
KEITH HART

44 Nomads and the Outside World
A. M. KHAZANOV. Translated by Julia Crookenden

45 Actions, Norms and Representation: Foundations of Anthropological Inquiry*
LADISLAV HOLY AND MILAN STUCKLIK

46 Structural Models in Anthropology*
PER HAGE AND FRANK HARARY

47 Servants of the Goddess: The Priests of a South Indian Temple
C. J. FULLER

48 Oedipus and Job in West African Religion*
MEYER PORTES

49 The Buddhist Saints of the Forest and the Cult of Amulets: A Study in Charisma, Hagiography, Sectarianism, and Millennial Buddhism*
S. J. TAMBIAH

50 Kinship and Marriage: An Anthropological Perspective (available in paperback/in the USA only)
ROBIN FOX

51 Individual and Society in Guiana: A Comparative Study of Amerindian Social Organization*
PETER RIVIERE

52 People and the State: An Anthropology of Planned Development*
A. F. ROBERTSON

53 Inequality among Brothers; Class and Kinship in South China
RUBIE S. WATSON

54 On Anthropological Knowledge*
DAN SPERBER

55 Tales of the Yanomami: Daily Life in the Venezuelan Forest*
JACQUES LIZOT. Translated by Ernest Simon

56 The Making of Great Men: Male Dominations and Power among the New Guinea Baruya*
MAURICE GODELIER. Translated by Rupert Swyer

57 Age Class Systems: Social Institutions and Politics Based on Age*
BERNARDO BERNARDI. Translated by David I. Kertzer

58 Strategies and Norms in a Changing Matrilineal Society: Descent, Succession and Inheritance among the Toka of Zambia
LADISLAV HOLY

59   Native Lords of Quito in the Age of the Incas: The Political Economy of
     North-Andean Chiefdoms
     FRANK SALOMON
60   Culture and Class in Anthropology and History: A Newfoundland
     Illustration*
     GERALD SIDER
61   From Blessing to Violence: History and Ideology in the Circumcision
     Ritual of the Merina of Madagascar*
     MAURICE BLOCH
62   The Huli Response to Illness
     STEPHEN FRANKEL
63   Social Inequality in a Northern Portuguese Hamlet: Land, Late
     Marriage, and Bastardy, 1870–1978
     BRIAN JUAN O'NEILL
64   Cosmologies in the Making: A Generative Approach to Cultural
     Variation in Inner New Guinea*
     FREDRIK BARTH
65   Kinship and Class in the West Indies: A Genealogical Study of Jamaica
     and Guyana*
     RAYMOND T. SMITH
66   The Making of the Basque Nation
     MARIANNE HEIBERG
67   Out of Time: History and Evolution in Anthropological Discourse
     NICHOLAS THOMAS
68   Tradition as Truth and Communication
     PASCAL BOYER
69   The Abandoned Narcotic: Kava and Cultural Instability in Melanesia
     RON BRUNTON
70   The Anthropology of Numbers
     THOMAS CRUMP
71   Stealing People's Names: History and Politics in a Sepik River
     Cosmology
     SIMON J. HARRISON
72   The Bedouin of Cyrenaica: Studies in Personal and Corporate Power
     EMRYS L. PETERS edited by Jack Goody and Emanuel Marx
73   Property, Production and Family in Neckerhausen
     DAVID WARREN SABEAN
74   Bartered Brides: Politics, Gender and Marriage in an Afghan Tribal
     Society
     NANCY TAPPER
75   Fifteen Generations of Bretons: Kinship and Society in Lower Brittany,
     1720–1980
     MARTINE SEGALEN, translated by J. A. Underwood
76   Honor and Grace in Anthropology
     Edited by J. G. PERISTIANY AND JULIAN PITT-RIVERS

*available in paperback